Budapest Blackout

Budapest Blackout

A Holocaust Diary

Mária Mádi

Edited by James W. Oberly
With a critical introduction by András Lénárt

THE UNIVERSITY OF WISCONSIN PRESS

The University of Wisconsin Press
728 State Street, Suite 443
Madison, Wisconsin 53706
uwpress.wisc.edu

Gray's Inn House, 127 Clerkenwell Road
London EC1R 5DB, United Kingdom
eurospanbookstore.com

Printed in the United States of America
This book may be available in a digital edition.

Library of Congress Cataloging-in-Publication Data
Names: Mádi, Mária, 1898–1970, author. | Oberly, James Warren, 1954– editor. | Lénárt, András (Historian), writer of introduction.
Title: Budapest blackout : a Holocaust diary / Mária Mádi ; edited by James W. Oberly ; with a critical introduction by András Lénárt.
Description: Madison, Wisconsin : The University of Wisconsin Press, [2023] | Includes bibliographical references.
Identifiers: LCCN 2022042505 | ISBN 9780299343101 (hardcover)
Subjects: LCSH: Mádi, Mária, 1898–1970—Diaries. | Holocaust, Jewish (1939–1945)—Hungary—Budapest—Personal narratives. | World War, 1939–1945—Hungary—Budapest—Personal narratives. | Budapest (Hungary)—History—20th century. | LCGFT: Diaries.
Classification: LCC DB992 .M33 2023 | DDC 940.53/180943912—dc23/eng/20221108
LC record available at https://lccn.loc.gov/2022042505

To the memory of

Barbara Henfer Walton Blankinship (1941–2021)

And to the memory of

Alfred Alexander Lakos (1937–2021)

Contents

List of Illustrations ix

Preface by Christina Blankinship Harrell xi

Editor's Introduction by James W. Oberly xv

A Critical Introduction by András Lénárt xxiii

Dramatis Personae xxxi

1 Observing the War from Budapest, December 1941–February 1944 3

2 The Invasion and Occupation of Hungary, March 1944 17

3 The Holocaust in Hungary and the Air War, April–July 1944 37

4 Hungary Tries to Leave the War, July–October 1944 119

5 Arrow Cross Coup and Nazi Terror, October–November 1944 183

6 The Battle of Budapest, December 1944–February 1945 228

7 Soviet Occupation, February 1945 271

8 After the Battle of Budapest, March–November 1945 284

Illustrations

MAPS

1 Hungary, December 1941, at the start of Mádi's diary 5

2 Budapest, December 1941–March 1944 6

3 Budapest during the Holocaust, 1944–1945 121

4 Budapest during the siege, December 1944–February 1945 229

FIGURES (FOLLOWING PAGE 110)

The opening page of the first volume of Mária Mádi's diaries, December 1941

Mária Mádi in Budapest, ca. 1941

The diarist's membership book in the Budapest Physicians Association

Daughter Hilda Walton, after her arrival in the US in the summer of 1941

Mária Mádi with the family dog "Joe," ca. 1940

Granddaughter Barbara ("Babu") Walton, ca. 1955

Floor plan for Mária Mádi's apartment at 19 Margaréta utca, Budapest

"Aluminum ribbon" that Mária Mádi found on Margaréta utca

Alfred ("Frédi) Lakos with his parents, ca. 1943

Irén Lakos in Milan, ca. 1994

Mária Mádi in the United States, ca. 1950

Mária Mádi's gravestone, Atlanta, Indiana

Preface

Christina Blankinship Harrell

It was midsummer 2012 when we found the diaries while cleaning out my parents' basement. They were a forgotten treasure buried beneath old grade school report cards and leftover ski equipment. Eager to take a break from the hauling and sorting, we turned our weary attention to the box full of my great-grandmother's diaries, written in perfect English with a fountain pen. Had we seen them before? Sure. My parents had casually discussed the existence of the diaries and told us that they had been written because no letters could be mailed into or out of Budapest during World War II. Had we understood their significance? Never. Of course, now the value of these sixteen diaries is clear to us: these are my great-grandmother's daily accounting of one of the darkest periods in human history.

And so began a long but delightful journey to ensure that the diaries would not be forgotten. My uncle Stephen Walton's tenacity and detailed follow-through have served Mária Mádi's witness well. Along the way he has come across a cast of skilled artisans, historians, and professors—all interested in furthering her remarkable story.

My mother, Barbara Walton Blankinship, is lovingly referred to as "Babu" in Mária Mádi's writings. Mária's family often referred to her as "Mami." Babu remembered the day Mami arrived at their house from Hungary after the war: "My mother was thrilled to pieces. We made everything just right in the house waiting for her. But I remember not knowing who she was when she arrived. This stranger (to me) held out her arms wanting to hold me, her first grandchild. It took many years for us to know each other. For me, she was a little intimidating even though she was very loving with me."

Babu recounted sweet days of visiting her grandmother while in college. She traveled from DePauw University in Greencastle, Indiana to Dublin, Ohio, to spend time with her grandmother on holidays: "She stenciled stars on the ceiling of the guest bedroom just for me. She took an interest in me. She asked me about my plans for the future. Mami was one of the few people who saw me as a young woman rather than a little girl. The time we had together was so important to me. She was very, very loving and caring—almost like she was making up for lost time." Mami's love for Babu grew deep and strong during Babu's early childhood, when they were separated.

Stephen knew his grandmother Mária for a relatively short time. She moved into their home in Houston around 1966: "She was an intense but highly intelligent person. She loved to talk with me about world travels, especially Greece. After her passing, we learned that she wanted my wife, Martha, and me to go to Greece with a gift from her will. We actually traveled all over Europe (including Greece), ending in Budapest. There we saw the flat she lived in and where Alfred Lakos was hidden. Then a phone call from Alfred came out of the blue." Alfred was just seven years old when Mária hid him and his aunt for several months in her Budapest apartment in 1944–45. Stephen recalled:

> He needed some information on the location of Mária Mádi's address in Budapest, which we had. As luck would have it, my wife and I had plans to attend a seminar in Atlanta near his home about two weeks later. We met Alfred for lunch. It was a wonderful get-together. I knew who he was from Mami's diaries, which I had kept untouched for twenty-five years. This meeting started a chain reaction of events. We decided to send the diaries to the United States Holocaust Memorial Museum (USHMM). Our contact was an archivist named Rebecca Erbelding. But before we relinquished them, we decided to read them. In diary number 12 of 16, on page 55, we first saw the name Fredi Lakos. Upon finding this, we connected Alfred, the survivor, with Rebecca, the archivist.

One spring day in May 2016, Stephen and his wife, their children and grandchildren, and Babu's children and grandchildren traveled to Denver to the synagogue where Mária was posthumously awarded the Righteous Among the Nations designation from Yad Vashem, Israel's Holocaust remembrance authority. This is an honor for non-Jews who risked their lives to save Jews during the Holocaust. Many of the sixteen hundred people in attendance that day were Holocaust survivors themselves, eager to pay tribute to this hero.

As we entered the synagogue that day with our young children in tow, we noticed some curious onlookers. They approached my son, Jack, inquiring, "Why are you here today?" He answered, "Our great-great-grandmother is Mária." Upon hearing this, several Holocaust survivors drew close to the children and placed their hands on them, saying, "God bless you! Do you realize you have the blood of a hero running through your veins?" These are words our children will never forget.

At that moment, I saw Fredi Lakos, who was standing in the synagogue, accompanied by his children and grandchildren. This was a surreal moment. It was not lost on all of us that they would not be in that synagogue without Mami's courage. In that moment, we were families reunited by one woman's courage in the face of darkness. Heroic lives unite us, and they start with "the next right thing."

Fredi recalled Mária telling him and his aunt Lacy to hide behind a huge mirror in her apartment when visitors came to her door: "She told me a few times never to go out on the balcony nor stand in front of the window! If recognized, she would be in 'trouble'! As a seven-year-old, I understood the word 'trouble'! Bless you, Mária néni! You saved us so that I can write today these recollections!"

At the awards ceremony that day in 2016, one of the dignitaries presenting the award stated that the word "righteous" is perhaps the most fitting word to describe Mami's actions, a word engraved on the award itself. That word is fitting in its simplicity. Babu noted, "The interesting thing about her is that she had no idea she was doing something heroic. She didn't do any of this to call attention to herself. She did what she knew was decent and right."

Barbara recalled Mami being fascinated by the study of trees in her later years. She remembered Mami planting oak saplings wherever she lived after immigrating to the United States. Mami was particularly fascinated by redwood trees. The thick bark of redwoods contains tannins, which help the tree resist danger. This is a thematic element running throughout Mami's life. She possessed the ability to see a threat and survive it while developing a strength and a beauty that long outlive her.

Our thanks to Rebecca Erbelding at the United States Holocaust Memorial Museum and James Oberly at the University of Wisconsin–Eau Claire. They trumpet this message of bravery and tenacity so that generations to come can hear it. In Mária Mádi's diaries we see a picture of contrasts: love and defiance, fear and deep courage, pain mixed with great beauty. These contrasts weave together a heroic narrative that brings our family immense pride.

May we remember the value of these same simple, decent actions in our lifetime. For in the remembering, we can work to shine the light of hope in the dark.

Editor's Introduction

James W. Oberly

The *Washington Post* featured the news in November 2014: "Defiant Hungarian Doctor Hid Jewish Boy as Nazis Scoured Budapest during Holocaust."[1] The story described a Christian Hungarian physician who hid a Jewish boy in her Budapest apartment for four months during the worst of the terror inflicted by the Hungarian Fascist Arrow Cross Party in 1944–45. Dr. Mária Mádi saved the lives of young Alfred "Frédi" Lakos and his aunt, Irén "Lacy" Lakos, even as she wrote in her diary about the occasional bother the young boy caused. The *Post* reported this news seventy years later because only then had Mádi's diaries become public after her grandchildren donated them to the United States Holocaust Memorial Museum.[2]

Born Mádi Kiss Mária Lujza (Louise) in 1898, Mária was the youngest of four children of Charles and Lujza (née Wimmer) Mádi. Her father served as the legal counselor to the Reformed Church in Hungary, the latest in a line of men who adopted the Calvinist creed. Her mother, however, was Roman Catholic, and the children were raised in that faith. The Mádi family moved from Hungary to England before World War I, where Mária spent time as a girl. The young Mária completed her secondary school studies in 1916 at the Veres Pálné High School in Budapest and then began medical studies that same year at the Pázmány Péter Catholic University of Budapest. In 1919 she married Lajos Henfner Felsőbüky. They had one child, a daughter born at the end of the next year, Hilda Felsőbüky. In 1922 Mária completed her studies for an MD degree, specializing in pediatrics. She recalled in a diary entry that she had sought to emigrate from Hungary to the United States in 1922 after earning her degree but that although her marriage was ending, she was still encumbered with a husband, and the United States would not accept her. Two years later, she and Lajos divorced, but by that date, Congress had enacted legislation that severely limited entry of new immigrants into the United States. Instead, she remained in Budapest, practiced medicine, and raised Hilda as a single mother. Her first assignment was in pediatric dermatology, but in 1928 she took a post in public health that was funded by the Rockefeller Foundation in Hungary. After 1936 she obtained an appointment in radiology at the prestigious Eötvös Loránd Radium and X-Ray Institute of Hungary.

English was Mária's second language, but she also spoke German, Italian, and French. In 1939 Hilda, just eighteen, married an American petroleum geologist named George Walton, who had been prospecting in Romania and Hungary for one of the Standard Oil companies. The couple left Europe for the United States in the summer of 1941. After Hilda moved to the United States, Mádi tried for the second time to secure an immigration visa to enter the United States. US authorities refused her, and although she had a son-in-law who was a US citizen, she still had siblings in Hungary who might want to follow her, an outcome not favored by US immigration officials.

In December 1941 Mádi had been out of work for a year from her position as a scientist at the institute. She suffered from anemia and was regularly hospitalized in 1941. Consequently, she had to give up the family villa on Rezeda utca near Budapest's Gellért Hill. Mádi moved to a small flat on Margaréta utca in the Németvölgyi neighborhood of the city's 12th District. With the March 1942 wartime mobilization of Hungarian civilians, Mádi was appointed by the Budapest Municipality Committee (city council) to serve as an emergency room physician at the Szent Rókus General Hospital.

The December 1941 break in diplomatic relations between Hungary and the United States also ruptured private family communications. On December 12 US navy censors moved to seize control of all international telegraph lines going from the United States to continental Europe. That ended any chance of Mádi exchanging telegrams with Hilda and George. Soon thereafter, the US post office stopped sending international mail to most of Europe, that is, anywhere deemed to be under German control or in alliance with Germany and Italy. The exceptions included the neutral countries of Portugal, Spain, Sweden, Switzerland, and Turkey. In turn, the Hungarian post office stopped sending international mail to the United States. Letters Mádi had posted to Hilda on November 26 and December 1 and 6 came back undelivered. The last communication Mádi received from Hilda had arrived in November with a single snapshot of the new baby granddaughter, Barbara. Thereafter, writing a daily diary in the form of thoughts directed to her family in the United States was the only way that Mádi could communicate with her loved ones.

The first entry on December 23, 1941, read, "Since we are at war with the States, there is no hope for me to join you, my only ones. My first thought was: at least five years." Mádi's phrase "we are at war with the States" referred to the declaration of war that Hungary issued on December 13 in concert with its Axis partners, Germany and Italy, which did so in support of Japan's war against the United States. The next thought in that opening sentence, "there is no hope for me to join you, my only ones," referred to Mádi's efforts to get an exit visa from Hungary and an entry visa from the United States to join her daughter and son-in-law. Finally, her prediction of a five-year separation was correct. Not until December 1946 did Mádi board a Pan American World Airways Clipper airplane from Paris and fly to New York to be reunited with Hilda, George, and young Barbara.

The doctor called her diary "Budapest Blackout" and hoped that "on the other side" of the divide her family was safe in the States and, like her, was writing down thoughts and feelings. Near the end of the first volume of the diaries, Mádi explained that she did not title the diaries "black-out books" because of a fear of air raids; instead, "I choose this name because it symbolizes our life . . . something like a black-out of souls."

There was no blackout of news and information that Mádi could collect, at least for the first three years of the war. She listened daily to the BBC's Hungarian-language service, broadcasting from London. When her short-wave radio could pull in North America signals, she heard news from CBS and NBC. Many diary entries include her observations on the programs she heard, who said what over the airwaves, and how they said it. Hearing General Dwight D. Eisenhower's voice broadcasting to occupied Europe reminded the doctor of her son-in-law's American-accented English.

A month after beginning her diary, Mádi investigated how she might somehow correspond with Hilda across the official postal blackout. A friend visited the apostolic nunciature in Budapest and learned that the pope had volunteered the Vatican's assistance in working with the International Red Cross in sending postcards, limited to messages of twenty-five words, between families in the United States and Axis Europe. Mádi marveled that the pope was generous enough to "help people of all religions" with their transatlantic messages. She promptly filled out the message form and trusted the Catholic Church to get it delivered to Hilda. It did, but with a year's delay. The reply Mádi received from Hilda via the Vatican–Red Cross connection took another two years to reach Budapest.

Informal, ad hoc connections through neutral European countries, especially Sweden and Switzerland, worked better. On June 22, 1942, Mádi received a letter from Hilda, "the greatest event for me since the war broke out," as she wrote in her diary. The letter from America came via Dr. Pál Sebestyén of the Hungarian Foreign Office, who retrieved it from a Swedish contact. Hilda's letter, dated May 3, included news that George had relocated the family to Shreveport, Louisiana, for petroleum engineering work. The letter included photos of young Barbara. Some of the complexity of the mother-daughter relationship came out in a June 22 diary entry: "I read and re-read your letter. Every word has double meaning for me—it means what you say and it means that you all love me." Visits that summer to her dying ex-husband, Lajos, caused Mádi to think more of the child they had made together. On the last day of August 1942, Mádi received news that a Foreign Office colleague of Sebestyén had three letters from America to relay. On September 2 the doctor received the letters, one postmarked June 4 and two postmarked June 18. She was overjoyed upon receipt of the letters, which included additional photographs of Barbara.

Mádi's diary writing might have ended in the summer of 1942 had she believed that the Swedish connection could be regularly repeated. She rightly surmised, however, that Sebestyén could rarely get to Sweden. A letter from Hilda reached Mádi on September 22, 1943, prompting a diary entry: "A letter from you! (dated July 14). And what a sweet letter, full of impulse and love. Life can be bright sometimes, still." After the 1943 letter from America, Mádi received only one more letter from Hilda until after the end of the war. The diary continued as her way to write to Hilda.

The practical physician wrote in a schoolchild's lined paper notebook in a clear hand with a fountain pen, so long as that instrument held out and ink was available, averaging about two pages of manuscript per day. Sometimes at the end of a night's writing she reviewed her writing, striking out some words and inserting others with the same ink. In 1969 she revisited her diary, editing in pencil, inserting frequent asterisks with explanatory notes at the bottom of the page. Readers of this abridged volume will find the 1969 annotations of her diary entries placed in footnotes.

Very rarely did she falter in her diary entries in English. On May 30, 1942, she wrote an entire entry in Hungarian, her first to that date, with the phrase "I need to write in Hungarian." That entry came at the end of the copybook. The language of the present for Hilda and George and for Barbara's future was English. Several days passed before Mádi acquired a new lined book and began writing again on June 4 in English, not to stop for another forty-one months.

Hilda and George Walton were able to follow, if at a distant remove, Mádi's life in wartime Budapest. In 1943 and 1944 Mádi wrote checks on George's US bank account. When Hilda left Hungary for America in 1941, she left behind with her mother some of her husband's blank checks. Mádi wrote in the diary, "George, dear, I had to sell one of your cheques for $50." Mádi wrote that she needed the money to clear up some bills. She regularly wrote in her diary about the low pay she received as a physician, just 340 pengö per month at the start, raised to 430 pengö per month in 1943. She calculated in her diary that the amount was the equivalent of thirty-three dollars per month.

This volume contains about one-quarter of all the diary entries Mádi wrote between 1941 and 1945. A few entries are included from the period between

December 1941 and February 1944. They give the reader a sense of her thinking at the start of her enforced separation from her family. Early in the first diary she wrote, "Now I begin to think of it: though involuntary, but my staying here these years will be a very exciting adventure. I am going to see, to hear, to witness everything and to tell you all about it. At the end we (or you) shall see whether my Kassandra feelings were right. Nobody believes me, but this used to be the lot of Kassandras."

Many of Mádi's diary entries from March 1944 through February 1945 are reproduced in this book. In those eleven months, she completed notebook number 6 and filled nine more, writing at least as many pages as she had in the previous twenty-six months. She increased her diary entries because in rapid sequence she lived through the German occupation of Hungary, the destruction of Hungarian Jewry, the war of the Allied air forces on Hungarian targets, the siege and the Battle of Budapest, and, finally, the Soviet occupation. At the start of this cascade, she wrote Hilda directly in her diary, "I hope, I shall be able to go on, as I told you at the beginning. I am going to be a witness."

The diary entries in this abridged volume include Mádi's writings on the Holocaust, such as the issuing of decrees by the Hungarian government in 1944 meant to, in her words, "twist on the Jews." The reader will learn how she worked to provide Jewish colleagues and friends with food, shelter, documents that would protect them, and human compassion. The diary entries published here also show her views on the political situation in Hungary and the course of the fighting on the different World War II fronts. This book includes many of the diary entries describing the air raids and warnings of air raids that she experienced in the year of the German occupation of Hungary from March 1944 to February 1945.

This volume excludes much of the mundane writing that the doctor did in speaking through her pen to Hilda and George Walton, such as daily weather reports, details of gardening, and accounts of persons known to Hilda from before 1941. The diaries have extensive detail on shopping for food and necessities and the cost of living that Mária Mádi experienced from 1941 on, and most of those entries are omitted from this abridged volume. The doctor also wrote frequently of her own health or, rather, her ailments and of details of her work as a physician at several locations in the capital city; these entries have also, for the most part, been omitted from this volume. Readers who wish to pursue these topics may consult the full text of the manuscript diaries at the US Holocaust Memorial Museum, where they are preserved and in digital form. Excisions of diary entries for this abridged volume are indicated in the text by bracketed ellipses.

This abridged volume of Mádi's diaries includes only a few entries written after February 1945. Water, telephone, and electricity had slowly been restored to Budapest residents. However, food remained in short supply for months. By the summer of 1945, she had begun to receive regular packages from Hilda in the United States. Her daughter sent food, cigarettes, and even a new pair of shoes from the Bonwit Teller department store in New York. Hilda slipped some US currency into the parcels. Mádi welcomed dollars, which had value in Budapest, unlike the rapidly depreciating Hungarian pengö.

Mádi kept her diary until November 5, 1945, a few weeks before the resumption of regular mail service between Hungary and the United States. She wrote a final entry to Hilda: "This is the end with scribbling. Last night I addressed my first direct letter to you, from now on there is no more sense in writing this diary." After immigrating to the United States in 1946, Mádi took employment as a staff physician at Westborough State Hospital in Massachusetts from 1947 to 1952, then relocated to Ohio to take an appointment as a staff physician at Columbus State Hospital. The writer John Bartlow Martin interviewed her for his 1959 book, *The Pane of Glass*, about the treatment of schizophrenia. He described her as "an intense Hungarian woman of restless intellect" who was the most effective physician on staff for her patients on the chronic ward.[3] She was a leader at Columbus State Hospital in ending the use of lobotomy and of halting abusive and punitive uses of electric shock therapy on chronic patients. Instead, she advocated for treating mental illness through newly developed drugs that became available in the 1950s. She foresaw that many patients could be released from state mental hospitals if they could receive pharmaceutical treatment at community clinics.

In 1946 Mádi brought with her from Hungary the sixteen volumes of diaries as well as family papers and photos. After retiring from Columbus State Hospital in 1966, she moved to Houston to live with Hilda and George Walton. One of her visitors in Houston in 1967 was Irén "Lacy" Lakos, who had moved to Milan, Italy, after the war. Alfred Lakos was also reunited with Mádi in the late 1960s after he fled Hungary following the 1956 Hungarian Revolution.

Mádi's diaries speak to readers today about loneliness, deprivation, and fear in wartime Budapest. Across time and space, the words she wrote in her diaries address readers today: "[S]till I firmly believe in love, in fine individuals, in beauty, goodness." She was a correspondent in an imagined exchange of letters with her daughter, who was safe in America, even as she was a witness to destruction and death during the regency of Admiral Miklós Horthy, the Arrow Cross Party terror, and Red Army occupation. We read Mádi's diaries with the foreknowledge that when she was called upon to act courageously and save lives at the risk of her own, she did not hesitate.

Starting in December 2018, a team of transcribers from the University of Wisconsin–Eau Claire (UWEC) and Károli Gáspár Református Egyetem (KRE,

Károli Gáspár University of the Reformed Church in Hungary) met with Stephen Walton and Alfred Lakos to discuss transcribing the diaries into a typescript to make them accessible to the public. The transcribers began their work in Budapest in early 2019 and continued the rest of that year in Wisconsin and in Hungary as students from the two institutions worked from the museum's digital scans to transcribe all the diary entries. The transcribing work concluded in 2020, and UWEC donated the complete set of transcripts to the museum. That transcribing work included all the diary entries in both English and Hungarian and all the newspaper clippings in Hungarian. The UWEC transcribing team included Elizabeth Fa Jing Peterson, Hannah Lahti, Chue Tu Her, Katherine Ciolkosz, Cade Lambrecht, and Josh Fabos. At the KRE, Dóra Sárkány, Krisztina Milovszky, Alexandra Sümegyi, Noemi Puchinger, and Laura Suszta did transcribing, supervised by Drs. Nóra Nádasdi and Katalin Kállay, with additional help from Drs. Judit Nagy and Miklós Vassányi. Zsigmond Hunor of Székelyudvarhely / Odorheiu Secuiesc, Erdély/Transylvania, Romania, transcribed all the Hungarian-language newspaper clippings in the diaries, with his transcriptions donated to the museum. UWEC's International Fellows Program, led by Jeff DeGrave and Kimberly Reed, along with the UWEC Department of History, led by Louisa Rice, provided essential grant funding support for the transcribing and editing project.

The entries selected for this book incorporate Mádi's editorial changes made in the late 1960s. She was not consistent in her spellings of English words, especially later in the war. She sometimes struggled to write of people and places she heard on English-language broadcasts, attempting to produce on paper the phonetic sounds she heard on the radio. The entries in this volume keep her sometimes idiosyncratic English spellings. Readers will find [*sic*] inserted to indicate that the doctor wrote an entry as copied, even if, for example, she mixed up English pronouns in referring to people. Words underlined in the diary are rendered here using italics for emphasis. Entries are annotated, as needed, so the reader may follow her references more easily. Only a handful of passages were written in Hungarian, and those selected for this volume include English translations in the footnotes. She more frequently referred to Hungarian place-names in her diaries, for example streets in Budapest or provincial targets of American air raids. She was inconsistent about using diacritics, which have been reproduced as they appeared in her diaries. The editorial team of Maria Kubanyi Vincze, Sára Kaiser, and I checked all the Hungarian-language entries, place-names, and personal names for consistency of spelling. David Forrai offered valuable help in identifying family members whom Mádi befriended and assisted in wartime Budapest. William Oberly and Louise Merriam undertook careful readings of the diary abridgments.

NOTES

1. Michael E. Ruane, "Defiant Hungarian Doctor Hid Jewish Boy as Nazis Scoured Budapest during Holocaust," *Washington Post*, November 29, 2014.

2. The United States Holocaust Memorial Museum has scanned the manuscript diaries and made them freely available in its selections search page. See "I Am Going to Be a Witness: Maria Madi's Diary," accessed February 13, 2020, https://www.ushmm.org/collections/the-museums-collections/curators-corner/i-am-going-to-be-a-witness-maria-madis-diary. See also Mádi's listing in Yad Vashem's Righteous Among the Nations Database, accessed February 13, 2020, https://righteous.yadvashem.org/.

3. John Bartlow Martin, *The Pane of Glass* (New York: Harper & Brothers, 1959), 224.

A Critical Introduction

András Lénárt

War diaries always contain a degree of tension. They are like crime shows where the viewer knows the identity of the killer from the very beginning but still needs to see how the detective gets to the solution. The diary writer either survives to the end of the story or dies, as happened to Anne Frank, the most famous World War II diarist. The peculiarity of Frank's text is due to the author's young age, the combined presence of child and adult perspectives, the incompleteness of the diary, and of course the girl's tragic fate. The relatively early publication of the diary (1947) was equally important, as was the attention surrounding the Frank family, which personified assimilated and modern middle-class Jewishness. Anne Frank's book has become both a symbol and a reference: all other diaries are compared to it.

Mária Mádi, a forty-six-year-old radiologist in 1944, was an entirely different kind of person. She lived alone in a small apartment in the wealthiest area of Budapest, which by the mid-twentieth century had grown to a populous city due mostly to the contributions of its Jewish inhabitants over the span of the previous century. Mária was not Jewish—quite the contrary, in fact. She came from a noble family, with aristocrats among her wider relations. It cannot be denied that she was a special person. Once, after a pointless and ultimately frustrating reunion with *her* people, she reflected on how clearly different she was from them: "It is difficult to find an explanation for the fact: I can tolerate them only with utmost self-control. They are my own sort of people, that is, gentiles, the same social class and about the same education. Our roots, customs, environment, circumstances are almost the same. In spite of these, it is hard to endure their absolutely primitive talk."

Two weeks later, she summarized her personal philosophy in a few sentences to her twenty-four-year-old daughter, herself the mother of a three-year-old girl: "I know, how ridiculous it is, to give early Victorian advices, still I have to tell you this. I have seen many people, men and women alike, who, middle aged, got deplorably provincial in their way of thinking, though they were smart in earlier years. Your aunt Margit, Ibola and many others. The big danger is a happy, married life, when these people cease to think independently of their husbands or wives and an economically secure life when they trust papers and the whole world around, as just suited to their tastes and needs."

Mária Mádi fulfilled her own ideal: she was an educated physician, divorced, and a working woman who was economically and intellectually independent. This combination provided the conditions necessary for individual freedom, or at the very least gave her the means to resist the aggressive attempts of authoritarian regimes and dictatorships to harm people by propaganda and discriminatory laws. However, what sets this diary absolutely apart from other remarkable wartime ones is the language. It was written in English for the future family who decided to settle and live in the United States and consequently would not speak the Hungarian language. We might add that it was prepared for American readers without letting them or the family know about its existence. Presumably, after correcting the whole text one year before her death, Mária had the intention to leave a legacy/inheritance with no further instructions.

Mária's daughter, Hilda, married an American engineer and in April 1941 immigrated to the United States when her husband returned there, not long before the entry of Hungary and the United States into the war. Mária, who had spent some school years in England, had only vague ideas of the United States, but she tried to report not only to her closest confidants but also to the broader American audience information about the desperate situation in Hungary.

After World War I, Hungary suffered a terrible loss: two-thirds of its territory and consequently half of its population were assigned by the Treaty of Trianon to be part of either newly formed countries such as Czechoslovakia and Yugoslavia or absorbed into Austria and Romania. This shocking result of the war clearly defined the structure of internal politics. The party that would be able to rewrite this international judgment on the country, a judgment considered absolutely unjust by ethnic Hungarians, including Jews, would be supported by the people. After a brief period of social turmoil, characterized both by democratic achievements against the old regime and by attempts to establish a Soviet republic, after 1920 the nationalists, also known as the counterrevolutionary regime, consolidated their power. Political parties and leading politicians came and went, but the most important representative figure, Regent Miklós Horthy, stayed in power until the fall of 1944. The country and its politics were so obsessed with the idea of a complete (or at least partial) revision of the Trianon Treaty's national borders that all other issues or considerations became insignificant. Nazi Germany was the leading revisionist power on the European continent seeking to revise the Treaty of Versailles. When Germany explored its economic and political influence on Eastern Europe, Hungarian leaders did not hesitate long to accept the help of the Third Reich. In November 1940 Hungary signed the Tripartite Pact with Germany, Italy, and Japan, committing Hungary to armed conflict.

The favoring of Christian churches, conservative and anti-Communist ideologies, and the discrimination against Jewish people and against left-wing thinking did not come with the Germans; these elements were present in the Horthy regime from the beginning. In 1920 the first anti-Jewish law after World War I was passed in Hungary. The numerus clausus ("closed number" in Latin) statute limited the number of students at universities to the proportion of their minority group. The law was clearly directed against assimilated and Hungarian-speaking citizens with Jewish origins. If you were a Jew, you were defined by your religion, regardless of whether you had been baptized as a Christian, went to a Christian church, or were a believer or not. Due to international pressure from the League of Nations, in 1928 Hungary moderated its discriminatory law to an extent but never completely withdrew it, and in practice its adaptation depended on the management of the university. Nevertheless, antisemitic discrimination was not a peculiarity limited to Hungary. Jewish quotas in higher education were introduced in many countries, including Canada and the United States.

Antisemitism in Hungary increased after Adolf Hitler came to power in Germany and became virulent from the moment when the parliament passed an anti-Jewish law in 1938 modeled on Germany's Nuremberg laws. Constantly fighting with the Hungarian Nazi parties (the Arrow Cross and other racist mass movements), the conservative government became increasingly radical in two respects. The first objective was to satisfy the social demands of millions of poor and broken people, especially after the economic crisis in the early 1930s, with the promise of confiscating and redistributing the property of Jewish people or by restraining their business and favoring the "Christian" trade, schooling, and better public promotion. The other common objective was regaining the traditionally Hungarian territories in cooperation with the German expansion toward the East. This led to Hungary regaining territories from its neighboring countries between 1938 and 1941 (mainly as consequences of the Munich and Vienna agreements) by forming a dangerous coalition with the fully antidemocratic and oppressive German state. These dubious victories, obtained by the grace of the Axis powers, were welcomed both by people in Hungary and by ethnic minority Hungarians in the reoccupied lands. We know of footage taken by a Jewish amateur filmmaker in 1938 who traveled from southern Hungary to the northern town of Kassa/Košice on the occasion of the march of the regent and the Hungarian army, a filmed propaganda event for newsreels. The parade happened on November 11, just six months after the so-called first Jewish law was introduced in Hungary and the day after Kristallnacht, the pogroms that had taken place in Germany that significantly damaged the reputation of Nazi Germany abroad. The dream that many longed for came true, and the happiness was felt unanimously. Even the author of the diaries, Mária Mádi, an Anglophile who observed Germany with suspicion, approved of the territories being returned.

But hopes were very soon shattered. Jewish people with Hungarian identity in the regained territories became terribly disappointed as anti-Jewish legislation was extended to their lands. The new Hungarian rule did not really appreciate Jews' efforts to preserve and protect Hungarian culture and infrastructure against the influence of foreign sovereignties.

Hungary's fate was irrevocably bound to Germany. The country was on a track that had placed it into war on the side of Germany. The political leadership's aims of avoiding armed conflict worked for a while: the country got back part of Carpathian Ukraine from Czechoslovakia (1939) and Northern Transylvania from Romania (1940) without much resistance. However, Germany now had expectations of Hungary in return: the National Socialist Volksbund organization had to become the only legal representative organ of ethnic Germans in Hungary, and the composition of yet another anti-Jewish law was introduced with the sole purpose of satisfying German demands. Increasingly, Hungary had to export goods to Germany despite jeopardizing internal supplies. The shift from neutrality to total commitment to Germany became manifest in 1941 as Hungary renounced the peace treaty with Yugoslavia, which had been signed only four months earlier, and invaded the country hand in hand with the Germans. Germany wanted to secure the stability of the Balkans, which were at a boiling point, before attacking the USSR. Hungary regained more territories with ethnic minorities from Yugoslavia. The real turning point was the participation of Hungary in the long and bloody battles on the Eastern Front. After that there was no way back. Hitler dealt the cards cleverly, as Romania and Hungary competed for the mercy of the glorious Third Reich in the interest of gaining more land and influence.

Hungary, however, was not well prepared for warfare. During the 1920s, following World War I, Hungary was forbidden to maintain an army and to build up its armaments. The first military investments only started in 1938, and the country's human and economic resources were insufficient for offensive warfare. The Germans were aware of the weakness of the Hungarian troops and therefore assigned them policing roles in the invaded territories in Ukraine. With the Soviet counterattack at the beginning of 1943, the Hungarian army was devastated.

The newly appointed prime minister, Miklós Kállay, tried to ease Hungarian dependency on Germany and looked for ways to connect with the Allies, primarily the United Kingdom. The tactic of finding new allies among the enemies and leaving out the USSR was as hopeless as the policy of "armed neutrality" at the beginning of the war. Hungarian leaders were so deeply intertwined with Germany that after the Battle of Stalingrad (August 1942–February 1943) the gradual recognition that Germany could not win the war was not enough for them to face reality. Many Hungarian leaders found it impossible to imagine that Eastern Europe would fall under the Soviet realm. However, the Allies decided at the Tehran Conference (1943) to invade the European continent in France, the nearest country to England, rather than in Greece, as Mádi and some Hungarians wished. This meant that the overwhelming expansion of the USSR into Eastern and Central Europe was now inevitable. At this point, the Hungarian government should have started negotiations with the Communist enemy. This did not happen, and Prime Minister Kállay could not carry out the withdrawal of the one hundred thousand Hungarian soldiers from the front lines against Hitler's will.

Meanwhile, the rhetoric did not change too much. Anti-Jewish legislation continued, and many Jewish men who were drafted into the military labor service died after 1941 because of the hardship, deprivation, and deadly cruelty of army officers. Nonetheless, compared to people in other countries by the end of 1943, the vast majority of Hungarian Jewish people were still alive, and the country had avoided greater losses. And then came 1944, one of the most catastrophic years in the history of Hungary.

At the beginning of 1944, the victory of the Allies seemed certain. Much of Europe (many people, but not everyone) had been waiting for the Anglo-American landing and the pushing back of the Nazi army. The Allied landing location was of crucial importance to Horthy and the Kállay government, but their hopes dissolved completely. The problems of the country were immense. Was it possible to avoid the German occupation? Was it possible to avoid fighting with the Red Army and to receive guarantees that some territories outside the Trianon Treaty borders could be kept? Would it be possible to avoid the destruction of the country either by the Germans or by the Russians? Finally, there were the concerns of the Jewish citizens about their prospects. Was there a way for them to stay alive at home?

The problems exceeded the abilities of the Hungarian leadership. The Germans managed to keep Hungary under control and from making peace with the Allies and turning against Germany. All the progress and achievements backfired during 1944 and 1945. The German army occupied Hungary on March 19, 1944, and as Mária Mádi documented, the occupiers looted the country. The approaching Soviet army, during the bloody battles of 1944–45, also razed cities and towns. From the fall of 1944, the Soviets demanded continuous compensation for war damages incurred by the USSR. The Hungarian people did not protect their Jewish compatriots: 70 percent of Hungarians with Jewish origins perished following deportation to Nazi death camps or to labor services or due to being killed within the country.

The Gestapo arrived in March 1944 with prepared lists of people to arrest. Through the detention of the political elite, the Gestapo prevented any kind of serious resistance. Confinements were not limited to the liberal or left-wing politicians; aristocrats and former ministers were also under the warrant, including the most significant prime minister during the Horthy regime, Count István Bethlen (1921–31), and Miklós Kállay himself had to go into hiding at the Turkish embassy. Adolf Eichmann, the SS officer who was later captured, accused, and in 1961 condemned, and his Sondereinsatzkommando Eichmann unit met with his Hungarian counterparts, the new extremely antisemitic leaders of the Ministry of the Interior, László Endre, László Baky, and Andor Jaross. Together they organized the ghettoization and deportation of the Jewish people throughout greater Hungary with a tremendous rush of effort: by July 9, 1944, 147 trains had deported 437,402 Hungarian Jews to Auschwitz-Birkenau, according to German records. In July, due to protests of Christian churches and international political pressure, the regent intervened in favor of stopping the plan to deport the Jewish citizens of the capital, Budapest. The deportations ceased before their final round, but at the end of June, as Mária Mádi recorded in her diary, Jews in Budapest had to go into designated residential buildings for Jews, known as the yellow-star houses.

The summer of 1944 was full of hope after the Normandy landing and the advance of the Red Army. Everyone was counting the days, oppressors and hostages alike. How long would the final phase last? What would be destroyed and annihilated in Hungary by the occupying German power? What could be saved? How could people be rescued? How could they survive?

The leadership of the Ministry of the Interior worked with Eichmann to finally take out the Jews of Budapest. First on July 9, then on August 5, and finally around August 25, they planned to deport the Jews. On the first two dates, Horthy intervened, because of international political pressure and because he suspected a coup d'état by the gendarmes who had been massed in the capital, and he was busy driving them back. However, he did not put obstacles in the way of the deportation at the end of August, or at least there is no evidence of it. Romania's defection from the Axis to the Allies on August 24 caught the attention of the Germans and put the Hungarian leadership in a difficult position. Regent Horthy decided to appoint a new government only after the defection of Romania. The immediate effect was the stopping of any further deportation of Jewish citizens living in the capital. The attempt at ceasefire negotiations with the USSR was too slow and half-hearted. The new Lakatos government of Hungary missed the optimal date in the early days of September to declare a change of side and organize the armed resistance against the German invaders, who were temporarily confused because of the unfavorable events in Romania. The pro-Nazi Arrow Cross organized a coup in mid-October, realized largely through the intervention of the occupiers, and the majority of the army generals and officers stayed pro-German. They easily accepted the new joint rule by the Nazis and the Arrow Cross.

Mária Mádi hated the German invaders and blamed them and their Hungarian supporters for every possible thing that had gone wrong. Her diary documents the events and news on a daily basis. She was very well informed owing to the fact that influential people were among her acquaintances.

After the German occupation of Hungary, Mádi's entries increased to multiple pages per day, describing life in occupied Budapest, the establishment of ghetto houses, the need for protective documents, news of the war, and the deportation of Jews from the countryside. In October 1944, after the Arrow Cross coup, Mária ceased being a bystander and began hiding Jews, including a seven-year-old boy, in her small apartment. She spoke openly and honestly about the challenges of hiding her charges but was clear-eyed and resolute in her determination to do so. She kept writing during the most dreadful days of the Battle of Budapest (December 1944–February 1945), one of the longest and most devastating sieges of the war. It took more than fifty days for the Soviets to gain control over the capital. More than thirty-eight thousand civilians died, and 80 percent of the buildings were destroyed or damaged. According to experts, the Battle for Budapest was the final rehearsal for urban warfare before the siege of Berlin.

Mádi's main objective in writing the diary was to "be a witness" (March 26, 1944). To her, that meant being a witness to the war and, more importantly, to the Nazi (and Hungarian) persecution and deportation of Jews. Throughout the diary, Mádi acts instinctively and intelligently. She demonstrates solidarity by meeting Jewish friends in public, going to the ghetto houses, trying to comfort Jews, and delivering food and other necessities. She keeps quiet when others express admiration for the German army and ponders the chances of "final victory" while borrowing Churchill's books from the public library. She takes the risk of secretly listening to the BBC and comments on the news and human behavior with humor and sarcasm.

Mária Mádi was an independent-minded thinker and lonely individual in a toxic environment who used her relatively privileged position to help people. She was a quiet hero worthy of our great admiration, not only now but for generations to come.

Dramatis Personae

(listed in the order in which their names appear in the book)

Name	*Nickname/diminutive in the diaries*	*Comment*
George Walton	Geo	Son-in-law
Hilda Felsőbüky Walton	Hildukaim	Daughter
Barbara Walton	Babu	Granddaughter
Sebástyen family: Dr. Pál; his wife, Luzja "Lulu"; and their son, Pál	Sebes family: Apu, Lulu (also as mother, Mamu), and Api or Pali jun	Family friend and counselor in the Hungarian Foreign Ministry
Florence Walton	Flossie	Hilda's mother-in-law
Lajos Henfer Felsőbüky		Ex-husband and counselor in the Hungarian Ministry of the Interior
Irmus Marosy		Niece of Lajos Henfer Felsőbüky and married to Ferenc Marossy, an inspector in the Hungarian Foreign Ministry
Dr. Hanna Szábo		Dentist in Budapest and fellow member of the Women's Medical Association of Hungary
Andras Szerdahelyi	Bandi	Childhood friend of Hilda when the Mádi family lived at 18 Rezeda utca
Dénes Viczay	Dédé	Nephew; he was the son of Marguerite "Margit" Mádi Viczay

Name	*Nickname/diminutive in the diaries*	*Comment*
Lakos family: Irén, Laszlo, Karoly, and Alfred	Lacy, Irka, and Frédi	Irén "Lacy," also "Irka," was a Jewish friend; she sheltered with her nephew Alfred with Mádi, October 1944–February 1945
Horchler family: Elsa, Teresa, Ibolya, and Gizella	Teri, Iby, and Gizi	Family friends
Dr. and Mrs. Zoltán Németh		Neighbors at 19 Margaréta utca
Elly Hermanns and her mother, Amelia Brunansky		Neighbors at 19 Margaréta utca
Mária Pató		Neighbor at 19 Margaréta utca; she worked at the Magyar Amerikai Olajipari Részvénytársaság (MAORT, Hungarian-American Oil Company) with George Walton and Hilda Walton before 1941
Marcsi and Jenö Hajos		Friends; he was a journalist and was posted to Madrid in 1944 as press attaché
Erzsébet Tarnocsy	Bö and Böcsi	Jewish friend; she sheltered with Mádi at 19 Margaréta utca, October–November 1944
Kartal family: Emil and Erszike		Jewish friends
Pravdánéne	Auntie Pravda	Former housecleaner to Mádi at the 18 Rezeda utca; Ancy Pravda was her daughter
Dr. Irma Ormós	Mici	Pediatrician; she was a colleague in the Hungarian Women's Medical Association
Viktör family		Neighbors at 19 Margaréta utca
Tullia Bokor		Friend; she was the sister of Erszébet Toperczer, former MP in the Hungarian Lower House
Stefi Peregi		MAORT employee
Tercsi néni		Friend; children Eva Fidy, Pista Fidy, and Api Fidy

Name	*Nickname/diminutive in the diaries*	*Comment*
Gertrude and Rolf Nossak	Gerti	Austrian niece; Rolf Nossak was an official in the German Foreign Office
Vilmica Antal		Family friend, spouse of Lajos Antal, and sister-in-law of Istvan Antal, Hungarian minister of propaganda, 1944
Bingert family: Janos Bingert; Ivan, his son; and Ibolya, his daughter	Jancsi	Friend; he was employed at Hunnia Film Studios
Ilonka Krasznay Déghi		Mádi's tobacconist; married name Mrs. Janos Schmidt
Mici Adorján	neni (auntie)	Friend
Mr. and Mrs. Adolph Gorrieri		Neighbors at 19 Margaréta utca; both were pro-Nazi and pro–Arrow Cross
Elek Máthé and Klari Mathe	Elko	Friend; he was a clergyman in the Reformed Church in Hungary
Maria Kánya	Marika	Friend
Mr. and Mrs. Láng		Neighbors at 19 Margaréta utca
Pál Ubriszi		Neighbor at 19 Margaréta utca; he was a police official involved in the terror against Budapest Jews
Dr. Rózsi Timár		Physician colleague at the Social Insurance Institute; she was dismissed from her job in the summer of 1944 for being Jewish
Mr. and Mrs. Laszlo Székely		Neighbors at 19 Margaréta utca; Mádi delivered a child born to Mrs. Székely during the Siege of Budapest
Count Viczay	Kuri	Mádi's brother-in-law
Frigyes Horchler	Frici	Brother of Gisella Horchler
Mr. and Mrs. Lajtai		Neighbors at 19 Margaréta utca; both were pro-Nazi and pro–Arrow Cross
Pubi Szenczy		Nephew
Márta Waldbauer		Family friend

Name	*Nickname/diminutive in the diaries*	*Comment*
Klári Forrai		Jewish friend; married to Dr. Elemer Forrai and mother to sons Gabriel and Marcel Forrai
Barbara Rakovszky		Jewish friend
Zsigmund Stolcy		Friend; he was an official in the Budapest Police
Klári Bálint		Neighbor at 19 Margaréta utca; she shielded two Jews in her flat, October 1944–February 1945
Mr. and Mrs. Ferenc Benecze and their two children		Neighbors at 19 Margaréta utca; both were pro-Nazi and pro–Arrow Cross
Mrs. Csabonyi		Neighbor at 19 Margaréta utca
Marianne Halas		Friend, cousin to Mrs. Miklós Horthy
George Gyetvay		Cousin
Zorkóczy family: Dénes, Klara, and Marta	Dénes was known as Dini	Friends
Klári Bernauer		Jewish friend, sometimes referred to by her maiden name; her married name was Forrai
Ancy Somogyi		Cousin of Irmus Marossy, Mádi's in-law family
Mr. and Mrs. István Janik		Building janitor at 19 Margaréta utca; István was pro-Nazi and a member of Nyilas
Mikolay family		Neighbors at 19 Margaréta utca
Ernő Szabadhegyi		Acquaintance; he was a Jewish attorney helping the Kartal family
Mr. and Mrs. Janos Szücs		Neighbors at 19 Margaréta utca; both were pro-Nazi and pro–Arrow Cross
Pál Ruedemann		Director of MAORT and a former colleague of George and Hilda Walton

Budapest Blackout

CHAPTER I

Observing the War from Budapest, December 1941–February 1944

Chapter 1 includes a few excerpts from the six volumes of Dr. Mádi's diaries that cover the period from December 1941 to the end of February 1944. The first half of December 1941 was when the separate wars in Europe, North Africa, East Asia, Southeast Asia, and the North Atlantic combined into a global conflict. Hungary's membership in the Tripartite Pact called upon the country to declare war against the United States and Great Britain on December 11. The German defeat at the Battle of Moscow (December 1941–January 1942) forced the Germans to turn to allies such as Hungary to contribute troops for a renewed offensive in the spring of 1942. Mádi observed that the German foreign minister and the German chief of the general staff came to Budapest in January 1942, demanding new Hungarian contributions to the war on the Soviet Union. Mádi was working at the Rókus Central Hospital in the spring of 1942 and silently, almost mournfully, watched the unit of medical staff leave on horseback for the Russian front.

Hungarian forces advanced on the Don-Volga front throughout the summer of 1942. When the tubes in her radio burned out in October, she felt she had "only a slight idea what is going on in the world." She knew enough to report about the national concern for the Hungarian soldiers: "Now so many of the young people are out at the front lines, nearly every family has somebody to be anxious for. And to what end?"

What Mádi did not record in her diary was that the two hundred thousand soldiers of the Hungarian Second Army marched into Russia with an auxiliary labor corps of forty-five thousand Jewish men. The labor battalions, known as *munkaszolgálatosok,* of unarmed Jewish men did some of the most dangerous work at the front, notably clearing paths through Soviet minefields. When the Red Army encircled and destroyed the Hungarian Second Army at Voronezh in January 1943, Jewish men of the labor battalions were abandoned by their supervising officers and either killed or captured. Soviet forces saw the Jewish men as an invading force the same as arms-carrying Hungarian soldiers. One estimate places the number killed and missing in action at 80 percent of the Jewish men who set off for the USSR in 1942.

Mádi's vision of Hungary's future was one of bad choices leading to destructive consequences. She saw herself as a modern-day "Kassandra," a prophet whose warnings were destined to be ignored. She was convinced that the Americans would cede control of Eastern and Central Europe to the Soviets following the Axis defeat. Mádi wrote frequently of her memories of the brief but tumultuous Communist rule of Hungary in 1919. By the end of 1942, when the Germans were on the defensive at Stalingrad and in North Africa, she wrote: "Sound thinking people here all believe and hope for Allied success south of us but there is nobody (except jews) who is not against Bolshevistic spread towards west. . . . all depends upon which is going to get the best of Germany?"

Also in late 1942, Mádi wrote in her diary about attempts made by churchmen, both Roman Catholic and Calvinist Reform, to persuade the government to withdraw the army from the USSR and exit the war. The clergy demanded an end to Hungarian cooperation with the murderous German war on the Jews of Europe. Mádi's diaries show how much was known of the Holocaust in 1942. She was sure that Hungary would be punished after the war for allying itself with the criminal Nazi regime. Efforts by the Hungarian government to make a separate peace with Great Britain and the United States were unsuccessful, as President Roosevelt at the January 1943 Casablanca Conference demanded unconditional surrender of all Axis nations. The Casablanca declaration caused Hungarian prime minister Miklós Kállay to wonder how he could surrender Hungary to the Allies when the German army surrounded his country for a thousand kilometers on all sides.

Mádi waited impatiently for the Allies to open a second front in Europe. In July 1943 British, American, and Canadian armies invaded Sicily, prompting her to write of her "euphory." On July 10 she penned in her diary: "I do not want to rejoice beforehand but now I hope the end is coming . . . Looking back on these days last year, on their utter hopelessness, how wonderful to have news and events at last!" She hoped for an Anglo-American invasion of the Balkans, the so-called soft underbelly of Nazi-controlled Europe, that would bring English-speaking forces to liberate Hungary.

Her hopes in July, however, soon evaporated. On August 20 Mádi wrote, "Instead of allied invasion we may get bolshevik invasion, which is no maiden-dream." Events in the fall and early winter of 1943–44 gave Mádi more reason to despair about the fate of Hungary. She listened to reports of the meeting of the Allied foreign ministers in Moscow in October and wrote: "The Moscow conference has begun. What are we going to get out of it? Shortening of the war? Discussions about us, without us?"

The entries in chapter 1 and in subsequent chapters contain frequent references to a variety of people and places. Mádi often used nicknames for people familiar to Hilda, as well as the proper names of others she encountered either in person or via the press or radio. The "Dramatis Personae" identifies many of the individuals about whom the doctor wrote. Mádi also referred to geographical place-names in Hungary and in its capital city, Budapest. The footnotes to the diary entries identify many of these place-names. Map 1 shows Hungary as of the start of the diary in December 1941, by which time Hungary had regained territory lost under the post–World War I Treaty of Trianon to Czechoslovakia, Romania, and Yugoslavia. To Mádi's thinking, the most significant recovery was the Romanian province of Northern Transylvania, with its administrative capital, Kolozsvár. The map also shows some of the cities that are prominently mentioned later in the book when Mádi kept track of Allied bombings of both Hungary and neighboring Austria and Romania. Finally, map 1 shows the extent to which Hungary was surrounded by Germany and German power between 1938 and 1941. Austria had been absorbed into the Reich in 1938. The Czech homelands experienced the same fate in 1938–39, while nominally independent Slovakia became the first of the satellite states under German hegemony in 1939. German-occupied Poland became a conquered province later in 1939, as did Serbia in 1941.

Map 2 depicts Budapest, divided by the Danube River, with the Buda side on the west bank of the river and Pest on the east bank. The map shows the site in the Buda hills where the Mádi family had its city villa at 18 Rezeda utca

Map 1. Hungary, December 1941, at the start of Mádi's diary (Bill Nelson)

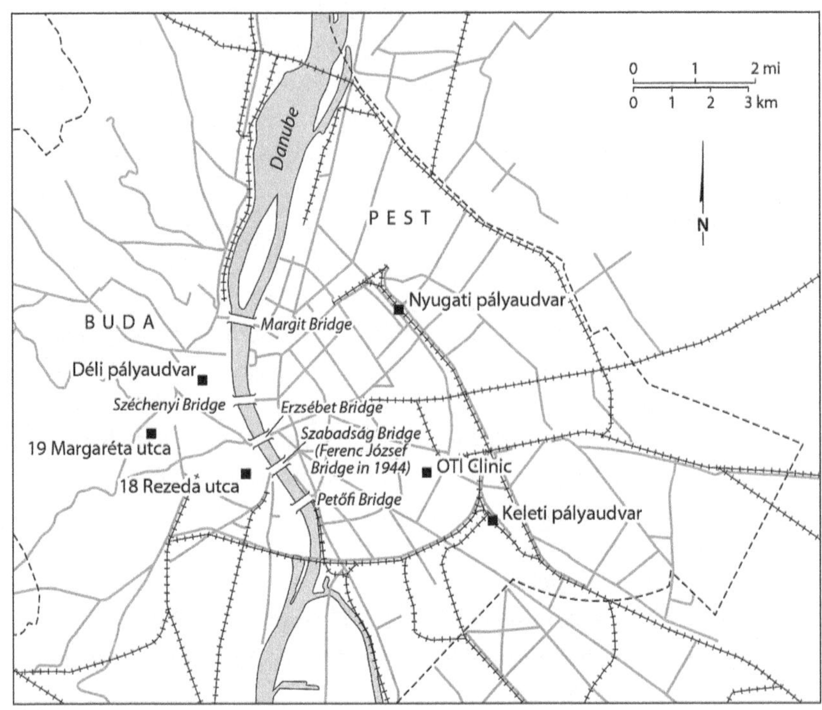

Map 2. Budapest, December 1941–March 1944 (Bill Nelson)

(street), as well as the small flat at 19 Margaréta utca where she lived from December 1941 to the fall of 1946, when she left Hungary for the United States. The map also shows the three railway terminals, Déli (South Station) in Buda and Nyugati (Western Station) and Keleti (Eastern Station) in Pest. Map 2 shows the bridges across the Danube that Mádi crossed by streetcar or on foot as she moved about the city. The map also shows the location of a place of work for the doctor at the Oti (National Social Security) building on the Pest side near Keleti railway station.

The connections of the Felsőbüky and Mádi families stretched to the borders of the old Austro-Hungarian monarchy and included German and Italian relatives. Mádi often mentioned members of the extended family in the diaries, although she disagreed with them regularly about politics and Hungary's part in the war. She made little effort to conceal her pro-Allied sympathies in conversations with friends, many of whom wished for a German victory. Mádi's niece Dr. Gertrude Nossak, a botanist, was married to an official in the German Foreign Office. "Gerti" and her husband, Rolf, came to Budapest; Gerti then spent a month doing field biology research in Hungary while Rolf continued to Istanbul on official business. While in Turkey, he found the opportunity to post a letter from Mádi to Hilda in the United States and on his return brought back delicacies such as coffee, cigarettes, and goose fat. Although Mádi welcomed the assistance and the goods, she worried that a telegram Rolf sent to Gerti care of the Budapest flat meant that she, Mádi, would "be suspected of Nazi sympathies."

Along with her close connections within Hungarian Christian society, Mádi had many Jewish colleagues and friends, especially doctors, dentists, and pharmacists. She knew some of the members of the extended Weiss-Kornfeld-Chorin family, the proprietors of the leading manufacturing establishment in Hungary. She was particularly close to Baron Alfons Weiss, a former neighbor on Rezeda utca, and fondly called him "Ali." Despite her friendships with Jewish individuals, she sometimes expressed her dislike of Jews as a social group because of what she saw as their loud ways of talking in public. One day in mid-1942, she entered the venerable Gerbeaud Café but soon left because she was unable to abide the "terrible noise, this sort of singing speech, which is so characteristic of Jews." Politics and the war, however, drove her closer to her Jewish acquaintances. At one point, she wrote of her pro-German friend Gisella "Gizi" Horchler: "It is a sordid effect of German propaganda that one becomes alienated from people, like Gizi, the best of friends, with whom one has much more in common with regards taste, style, surroundings, as one has with Jewish friends, to whom one must be attracted because of common views on events."

Waiting and war-weariness are the themes of many of the diary entries between December 1941 and February 1944. She reported on what she read and heard around Budapest in conversations with people whom Hilda knew. Mádi repeated rumors she heard, and she listened to the radio as much as possible to gather news from different sources, even as she scoffed at the demands that both the Axis and Allies placed upon Hungary. Her diary reflects the acute position of little countries in Europe caught between great powers. By early 1944 her "Kassandra" feelings had begun to sharpen. She feared that, for Hungary, the war would not end peacefully; instead, the country and its people would suffer untold catastrophes. The last entry in the chapter contains the doctor's lament that she was "tired of being sick, with no money and without adequate footwear," even as she caught herself in her self-pity, adding, "All my complaints are ridiculous, I am perfectly aware of it."

For Further Reading

Readers interested in learning more about Mádi's Hungary and Budapest between December 1941 and February 1944 may consult some of the following works. Evan Mawdsley, *December 1941: Twelve Days That Began a World War* (New Haven, CT: Yale University Press, 2011), offers a helpful broad view of how the different regional and even continental wars from the 1930s merged into one global conflict in December 1941, including how Hungary came to declare war on the United States and the United Kingdom. Mária Ormos, *Hungary in the Age of the Two World Wars, 1914–1945*, translated by Brian McLean (Boulder, CO: Social Science Monographs, 2007), provides a summary of events that explains the place of Hungary as a little country caught between its ambitions for territorial revision of the Treaty of Trianon and the larger powers of Europe. Mádi's diary entries between 1941 and 1943 contained much commentary on what she saw as the justified reclaiming of the territories lost at Trianon. Two books, Holly Case, *Between States: The Transylvanian Question and the European Idea during World War II* (Stanford, CA: Stanford University Press, 2009), and Leslie Waters, *Borders on the Move: Territorial Change and Ethnic Cleansing in the Hungarian-Slovak Borderlands, 1938–1948* (Rochester, NY: University of Rochester Press, 2020), recount the history of the Hungarian reoccupation of Transylvania and southern Slovakia, respectively, that Mádi applauded. Her diary entries show awareness of the fate of Jewish men drafted into the labor service during the war, especially for service in Ukraine and Russia. Robert Rozett, *Conscripted Slaves: Hungarian Jewish Forced Laborers on the Eastern Front during World War II* (Jerusalem: Yad Vashem Press, 2014), tells this history. Finally, Cecil B. Eby, *Hungary at War: Civilians and Soldiers in World War II* (University Park: Penn State University Press, 1998), recounts oral history memories of Mádi's Hungarian contemporaries who lived through the war years.

~

DECEMBER 23, 1941.

Since we are at war with the States, there is no hope for me to join you, my only ones. My first thought was: at least five years.[1] . . . May be much more and who knows whether we are going to survive all, what is going to happen. Geo,[2] whom I have seen last as a youth will become in these years somebody

1. Mádi left Europe for the United States on December 9, 1946, just shy of five years after this diary entry. See Immigration and Naturalization Service passenger arrival form for Madi-Kiss, Maria Louisa, accessed April 21, 2021, http://www.ancestry.com/.

2. George Walton (1912–2001), son-in-law of Mádi, petroleum engineer with Carter Oil Company, formerly petroleum engineer with Magyar Amerikai Olajipari Részvénytársaság (MAORT, Hungarian-American Oil Company).

whom I do not know, Hilda[3] left me as a girl, almost child, exuberant with the joy of life—well, she will be a mature woman, let us hope, she will be spared the loss of them, whom she loves. You remember? Geo did not like our not going to church on Sundays, now I go almost every day and pray for him, that he may be spared from the horrors of war. This military service act of the U.S. was a worse blow for me than being separated from you for years. Now, Barbara[4] will be perhaps in school, when I see you again. At best, there will be a tremendous gap between us, in our way of thinking. If we are going to meet ever.

DEC. 29, 1941, MONDAY.

Since the declaration of war (dec. 11) I got back two of my own letters addressed to you, from dec. 6 and dec. 1.[5] This afternoon my letter to you from Nov. 26 came back! It never left Budapest in such a time. It was a sort of farewell letter, now not even this could reach you.

JAN. 7, 1942.

I have to forget all about you, impossible to live burdened with all loving memories and to live without any hope. It is a sort of Kassandra[6] feeling but mark my words, it will be like this: some day, should the present East European military situation change, the Russian army must not even be near us, local Soviets will seize the power in all European countrys with the exception of France and perhaps Switzerland. These two countrys will get an immediate help from the West. I do not know whether this soviet system is going to last or will be only temporary but I think the middle classes will not live through this intermezzo. I think Middle-and-Eastern Europe was sold at the recent Moscow-conference.[7]

---

3. Hilda Felsőbüky (1920–89), daughter of Mádi, married George Walton in 1939.

4. Barbara Walton (b. 1941), daughter of Hilda and George Walton. Often referred to in the diaries as "Babu."

5. The United States suspended postal, telephone, telegraph, and cable services to Hungary on December 11. See Louis Fiset, "Return to Sender: U.S. Censorship of Enemy Alien Mail in World War II," *Prologue* 33, no. 1 (2001); Lawrence Sherman, ed., *The United States Post Office in World War II* (Chicago: Collector's Club of Chicago, 2002).

6. Kassandra/Cassandra was Priam's daughter in ancient Troy. Cassandra's fate was to prophesize the future but to have her warnings of doom ignored. See Euripides's portrayal of her in *The Trojan Women.*

7. The conference in Moscow (September 29–October 1, 1941) was hosted by Vyacheslav Molotov and attended by Lord Beaverbrook, representing the UK, and by Averell Harriman, representing the United States. An agreement on supplying the USSR with tanks and warplanes from US and UK stocks was reached. See Ambassador Steinhardt to Secretary of State, October 1, 1941, in *Foreign Relations of the United States, 1941,* vol. 1, *General, the Soviet Union* (Washington, DC: Government Printing Office, 1959), document #786.

You may imagine how agreeable it is to hear some over-zealous radio commentator refer to us as "those gangsters" that is, the small European nations.

It is believable that there was a time when lots of foreigners came to Budapest by the Vienna ship and the city was all lights and life, sparkling with gayety of peace time. Tomorrow Ribbentrop is coming to Budapest, one hears to guess that they want a general mobilization in our country.[8] The second step to exhaustion. The first is the rationing.

JAN. 27, 1942, TUESDAY.

Now I begin to think of it: though involuntary, but my staying here these years will be a very exciting adventure. I am going to see, to hear, to witness everything and to tell you all about it. At the end we (or you) shall see whether my Kassandra feelings were right. Nobody believes me, but this used to be the lot of Kassandras.

MARCH 8, 1942, SUNDAY.

Had lunch with Sebestyéns. They are nice and kind. Apu[9] travels a lot, came just home from two weeks in Berlin (could not go anywhere because about 6 p.m. he had still work and the theatres begin about this time), goes next week to Rome, then to Switzerland and from there again to Berlin. This Switzerland business is very important for me, he takes a letter from me for you, gave an address, where you can write all the time and without my asking him, said, he is going to cable you and telefon your answer immediately home. Is it not awfully good of him? I could bear this situation so much better if I had occasionally some news from you!

JUNE 22, 1942, MONDAY.

The greatest event for me since the war broke out the first letter from you since last Nov. 10th, dated May third. It came through Stockholm . . . I gave up hope entirely from this address but of course it did not come by mail to this country, very cleverly. How good to know that Geo is working at Shreveport instead of military service! Babu crawling and being naughty! From these factors I can guess that you are happy. You mentioned your vacations are planned

8. "Ribbentrop Confers in Hungary's Capital," *New York Times* (hereafter cited as *NYT*), January 6, 1942. Joachim Ribbentrop, German foreign minister (1893–1946), indicted, tried, convicted, and executed for conspiracy against the peace, crimes against peace, war crimes, and crimes against humanity by the International Military Tribunal, Nuremberg.

9. Sebestyén Pál (1893–1973), lawyer, diplomat, and undersecretary in the Ministry of Foreign Affairs. See *Magyar Életrajzi Lexikon* (Hungarian dictionary of biography, hereafter cited as *MEK*), accessed April 21, 2021, https://mek.oszk.hu/00300/00355/html/index.html.

for June at Atlanta—so may be you are there today, when very probably Apu's cable will reach Mother Flossie.[10]

SAME NIGHT.

I read and re-read your letter. Every word has double meaning for me—it means what you say and it means that you all love me.

JUNE 23, 1942, TUESDAY.

Tomorrow Babu will be ten months old. Her height of 67 cm-s (by now she may have grown more) is unbelievable. I measured all the furniture in my apartment to see her proportioned to them and I am amazed. It is as I have told you before: with your letter and news comparatively recent (May 3rd) I find life more easy to bear. This was an almost cheerful day for me though I know very well, months may pass again without news.

AUGUST 7, FRIDAY.

I was told that your Dad[11] is in a private nursing home so this morning I went with Irmus Marosy[12] to see him. He is very ill, a chronic gastric inflammation plus (shrinking) cirrhosis of the liver, it seems he had been drinking too much these last years. It was a pity to see him with 30 kg-s minus, shaking hands and nearly unable to speak because of the continuous nausea. We cheered him up a bit, made jokes. You are not going to see him again.

SEPT. 8, TUESDAY.

I have to tell you that your Dad passed away quietly on last Saturday, at 12:15 noon. He will be buried on Thursday at the churchyard of Nagykovácsi.[13] The day before he was operated on and it turned out it was a tumour of the stomach.

DEC. 17, 1942, THURSDAY.

A joint declaration was made by the States, Great Britain and Soviet Russia against slaughtering of jews in Poland by the Nazis.[14] I entirely agree with the sense of it though do not know will the declaration help anything at present, further: why was it not made before and thirdly why did Great Britain let

---

10. George Walton's mother, who lived in Atlanta, Indiana.

11. Lajos Henfner Felsőbüky (1883–1942), advisor to the Ministry of the Interior. He and Mádi were married in June 1919. They separated in 1924, and he was granted an annulment in 1927.

12. Irma Marosy, niece of Lajos Felsőbüky.

13. Suburban Budapest, a Swabian village and part of the Tisza family estate, one of the biggest landowners in Hungary.

14. "11 Allies Condemn Nazi War on Jews," *NYT*, December 18, 1942.

happen to the unfortunate ship with 700 jews before the coasts of Palestine, what happened?[15] [. . .]

JAN. 20, 1943, WEDNESDAY.

Yesterday the Russians announced the capture of 22,000 Hungarians (about the 12 Jan.). God knows only how many of our friends have been there? Hanna's husband was there, south of Voronyezs,[16] Bandi Szerdahelyi[17] too. Not half of them will survive the strain of exposure and hunger of prisoners. Hanna worries herself to death.

JAN. 27, 1943, WEDNESDAY.

The Stalingrad German army lives its last hours. It will prove the biggest blunder of Hitler's leadership not to have left them surrender. Not as if surrendered their fates would be different as it will be now, but because the loss would not weigh on Hitler's conscience (is there such a thing?) but on the Russian's. Two hundred thousand men after all. And I am sure among the Roumanian troups thousands of Hungarians must be, from Transylvania.

FEBR. 4, 1943, THURSDAY.

Dédé[18] was here last night, he was at home to say goodbye before going to the frontline, but I have a slight hope their departure will be further delayed as with regards to Russian encirclement there is no positive knowledge of the whereabouts of our troops. Gen. Nagy[19] Secretary of war allegedly has said "dögöljenek meg a németek."[20]

FEBR. 19, 1943, FRIDAY.

Goebbels last night speech was rather menacing towards everybody.[21] People present announced the ten questions put to the German people, naturally in the

15. "Jews of Palestine Mourn Refugee Dead: Black Sea Ship with 700 Lost," *NYT*, February 28, 1942.

16. Battle of Voronezh (January 24–February 17, 1943), at which the Red Army encircled and destroyed the Hungarian Second Army, which suffered ninety thousand killed, wounded, captured, and missing. "A 2. magyar hadsereg (1942–1943)" (*MEK*, http://mek.oszk.hu/02100/02185/html/63.html).

17. András "Bandi" Szerdahelyi was a childhood friend of Hilda. The Szerdahelyi family lived on the Gellért hill, near Mádi's old home on Rezeda utca.

18. Maria's nephew, son of her sister Marguerite, countess of Viczay.

19. Vilmos Nagy (1884–1976), minister of war for Hungary (1942–43) (*MEK*).

20. "Let the Germans all be killed."

21. Speech of Joseph Goebbels, German minister of propaganda, February 18, 1943, at the Berlin Sportpalast, https://en.wikipedia.org/wiki/Sportpalast_speech.

affirmative. Goebbels just mentioned that all nations "available" will be "used" in the future not so "superficially" as until the present. I hear that next week our factories began 12 hour work-days, I hear about civilian mobilization, etc. By the way, some people say that even our iron plants are turning out submarines.

Day by day our soldiers on leave from the front line were told by the radio to report at the railway station to be sent back to Russia [. . .] I hope not. I hope our government will not give way this time to Jerry's[22] demands.

FEBR. 23, 1943, TUESDAY.

I could not sleep this morning so I switched on the radio and listened to the last news of the North American service of the BBC,[23] this finished I changed the wavelength to Budapest—it was 6 a.m. and there messages were on to the frontlines. All to soldiers, whose post numbers were beginning with two hundred. We know, nearly all these troups were lost at Voronyezs[24] and at Kurzk. It sounded like a ghost story. Mothers and wives clinging to the last straws of hope.

JULY 25, 1943, SUNDAY.

Mussolini has resigned! Nonsense, that Badoglio[25] will carry on the war. It can't last a week more in Italy, without Mussolini's immense prestige. Not even with his prestige could it last for long. War will have an end in Italy in a short time. What consequences next? Atlantic invasion or no invasion, the next step probably, no, surely will be some strong action on the Balkans, Bulgaria will have to decide and it is no question on which side she is going to decide. So may be in two or three weeks time we can be in the foreground of events. Dear! Getting nearer and nearer to you every day.

AUGUST 19, 1943, THURSDAY.

Second[26] BBC news the people of Europe were told to get ready for Europe's invasion, whatever that means. Now is something really important to happen

---

22. Mádi referred to Germans as "Jerry" and later simply as "Gs."

23. It was not illegal for Hungarians to listen to foreign broadcasts, even from enemy stations, until March 1944. Mádi regularly listened to the BBC, the Voice of America when she could get it, and Radio Kossuth, the Hungarian-language service of Radio Moscow. Zsuzsanna Ozsváth recalls that when she was a child her family "listened to the BBC every day . . . and followed the war on the map" (Zsuzsanna Ozsváth, *When the Danube Ran Red* [Syracuse, NY: Syracuse University Press, 2010], 67).

24. Reference to the Battle of Voronezh (January–February 1943).

25. Marshal Pietro Badoglio (1871–1956), former chief of staff of the Royal Italian Army, replaced Mussolini as prime minister after the king dismissed the Fascist leader.

26. Mádi made attributions about information with the word "Second." She later edited some of these to read "According to."

or is it just bluff to put the Germans off the scent? I believe rather the first alternative.

AUGUST 20, 1943, FRIDAY.

Since four years things are turning from bad to worse for humanity and for me. Four years ago, on your engagement day we felt already that something is in the air, three years ago it was the last days of our farewell, and Geo was not with us. Two years ago I still hoped to join you.[27] Last year, well, then there was no more hope left for me. This year there is more hope but we are living under the imminent menace of air raids. What life.

From the Foreign Office[28] I have heard that allegedly the allies are not going to land on the Balkans nor have anything to do with any of the Balkan nations because of Russian jealousy. This may mean good for Hungary because in this case Yugoslav insurgents will not be organized against us but may mean bad also as instead of allied invasion we may get bolshevik invasion, which is no maiden-dream.

AUG. 25, WEDNESDAY.

There used to be some misterious messages on BBC's French service, like this: Georgine n'a plus des bottines. Or: Éduard va promener l'aprés midi. We used to guess the meaning of these messages but got to the conclusion that though it is not impossible to imply some real meaning to them, it is more likely just a jig-saw puzzle (keresztrejetvény) for the German braintrust. Last night BBC's Hungarian service announced a special message for us: We hope there will be cherry-rétes[29] on Sunday. Now I am almost positive about it, there will nothing happen on Sunday.

DEC. 31, 1943, FRIDAY.

Thanks God, I do not feel at all moved or sentimental at the close of the old year. It was an abominable span of time, so the sooner the better to get rid of

27. Mádi applied for an exit visa from Hungary and an immigration visa to the United States in August 1941. She was granted the first but denied the second by US officials.

28. Mádi's reference to the "Foreign Office" was to Hungary's Ministry of Foreign Affairs. Her friend Pál Sebástyen provided her with his insights into the war.

29. Cherry-rétes was a Hungarian pastry specialty. On the use of short-wave radio code words and numbers for one-way communication with clandestine agents, see Leo Marks, *Between Silk and Cyanide: A Codemaker's War, 1941–1945* (New York: HarperCollins, 1998).

it. A few hours and it will be finished and this time I have big hopes for the next one.

JAN. 1, 1944, SATURDAY.

Cincinnati, Ohio is on my radio. Very unusual event. I have just heard a fairly good round up of last year's political events. A rather cold, but radiant, sunny day. At noon I went up to Bástya sétány[30] all sunshine and people this typical "buda" sort, gentiles, some beautiful young women, nice blond babies, funny dogs, high officials (middle aged) and young air corps officers. Two SS men walked vis-à-vis these nice people of ours (they like the good confectionery shop Ruszwurm near by)[31] and they looked green with jealousy. Yes, in spite of their "European fortress," people here are still rather happy and grow day by day in loathing these parasites of Europe.

JAN. 12, WEDNESDAY.

President Roosevelt spoke yesterday about a general mobilization of all working forces.[32] I do not understand this. If this mobilization is necessary (130,000,000 people!) to win the war, why not before? If not, so why do it now, when at least a year will be needed until the results can be felt. Generally the war's end, at least European war's end, is hoped for in this year. Is this mobilization meant just for the fall's electoral campaign? I can't help to think of the postwar period, how difficult will be the demobilization of these masses and their return to normal working conditions.

The execution of Ciano,[33] de Bono and the other three took place at Verona though a day before it was announced, they were transferred to Cremona. It seems the Germans feared interference in the last moment. It is a shame as they had to die because they objected to the German influence and against war. Mussolini tries to wash himself white: he is ill at his villa at Garda lake. A nice grandfather, who killed the father of his grandchildren. Much like good old renaissance—Borgia times.[34]

30. Bastion Promenade in the Castle District of Buda.

31. Bakery and confectionery shop in the Castle District of Buda.

32. "President Asks Civilian Draft to Bar Strikes," *NYT*, January 12, 1944.

33. Count Galeazzo Ciano (1903–44), Italian foreign minister (1936–43) who was married to Mussolini's daughter. Tried, convicted, and executed by a court of the Italian Social Republic (Fascist) in 1944. See Ray Moseley, *Mussolini's Shadow: The Double Life of Count Galeazzo Ciano* (New Haven, CT: Yale University Press, 1999).

34. A reference to the Borgia family of Pope Alexander VI (1492–1503) and the intrigues associated with that family.

I am tired of being sick, with no money and without adequate footwear, when outside snow is high on the streets. The soles of my shoes have holes on them, what is not so bad in dry weather, but very disagreeable in snow or rain. Besides no coffee to cheer me up. All my complaints are ridiculous, I am perfectly aware of it. All this has no importance at all and no meaning whatever. It is but my dear own self, who feels uncomfortable. For the second time I have asked for rationed leather-soled footwear, but in vain. Authorities seem to believe, MD's do not need shoes [. . .]

CHAPTER 2

The Invasion and Occupation of Hungary, March 1944

Chapter 2 includes much of what Mádi wrote in her diaries about the occupation of Hungary by the German army in March 1944. Mádi renewed her pledge to Hilda to "be a witness to everything," and she soon increased the volume and extent of her writing.

In early 1944 the government of Hungary, led by Prime Minister Miklós Kállay, asked the British and Americans through intermediaries about surrendering to the Allies without suffering Soviet occupation. The Germans were aware of the peace feelers extended by the Hungarians, and Hitler summoned Regent Miklós Horthy to a conference in Salzburg, ostensibly to discuss military strategy, the weekend of March 15–17. Instead, the Germans detained the regent and held him for several days. The Germans massed troops on the old frontier between Austria and Hungary, and while Horthy was Hitler's guest prisoner, the German army marched into Hungary on March 19.

Mádi called the arrival of the German army an "invasion," but on reflection more than two decades later, when she edited her diaries, she crossed out that word and substituted the word "occupation." The difference is significant. The German army between 1938 and 1944 marched into many countries. Some invaded countries were destroyed, most notably Poland, where the Germans and the Soviets crushed armed resistance, dissolved the Polish state, and treated the people as conquered subjects to be displaced, enslaved, or killed. Some German moves were bloodless occupations, with the local population welcoming the German army as friends, notably during 1938 in Austria and in the German-speaking part of Czechoslovakia. During some invasions the Germans had to overcome brief armed resistance, but the invaders soon found local political and military collaborators, such as Vidkun Quisling in Norway. By the 1960s Mádi had come to see the March 19, 1944, arrival of the German army in Hungary as more like the Norwegian experience than the Polish one.

In the weeks leading up to March 19, Mádi reminded Hilda and George Walton that Hungary had joined the German-led Axis not because of any great enthusiasm for Nazism but because of the lack of any alternatives. On March 2 she wrote that "some fatheads and especially bribed politicians, big industrialists" welcomed Hungarian participation in the Axis-launched war against the USSR, "but the majority of the people did never share their illusions. The cause of this joining was much more our hopeless position, encircled totally by German troups [*sic*]." Mádi wrote of the pro-German sentiment among many of her friends, relatives, and acquaintances. She estimated that "about 50 percent is pro-German, 25 percent pro-allies and 25 percent anti-German but so much afraid of bolshevism that they are undecided. I have excepted Jews or those of Jewish origin, because that is absolutely clear. They must be anti-Nazi." Hers was an admittedly unscientific poll, but she put her finger on one strand of public opinion, those "so much afraid of bolshevism." The arrival of the German army on March 19 was cast by both Germany and the new Hungarian government that had emerged by March 22 as a stand against godless Communism and a defense of the idea that Hungary was a Christian nation, a belief that had taken strong root from 1914 onward.

That Jewish Hungarians "must be anti-Nazi," the doctor recognized immediately on March 19, as the arrival of the German army, along with the German Gestapo, put Jewish lives in immediate danger. March 19, 1944, provided the opportunity for the long-suppressed National Socialist, Fascist, and antisemitic parties in Hungary to cooperate with the German war on the Jews. That very first day of the occupation, Mádi wrote of her fears for the lives of her Jewish friends, Irén "Lacy" Lakos, Emil Kartal, and Klári Forrai. The next day, the twentieth, she spoke with her neighbor Mária Pató, who had been a work colleague of Mádi's son-in-law, George Walton, about the Gestapo arrests of Jews. On the twenty-first, Mádi feared that the Gestapo had detained her friend Baron Alfons Weiss (he was actually still at large) and the textile businessman Leó Goldberger. Hungary's three-quarters of a million Jews, whose lives had been protected by the Kállay government, were suddenly in jeopardy. SS men who accompanied the German army took over the administration of the suburban Kistarcsa detention center and quickly made it a concentration camp for Budapest Jews.

The excerpts from Mádi's diary from March 19, 1944, reveal her hope that Hungary's government and its people would resist the German occupation. She tempered that hope with the observation that "of course, we must not nurse any false illusions, there will be people who are willing to collaborate with the Nazis." Still, over the next several days, she wrote of stories she heard of resistance throughout the country, even an expression by a pro-German friend that he hoped "90 percent of the Hungarians will resist."

All the stories of resistance proved fleeting, however, and she soon recognized that Hungarians acquiesced, even if grudgingly, to the presence of the German army in their country. Mádi's diary entries from the spring of 1944 reveal her understanding of some of the reasons behind the acceptance on the part of most Hungarian people to the German occupation. One reason was that a significant portion of the Hungarian population was of German ethnic origin, descendants of eighteenth-century peasants from Germany who settled in Hungary after the expulsion of the Ottoman occupying forces. They were known in Hungary as "Danube Swabians" (Dunai svábok). Mádi knew many such individuals personally, and she related to Hilda and George Walton in a March 26, 1944, diary entry that a former colleague of theirs at the Magyar Amerikai Olajipari Részvénytársaság (MAORT, Hungarian-American Oil Company) office had voiced the opinion that "she is very happy the Germans came, there will be order in the country! She is sváb, of course." The ethnic German component of the Hungarian nation was especially well represented in the officer corps of the Hungarian army and war ministry.

The diary entries from March 1944 show Mádi struggling to learn news of the occupation and the resulting imposition of a German-directed government, even as Regent Horthy after three days gave his approval to the appointment of new Far Right figures and the dismissal of many conservative but not pro-Nazi officials. She found the radio broadcasts of the BBC and Voice of America lacking any means of help to Hungarians who might try to resist the occupation. On the other hand, German propaganda through newspapers and over the radio was effective in convincing many Hungarians that the occupation launched on March 19 was necessary and proper. She noted in her diary that the Germans were tireless in repeating their message that Hitler and the Nazis had taken Germany from abject defeat and humiliation to a state of prestige and prosperity. German propaganda in March 1944 promised the same for Hungary, now under German military protection from the Soviets. Mádi dismissed the promise of prosperity by the Germans as "industrial propaganda stuff: butter made out of the air and stockings made out of coal!" A neighbor of Mádi in the 19 Margaréta utca building expressed an expectation of prosperity: "[Y]oung Mrs Viktör told me day before yesterday she hopes now the Hungarian pengö will have its value!" The doctor believed that those who hoped for an increase in the value of Hungarian currency were very misguided; she called such thinking "stupidness." Despite this, she recognized that German propaganda was more persuasive than Allied propaganda.

Mádi's diary writings are filled with shrewd appraisals of the character of people she observed. As the names of the personnel of the new government were announced, she commented about the low quality of the character of the appointees. One was "compromised in some ugly affair." The list of cabinet members she dismissed as "[t]hese scoundrels!" including one of Hilda's cousins on her father's side, of whom she said, "I thought him more cunning" than to get mixed up with the collaborators. She regarded many of the people living in her Margaréta utca apartment building as persons whose "social standings in peacetime could be called mediocre" but who after March 19 "play high and mighty," with one neighbor having a second telephone line installed and others being chauffeured around the city in private cars. On March 27 she wrote about her neighbors: "The basest instincts are coming to surface now." She suspected a neighbor in the apartment building of spying on her. She recoiled in disgust at how the husband of one of her friends was "gloating over the news" of the German occupation. Perhaps the most poignant comment to be found in the doctor's diary for March 1944 was the cry from her heart addressed directly to her daughter and family in America: "[H]ow terribly happy I am because you are out of this!"

For Further Reading

Readers who wish to learn more about Regent Miklós Horthy may consult Thomas L. Sakmyster, *Hungary's Admiral on Horseback: Miklós Horthy, 1918–1944* (Boulder, CO: East European Monographs, 1994). For the regent's dealings with Hitler and the German government, see Mario Fenyo, *Hitler, Horthy, and Hungary: German-Hungarian Relations, 1941–1944* (New Haven, CT: Yale University Press, 1972). Historians continue to debate the role of the regent and the Hungarian nation in acceding to and not resisting the German occupation of March 1944. A valuable summary is in István Deák, "A Fatal Compromise: The Debate over Collaboration and Resistance in Hungary," in *The Politics of Retribution in Europe: World War II and Its Aftermath*, edited by Istvan Deak and Tony Judt (Princeton, NJ: Princeton University Press, 2000). Mádi's diary entries after March 19, 1944, show a frustration with what she regarded as the clumsiness of Allied radio propaganda that commanded Hungarians to resist the German occupation. David Garnett, *The Secret History of PWE: The Political Warfare Executive 1939–1945* (London: St. Ermin's Press, 2002, reprint of the 1947 edition), covers the history of British broadcasting and leaflet dropping over Axis countries by one who participated in its planning.

~

FEB. 24 [1944,] THURSDAY.

Barbara two and a half years old. She is riding a tricycle, next I shall hear about her, she will drive a car.

Step by step a German net is built inside the country. The barracks I told you about when going from our old home toward Mihály[1] are German military

1. A reference to Mihály utca in the 1st District (*kerület*) of Budapest, near the Gellért Hill and the Mádi family house at 18 Rezeda utca, where Hilda was raised. See map 2.

barracks as I am told. At Somlöi ut[2] an empty house is occupied by the German officers and they put the Hungarian janitors out of the house. How I hate all this!

FEBR. 25, FRIDAY.

The day began with an alarm at dawn at 3 a.m. [. . .] Some people state to have heard the sirens, I did not, with many others. Then flack[3] was heard in two phases [. . .]. In spite of all, I am charmed by the sight of certain people, how they enjoy now their "splendid Germans" and all this friendship with Germany. They got what they asked for.

Gizi[4] was here tonight and had tea with me. She can't help, is feeling pro-German, I can well see on her attitude towards events. These people, who have been so enthusiastic about German achievements two years ago are disgusted now, when things are turning against them. It seems to be the "moral" attitude, now they realize, how many people are dying in the air raids (they never had a thought for them when in 940[5] London was blitzed), but again do not give a consideration to the fact, that in these days London is getting the weight of really new weapons. The meanness is exclusively on allied side, to raid innocent people.

FEBR. 26, SATURDAY.

It is a sordid effect of German propaganda that one becomes alienated from people, like Gizi, the best of friends, with whom one has much more in common with regards taste, style, surroundings, as one has with Jewish friends, to whom one must be attracted because of common views on events. [. . .]

FEBR. 28, MONDAY.

I spent last night with re-reading your married-life letters from Zalaegerseg, Kaposvár, Dunaföldvár, Szombathely, Nagykanizsa[6] and Romania. I felt really surprised how could I write you twice some nasty letter, as it turns out from your answer, then again surprised how could I hold you in spite of all; you two were holding fast together but still were very attached to me. And Geo's letter, before you started for Romania: "if something does happen, you can be sure that I will protect Hilda with my life, my future, or my everything." In the same

2. *Út* and *utca* are Hungarian for "road" and "street," sometimes shortened by Mádi to "u."

3. "Flack," sometimes spelled "flak," was a term for antiaircraft fire.

4. Gizi is the diminutive of the Hungarian name Gisella. Gizi was a cousin of Mádi.

5. Mádi regularly left off the "1" before the year in dates.

6. Places in Hungary with oil explorations by MAORT and where George and Hilda Walton worked.

letter he gives a very witty picture about Hungarian militarism of those days as seen from outside. And you, inviting me in verse to visit you on your birthday "nélküled egy születésnap olyan, mint Joe ha névest kap."[7] These remained few things one can believe in. but still I firmly believe in love, in fine individuals, in beauty, goodness, inherited traditions. In improvements I believe only individually, the average seems deteriorating or else dictatorial systems could not have been formed with such success as we had to witness.

MARCH 2, THURSDAY.

BBC commentators often mention the satellite countries (among them Hungary) in these days. They saw we have joined Germany three years ago in the conviction Hitler will be master of Europe. This is all wrong. Sure, there had been some fatheads and especially bribed politicians, big industrialists, who hoped for this but the majority of the people did never share their illusions. The cause of this joining was much more our hopeless position, encircled totally by German troups (as W. N. Ewer[8] comments too) on the one hand, on the other hand the disastrous situation in what countries found themselves, who hoped for allied help, see Poland Yougoslavia, Greece, etc. In the long years of unpreparedness (1939–42) the prestige of the allies suffered a lot all over the world and this fact was used well by German propaganda.

American progress on the Pacific is splendid and I hope they are going on with it until the Philippines and Dutch East indies.

Not being any more nomads, no use the repeated admonitions of BBC regarding future raids over Budapest.[9] People simply have to stick to their homes. It will need a lot to chase us from the only secure corner of our lives from our houses. Unwillingly I write it down with the hope when you read this it will be again all right. I was informed today that I shall get no more salary from the municipality.[10] Now insecurity is beginning all over again, the problem how to settle rent, food, electric, etc. tomorrow.

MARCH 3, FRIDAY.

I made long walk with Lacy[11] this morning and told her about the present situation, she is going to lend me thousand Ps to hold out until I can get some

7. Without you, a birthday is rather like if Joe [the family dog] did not have a name.

8. William Norman Ewer (1885–1977), British writer and Communist.

9. The Hungarian service of the BBC urged Hungarians to flee their homes in anticipation of the Russian offensive approaching the Carpathian Basin.

10. Mádi's employment in the Emergency Department at Rókus General Hospital ended in March 1944.

11. Lacy, also known as Irka, was Irén Lakos, a Jewish friend of Mádi.

suitable work. It is good of her and is a great help as I am rather helpless these days.

The afternoon I was invited to the Horchlers.[12] Iby, Iván, Dr. Decri, Lajos Farkas were there for tea. Politics seem to be inevitable and it is from Scylla to Charibdis, I am not astonished on poor Pubi's ideas (he is sure the Finns will never break with Germany, Germans need only this summer for final victory, etc.) but Iby told a story how the stones of the old monastery of Monte Cassino were already out in the states and they will be used for construction![13]

Seeing the childishness and credulity of public opinion in good middle class circles, one must really get to the conclusion that terms must be dictated, not discussed with them. Sure, it is not so with many people but the Horchlers' German sympathies make them blind and they just believe what she has read in some dirty pamphlet.

MARCH 4, SATURDAY.

I tell you a joke Iván told us yesterday: in 1960 a newspaper fixes prizes for a jigsaw puzzle competition. First prize a roast chicken leg, second three potatoes, third 10 minutes use of the electric current. The prizes are won, the winners interviewed. The first won by a family of five. They had soup the first day, the second day and third day they ate the leg. The fourth day they chewed the bones. The fifth day they gave it to the office for raw material collecting. Similar with the potatoes. The third prize, after long meditation, as how to use best the current decides to switch on the radio and just the voice of America is heard. Hungarians if you still go on serving Germany. . . .

MARCH 5, SUNDAY.

Such a terrible snowstorm! Since about 2 p.m. it was raging and at last about 7 p.m. I had to start off from the Sebestyéns where I spent the afternoon. They gave me skiing boots and a big woolen scarf to wrap my head and face in. I have an idea what last winter's Russian frontline was like.

MARCH 6, MONDAY.

The afternoon I was invited in our house to Mrs Németh[14] and met there two ladies living in the same house, mother and daughter, whom people believe to

---

12. The family of Henrik Horchler, a petroleum engineer.

13. The reference to the clashing rocks of Scylla and Charybdis from Homer's *Odyssey* meant being caught between two bad outcomes. In the Battle of Monte Cassino (January–May 1944), the twelfth-century Italian abbey was destroyed by Allied bombing.

14. Mrs. István Németh, upstairs neighbor of Mádi at 19 Margaréta utca.

be German but they are not.[15] The mother is Austrian and the daughter (widow) Dutch by marriage. They loathe the nazis more then anything so we agreed and enjoyed having a conversation.

MARCH 8, WED., 10 A.M.

Dr. Gerde[16] just 'phones he has a letter for me. Oh, my Dearest, what happiness! I do not have an idea from which date it comes but it is from you! I have to hurry up and run to Andrássy ut as quick as possible. You are clever and wise to use this address continuously without getting new letter from me. I have some difficulty in sending letters just now but Apu promised to arrange it for me somehow.

SAME NIGHT

I got my letter it is dated the 19 January and there are two snapshots of Babu in it. . . . It was so unexpected and recent and lovely. I feel your love all the time and your loving care and be sure it helps a lot. At last Geo signed this letter again, it is ages and ages I have not seen his handwriting. Thank you both!

MARCH 11, SATURDAY.

Most fantastic sorts of German propaganda are on the air . . . the English are so wicked, they deserve it because they used to bait crocodiles in India with negro children (!) Again another item, last week's German raids over London caused a serious war fatigue in England (there may be something in this) but all the raids over Germany make the German population even more determined. German effort to hold Argentina on any price points to the importance of this country in their plans. I am told, the leaders have deposited their fortunes there and very probably mean to fly over, when everything lost here. In the mean time why not go on?[17]

I have made statistics about people's opinion among my friends, acquaintances, relatives, etc from all social strata and I have found that about 50 percent is pro-German, 25 percent pro-allies and 25 percent anti-German but so much afraid of bolshevism that they are undecided. I have excepted Jews or

15. Elly Hermans and her mother, Albina Brunowski, upstairs neighbors of Mádi at 19 Margaréta utca.

16. Oszkár Gerde (1883–1944), international lawyer and former Olympic fencing champion for Hungary. His home at 25 Andrássy út was on the most fashionable boulevard on the Pest side of Budapest.

17. Mádi's subsequent annotation: "P.S. 1969. This is what happened."

those of Jewish origin, because that is absolutely clear. They must be anti-Nazi. [. . .]

MARCH 13, MONDAY.

There are rumors in town about allied peace terms for Germany. I am rather sceptic about it and even in case there would be some truth in these rumors, I can not believe the allies would treat with the Nazi gang on the other hand the gang will not give way to any other government [. . .] I went to the social Insurance building,[18] to look around for some part time work, 2–4 hours per day. I think, there will be some in a few weeks, if only I shall be able to work. Because of some knitting I went to see the Marosys, they told me that yesterday Pista Antal[19] (minister for propaganda) advised them to leave Budapest, because by Easter Bpest[20] will be dangerous to live in. What could he mean by it?

MARCH 17, FRIDAY.

This morning we went for a walk with Maria Pató[21] on the Széchenyihegy, she has a few days vacation. As soon as we were up, just having a coffee at Hotel Gyopár, the air raid sirens sounded and we were sent to the shelter [. . .] As usual, we were told nothing in our radio news service. I am afraid these German airfields are used to chase allied planes flying over the country and if this happens, we shall be raided in no time.

SAME NIGHT.

For tea with Mrs. Hermans (the Dutch lady in the house) and her mother [. . .] They are nice people, furnished beautifully with old Dutch mahogany furniture.

MARCH 18, SATURDAY.

I did not go out the morning as I did not want to be caught somewhere in a shelter. [. . .] Coming home from them I dropped in on Bö,[22] she is the same

18. Országos társadalombiztosító intézet (Oti, Hungarian social insurance). The National Workers Health Insurance Agency was located on Fiumei út near Keleti pályaudvar (Eastern Station).

19. István "Pista" Antal (1896–1975), minister of justice in 1944. He was convicted of war crimes by the People's Tribunal in 1945 but not executed; instead, he served fifteen years' imprisonment (*MEK*). István Antal's brother, Lajos Antal, was married to Mádi's former sister-in-law.

20. Mádi called Budapest "Bpest" throughout the diaries.

21. Upstairs neighbor at 19 Margaréta utca. She was an employee at MAORT and a former acquaintance of George and Hilda Walton.

22. Erzsébet Tarnocsy, a Jewish friend of Mádi.

as usual, all hope for the end of the war this year. She has no news of Laci and András[23] since October.

After 9:30 p.m. the streets were so dark, I could hardly find where to go this five minutes distance. Bö has some information that German troups are ready at the Hungarian border to occupy the country in case we should try to get out of the war. Well, it was easy to step in but it is rather difficult to get out.

MARCH 19, SUNDAY.

This is about what we heard. The day before yesterday our regent[24] was called to Hitler's headquarters with Ghyczy, the minister for foreign affairs.[25] [. . .] The regent is guarded by German soldiers, who crossed the border at 3 a.m. All G. troups, meant for the east and the south were spread here in the country along the railway lines. About 11 a.m. a so called crown council began, with all cabinet ministers present and the regent. It still lasted when Apu left for home. The government abdicated, Kállay[26] did not form another cabinet, neither Imrédy[27] (There are some rumors this afternoon in town that Reményi-Schneller[28] or Homan[29] will be premier) We do not know yet whether the regent has abdicated or not.

Of course, we must not nurse any false illusions, there will be people who are willing to collaborate with the Nazis. By the way, not only the transdanubian[30] parts but the whole country is being occupied they are at the radio center, general Post office, Police headquarters, etc, etc. The Gestapo began to search

23. Bö's sons. They were drafted into Jewish labor service battalions for wartime construction, engineering, and sometimes mine-clearing work. See Randolph Braham, *The Politics of Genocide: The Holocaust in Hungary*, 3rd ed. (New York: Columbia University Press, 2016), 1:287–89.

24. The regent was Miklós Horthy (1868–1957). He was head of state of the Hungarian government in the absence of a hereditary monarch (*MEK*).

25. Jenö Ghyczy, Hungarian foreign minister (1943–March 22, 1944) (*MEK*).

26. Miklós Kállay, prime minister of Hungary (March 1942–March 1944) (*MEK*). See his memoir, Nicholas Kállay, *Hungarian Premier: A Personal Account of a Nation's Struggle in the Second World War* (New York: Columbia University Press, 1954).

27. Béla Imrédy (1891–1946), former Hungarian prime minister (1938–39) and minister for the economy (1944). Indicted, tried, convicted, and executed for war crimes by the Budapest People's Tribunal (*MEK*).

28. Lajos Reményi-Schneller (1892–1946), indicted, tried, convicted, and executed for war crimes by the Budapest People's Tribunal (*MEK*).

29. Bálint Hóman (1885–1951), former minister of education (1939–42) who was indicted, tried, and convicted by the People's Tribunal in 1946 and sentenced to life in prison (*MEK*).

30. Hungarian region(s) west of the Danube River.

the house of some politicians Bethlen[31] they could not find, he fled somewhere [. . .] All this and still nothing is told to the public. Not in the radio news, neither in tonight's papers.

All morning was spent by Apu & his colleagues in burning documents.[32] The afternoon I dropped in on Lacy and the Kartals,[33] they will suffer, I am afraid and I do not hope to be able to help them. Our radio fell silent at 12:30 p.m., this lasted until 3 p.m. between air-danger was signaled (the Klagenfurt raid went on). At 3 p.m. the usual musical signal was given then one of the announcers began the news but after three or four words about the eastern situation she was interrupted and there was silence again for forty minutes. Then the news were read, but as I have mentioned already, nothing about the most important recent events. From then on the radio went on but not its usual program, only some pall-mall of records. [. . .]

MARCH 20, MONDAY.

At 7 a.m. BBC still not suspecting anything. Coming home last night about 7:45 p.m. four big military trucks were waiting in our dark and quiet street, high walled and covered up, as though for human transport. I suppose soldiers on leave were gathered from the houses.[34]

Without newspaper or radio here in Bpest everybody knows about everything. Most people are very downcast. [. . .]

I have seen G military trucks near the south railway station this noon, and a crowd gathered on the other side so from the streetcar I did not see more. Terrible what things may happen. I am worried for my friends. At 10 I heard the first news from abroad about the occupation. . . . At Budaörs aerodrome[35] yesterday morning German parachuters were dropped. They came in swarms, disarmed our soldiers, broke into the depots ate and drank plenty and got drunk.

---

31. Count István Bethlen (1876–1946), prime minister (1921–31) and life peer of the Upper House of the Hungarian Parliament. He was captured by the Red Army in 1944 and deported to the USSR, where he died in a military hospital (*MEK*).

32. The daughter of Foreign Office counselor Aladár Szegedy-Maszák recalls learning that her father spent long hours at the ministry burning documents on March 19 and 20 before the arrival of the Gestapo. Marianne Szegedy-Maszák, *I Kiss Your Hands Many Times: Hearts, Souls, and Wars in Hungary* (New York: Spiegel & Grau, 2013), 120.

33. Family of Emil Kartal, former official in the Ministry of Education.

34. Mádi's subsequent annotation: "P.S. 1969. Or Jews?"

35. Budaörs, located southwest of the city, was the international airport for Budapest in the 1930s before Ferihegy airport opened.

MARCH 21, TUESDAY.

Pravdánéne[36] was here this morning.[37] [. . .] They are not all pleased with recent events and she came to have my opinion. As I did not want to destroy your wartime letters I made a packet of them and gave them to her, to take care of them. There is nothing dangerous in these letters but one would have to explain, how they got here.

Néne coming home has seen armed German soldiers (several carloads) enter the building of some Jewish office at Sándor square, they brought out many boxes and packets, etc, people said it was all gold, well, these are rumors [. . .]

Since yesterday Jews were rounded up everywhere, at first the big ones. I hear poor Ali is among them, then Goldberger[38] and the others. They were taken to Police Headquarters but according to Randi, who act as an interpreter, there was no Hungarian even near them the Gs isolated them entirely.[39] You may imagine what these brave Gestapo men earn in these days with all these detentions and house-searchings. They hope I suppose to insure their future and their old days.

Now the half a million German troups who invaded Hungary will have to go at least partly to Roumania, if it is still possible to hold them from collapse. It is believed here that in a short time general mobilization will be forced upon

36. "Auntie" Pravda, a former servant of Mádi's family.

37. The Citadella was the summit of the Gellért Hill and near to the Mádi family house at 18 Rezeda utca, as shown on map 2.

38. Ali was Baron Alfons Weiss of the Weiss family of Hungary, co-owner of the Weiss-Manfred Works armaments factory in Csepel (suburban Budapest). Leó Goldberger (1878–1945) was a textile businessman. For the expropriation by the SS and the German Foreign Office of the Weiss-Manfred Works, see Braham, *The Politics of Genocide*, 1:516–24. See also the account by Baron Móric Kornfeld, who wrote a chapter in his postwar memoirs titled "The History of Ten Weeks in 1944: Budapest-Oberlandzendorf-Mauthausen," about the arrest and expropriation of the property of the extended Weiss-Kornfeld-Choric family: *Reflections on Twentieth Century Hungary*, ed. Ágnes Széchenyi (New York: Columbia University Press, 2007), 146–89. See also Szegedy-Maszák, *I Kiss Your Hands*, 122–29. Contrary to Mádi's belief, Baron Alfons Weiss managed to elude arrest by the Gestapo after March 19 but eventually turned himself in as part of a complicated exchange between his extended family and the SS. See Yehuda Bauer, *Jews for Sale: Nazi-Jewish Negotiations, 1933–1945* (New Haven, CT: Yale University Press, 1994), 201–4.

39. As early as the second day of the occupation, Hungarian authorities deferred to the Germans on arrests of Hungarian Jews. See Braham, *The Politics of Genocide*, 1:420. See also Kornfeld, *Reflections*, 151–61, for how German SS personnel, not Hungarians, arrested him and about three thousand other Hungarians within the first few days of the occupation. See also Szegedy-Maszák, *I Kiss Your Hands*, 130–33.

us, if it is true that Sztójay[40] our former minister to Berlin accepted the premiership he will be willing to serve them on every line. [. . .]

MARCH 22, WEDNESDAY.

The majority of the G. troups, which invaded Hungary are very young and have not seen any fighting yet. They come from Austria and from France.[41] The radio alert of last night ended soon after I finished writing my notes.

Snowstorm and lasting snow again on the streets. Gizi came here the afternoon, later I went to Rami for cigarettes still no Daru but I got hundred Darlings.[42] I am afraid all our tobacco (no all other things) will be pillaged by Jerry. One RM is stabilized on 160 p! coming home I met Mici Ormos my med colleague. There are some fresh news about Bethlen, they have him, it is stated and Peyer,[43] the social democrat leader too. Anna Kéthly MP[44] has been killed so was Bajcsy-Zsilinszky[45] too.

Allegedly Keresztes-Fischer,[46] your daddy's cousin, minister for the interior committed suicide. Some news say that all Imrédy will accept premiership, because the Gs promised to get out in two weeks time! The new minister for the interior would be Ruszkcy, he had a German name before and is compromised in some ugly affair. In spite of all rumours it is very significant that after more than three days there is still no new government.

Not only Jews are rounded up but Polish, French and Italian refugees too, today I hear, thirty-seven Polish corpses are in the morgue. One of them was shot yesterday on Fö utca. Is it not unbelievable? Our peaceful utca where we used to live years long, where I went to school as a child and now unhappy chased people are shot there with machine guns.

---

40. Döme Sztójay (1883–1946), prime minister of Hungary (March 1944–August 1944), indicted, tried, convicted of war crimes by the Budapest People's Tribunal, and executed (*MEK*).

41. Braham, *The Politics of Genocide*, 1:386–87.

42. Rami was Mádi's tobacconist, Mrs. István Friedrich. Daru and Darlings were cigarette brands. See the 1941 *Budapesti telefonkönyvek* (telephone and business directory).

43. Károly Peyer (1881–1956), interior minister (1919) and longtime leader of the Magyarországi Szociáldemokrata Párt (MSZDP, Hungarian Social Democratic Party) (*MEK*).

44. Anna Kéthly (1889–1976), MSZDP leader.

45. Endre Bajcsy-Zsilinszky (1886–1944), newspaper editor and member of the Hungarian Parliament. Opposed Hungarian participation in the Axis war. Arrested by the Gestapo, March 19, 1944, and executed by the Arrow Cross, December 1944 (*MEK*).

46. Ferenc Keresztes-Fischer (1881–1948), interior minister (1938–44), arrested by the Germans in March 1944 (*MEK*). See also Jenő Lévai, *Black Book on the Martyrdom of Hungarian Jewry* (Vienna: Central European Times Publishing Company, 1948), 78.

People say that the Gs perfect lists about officials at Companies and Banks. The Jews rounded up are taken to the Tolouchház and Kistarcsa.[47] Still no word about events either in the papers or on the radio. We were not even told that the former government resigned. Our radio news service is full with threats on Jews.

8 P.M. SAME NIGHT.

Alert on the radio. Between the danger signals the G radio program gives broadcasts in its highbrow musical propaganda. I am told that the air defence of Budapest will be five times as much as it was before (Not enough fighters!). [. . .] all the G rubbish and their industrial propaganda stuff: butter made out of the air and stockings made out of coal! Pray if it is all so simple, why don't we have any? Not even coals?

9 p.m. our radio announces the forming of the new cabinet, premier Szótjay, minister of justice Antal István! Too bad I thought him more cunning. These scoundrels!

More than three and a half days passed since the occupation and tonight only the announcement, not more than German troups arrived on mutual agreement to our country to strengthen war efforts. Horthy is continuing as Regent. Here is the cabinet list: premier and foreign secretary Szótjay [. . .] justice Antal István.[48]

Since Sunday only inhabitants of the Fortress hill[49] may come and go there. Jews may not leave Bpest. All trains, boats, streetcars have to wait at city limits until Gestapo men with the help of our own police men look at identification cards. Jews are taken off all vehicles. [. . .]

A very conservative gentleman exclaimed upon the first news of the occupation: in two months time there will be nobody who would not cheer the Russians coming in!

Among the many bad news I have to tell you something nice. Szöszi the former fiancé of poor Janci has a friend, an engineer who joined up with Maort

47. Kistarcsa was a Hungarian concentration camp outside Budapest that incarcerated Jews in 1944. See Braham, *The Politics of Genocide*, 1:482–84; and "Budapest," in *Holocaust Encyclopedia*, https://encyclopedia.ushmm.org/content/en/article/budapest.

48. "A Puppet Cabinet Set Up in Hungary: Field Marshall Szotjay Becomes Budapest Quisling Premier; Premier Antonescu Summoned to See Hitler," *NYT*, March 23, 1944. Premier Antonescu was General Ion Antonescu (1882–1946), wartime leader of Romania (1940–44) who was arrested, tried, convicted, and executed for war crimes.

49. Fortress Hill was also known as Citadella.

and is working at Lispe.[50] One of the workingmen told him sometime ago: God give that the American gentlemen come back. To work with them was a pleasure.

MARCH 23, THURSDAY.

Members of the former G legation to Budapest with Jagow[51] as minister, were called back and others sent in their place. They bring us several hundred thousand out-bombed G persons. Before the occupation they forced half a million grown ups adults though we had two hundred thousand out bombed G children already. There is some talk about Iván Héjjas[52] who allegedly is organizing partisans inside the country. Kossuth[53] festivities were planned for the 20 March throughout the country. Kossuth was the symbol of all enemies of the Germans. [. . .]

I gather that the Hungarian minister for Sweden refused to recognize the present government. I wonder what will happen with them in Ankara, Bern and Lisbon? Hairdressers are limited to a smaller amount of current[54] as they used before. So even to be accepted by a hairdresser for a shampoo is a treat to be specially appreciated.

There are some people in this house, whose social standings in peacetime could be called mediocre. Now either by importance of their industrial companies or with aid of military service they feel and play high and mighty. There is a shortage in telephones lines all over country. People next door have two lines. One ordinary, another for military purposes. The same with traffic. These people were content to ride on street cars before, now they use military cars or industrial cars in all hours of the day.

I was always convinced that the worst thing about Jerry is his not having any sense of humour. Their propaganda tells us seven times a day that Hitler lifted Germany out of abominable conditions to welfare and moral heights. This they promise us for cooperation.

---

50. Lispe was the site of a Hungarian oilfield where George Walton had worked. At the February 1945 meetings in Yalta, the United States indicated its interest in seeing MAORT restored to Standard Oil Company management and direction. See *Foreign Relations of the United States* (Washington, DC: Government Printing Office, 1945), vol. 5, 244.

51. Dietrich von Jagow (1892–1945), German ambassador to Hungary (1941–44).

52. Iván Héjjas (1890–1950), leader of the White Terror in 1919–20, sentenced to death in absentia by the People's Tribunal in 1949 (*MEK*).

53. Lajos Kossuth (1802–94), leader of the Hungarian Revolution of 1848–49 against Austrian Habsburg rule.

54. Electricity.

There are some whispered news that the garrisons of Szombathely and Újvidék resisted the occupation. I hope to hear more about this time. The Rimamurányi Iron ore Co,[55] which had large offices and in fact its center at Bpest, is going to move out from here.

Oh, Hildukaim,[56] how terribly happy I am because you are out of this!

Air raid alerts on our radio seem to become an everyday affair. Since Jerry is here, we had it every morning and every evening.[57] Now Beszterce, Szamos and Maros are called probably Soviet cargo planes are flying over to Tito.[58]

MARCH 24, FRIDAY.

Coming home I have seen something on the streetcar, what would be unbelievable before. A Jewish labour-service[59] man stood at the end of the car. I stood there too. At the Marguerite Bridge an officer of the air corps got up, the Jew saluted him, military fashion and then the air corps man made some friendly remarks about the weather addressed to him. They were no acquaintances, it was clear, he only wanted to demonstrate his sympathy. Getting out, he again greeted friendly fashion.

Bibi Beck, husband of Elsa Horchler 'phoned news on Sunday to Ancél Telkes, husband of Teri Horchler former a big "nyilas"[60] and pro-German. Bibi gloating over the news, but Ancél said with passion: I hope 90 percent of the Hungarians will resist. So after all there is some hope of national resistance. At Koloszvár[61] there were clashes between the local garrison and the G troups.

55. Rima-Murányi Iron Co. was a Finnish company.

56. My Hilda.

57. The German occupation of Hungary in March 1944 coincided with the Fifteenth Air Force's readying of bases at Foggia on the Italian Adriatic. From Foggia, the range of B-17 and B-24 bombers extended to the southern parts of the German Reich, Hungary, Romania, and Yugoslavia. The official history of the Fifteenth Air Force says that daily bombing of Axis targets had to wait until winter weather cleared over the Alps. By April 1944 Hungary had become a frequent target because of its oil-producing, oil-refining, and manufacturing capacity. See Wesley Frank Craven and James Lea Cate, eds., *The Army Air Forces in World War II* (Chicago: University of Chicago Press, 1952), 3:26, 261.

58. Josip Broz Tito (1892–1980) was the general secretary of the League of Yugoslav Communists and leader of the military resistance to Axis occupation of Yugoslavia (1941–45). Beszterce, Szamos, and Maros were cities in Northern Transylvania. They were under Hungarian rule from 1940 to 1944.

59. Article 230 of the 1939 law expelled Jewish men from the armed forces but subjected them to compulsory labor work under army control (the Munkaszolgálat). See Braham, *The Politics of Genocide*, 1:287–88.

60. Nyilas refers to the Arrow Cross, or Nyilaskeresztes Párt, which was the antisemitic and Fascist political party.

61. Kolozsvár was the capital of Northern Transylvania from 1940 to 1944.

At 8 p.m. Mrs. Hermans and her mother, later Mrs. Németh came. We have agreed upon it before. It is funny, but you never can plan now any program without the interjection: in case there is no air raid.

8 orai. Ujság and *Esti Kur* does not appear any more, these were the so called Jewish papers. Mrs Hermans heard G. news in their radio, according which Gs promise the Hungarian population that in case of bombardment people will get all the Jewish houses, furniture and all. They always appeal to the lowest instincts but seem to forget that even Jewish houses are liable to be destroyed by raids.

MARCH 25, SATURDAY.

Giescking[62] has been rather coldly received at Stockholm. He is one who used to travel with his own musical concert piano and does not play on any other piano. I can understand the bitterness of the Swedes . . . Though one must never forget that with before not long the Swedes were very agreeable and helpful to Germany. I hope my radio tubes will last because else we are entirely cut off from world news. I hear on BBC that Argentina is nicely rounding up axis spies. She yielded after all to allied wishes.

I have listened to some American flyer's voices on BBC. Never have I heard sadder voices. If must be a terrible life and continuous risk. Again people's stupidness: young Mrs Viktör told me day before yesterday she hopes now the Hungarian pengö[63] will have its value! I was so taken aback, what sort of mental process would lead her to this conclusion, that I gave up to explain. Beside the looting of the country, we have to pay all expenses of the occupying army.

Cordell Hull's calling Hungary will never be heard by the majority of our population. BBC said they are not sorry for the Hungarians but for the refugees.[64] I had luncheon with Tullia, she wanted me to spend the whole day with her but this I could not stand. After lunch she had to nap, I read a book then we went for a walk on our old hill, but it is no pleasure any more, everywhere German soldiers. Citadella ut (the new one leading from Búsuló to Mihály utca) barricaded with G trucks.

At 8:30 p.m. Marie Pató came here, I hurried home. She has been very nervous these days, there seems to be some Jewish blood in her and poor soul she is much afraid. I hope nothing serious will happen, though people may be very disagreeable at the office. She tells me the majority of people at Maort are anti German now, but there are some for example, Stefi Peregi, who said today,

62. Walter Wilhelm Gieseking (1895–1955) was a German pro-Nazi pianist. Zsuzsanna Ozsváth recalls attending a concert performed by Gieseking in Budapest shortly before the March 19, 1944, occupation. The audience was comprised mainly of German officers. See Ozsváth, *When the Danube Ran Red*, 79.

63. Hungarian currency. Its prewar value was five pengö to one dollar.

64. "Hull Urges Hungary to Rise against Nazis," *NYT*, March 25, 1944.

she is very happy the Germans came, there will be order in the country! She is sváb,[65] of course, Peregi is a new name.

MARCH 26, SUNDAY.

I suppose it is G propaganda for simple souls, that allegedly our troups are occupying Southern Transylvania, being at Arad and Temesvár. This is nonsense I am sure.

Until now we got our flour rations for two weeks ahead, yesterday we were told to take them out for the coming two months. it seems local authorities try to save something for us before all food is taken out of the country. German food-specialists are already here to grab whatever they can. [. . .]

There are people who are so much afraid of house searching that they burn every English print, even books. I could not do this, did I, it would be the first to burn these letters, written to you. But I hope, I shall be able to go on, as I told you at the beginning. I am going to be a witness. One can hear noises from the neighbouring apartments and one hears the shortwaves disturbing (jamming) noises! Neighbours too are listening to other stations!

9:50 p.m. Churchill just finished his speech.[66] A world of difference between him and Nazi leaders: these are showing off, he began with short comings and disappointments. His voice is not so clear as it used to be. I had the impression as if he had had minor apoplexy. The signs of which have not cleared yet. Interesting that he spoke relatively short about Russia and not on the same footing on which he mentioned the States and Britain. . . . he did not mention all the time the second front. Is it to be hoped that next month it is going to begin really? Somehow I believe: yes.

MARCH 27, MONDAY.

2:40 p.m. snowing densely again. Our 2:30 p.m. news service is thundering not so much against Jews this time but against the gentiles who forgot themselves so far, as to be friends of the Jews. This is an index of resistance [. . .]. Bö mentioned today that in his broadcast yesterday Churchill seemed to be as confident about Hungarian resistance as we are about western invasion.

I am told that prof. Kornis's[67] philosophy lecture was a big demonstrative affair at the University. He is under custody but they let him go on lecturing. The audience cheered him, cheered and all embraced the Jewish students.

65. Swabian, that is, German.

66. "Address by Prime Minister Churchill on War and Conditions in Britain," *NYT*, March 27, 1944.

67. Kornis Gyula (1885–1958), philosopher, university instructor, and president of the Hungarian Academy of Sciences. He was arrested by the Gestapo in 1944 and imprisoned until 1945 (*MEK*).

Lacy's brother was offered a job by Jerry with the intermediary of the Jewish Rel. Office.[68] They want an architect, a road building and a mining engineer from the Jews. May be it would be a life insurance for him but he declined.

The basest instincts are coming to surface now. In a letter addressed to the editor of *The Pest* Boldiszár Horváth[69] (may be the letter is a forgery) urges that when there is an alert going on our radio people should not be permitted to listen to lectures or music. Jerry's spirit is beginning to show itself.

I found the espressos of the city almost empty, though a week before they used to be full. The waitresses say it is since the occupation that people do not come anymore. As I drank my coffee at Monpti in the heart of the city, a G armed truck passed on the Petőfi Sándor street. Some of the people shuddered with disgust.

May be I am developing a persecution complex, but tonight as Mrs. Németh came to see me and she has eager eyes and look for everything, I felt a bit uneasy, whether she is not spying on me already.

MARCH 28, TUESDAY.

The pawnshops are full with work, it seems the Jews realized only now that their property is in danger, they are pawning silver, jewels and Persian rugs. Heaps of them. Safes are closed before everybody, Jew or Gentiles just the same. Some Jews are trying to get Hungarian officers, to rooms in their apartments. It will be late, though, I think enforcement of G laws will turn them out of their places. Your friend Eva's mother air corps officer was informed today, that his telephone will be taken tomorrow. So the Kartals.[70]

The trans-Tisza part of the country, together with whole Roumania (no borders any more) is G military operation ground and under G military government.[71] [. . .]

---

68. The Budapest Jewish Council, formed on German orders on March 21, 1944. See Braham, *The Politics of Genocide*, 1:418–79; and "Budapest," in *Holocaust Encyclopedia*.

69. Boldizsár Horváth (1897–1970), orthopedic surgeon. From 1932 to 1963 he was the chief doctor of the orthopedic surgery department at the Szent János Hospital.

70. Emil Kartal was a Jewish official in the Ministry of Education. The Kartals were family friends of Mádi. For the expropriation of Jewish property by the Germans, see Braham, *The Politics of Genocide*, 1:516–27.

71. The Tiszántúl (Trans-Tisza) region was the territory east of the Tisza River and continuing into Transylvania. In 1940 the Second Vienna Arbitration gave Hungary the northern half of Transylvania, reversing in part the Trianon Treaty of 1920. The Paris Peace Treaty of 1947 reversed the Vienna Arbitration and restored the borders between Hungary and Romania to their 1920 status.

MARCH 29, WED.

A busy day. Pravdáné here the morning, got her injection. We left together, though I felt poorly, but promised Tercsi néni[72] to see her. [. . .] Tersci lost much of her weight and is very miserable, just looking at her. They will be stigmatized with the yellow star very probably in the near future.[73] I do not approve of mixed marriages but one should not break up families and make them miserable. Erzsi and Emil had to be seen too. It is so little one is able to do for them, just a little sympathy and may be in a few days even this will be forbidden. We agreed upon postcard and we can meet in town somewhere, I hope, even if the new "laws" come. [. . .]

The mayor of Bpest Homormay[74] . . . resigned so many provincial chiefs and several diplomats (outside the country) have not recognized the new "government." Good for them. I heard a remark about BBC & Co urging us for resistance. It is all right talking resistance from London but here any act will be followed by killing so many innocent hostages.

In our old home and in the former homes of the Sebes' G soldiers are in large numbers since yesterday. I am sorry for the place. Passing the Gellért hotel[75] this afternoon, I have seen about a hundred G parachuters at the bath entrance, some trucks too. [. . .]

Dr. Scherf just called me on 'phone he got some news from Gerti[76] about her coming on April 20 to Budapest. I am not enthusiastic. Bö rang me up too, she wants me to do something for her. Of course, with pleasure, I told her.

Soviet troups about fifty kms from the Hungarian border about 100 kms from Rakó, where I spent a couple of weeks in '41. [. . .] It is surprising, how fast they are, there can't be much resistance at those parts.

I hear that at the house of Ali the Gs took inventory of everything, until the last handkerchief and left it there on the responsibility and under care of Teta, their old G nurse.

---

72. Auntie Theresa.

73. The cabinet of the new Hungarian government approved a series of anti-Jewish measures on March 29, 1944, including the mandatory wearing of a yellow star on outer garments beginning on April 5. See Braham, *The Politics of Genocide*, 1:492–97.

74. Homonnay Tivadar (1888–1964), Christian Socialist politician and mayor of Budapest (*MEK*).

75. The Gellért Hotel was a spa resort on the Buda side, close to the former Mádi home at 18 Rezeda utca.

76. Gertrude, Mádi's Viennese cousin. Gerti was married to Rolf, an official in the German Foreign Ministry.

CHAPTER 3

The Holocaust in Hungary and the Air War, April–July 1944

Until March 1944 Hungary did more than any other German ally to protect its three-quarters of a million Jewish citizens against deportation and death. Hungary was able to avoid participation in the murder of its own Jews because it maintained its national sovereignty and protected Jewish Hungarians as citizens, even if second-class citizens. However, after March 1944 occupied Hungary enthusiastically participated in the Holocaust, and its management of mass murder was the most thorough of any German ally, with more than 750,000 persons stripped of property and state protection and more than 430,000 of them deported to Auschwitz-Birkenau, where most were murdered. The entries in chapter 3 show Mádi as an observant recorder of the Holocaust in Hungary as it happened before her eyes.

Jews were prominent in the Hungarian half of the old Dual Monarchy. The 1910 census counted more than eighteen million subjects in the kingdom of Hungary, with almost one million of them Jews. They were present in every county of the kingdom, with some two hundred thousand Jews concentrated in Budapest. Hungary lifted restrictions on Jewish civic participation in 1869, and during World War I, Jews became more integrated into the life of the kingdom. Hungarian became the preferred language of Jews, and they excelled in the learned professions and in business. During World War I Jewish men served widely in the armed forces both as officers and in the ranks. At home, Jews were prominent in war relief efforts.

What made antisemitism more virulent than passive in Hungary was the brief but bloody Communist dictatorship that was inspired by the Bolshevik Revolution in the former Russian Empire. Jews were prominent in the Hungarian Communist regime, and, as in Russia, there was a fierce civil war between "reds" and "whites." Unlike in Russia, in Hungary the whites won, and in 1919 and into 1920 they imposed a "white terror." Scholars estimate that the whites imprisoned up to seventy thousand suspected Communists and summarily executed from fifteen hundred to five thousand people, many of them Jews.

The Horthy regency held parliamentary elections in 1920, and one of the first actions of the new body was to pass a numerus clausus (quota) law limiting

Jewish enrollment in the universities of Hungary to the proportion of Jews in the Hungarian population, just 6 percent after the Trianon shrinkage of the country. Prime Minister István Bethlen, who led the parliament from 1921 to 1931, resisted additional antisemitic legislation. Starting in 1932, the ministries that succeeded Bethlen instead sought assistance for the Trianon revisionist project from Fascist Italy and, after 1933, Nazi Germany. Prime Minister Gyula Gömbös favored Nazi-style race laws, and after his death in 1936 the Hungarian parliament passed a series of increasingly restrictive laws that limited Jewish participation in civil society. A 1938 law extended the numerus clausus quotas to licensed professions, such as physicians, and a 1939 law further limited Jewish economic opportunity. The prewar Hungarian restrictive laws defined Judaism as a religious choice, not as a racial category, as the Germans had done with their Nuremberg laws.

Some Jews converted to Roman Catholicism or to Calvinist Protestantism in response to the 1938 and 1939 laws. In 1941, soon after Hungary declared war on the Soviet Union and joined the Nazi war against so-called Judeo-Bolshevism, the parliament revised the anti-Jewish laws to classify even baptized, converted Jews as Jews by race, following the German example. Whereas more than one hundred thousand Hungarian Jewish men served in the armies of the Dual Monarchy in World War I, no Jewish men were allowed to serve in the Royal Hungarian Army from 1938 onward. Instead, they were subjected to conscription into labor battalions under army control.

Regent Horthy's appointment of the government of Döme Sztójay on March 22, 1944, began the radical Hungarian part of the Nazi Holocaust. A few hundred Gestapo and SS men rounded up prominent Jews. They also demanded property from the Jewish Council the Gestapo had selected, but the Germans needed more. They needed the active collaboration of a pro-Nazi government able to use the power of the Hungarian state in the war on the Jews. The Sztójay regime did not work through the Hungarian parliament, many of whose members had been arrested in the first few days after the German arrival. Instead, the government issued decrees that had the force of law. Starting on March 22, Mádi's diary chronicles the decrees directed against the Jews of Budapest and of Hungary. On that day, Jews were forbidden to leave the capital. They were also forbidden to drive cars. They had to surrender radios to the police. Next, they had to register all their property with the Jewish Council in preparation for confiscation by the Hungarian state. Jews had to give all but one change of clothing to the Hungarian police, with the surplus clothes supposedly for redistribution to German victims of Anglo-American bombing across the Third Reich.

At the beginning of April 1944, the Sztójay regime imposed the physical segregation of Jews from Gentiles in Budapest and soon after in the rest of the country. The government decreed that Jews could not employ non-Jews as servants, a cruelty that caused Mádi to write, "These maids behave wonderfully in all these families, they are faithful, are crying out their eyes, because they have to leave." Next, the government banned non-Jews from visiting Jews, a decree that Mádi ignored as she set down in her diary, "It is day by day that I go to them now, they are the most miserable and I fear, they have plans of suicide in their minds." At the same time, rumors began that the Ministry of the Interior would require all Jews, broadly defined by Hungary's 1941 Nuremberg-style laws, to display a prominent yellow star on their garments when in public. The yellow-star decree was issued on April 5. Mádi wrote of her friends, "They are sick with shame and fear, marked thus, they may be set out to any brutality." The repression of the Hungarian government extended to the whole population, as the Hungarian government issued a decree making it a criminal offense to listen to the BBC, the Voice of America, or Radio Kossuth from Moscow, a decree that Mádi promptly disobeyed.

Mádi's posting at Szent Rókus Hospital came to an end when some of the staff physicians whom she had replaced in 1942 returned from service in the Hungarian army. In April 1944 she took a physician's job with the National Social Security Administration "Oti" (Országos társadalombiztosító intézet), where she saw patients with workers' compensation claims. Mádi replaced a Jewish physician at Oti who was dismissed because of her racial classification. Daytime air raids often caused Mádi to seek shelter at Oti, which was located uncomfortably close to the Eastern Station, a prime target of Allied bombers.

Even as life became more oppressive for the Jews of Budapest, the Hungarian government began the roundup of Jews in provincial towns and cities on April 15. Jews were forced into segregated ghettos in preparation for deportation to Auschwitz-Birkenau. The rural police of the Ministry of the Interior, known as the gendarmerie, oversaw the segregation of Jews and the forced march of ghettoized Jews to railheads for deportation. Mádi soon became aware of the ghetto orders, writing in her diary on April 29 about events in the city of Kassa (Košice) in the Félvídek region of northern Hungary, now present-day Slovakia: "It would be the duty of a diary to register all events around me. Every day new orders and regulations are published, almost everyday new atrocities and cruelties happen it is difficult to register them all and too painful too. As an outstanding feature is the case of 12000 Kassa Jews, who were driven out of their home and out of town, into the open hill sides, no shelter, no water, all with but one small bag." News came to Mádi in Budapest of other countryside ghetto roundups of Jews and subsequent deportations. In June she met a friend who related the horrors of what happened in the western Hungarian city of Györ, not far from Vienna: "All Jews, men and women were searched naked before military commissioner for jewels, women and girls even by mid-wifes. Then they were driven out of their houses, over the streets of the town, like cattle into an empty brick kiln, waiting for deportation." In June 1944 Mádi learned of the mass murder in the gas chambers of Auschwitz-Birkenau.

In 1943 Prime Minister Kállay had worked out a nonviolent modus vivendi with British and US air forces. Until March 19, 1944, the Hungarians agreed not to shoot at Allied aircraft overflying Hungarian territory, even as bomber squadrons used Lake Balaton as a rendezvous point in preparation for repeated attacks on Austria. When US and British flyers were downed on Hungarian territory, the Kállay government agreed not to turn over the airmen to the Germans. In turn, the Anglo-Americans did not bomb Hungary. The German occupation ended the informal truce, and the air war against Hungary soon began. On April 2–3, 1944, the US Fifteenth Air Force, based at Foggia, Italy, sent 450 B-17 and B-24 bombers to attack the railyards of Budapest and the oil-processing plant at Csepel Island in the southern part of the city. The destruction in Budapest was considerable, even as Mádi wryly observed, "How nice to know that Americans have been so near to us." Mádi was at home in her flat at 19 Margaréta utca when the American bombers struck on April 3. She and her neighbors had to go to a makeshift basement shelter: "We just came up from the shelter, where we spent three and a quarter hours, Allied planes came in several waves since 11 p.m. [. . .] The shelter is cold, smelly and too small for more than thirty people, among them some busybodies. No night fighters could be heard. When the noises got worse, I could notice my legs shaking, though partly the cause may be cold."

For the rest of 1944, Budapest was under regular air raid alert. US, British, and Soviet aircraft repeatedly flew over the city, sometimes to bomb, sometimes to photograph, and sometimes simply to pass en route to other targets in Hungary, Austria, and Romania. The Hungarian radar defenses could not distinguish among the different purposes of the flights. Civil defense officials regularly sounded sirens and made use of Radio Budapest to signal residents to take to the shelters.

The Allied air attacks on Hungary led the Sztójay regime and the German occupiers to intensify their war on Hungarian Jews. On April 7, Good Friday that year, Mádi wrote: "The nazis understand to twist on the Jews after every move of the allies. After the Monday daylight raid they summoned the Jewish Council and told them to release 500 apartments for the use of the bombed out

Gs [Germans] in 24 hours. Next day the Council could not report more then 380 flats, two members of the Council were taken as hostages. The Council was told to evacuate not 500 but 1000 apartments in 12 hours, if not, their hostages will be shot." Hungarian officials seemed to believe that the Jews of Budapest were somehow in contact with the Allied air forces, even to the extent of directing the bombers from ground positions. The Hungarian government issued decrees prohibiting Jews from entering bomb shelters, thereby exposing them to death from the air. Later in April, Mádi wrote: "Every day some new cruelties. Last night two hundred and fifty well to do Jews and Jewesses were called to work (with a rug and a pail) and it is believed, they will have to work and to live close to the target areas. . . . Our news service—I feel sick listening to it. Lies without any scruples."

Christians, or "Gentiles," as Mádi called herself and others who were not Jewish, were forbidden to enter yellow-star houses. That did not stop the doctor, who regularly visited her Jewish friends in yellow-star houses, delivering food, cigarettes, and medicines to them. Moreover, she carried appeals from them to the consulates of the neutral powers such as Sweden and Switzerland, asking for diplomatic protection. She also shared identity papers with friends in yellow-star houses, giving Hilda's birth certificate and other documents to an "alterego" who was then able to pass for "Gentile."

By late June the news of ghetto roundups, deportations, and yellow-star houses had produced both an international and a domestic outcry. Mádi did not know of the international protests of President Roosevelt, British foreign secretary Anthony Eden, and the pontiff, Pius VI. She assumed, however, that the massive air raid by US bombers over Budapest on July 2 was in response to Hungary's war on the Jews. She reported that Hungarians were shocked to be the targets of Allied bombing. Her pro-German friends and relatives in Budapest "never believed for a moment, this could happen to them." That night she wrote in her diary: "People feel that all the cruelty towards the Jews—well, serves them right or in the best case, very sad, but what can we do? Their own suffering or inconvenience is something monstrous. On the other hand Jews are relieved, hearing the sirens. Thank god, they say. During a raid no detectives and no gendarms come. We have peace as long as a raid lasts."

In mid-July Mádi learned from her friend in the Foreign Office, Dr. Sebestyén, that the king of Sweden had written Regent Horthy a letter protesting the treatment of Jews. She paid close attention in June to the news that Cardinal Jusztinián György Serédi, head of the Roman Catholic Church in Hungary, "in the name of the whole Roman catholic priesthood turned with a memorandum to the present government. So did the council of Hungarian protestant churches. They both rose their protests against cruelty towards Jews." The deportations from the countryside ended, and the trains stopped running from Hungary to Auschwitz-Birkenau. However, the air war by the Allies against Hungary continued, and the Jews of Budapest, who had earlier largely escaped deportation and murder, faced new dangers as the war came nearer to the country and its capital.

For Further Reading

The scholarly literature on the Holocaust in Hungary is extensive and growing. Readers of Mádi's diary may wish to start with the volume by Randolph Braham, *The Politics of Genocide: The Holocaust in Hungary* (Detroit, MI: Wayne State University Press, 2000), a condensed edition that summarizes his earlier two-volume work. Mádi kept track in her diary of the various antisemitic decrees that the German-backed government of Hungary began introducing in March 1944 and throughout the summer. Zoltán Vági, Lázsló Csősz, and Gábor Kádár, *The Holocaust in Hungary: Evolution of a Genocide* (Lanham, MD: AltaMira Press, 2013), reprints and translates into English many of those documents. Mádi wrote particularly about the crisis in housing in Budapest created by the government's "yellow star" segregated housing decree of June 1944. Tim Cole, *Holocaust City: The Making of a Jewish Ghetto* (London: Routledge, 2003), tells the history of that decree and the ensuing scramble among non-Jews to grab for themselves flats and houses that were seized from Jews. Readers who wish to understand the geography of the yellow-star houses should consult the important digital mapping project Yellow-Star Houses, http://www.yellowstarhouses.org, where the almost two thousand houses segregated for Jews only are identified. The world of Hungarian Jewry where Mádi's friends and professional colleagues lived is described in Ferenc Laczó, *Hungarian Jews in the Age of Genocide: An Intellectual History, 1929–1948* (Leiden, the Netherlands: Brill, 2016). Mádi was generally favorable in her diary entries to the role of the Roman Catholic Church and the Reformed Church in Hungary in standing up to the antisemitic government policies and deportations. Paul Hanebrink, *In Defense of Christian Hungary: Religion, Nationalism, and Antisemitism, 1890–1944* (Ithaca, NY: Cornell University Press, 2006), details the long history of the churches in promoting antisemitism and of turning their backs on Jewish suffering, at least among those Jews who had not converted to Christianity. Finally, Mádi dutifully recorded the air raid alerts and reports of bomb damage in Budapest and around Hungary during the summer of 1944. The official history of American bombing missions over Central Europe is in Wesley Frank Craven and James Lee Cate, eds., *The Army Air Forces in World War II* (Washington, DC: Government Printing Office, 1951), while Tom Faulkner, *Flying with the Fifteenth Air Force: A B-24 Pilot's Missions from Italy during World War II*, edited by David L. Snead (Denton: University of North Texas Press, 2018), is a memoir of a young American pilot who flew missions from Foggia, Italy, over Austria and Hungary until his plane was shot down.

~

MARCH 30, THURSDAY.

In the secret of my heart I felt all the time that without the G invasion of our country, as undesirable as it is, peace won't be reached. So am I with the Soviet troups. I am convinced, many calamities will be caused by them but peace won't come to us without these stages. With two subsequent invasions of our country survival will be problematic, that is sure. But who cares? We begin to be so indifferent about everything.

Some people in terror do rash and inconsiderate acts. The usual postman came yesterday to Erzsike's door, all drunk and told the maid that next house a Jewish lawyer and his wife left their eight room-flat in a hurry, gave their servant a thousand Ps and told her to stay there. The servant girl, left alone began to drink cognac and liqueurs, invited the mailman to join her, etc. Now, what could these people gain by going away even if they have false papers and can get out of Budapest?[1] They will be caught by Jerry somewhere else and will be treated as suspicious persons even worse, because they ran away. [. . .]

Today Irmus asked me to come and discuss things with them. Poor Lajoska[2] is worse again, they asked my opinion. As nearly always when I go there Szöszi comes in too. She told us about a friend of her at Tétény, who with family is living in a country house there . . . The Gs have plenty of champagne, oranges and chocolate but never offer any to their hosts, not even to their little daughter 1 ½ years old, with whom they used to play. The cook got angry seeing this stinginess and told the one of the men, you like to play with the child but would not give her one single orange. So the soldier brought out next time from the officers room two slices of orange.

It was Szöszi too, who told me for absolute certain that the Gs have saved us from a communist plot, which English parachuters planned to organize (by force) here in Budapest. I could not help laughing and as I am still not cautious enough, tried to explain her the absurdity of the idea. She was offended.

1. Mádi's subsequent annotation: "1969: I was wrong."

2. Lajos Antal, brother of István Antal, minister of justice under the Sztójay regime (*MEK*).

The G. propaganda in the Hungarian radio told us that Hungary has decided its fate, hundred percent! They did not ask me neither any of my friends or acquaintances. Pray, who was it, who made the decision?

New "legislation" began today by a new definition of being a Jew or not. I am afraid, poor Natszler[3] will be among them and he seriously ill too. No gentile servants can work for Jews any more. Others to follow.

I have told you before that teaching at our schools started the 1st day of November, 943. Now today we are told that tomorrow the 31st of March the curriculum will be finished. The good old G system for education. Five months, together with Xmas holydays! In tonight's papers I see that in Roumania the situation is the same. So Jerry is counting on real war in these parts. Csernowitz[4] was taken today by Soviet troups.

Vilmica told me the story of their taking an oath on their duties as rescue parties' heads in houses (légó parancnok)[5] in case of air raids. They got an invitation for a certain date, but were told, there will be severe fines and punishment if they do not appear. Getting to the place, they were herded into a big room, door closed upon them, guards at the entrance so nobody could get out and then they had to take an oath. She was so furious with this treatment she did not repeat one word of the oath.

Coming from Sándor street I went to Gellért bath, to renew my free ticket for the season. I asked them what the crowd before the entrance yesterday was. So they at the office explained it was nothing unusual, everyday G soldiers come to the "fürdő"[6] not only in hundred-groups but sometimes five hundred. They have free use of Rudas, Szécheny. They wanted the Hotel Gellért for GHQ but could be persuaded to take Astoria for such and accepted at Gellért only sixty rooms. I went in to see the bath itself, it was disgusting, full with them, the personnel complains how impertinent they are. As they are, at least many of them (so say G med. papers) infected with venereal diseases, it is dangerous to go there anymore. At early hours, for sunbath it will be possible still but no more swimming, I am afraid.

---

3. Ervin Natzler, a Jewish lawyer, sometimes represented the extended Weiss family. The March 29 law defined which Jews were required to wear the yellow star and which were exempt. See Braham, *The Politics of Genocide*, 1:494–95.

4. Csernowitz (Czernowitz/Cernauti/Chernivtsi) is a city in present-day Ukraine. For the Soviet success there that Mádi noted, see "The Russians Return," *NYT*, March 31, 1944.

5. Air (raid) commander. With the occupation of Hungary by the German army, the tacit ceasefire between Hungary and the British and American air forces came to an end. Hungary became a military target of the Fifteenth USAAF and the Royal Air Force squadrons based at the Foggia complex on the Italian Adriatic. Daily bombing raids on Hungary began on April 2. See Craven and Cate, *The Army Air Forces*, 3:172–77.

6. Medicinal hot-springs bath.

MARCH 31, FRIDAY.

12:30 p.m. Dédé just left, he was here to say goodbye as tomorrow he must be off for the front line. [. . .] I told Dédé what I could, not to go into things not to compromise himself on the side of Jerry. I hope he believes me when I told him, that future events do not depend on our standing by the side of the Germans. I hope he will not be taken out of the country anymore. The frontline being at the foot of the Carpathians.[7]

The afternoon I went to see Emil and Erzsike,[8] I could stay but a short while, ran home, to find Bö here waiting for me. She staid an hour, then we had our raid exercise down in the shelter. I urged all inhabitants of the home to get if possible more $CaCl_2$ powder for possible burns.[9] I understand, that Elma, our French friend is talking about me. So I thought before. I can not trust her. She may be spying on us for Jerry. This is a dangerous affair for me. Jews will have to wear the yellow star from April 5th on. They are sick with shame and fear, marked thus, they may be set out to any brutality. Emil asked my advice today, whether to stay at home or to fly, leaving behind Erzsi and her mother in law. I told him, I personally believe it to be more safe to stay and disappear only for the final act. Maybe I am mistaken, advice one can not give in these matters.

APRIL 1, SATURDAY.

Listening to this morning's Voice of America [. . .] U.S. air attacks on the Paras islands is splendid, the war seems to take big steps there.[10] So the Soviet here. According to this mornings news they are already before two Carpathian passes: Tatár hágó and Radnai szoros.

For a short time, on my way home from Rákospalota I dropped in to the Kartals, then home, here Mrs Hermans came to see me, then I went over to the Horchlers and told them, how to impress Elma on their next French lesson. Ervin Natzler died suddenly. He was seriously ill, but this sudden death seems to be timed too exactly, I believe, it was suicide. He was of Jewish origin and could not survive the yellow star and other humiliations. An honest man

7. Mountain range in Central and Eastern Europe stretching in a semicircle from present-day Slovakia to Serbia. After Voronezh in 1943, Hungarian troops had pledged to defend the mountain passes against possible Soviet advance.

8. The Kartal family. The marriage of Emil and Erzsike was mixed: he was Jewish, she was a Gentile.

9. Calcium chloride was used as a topical treatment for skin burns.

10. A reference to the US Navy bombing of the Japanese base at Yap in the Palau Islands in the Central Pacific. See Craven and Cate, *The Army Air Forces*, 3:294–99. Mádi spelled phonetically based on what she heard over the radio.

passed away with him. His man servant found him dead in his armchair, with the Bible on his lap.

APRIL 2, SUNDAY.

I was wide awake at 6 a.m. so better do something. Iby 'phoned yesterday, we shall meet this morning at Natzler's funeral, at 11:30 a.m. at Farkasrét cemetery.[11] Until then I shall have to do some packing of suitcases, meant for the cellar in case of raids, to clean, to have a hot bath (only Sunday), to dress up warm, because since yesterday the weather has cleared up.

Now, to sum up some impressions, gathered by chance: parallel with the official antisemitic propaganda, a real philosemitic wave is arising, people (uncle Béla, Daisy, the friend of Paula Br.) switch off the radio when the stuff begins and do whatever they can for Jews and try to be extremely nice to them. Working men are grumbling against Jerry's arrival and plundering. Shops—except for G. soldiers—are rather empty, business is killed. Jews are told by their central committee that except for two clothes per person, they will have to give up all their clothes, which will be sent to the blitzed German population—there were rumours in town yesterday that Soviet troops would be already at Kőrösmező and Rahó, inside the country, Kassa would be evacuated. Still no reliable news about Roumania. The Germans deny that signs of general collapse are showing there. This certainly must be taken for the affirmative.

Since the invasion of our country Jews may not leave the premises of Bpest. In the first days G. soldiers did check people's identity on every possible way out of town: railways, streetcars, the few still existing buses and even paths for hiking. Yesterday, going to Rákospalota I noticed that at the customs line only two Hung. policemen were posted, one of them got on the street car, asked politely for identification cards but scarcely gave a glance, and was out again. It seems our authorities want to give opportunity for those, who want to slip out.

The funeral of poor Natzler was a dignified affair, no speeches but the Circumdederumt.[12] Many flowers, many friends. Only an uncle (nyug. vezérőrnagy),[13] Székely, his partner for a quarter of a century and as I was told an illegitimate son. He may be about twenty-six.

I met there Dr Kabakovics, my other attorney, Piroska Kálmán and the Bingerts all three, János,[14] Iby and Iván. Jancsi is shocked by events, it seems.

11. Farkasréti temető was on the Buda side of the city.

12. Sixteenth-century music composed for a funeral service.

13. Major general, retired.

14. János Bingert, Hunnia Film Company executive.

Two years ago he preached G. victory, it did not matter, he said, whether it is a sacrifice of five million youths. Now Iván is nearing twenty, until now he was an apprentice at the film studio but recently his father began to take his law studies seriously. It could be an excuse to have him for a while from military service.

Lunch with the Sebes. Apu had to accept the post as deputy foreign secretary (with the exception of political and press matters). It is not good but he says, it saves him for the present from arrest. Whether it will save him from trouble in the future? After Easter they will be transferred to Balatonfüred, as the plans go temporarily.

It is generally believed that this government is too tolerant toward Jews and will be chased by Jerry in a few days. The afternoon I dropped in on Lacy, did not find her home but her brother. There is no trouble yet. Then I hurried to the Fidys.[15]

According to "new order" Tercsi néni would have to wear the yellow star, with her husband and children going on for gentiles. She is desperate, I tried to calm her by the news of a coming change in rules, cases like her will be taken for Jews though, but won't have to wear the star. I am told, it is coming tomorrow. After five minutes I left them, home Elly Hermans called for a few minutes, then evening Maria Pató. She has a quarter of Jewish blood in her, so the new order does not touch her legal standing, in spite of this, some people are rather mean to her at Maort. Miss Osán for one. Poor thing, yesterday she found a yellow star in her office drawer. How wicked some people can be.

The next G. plan would be to hold a stable line against the Soviet offensive: north about the same as now west of the Pripjet marshes, the Carpathians, the Focsani (Romania) triangle and the Danube delta.

G. Gestapo headquarters had been at the Hotel Astoria in the first days of the invasion occupation. Not now. They change the place every four or five days. Secret radio stations seem to be at work here again as today at 5 p.m. the "*Hétfő*"[16] newspaper got on the streets with a government announcement and at 8 p.m. BBC news quoted already from it. As of today, listening to foreign stations is forbidden. Penalty 6 months of prison *and* internment.

APRIL 3, MONDAY.

At 10:30 a.m. the Bpest syrens were sounding, I hesitated to go down to the shelter but when a strong antiaircraft could be heard, I decided and went. We sat there for two hours, AAC[17] could be heard, sometimes strong, then again

15. Béla Fidy was a ministerial counselor.

16. Monday.

17. Antiaircraft, that is, "flak" or "flack," as Mádi spelled it.

nothing, but bombs dropped I could not distinguish. The man folk, who felt very important said, they heard it once and stated, it must have happened somewhere round the Buda mountain circle. If it is so, it must be small caliber bombs, I could notice no vibrations. After the alert I heard people say, they have seen many foreign planes in fifteens of a row flying over us. How nice to know that Americans have been so near to us. At 2 p.m. BBC[18] announces that fierce air battles were fought over Hungary and Bpest. At 3:20 p.m. our radio Bp announces mines on the Danube from 1740 km until 1765 km.[19] So there were mine laying operations. At 3 p.m. BBC spoke in detail about air battles over Budapest. Well, we are not yet told anything, what happened, but if this is all, it won't be so bad. From today on, we shall have black out at 7 p.m. summer time, that is 6 p.m. normal central European time, street-black out from 9 p.m. summer time, that is 8 p.m. normal Central European time. Having been in town, I gather, there has been really a serious raid over Bpest. Funny, how little we heard the noises. The freight yards of Ferencváros was hit[20] and some oil depots are still burning there.[21] A municipal house at the end of Üllői ut, Csepel, Kispest, the Horticultural School at Gellért hill got bombs. The official announcement speaks about "terror"—raid and casualties. I have seen Erzsike again. Emil has some hope to be exceptioned on behalf of his behavior during the 1919 communist régime. A two sided weapon: if it is some help now, it will be the worse at another turn of affairs.

Number 5 and 11 streetcars are not running. At 8 p.m. my phone still not in function. At 8:15 p.m. I got a line after all. I had to tell Iby,[22] why could I not go and see her today, as I have promised. She says, there is no trouble with them but Irén Zilahy, wife of prof. Benedek died in her villa at Himfy utca, Gellért hill. The shelter was hit. [. . .]

Maria Pató came home with fresh news. She made a tour with a friend round the damaged places, they have been out at Csepel,[23] to see Pestszenterzsébet fires burning. [. . .] Somehow I had an idea that after having started big fires, a night raid may follow. At 9:30 p.m. our radio broke off and is signaling alerts

18. Mádi continued to listen to the BBC, Voice of America, and Radio Moscow, despite the new law forbidding Hungarians to listen to enemy broadcasts.

19. Kilometers upstream from the Danube Delta on the Black Sea.

20. Mádi's subsequent annotation: "1969: entirely erased."

21. "More than 450 B-17's and B-24's bomb aircraft factory and M/Y at Budapest" (Kit C. Carter and Robert Mueller, *The Army Air Forces Combat Chronology* [Washington, DC: Air Force History Headquarters, 1973], April 3, 1944, hereafter cited as *CC*).

22. A diminutive for Ibolya, or "Violet," Horchler.

23. An island in the Danube downstream from present-day Pettöfi Bridge (see map 2). It was the site of a Shell Oil refinery plant, a repeated target of US bombers in 1944.

on the south side of the country. I dressed up all fresh, in case I should loose all my things, to have the most useful clothes on me.

APRIL 4, TUESDAY.

We just came up from the shelter, where we spent three and a quarter hours, Allied planes came in several waves since 11 p.m. Sometimes it sounded rather bad. My impression is, that it must be more serious than the morning raid. The shelter is cold, smelly and too small for more then thirty people, among them some busybodies. No night fighters could be heard. When the noises got worse, I could notice my legs shaking, though partly the cause may be cold. Scenery: clear, beautiful, moonlit night.

I dropped on to Tercsi néni, she was disconsolate desperate because of the star she would have to wear from tomorrow on. I told her, she will be exceptioned, but she did not dare believe me. Tonight our news service brought the news really, she called me immediately and thanked for telling her ahead and saving her two days anguish. [. . .] From her I went to see Lacy (all this, because from tomorrow on may be we shall be forbidden to visit Jewish friends, but I am at the end of my strength). They often asked me to lunch with them but somehow I could never accept, so today I told them I should like to lunch with them. Lacy was just learning gyurttészta[24] from their servant maid as from the end of April they may not engage gentile servants any more. These maids behave wonderfully in all these families, they are faithful, are crying out their eyes, because they have to leave. Lacy and Károly are not going out on the streets for at least three days. From Lacy I went to Erzsike. It is day by day that I go to them now, they are the most miserable and I fear, they have plans of suicide in their minds. [. . .]

At Csáky utca[25] drunken G. soldiers went into a house and to a certain Jewish family, told them to give out once three thousand pengös and values, left with a paper in hand, list of Jews living at the same house. These soldiers would be shot by their own authorities, if reported, but who dares to report, and how to find them? It is an indicator, how they used to behave in other countries and I fear, it is only a question of time, they will be authorized to behave like this here too. At Kispest a barkeeper refused to serve two G. soldiers, as it was his duty. One of them stabbed him and then the barkeeper's son killed both. Emil's two nieces (about 15 and 16 of age) the family tries to put into some convent or mission house, to be protected against atrocities, what happened before in Slovakia.

24. Mádi's subsequent annotation: "1969. to make noodles."

25. Hegedűs Gyula utca in present-day Budapest.

Night's raid was chiefly over Csepel. Two war plants have been hit, there is talk about 1000 casualties. One Maort clerk lost his wife and four children, besides all, what he owned (the Company gave him 500 P.! for compensation) The case was serious, sure, today big yellow posters tell the population that Budapest and surrounding industrial places will be evacuated (freight cars, free fare, 150 kg luggage/person) but certain branches of occupation and some professions (medical of course included) may not leave the premises. I do not intend to go away but if my place would be ruined, it is outraging, not to be able to go away. [. . .]

Fourty seven G. officers were hit yesterday at Budaörs airport. Bucharest got her first raid today. I always believed, they will have it before Budapest.

Something to be mentioned: in Bpest no big caliber bombs and no incendiaries were dropped (no machine-gunning either). Jerry mentions 16 raiders shot down over Bpest. Well, the official examination committee had to go out to one case, to Ócsa,[26] where one of our fighters was brought down, allegedly by Jerry. The daylight raid was made by about 200 liberators.[27]

APRIL 5, WEDNESDAY.

The Allies, especially England seems to be so anxious about the fate of Jews and refugees in Hungary. It will be only the terrible slowness of the allies, if they won't survive nazi occupation in this country. Russia is doing her job, but on the other side nothing happens. These people will have to die only because of the cautious moves (or immobility?) of allied armies on the western side.

I spent a quiet day, I felt exhausted after the excitements of the last days. All is done, what could be done, today the yellow stars appeared on the streets, a few only, most people feel ashamed to look at. The first nice, rather warm day, sunshine and showers chasing each other. [. . .] Homesick for a garden, where you can watch the grass grow and buds coming out, have space to look round and far. But chiefly homesick for you, my Dearest, you, the best in my life, who are sunshine and space and grass and buds and all—all beauty of my life. It is so lovely though, to know that even if far away, but you exist, have Geo and Barbara and still have your thoughts sometimes here, around me. The bonds between us are indissoluble.

Hanna told me that under the blitzed houses round the freight yards of Ferencváros people today still were living, but the salvage work can not get to them. Knocking and scraping noises are still heard from under the ruins.

26. A suburb southeast of Budapest.

27. "Liberators" refers to USAAF B-24 bombers.

APRIL 6, THURSDAY.

About 60 mtrs[28] from the house I am living in, there is a school building (you remember, may be, with the statue of Uncle Bear—Mackó úr), here the G.s are storing explosives. [. . .] Almost all the school buildings in the country are occupied by G. troops.

I have seen Mrs Déghi, Ilonka,[29] she put some cigarettes aside for me, they are scarce. Rami too. Met Rózsi Némethy, a leader and former classmate, went to the grocer Raki and assured them of my sympathy. They were pleased. Met Mici néni (Adorján) and Hanna by chance. Mrs Németh with her baby daughter Zsuzsi left here today, they are evacuated to Gödöllő.[30] Ilonka told me how Keresztes Fischer and his brother were arrested by the Gestapo and taken to Dachau.

A bit too much of popularity. Maria Pató comes daily. Today twice, other people from the house, Ancy was here to ask me for Good Saturday, the evening. She is very nice and came, I am sure, to prove their friendship. They can't help, especially her sisters and brothers, to feel German. I can see ahead the time, when I shall feel my duty to go and see them, just the same as I have to see now Jewish friends. [. . .]

All this noise about evacuating is of course almost nonsense as so many people, medical, teachers, pharmacists, transport and all sorts of war workers, bakers, butchers, nurses, and many others may not go, wherever they happen to live. Tonight at 8 p.m. (an hour after black out time) I had to go out to mail some letters. In the school opposite us (it is not even 50 steps) two big windows were bright, lighted by Jerry, like in good old peacetimes. [. . .]

I felt often suspicious towards the loud nationalism of our upper middle classes, somehow it smelt after fear of loosing their privileged situation. Now these people, by greeting the G. invading troups with relief, have disclosed the fact how utterly indifferent they are to the national interests. There is nothing else important for them, but their wellbeing, influence, and power. See the Zorkóczys, Becks, Bingerts, etc.

APRIL 7, GOODFRIDAY.

The nazis understand to twist on the Jews after every move of the allies. After the Monday daylight raid they summoned the Jewish Council and told them

---

28. Mádi's subsequent annotation: "1969. No, much less."

29. Mrs. Janos Schmidt (née Degi) owned a tobacconist shop at Tisza Kalman Square (*Budapesti telefonkönyvek*), which is now Pope John Paul II Square.

30. A suburb northeast of Budapest and former summer home to the Habsburg monarchs.

to release 500 apartments for the use of the bombed out Gs in 24 hours. Next day the Council could not report more then 380 flats, two members of the Council were taken as hostages. The Council was told to evacuate not 500 but 1000 apartments in 12 hours, if not, their hostages will be shot.[31] [. . .] Besides these so called legal measures the looting of some Jewish houses at different parts of the town is an everyday affair now. Drunken G. soldiers go to different flats (Újpest[32] is their favourite now) and ask for money and valuables. They go at night.

A new order appeared in today's papers: Jews have to give up their radios, within three days.[33] They are not permitted to sell or give it away.

The whole capital was flooded yesterday by yellow posters drawing of hammer and sickle = Star of David. Meaning: communism and Jews are the same. Today there were scarcely a few to be seen. They were damaged or disappeared entirely. Seeing the fiasco Jerry ordered to remove them, those that were left. One of my friends, seeing a poster-man scraping the remnants of a yellow poster, inquired and was told they have orders to remove them without a trace. What next?

APRIL 8, GOOD SATURDAY.

Rather cold, rainy morning. No alarm on our radio but G. bombers raging over us at a low level, just as they did on the day of invasion. Has something happened inside the country? Our "great allies" are capable of anything.

Good old times, when a gentleman could afford to be an antisemite! Exclaimed a friend sometime ago. This is the situation: in these days you can't help to feel for them, whatever your feelings may have been before. Besides, it is only a question of time, we Hungarian gentiles may get the same treatment, see occupied countries.

At Mártonhegyi ut 38 (some time ago it belonged to the Liebsteins) a Polish refugee lived with his Hungarian wife and child.[34] I was told today, he too was rounded up by Jerry, on every occasion the pretext is an English spy.

APR. 9, EASTERS SUNDAY.

An alert began here at 10:12 last night. I dressed and was all prepared to go downstairs but did not go. Staying in my place was so much better. There were but distant noises, mostly AAC. [. . .] As to what happened, we do not know yet.

---

31. Braham, *The Politics of Genocide*, 1:484–85.
32. District on the Pest side of the Danube, north of the Margit Bridge (see map 2).
33. Braham, *The Politics of Genocide*, 1:496.
34. Mártonhegyi út, in the 12th District, where Mádi lived.

About last Monday's raid over Bpest, casualities are said to be between 1000 and 5000.

SAME NIGHT.

Hanna Sz. and Maria Pató here the evening. The morning Anni Pravda came with a beautiful rose coloured hyacynth and some mákos-diós[35] from her mother. She is promoted to a clerk in the optical factory, is very happy and feels it as a social elevation.

I understand, Jerry still do not have Bethlen neither Kállay, nor Ali. Bethlen somewhere hiding, at the Bpest Turkish legation[36] and Ali is sleeping every day at another house, day time walking on the streets.

M. Pató tells me, last night during the raid a G. sergeant came to our shelter and offered to cheer them up, played his accordion and danced, told tales about Paris, Russia, etc. The Gorrieris (horrid people) gave him rum to drink and were charmed with him, thank God, they can't speak German.[37] I am sure, the soldier understood Hungarian and came to spy on our house, after an hour went over to the next house's shelter.

They must be in a desperate need of men, as they want to draft all Hungarian youths with a German name (to be exact, all, who have three grandparents with German names) to their SS. The Hung. government is trying to specify on who is registering themselves as German. Sure, they induct in to their SS such dirt and idiots, that this alone must mean their losing the war. [. . .]

Lulu Sebestyén has a splendid story about last night's raid. In their house all people were gathered in their shelter, iron door closed, when a young mother, her baby on her arm and the heavy (full of belongings), baby carriage ahead, descended slowly and carefully the stairs. At the last flight of stairs she lost controle of the carriage which rolled down and reached the iron door with a bang. She got down with her baby after a while and entering the shelter, found it empty. All people escaped on the emergency door believing the terrible knock on the iron door was a bomb. [. . .]

The story of the yellow posters: the propaganda fellow (Antal) has put them on the streets. Yesterday morning at a ministerial council Jaross, minister for the interior, got into fits of rage and ordered them to be removed, as according

---

35. A Hungarian pastry made with poppy seeds and nuts.

36. Kállay, *Hungarian Premier*, tells the story of how he and his wife were sheltered in the Turkish embassy in Budapest from March through October 1944, at which time the Arrow Cross invaded the embassy and arrested him.

37. Adolph and Mrs. Gorrieri, the janitor and his wife in the 19 Margaréta utca apartment building. Mádi's subsequent annotation: "1969. They do, only not too much."

to him people will believe it to be bolshevic propaganda. Policemen had to tear them down, they got into fight with "nyilas,"[38] allegedly several casualties on both sides.

APRIL 10, EASTER MONDAY.

Some other bad item for this part of the town is (besides the next school loaded with explosives), that the G. commander in chief of all Eastern european operations, a general Weiss is having his headquarters at one of the big hotels at Sváb-hegy.[39] Every few days they change into another hotel, after the experiences of Taormina and Frascati.[40]

Our diplomats in Stockholm, Helsinki, Madrid, Lisbon and Bern resigned.[41] As to how they did it, is characteristic of different people's different minds. There was one who left his post and everything, money, secret code, etc. There was one, who took the code and left the money. Again another, who left the code and took the money, another, who took both [. . .] Dissident ministers in the different capitals are communicating with each other by means of the secret code. Young Éliász is among the dissidents and by this he endangers his father and family here. He very probably believed his father under arrest already, but until now he is not, though chief of the Bpest police.

Jerry's controle of telephon talks is like that: There are certain lines (Apu's for example) on which they are hanging on continually. When somebody calls these, they listen to the talk but do not know, who was calling, except when the other is under observation too. Other lines are checked off and on. Often one can hear during a telephon talk, that someone enters the line. The wisest thing is to hang up then.

APRIL 11, TUESDAY.

Béla, the nephew of Pravdáné is an accomplished goldsmith, earned very well for a time and went to Miskolc[42] into a good job. Now he is at home or here with Pravdáné, because there is no gold, neither silver, to work with. The stupid contemplates to enter the SS. [. . .]

---

38. The Arrow Cross Party, a Nazi-like political party founded in Hungary in 1935.

39. Field Marshal Maximilian Weichs (1881–1954), commander of German army forces in the Balkans. "Sváb-hegy" (Swabian Hill) was a neighborhood near Mádi's apartment.

40. Taormina was a town in Sicily that was the headquarters of German forces; it was bombed by the Allies. Frascati, Italy, was the headquarters for the German Mediterranean Command; it was bombed by the Allies in September 1943.

41. See Szegedy-Maszák, *I Kiss Your Hands*, 162, for the resignation of the Hungarian ambassador to Portugal, Andor Wodianer.

42. City in northern Hungary (see map 1).

Elly Hermans came, I gave her tea, we talked events over, then the telephone rang, Apu was calling to go and see them as quick as possible. I knew the instant, it must be a letter from you, as his voice was laughing and excited. After Mrs Hermans left I walked over in a drizzling rain, heavy clouds darkening the sky but very springlike. It was a letter from you (Jan. 21) two days after your last one. Thank you, dear! Babu's "absolupy" is delightful. I always hoped she would call you George and Hilda, so I may be Mamy for her too. I don't believe you could be more good looking then before, but this is, may be, a lack of imagination on my part. It is a wonder, this letter could reach me, how, I do not know, I did not meet Apu yet. But sure, this was the last, until the end of the war.

APRIL 12, WED.

From 11 a.m. on a raid over the country. Alarms are given like that: Kanizsa, Zala, Veszprém, Győr, Sopron, Pécs, Baja, Bácska, Szeged, Földvár. They seem to fly in zig-zags, to shake off the fighters. After some zig-zagging the few fighters were out of fuel.[43]

11:50 a.m. Alarm over Bpest. Staying home. A few minutes after the sirens sounded, two G. soldiers (SS) entered our house. I could not repress a smile, as this time they won't find any drinks, nor people enthusiastic for them. I do not think there could be more then a dozen of people down the shelter. But I have not seen G.s going to the other houses. These two went after about ten minutes to the neighbouring house. In half an hour all was finished, no shots or explosives could be heard.

Yesterday morning some G. soldiers rounded up Jews on the Dohány and Dob utca and took them to their place near (very probably the school of Dohány u. or Wesselényi u.)[44] and made them scrub the floors and wash dishes. . . . One, who tried to run away, was treated cruelly. Do you notice, how low we have sunk, to discuss coolly such things.

Reading now Achtung, Europa. Thomas Mann's book[45] is, in spite of his violent antagonism, very German. It reminds me of myself, when I try to defend some Hungarian acts in spite of myself. He does not see the most important point: nowhere on the earth could naziism have such a success, but in Germany.

---

43. The Fifteenth Air Force sent 535 bombers to attack Budapest and other Hungarian cities (*CC*, April 12, 1944).

44. Dohány, Wesselényi, and Dob were streets in the 7th District of Budapest, in the Jewish Quarter.

45. A 1938 collection of Thomas Mann's essays.

Would you believe it, that after a raid over us, just a few hours later, people go to the pictures? So it is and no mistake. Today's raid was meant chiefly for Wiener Neustadt, as I understand. But Vienna did not get any bombs until now. Could we hope the same for the inner parts of Bpest? I believe, yes. Vienna has, I suppose, a more fortunate distribution of the industrial areas, all well outside of the city proper.

Beethoven's D major violin concerto on our radio, how I love it. Life could be lovely with peace and sunshine and music. By the way, George darling, I have listened yesterday to general Eisenhower on BBC. I have to tell you, he is the second American, besides you, whom I understand with difficulty.

9:30 p.m. a raid over the south side of the country is signaled. We have to prepare again for the shelter. I feel quite cheerful. Without this stage the war will not be over. The sooner, the better, if we have to go through. Bácska—Baja were alerted first, then, after ten minute interval Kanizsa—Zala, a few minutes later Földvár (that means Dunaföldvár)—Szeged. Our Beethoven concert was interrupted. Pity. At 9:55 p.m. it is Szolnok. 9:57 p.m. Veszprém, 10:03 Karcag, 10:05 Bpest (no alarm yet, only nuisance flights), 10:15 Miskolc, 10:30 Eger, 10:35 Győr, 10:40 Nyírség—in the meantime I have cleared a way antique china pieces which used to be on the grandfather-shelf, I put them into a wooden box, between cushions—a distant, single noise of an airplane motor can be heard—at 10:58 alarms over Bácska, Baja, Kanizsa, Pécs are cancelled (I did not hear Pécs mentioned before). Földvár, Nyírség, Veszprém, Zala too (11:04). It seems, there will be no trouble tonight. 11:10 Budapest, Karcag, Szeged, Szolnok: légoltalom pihenj.[46] So I go to bed now. With a headache.

STILL THE SAME NIGHT, BUT APR. 13, THURSDAY.

At 1:30 a.m. we were awakened by the sound of the sirens. Not very long after much noise, bombs and AAC could be heard.[47] I had no intention to go down, though, I have to confess, the noises were so strong, that I did not dare to open the blind. Idiotic. Then people from below came to get me, it seems, as a physician. I am valuable for them. [. . .]

At 10 a.m. BBC mentions large scale air operations all over Europe, Hungary or Bpest not even mentioned. At 10:40 a.m. Bpest radio went off the air, it seems to begin anew.

46. Mádi's subsequent annotation: "1969. Cleared."

47. "535 HBs (largest HB mission to date by Fifteenth AF) bomb A/F aircraft factory, and rolling stock plant at Gyor, Vecses and Tokol A/Fs and Repulogepgyar aircraft components plant at Budapest" (*CC*, April 13, 1944). The abbreviation "HB" referred to heavy bombers.

12:45 p.m. still nothing but distant explosions and very little AAC. A warm sunshine on the deserted streets, a cat walking slowly on the sidewalk, neither she, nor the birds have a clue of danger, though the noises become louder and louder.

12:53 quiet again. An SS sergeant entered our house, only ours, no other soldiers with him. This is the fourth time they come here. Is there a special reason?

1:07 p.m. the explosions got rather close, in these moments I hide this book into my shelter-bag. Somehow the only consolation for me are these pages. You will know, what happened with and around me. [. . .]

1:25 p.m. sharp AAC (some stray bombers seem to pass high above) but in the yard across a hen laid her egg and triumphs loudly over the achievement. Last night some people in our shelter discussed the "possibilities" of Hitler attacking New York by air. This hen has more brains.

1:35 The raid over Bpest at an end. People are creeping out (a bit impressed) of their shelters and life begins again. As a psychological experiment: I did not feel death near yet, only danger.

SAME NIGHT.

Elko[48] was here the afternoon. They could not get into the Eastern station, it got several bombs the night. [. . .] Jerry begins again his old joke about explosive playthings and toys (Stated, they are dropped by allied planes). I am sure, these dolls and boxes and fountain pens are "made in Germany" if they exist at all.

Since two days again and again rumours circulate about the invasion. Nothing on BBC so I am afraid, it is just a "Wunschtraum"[49] of the Jews, though one can hear it in gentile circles too. [. . .]

APRIL 14, FRIDAY.

A new German expression: offensive defence.

Have seen Ilonka Krasznay (60 Daru) and Tercsi néni. Api, who is an investigator for the air corps, has to see accidents, casualties and circumstances, has a story about a Balaton poacher (orvhalász), who found the crew of one aircraft. The pilot was badly wounded but managed to land his aircraft on shallow waters. The plane went partly down and they had to call help. The fisherman, *believing them to be Germans*, hit one on the head, then, somehow noticing the

48. Elko was Máthé Elek (1895–1968), a Reform (Protestant) minister (*MEK*). He was the author of the 1942 book *Amerikai magyarok nyomában* (Following the American Hungarians), an account of his travels to Hungarian immigrant communities in the United States in 1939 and 1940.

49. Pipe dream (German).

difference, went to their aid. They were handed over the Balatonkiliti G. airport. I hear, most of these boys are New Zealanders. Api says, they are doing their job splendidly, a perfect precision flight(?) (iskolarepülés), good aiming too.

Today the first pleasant warm day.

After supper I was with Gizi & Co, when at 9:30 p.m. nuisance flights were announced over the south side of the country. I advised them to have a rest, before the dance, came home and walked into my place while on alert over Bpest: from about 10 a.m. till midnight. [. . .]

APRIL 15, SATURDAY.

On other week-days a terrible noise begins at 7 a.m. in the yards of the opposite house. There are no vacuum cleaners and dust is beaten with bamboo sticks out of the carpets. The best side of these night raids is, people are sleeping exhausted, no noises.

Last time's raid over Győr hit the Messerschmidt factory thoroughly, the Richard textile factory, something else too and the waterworks, so they have to take water out of the Danube. Fires were so big, the Bpest firemen had to go to help them. [. . .]

It is not enough, some people (decent people) believe in this explosive toys nonsense, but there are again tales about negro pilots[50] and white women doing the bombers' radio and machinegun service, this all with being shocked deeply. I do not know, is it less shocking, but do not see the fact that here (and elsewhere too) mostly women are making ammunition. Jerry's tendencies can be felt in the tales, that two negro pilots who landed here after a raid, were taken into pieces by the "outraged population." Now, the population seems to be rather meek after a raid and concerned only with safety and rest. The same tales were circulating in Italy about girl pilots being killed by the Italians, when things became critical there, before the invasion of Sicily. [. . .]

M. Pató told me yesterday that the night before a G. SS rang on her door and told a humdrum story about looking for a girl, a rendezvous missed, etc. Impertinence. I understand, the Gorrieries and Németh's (in absence of young Mrs Németh) had G soldiers as guests in their apartments.

Military sources know about a new G. effort, one and one half million of fresh G. troups, youngest ones, besides our own, thrown into the gaps of the eastern frontline. It is possible, they will be able to get some success temporarily. There is no field, the G. propaganda would leave untouched. [. . .] When a war machinery, after eleven years of the régime and after five years of war is working

50. German propaganda minister Joseph Goebbels had been warning the Axis against "negro pilots" since the summer of 1943. See "Black Incendiaries," *Pittsburgh Courier*, June 12, 1943.

with such perfect harmony, one can not help to identify the G. people with the régime. We must not be too sorry for them, when they will be down.

People are willing to accept almost anything, no wonder governments have the audacity to put any amount of weight upon them. When I explained to some friends before, that the only hope for Hungary would be a German collapse, before war reaches our premises, people hoped that the wonder (our country being undamaged) will continue. Now, when war is extended all over us, they accept the situation and put all their hopes in G. help.

10:10 p.m. Air raid alert signaled here. Searchlights, over the "off the air" radio Russian record (they disturb the Hungarian radio)—at 11:05 the affair seems to be finished. Nothing happened, but my stomach is a lot worse. I have been on the sofa all day.

APRIL 16, SUNDAY.

People, the great majority, I mean, behave nicely towards Jews. I heard only two or three cases when Jews with the yellow star were insulted on the streets. László Endre[51] a bad character, became secretary for the interior with the outspoken purpose, to attend Jewish affairs. This fact is forecasting the worst.

G. spread the rumours, that nowhere have they received so many denouncements, as here in Hungary. I believe it to be untrue, rather "kedvecsinálás,"[52] a "Wunschtraum" only.

I met Bö the morning, on a bench near the cemetery. I can not go to her and she better does not come to me.[53] Even so, walking together and sitting by her side, people stared at me.—Lunch with the Sebes.[54] Young Pubi still at home but soon his leave will be over and he will have to join his corps unit. Mamu and the children plan to go to the Balaton on the first of May, Apu will have to stay here, like myself.

10:22 p.m. The radio went off the air again. I have to grin. Last night it was Turnu Severin in Roumania and by daylight Ploesti and Bucharest.[55] In tonight's *Hétfő* paper I see that two ships were damaged over the Danube mines. They are laid easily and fished out with difficulty just now, as in a few days the Danube has risen to 7.50 mtr. Here the lower embankments are deep under water.

---

51. László Endre (1885–1946), minister of the interior (1944), indicted, tried, convicted, and executed by order of the Budapest People's Tribunal for crimes against Hungary (*MEK*). See Braham, *The Politics of Genocide*, 1:402–3.

52. Wishful thinking.

53. Mádi's subsequent annotation: "1969. She changed her mind about that later, feeling very lonely."

54. Abbreviation for the Sebestyén Pál family.

55. The Fifteenth Air Force sent 432 bombers against Romania, including the principal Romanian oil fields at Ploesti (*CC*, April 16, 1944).

Midnight. Air raid at an end. As long as I could watch it, it was like big fireworks, flares, AAC, somewhere in the direction of Csepel, later Kispest. Big fires. [. . .]

APRIL 17, MONDAY.

Just got a military postcard from Dénes and a letter from Marika Kánya. Dénes mentions the partisans. Marika has a story about blitzed German children (age 12–16) at Harta.[56] Their camp leader just mentioned them the possibility of going to church on Easter sunday. As they looked as not understanding the reason, the leader questioned them what do they know about Jesus. Only one of them could answer and this said proudly: Jewish origin!

Passenger ship travel is suspended in consequence to the mining operations on Danube and Tisza.

Since yesterday Jews have to declare all their private property: money, shares, jewels, oriental rugs, etc.[57] This will be followed by taking from them all, they have. I am afraid, this is only a stage in cruelty and their lives will be in danger. They, poor things, do not realize the utmost danger, they are concerned with their material belongings.

Gizi was here tonight. She confesses, her opinion is flexible, says mine is rigid. She always will be on the side of the winner.

APRIL 18, TUESDAY.

By chance I met Marguerite[58] in town. She wants to be released from "honvédelmi női munkaszolgálat"[59] because they want her to peel potatoes the whole time from 6 a.m. on. It has really more than a bit of soviet taste, not to have any other use for a countess, well educated too.

APRIL 19, WEDNESDAY.

[. . .] Pravdáné told me the latest G. propaganda Japanese pilots arrived here and defended Bpest at the last raid. They are so splendid that since then the allies do not *dare* raid again.

56. Part of the *Kinderlandverschickung* (children's evacuation to the countryside). Harta was a village south of Budapest with a large ethnic German population.

57. "Declaration and Sequestration of the Wealth of the Jews," April 16, 1944, as cited in Braham, *Politics of Genocide*, 1:509. The Sztójay government proclaimed that the confiscation of Jewish property "is one of our chief resources for our war-effort" (Lévai, *Black Book*, 188).

58. Mádi's sister, who lived in Magyaróvár, near the Austrian border. She married Count Viczay and lived on a landed estate.

59. Women's Military Labor Service.

Béla Kozma, Pravdáné's nephew went to the SS. You can't change human stupidity. He joined the SS in order to get out to the U.S.A.! It seems, they have promised him something like that.

APRIL 20, THURSDAY.

Every day some new cruelties. Last night two hundred and fifty well to do Jews and Jewesses were called to work (with a rug and a pail) and it is believed, they will have to work and to live close to the target areas. Money and valuables were taken from them and tonight their businesses too. Our news service—I feel sick listening to it. Lies without any scruples.

APRIL 21, FRIDAY.

The friend of Gerti, a Miss Annelise Richter phoned this morning I am convinced, she is a spy or snooper, she speaks Hungarian, gives German lessons, has a comfortable income, is living alternately in hotels or boarding houses. [. . .]

I have mentioned you before the next school building. Between it and our house there was a grassy lot, on which today I see big quantities of lumber. It seems, German barracks will be built in our neighbourhood. [. . .]

I am irritated with the attitude here towards bombed quarters. The regent went to see them five days after the bombing, Jaross, minister for the interior after seven days. The Pope was within the bombed areas in two hours.

Popularity is tiresome. Today Mrs. Hermans was here twice, then Maria Pató, the janitor, Mrs Láng (a shoemaker's wife) and our Ida were all calling for shorter or longer time. Sometimes I feel furious when the doorbell rings.

News spread in town again about the invasion, but nothing on BBC. I think it is only a Jewish make-believe they have no radios any more and their only hope is an invasion from the west. Would there be really something in the rumours, either this or the other side would have blurted it out.

APRIL 22, SATURDAY.

The morning I had an appointment at the Social Insurance building. There seems to be plenty of work and soon I shall be up to my ears in work again. [. . .] Again new regulations with regards Jews, it is a new blow every day. Yesterday it was their businesses, today it is their rations. From the 1 of May on they will have the ⅓ part of sugar, half of the fats, weekly one ration card of beef (10 dk), but we do not get more sometimes, so this is not much of a difference. The cruelty is, they are deprived of all milk (for patients), butter, eggs. Not as if we should get much from these. Don't think me sentimental because I am so terribly sick of these things. It is true, I am very sorry for my friends but the chief reason is this state of lawlessness, we are living in. It is only a matter of time and all these things may happen to us. It is possible, some of our own people enjoy these cruelties but even if they don't, they can not do anything to change it. It is the meanest thing that happened in long centuries and Nero was but an insignificant little amateur compared with the nazi gang. It seems very unreal, that I should join you ever.

APRIL 23, SUNDAY.

[. . .] 3 p.m. distant explosions and AAC, getting clearer. It seems to be a return journey from Austria. It is the AAC around Bpest now, very intense. There are the barking of automatic cannons, four in a series, the deep detonations of the Bofors[60] guns and then deep, roaring explosions, these must be bombs dropped.

3:05 they seem to have passed us. G. soldiers coming into our shelter again. Some going out. Sitting in my apartment, doors to the balcony wide open is like having a box for a theatrical performance. But how splendid the view would be from the old home![61] More dangerous too, that is true. [. . .]

Yesterday I got from a place butter, very cheap. 20 P/kg. It was not an excellent butter but still usable. The man had it from the Waggon Lits Co.[62] He travels with them, says, railways in south Hungary and Yougoslavia are more like a battlefield, craters, derailed locomotives everywhere. When air raids come over these parts, Tito's men come out of their hiding and do their job. Last time their whole business done in the dining car (from Bpest to Zagreb) did not amount to anything more than 200 Ps, so few people are travelling. [. . .]

APRIL 24, MONDAY.

It is George's day.[63] My thoughts were with you, Darling. Did Barbara congratulate you?

Nothing came of yesterday's night alarm, but people were up (most of them, not myself) until 4 a.m. when the alarm was called off. No wonder, they are jumpy, unhappy and tired. Serves them right. Not before long they cherished the idea of an air raid over New York, they could bear very well the idea of London raided, well, everybody should have its share. Let us see how heroic

60. Swedish-made antiaircraft weapon.

61. At 19 Rezeda utca, on the Gellért Hill.

62. A reference to the Compagnie internationale des wagons-lits, a Belgian firm that operated sleeping cars on international trains, including the Orient Express.

63. Hungarians celebrate both name days and birthdays.

they will be when their turn comes. In every house people have to watch the radio in turns, in case of alarm one has to ring every doorbell in the house. My turn is tonight from 2 a.m. until 4 a.m.

Seen Erzsike and Lacy. Later had an adventure one of these evenings. A G. soldier in black uniform stepped up to her on the street (8:30 p.m.) a very young boy (I suppose, under the influence) put his arms around her shoulder and walking by her side told her how he loaths the whole war and SS and circumstances—but do not tell anybody I told you!—how he was no SS but a Heimwehr (Austrian) and comforted her, how well the Jews will have it after the war. At the end he said Servus![64] She said servus too, they parted. All the time people coming the opposite direction were terribly sorry for her with the yellow star and walking with a G. soldier. They believed her to be in deadly peril. Such tragicomic events happen too.

New people at the head of our radio. No jazz any more. No Karády[65] films and plays. Rumours have it that she was executed, but I do not believe. Her boyfriend, general Ujszászy who was the head of Hungarian secret service here, ordered to detain arrest this Wesenmayer,[66] so called G. minister to Hungary a few months ago, when he was just a spy. Now in his turn, Wesenmayer ordered the arrest of Ujszászy and Karády.[67] They will make out of her a national heroine, after all.

These Germans in the neighbourhood seem to be crazy. It is 11 p.m. and through the closed shutters there come loud noises of military commands and marching. [. . .]

APRIL 25, TUESDAY.

What a day. I had to get up at 4 a.m. and watched the radio for an eventual alarm, which did not come until 6 a.m., as long my duty lasted. [. . .]

Else there is an astounding naivity in political aspects. They really believe that the Gs came to save us from bolshevism, they really believe that "the fate

64. "Szervusz" in Hungarian or "servus" in German is an informal, friendly greeting term.

65. Katalin Karády (1912–90) was a Hungarian film star. In 1944 she was arrested by the Gestapo on charges of espionage. See Braham, *The Politics of Genocide*, 1:484.

66. Edmund Veesenmayer (1905–77) was the German plenipotentiary to Hungary in 1944. He was convicted of war crimes in 1949 but only served two years in prison ("Ministries Trial," in *Holocaust Encyclopedia*).

67. See "Hungarian Notables Reported Slain by Nazis to Hide Secret of Horthy Role in Occupation," *NYT*, May 8, 1944, for reporting on the supposed execution of General István Ujszaszy and Katalin Karády. See also Bauer, *Jews for Sale*, 135–37, on Ujszazy's and Karády's contacts with Western intelligence in 1943.

of Europe" is to be saved just by our cooperation, etc., etc. The town, as small as it is, full with G. soldiers, armed cars, tanks.

APRIL 27, THURSDAY.

10:40 p.m. Sirens. I just began to have a bit of leisure, from 5 p.m. until 8:30 Hanne Toperczer sat here and exasperated me with her most narrow views, from 8:30 p.m. Maria Pató until 10 p.m. What a life.

At 11:45 p.m. alarm off. In the meantime I went up to the Hermans, the old lady is still sick and could not possibly go down. We sat there and had a good laugh over our heroes, sitting down the shelter.

At 10 p.m. BBC's German news announced that Stephen Antal, so called minister of justice was seriously wounded. I am not sorry for him but am afraid, at least twenty hostages will be shot in reprisal.

APRIL 28, FRIDAY.

This morning I got a telephon call from the Social Insurance Med. Service. They asked me to go and see them, whether I could take a certain med. work. May be it would be safer just to stay at home because those parts of the town are on the margin of the industrial areas, but again, on the other hand, if I do no work at all (not being just moribund) they, I mean G. authorities could recruit me for their war work. I think, this was the thing to do, I went, had a talk with them and accepted. It was so urgent, I had to stay there immediately for the ordination (office) hours, 12–2:30 p.m. there worked two M.D.s before one is called up for military services, the other, being a Jewess, will be probably dismissed, independently, whether I accept or not.[68] I discussed the situation quite openly with her and she was on the same opinion.

Nightmares again: her husband, a lawyer (converted at the age of four, now 54 years old) was taken yesterday from their home for labour service. His last question to her was: is my prayer book in my bag?

APRIL 29, SATURDAY.

Everything all right with my work.

It would be the duty of a diary to register all events around me. Every day new orders and regulations are published, almost everyday new atrocities and cruelties happen it is difficult to register them all and too painful too. As an outstanding feature is the case of 12000 Kassa Jews, who were driven out of their

68. On the forced unemployment of Jewish professionals, see Braham, *The Politics of Genocide*, 1:492.

home and out of town, into the open hill sides, no shelter, no water, all with but one small bag. This followed the visit of Endre László, secretary of state for the interior. The mayor of Kassa, Alexander Pohl,[69] tried to intervene for the Jews in the Home Office, Endre promised to go and see for himself, he went in fact and found the affair all right, very satisfactory. Pohl was removed from his job, his deputy is acting for him.[70] The other feature of today is the index on Jewish and other antinazi-authors and their books. They will not be burnt publicly as in good old nazi times in Germany but will be bought up on waste-paper prices by the mills.[71]

It must be said for Gizi, Ancy and especially for Lujzi, they are really sorry for the Jews.

APRIL 30, SUNDAY.

An unexpected call by the mail man: (it is Sunday) he delivered the box with my usual eggs supply, sent by your aunt Margit regularly. We have so little protein on rations, no meat, no eggs, some beans and peas, but this only door is still open: if you have somebody in the country side to supply with eggs (there amidst the agricultural population it is more easy to get some) you can get a package, under two kgs. This is the last day for evacuation trains to leave Budapest. It is stated, a hundred thousand people left Bpest, I have no means to check whether it is correct or not. Sure, an everyday spectacle on our streets are trucks and horse carts loaded high up with all sort of furniture and odd objects.

Lots of daily papers and magazines were prohibited by the new régime. Kovácsné Tüdős Ilona's *Tejgazdasági Szemle*, Mrs Stephen Kiss's *Vendéglősök Lapja* and above all *Mozi Ujság*,[72] edited by Jenő Hajós, who could not be pro-German enough! These papers had not the slightest political leaning it is funny to watch, how some people, who helped the present situation to life, get under the wheels themselves. [. . .]

---

69. Alexander Pohl was the mayor of Kassa/Košice from 1939 to 1944. He was installed in office after the First Vienna Arbitration (1938) (*MEK*). See map 1.

70. Braham writes that, contrary to Mádi's diary impression, Mayor Pohl actively oversaw the roundup and internment of twelve thousand Kassa Jews in a temporary ghetto. See *The Politics of Genocide*, 1:546–47. Less than 5 percent of the Kassa Jews survived ghettoization and deportation to Auschwitz-Birkenau.

71. See Lévai, *Black Book*, on the ban on publishing books by Jewish authors (169–70) and the pulping of the paper used for Jewish books (190).

72. *Tejgazdasági Szemle* (Dairy business review), *Vendéglősök Lapja* (Restaurant journal), and *Mozi Ujság* (New film magazine).

SAME NIGHT.

The afternoon I went to see Tercsi néni, as she seemed a bit hurt, since I could not see her for about ten days or so. I am tired by who can tell, how long shall I be able to see them and do this charitable visits? His [*sic*] son, Api will be retired (aircraft), because of her origin.

Coming homewards on the streetcar I have seen two drunken G. soldiers, young peasant boys they were. They were rather noisy and engaged in talk a Hungarian soldier (all ranks and files) who was sitting across and reading a newspaper. One of the G.s pointed with his finger on the paper and shouted: don't believe a word they are lying all the time! Not a word is true! The Hungarian did not understand and told them rather indignantly to speak Hungarian if they wish to be understood, then the G. began shouting again don't believe a word, they are all lies . . .

MAY 1, MONDAY.

At 8:30 p.m. Elly Hermans here. She wants to get out of the country, just the same as myself, she to Holland, I to the States. How long shall we have to stay here? She, may be, not so long, for as a Dutch subject she will be able to get there shortly after the war. Not so myself. I should like to know, do you get your citizenship this year or only after the elapse of five years living inside the States?[73]

I shall have to get up at 4 a.m. tonight, in order to listen to the radio for the benefit of people in this house. At 6 a.m. I can go back to sleep, if only I can. No "légó" until now. Did I tell you about the intimate relations of Endre László and Crouy Lincsi? I am sorry for her, was a nice girl and now to associate with this sadist, well, too bad.

MAY 2, TUESDAY.

[. . .] The usual work, before I met Hanna (Szabó), afterwards I had to see Erzsi Kartal [. . .]

Erzsi tells me, they receive so much kindness on part of their gentile friends and aquaintances, they never had before. Milk they get more then before. But their situation is more grave as ever. In many towns Jews are forced into ghettos, sooner or later Budapest will follow and, I am afraid, there will be no more escape from there.[74] [. . .]

---

73. Hilda Walton became a US citizen in April 1943 in Shreveport, Louisiana.

74. The internment of Jews in Transylvania, Subcarpathian Ruthenia, and Northeast Hungary began on April 15, with deportation trains running to Auschwitz-Birkenau nonstop from the end of April to the beginning of July, carrying an estimated 437,000 Hungarian Jews. See Braham, *The Politics of Genocide*, 2:595–613.

We heard talk about how rich Jews were helped out from Slovakia into Switzerland by the Gestapo, for big sums of money.[75] Now I am told there exists a G. colonel, with one committee at our Hotel Bristol[76] residing, who helps Jews to get to Bucharest for twelve thousand Ps a head (I do not see any phantasy in getting to Bucharest) but helps them to get to Tito for nothing, "thinking of the future."

MAY 3, WEDNESDAY.

Several people observed that the G. occupying troups (ranks and files I mean) have no Hungarian money, at least, nothing worth mentioning. The Gestapo yes. They buy in shops big amounts, even embroideries, but the simple soldiers have very little Pengős and much RMarks.[77] As our country has to pay the high cost of occupation troups, it is interesting to watch, how the nazis cheat out their own men of the possibility to get something for their pay. [. . .]

Yesterday I had to wear my furcoat, today it was almost hot, I came home without stockings, as my last pair got holes on the way to the dispensary hospital. What on earth am I going to do with regards stockings, I do not know.

MAY 4, THURSDAY.

After the case of Marcsi's husband, it is Jancsi Bingert today. In spite of his being rather pro-German, he is removed out of his position as director of Hunnia.[78] [. . .] Personal grievances and revenge get splendid opportunity in these days. I rang them up and congratulated them on the occasion. May be, this will help him, who is a decent fellow and was never mean with Jews, to get back to his place after the war. May be, but not sure.

MAY 5, FRIDAY.

At 0:30 a.m. I was awaken by the sounds of sirens. In a comparatively short time, not quite half an hour later AAC could be heard. Probably partly a return journey from over Vienna, as from Sopron on all our towns were alarmed, but

---

75. This is a reference to the so-called Kasztner train, the agreement between the SS and Jewish Council member Resző Kasztner: the SS would provide up to fifteen hundred Jews with emigration papers to reach a neutral country, and in exchange, the Jewish Council would implement SS orders about ghettoization. See *The Kasztner Report: The Report of the Budapest Jewish Rescue Committee, 1942–1945* (Jerusalem: Yad Vashem Publishing, 2013); "Rudolph Kasztner," in *Holocaust Encyclopedia*; and Bauer, *Jews for Sale*, 197–200.

76. Hotel Bristol, located near the Eastern Station (see map 2).

77. RMarks were Reichsmarks, the German currency. The preoccupation conversion rate was two pengö to one RM.

78. Budapest film studio built in 1912.

was very probably a raid over Bpest too, as after having finished off we could see fires from the Újpest direction. At 2 a.m. alarm off. In two minutes I was in bed again. The opposite house buzzed like a beehive disturbed for about a quarter of an hour, then noises gradually subsided with the exception of two housewives: they sweetly chattered on as it would be noon or afternoon and they being on the market. [. . .]

SAME NIGHT.

It is believed that last night's raid was perhaps the biggest and most widely spread until now.[79] Factories in every part of the town, West railway station, the house next Scala movie, the square before St Stephens bazilika, Tisza István street, Mária Valéria street, etc, etc,[80] were hit but with small calibre bombs or incendiaries. [. . .]

My colleague, Dr Timár[81] was insulted today on the streetcar because of the yellow star.

MAY 6, SATURDAY.

0:10 a.m. Since about 10:30 p.m. our radio went off the air with warnings to Bácska, Baja. It seemed to be a slow affair, so I went to sleep. Just after midnight I had to awake as very large explosions could be heard, though from a big distance. [. . .]

At 0:35 radio continues with news. Quick to bed.

SAME NIGHT.

My med. colleague had her weekend day off, so I had to carry on with work. There is not much to do, since the airraids make people nervous, and not so many come to the office as before. [. . .] The afternoon a telephon call from an unknown lady for a Mr Ubrizsy,[82] living in the same house (I scarcely met him in the shelter, but this does not prevent people from giving my name and number to their friends).

Mrs. Láng talked to a G. soldier in a shop. The soldier said: I have been in Holland, Belgium, Poland, France, Greece, Italy, and Russia, but just the same, "krepieren muss ich,"[83] that is sure. They have lost their faith.

79. The Fifteenth Air Force reported no raids over Hungary. Instead, the raid was by British RAF bombers. See "War News Summarized," *NYT*, May 4, 1944, 1.

80. Locations in Budapest's 5th District.

81. Mádi's colleague at Oti.

82. Pál Ubrizsi, resident at 19 Margaréta utca and district leader of the Arrow Cross Party. See Braham, *The Politics of Genocide*, 1:482. Ubriszi was the cousin of the deputy minister of the interior, László Baky (Braham, *The Politics of Genocide*, 2:529–33).

83. I must die (German).

MAY 8, MONDAY.[84]

I inspected the damage done last Friday night in the city: corner of Tisza István u. and József tér,[85] the house of Erdélyi vendéglő.[86] It looks like an unfinished house: all windows and the doors missing. The fire was from the inside and demolitions too. Another house hit was next to Ritz, only the fourth and fifth floors were hit, it was a "dépendence" of Ritz so I hope, German officers lived there.[87]

Today after my work I went up to see Pravdáné, living nearby Eastern Station, where I have to change the streetcars. Afterwards I met Mamuci and helped her shopping. There is not much what you can buy but surely more then a few weeks before, because Jews have to sell now what they can and they do not hide their wares. Such a drop in gold prices, two months ago one gm of gold costs 80–100 P, now they throw it after you for 15–20 P, official price 15 P. [. . .]

Meanwhile such little things as women's compulsory labour service from the age of 18 until 30 and university students' compulsory labour service are introduced. Just by orders.

MAY 9, TUESDAY.

At last I got my birth certificate today, having gone for it five times in more then two weeks. People seem to be mad about their certificates, lines are waiting before the office. After my office hours I had lunch with the Kartals. Erzsike insists on giving some angora wool for Barbara, it will be a nice pass time to knit it for her. I shall have to do it for a five years old child, as it is not very likely, I could send it to her before this age. Bucharest got three severe raids in these days.[88] People here are taking it for sure that it will be our turn again. [. . .]

MAY 10, WED., 2 A.M.

I have the vigil for two hours this night, I was awakened by my neighbour Székely, at 2 o'clock and have to wake Mrs Gorrieri (the "lady" with the G. SS friend) at 4 o'clock. This is again the sort of idiocy we are used to, because the siren is loud enough to wake the dead in their graves, but no, in every house there must be a vigil from 10 p.m. until 6 a.m. Extra anxious people want to

84. Mádi had a diary entry on May 7 but the text was about mundane family matters and not included in this abridged volume.

85. Square.

86. Transylvanian restaurant.

87. Mádi hoped that the building adjacent to the Ritz would collapse and in doing so bring down with it the hotel where the Germans were billeted.

88. The Fifteenth Air Force bombed Brasov, Northern Transylvania, with 300 planes on May 6; 420 bombers attacked Bucharest on May 7, 1944 (*CC*).

be awakened even in case of disturbing flights, when the sirens are not yet sounded, some even earlier. As it is absurd and I am not deaf, I try to get in the meantime some BBC news. Sebastopol has fallen on the third day of its actual siege,[89] I suppose, the Germans hoped to hold out longer, as their news service did not prepare the public yet for this "change."

Discipline among the G. troups is not the strongest. I have seen with my own eyes a "Befehl—Parancs"[90] on both G. and Hungarian languages in several shops, in which it is forbidden there to exact from merchants wares above rations.

The latest about illegal actions is: G. authorities announced in papers and radio that who ever gave credit to G. soldiers or had been taken wares away from March 19 until April 8 should report on given place with invoice, or eyewitnesses. [. . .] Announced was too that requests should be made until the 20 May, later all claims are nil. Several merchants, among them Jews, went to claim their rights but they were arrested by G. authorities on the spot, instead of being paid.

SAME NIGHT.

I was but a quarter of an hour late for my work, alarms went on the radio but no more sirens at Bpest. I understand that it was Austria (Weinernaustadt) this time, may be some places in Hungary too, perhaps Pécs.[91]

Seen Lacy and Károly. Supper with Gizi & Co. I had to buy the most expensive stocking of my life today, I have none and the only shop, Kerpel, which used to sell me one pair monthly, being Jewish, was closed. [. . .]

In the meantime I tell you that 18,000 Jewish shops were closed at Budapest, out of which 600 will be reopened, the others will be stolen, pillaged. You may imagine what a loss this will mean to the national income.

In the pause, as long the radio does not give the alarms, we can hear beautiful Russian records. Our announcer has to tell us from time to time. Ladies and gentlemen, the danger is still prevailing, the music you hear is not radiated

---

89. Sebastopol or Sevastopol, a Black Sea port and the site of a lengthy battle in 1944. See "Siege of Sevastopol," *NYT*, May 9, 1944.

90. Both words mean "command," the first in German, the second in Hungarian.

91. Wiener Neustadt, an industrial city south of Vienna, was the site of several German aircraft factories. The Fifteenth Air Force began bombing Wiener Neustadt in November 1943 from bases in Sicily. Later, after the relocation of the Fifteenth and of RAF Bomber Command to Foggia on the Italian Adriatic coast, Wiener Neustadt became a regular, repeated target. Four hundred US Army Air Force bombers attacked Wiener Neustadt (*CC*, May 10, 1944). See map 1 for Wiener Neustadt's location and the location of the Hungarian city of Pécs.

by Bpest I. During the first raids our radio gave popular records to suppress Russian programe but now, it seems, they must use the electric energy somewhere else.

0:30 A.M. (MAY 11, THURSDAY).

[. . .] My next door neighbours, the Victors traded their radio set in for a seven valved tube big set, Jewish property, with help of some military organ. It is funny how some people have no sense of decency. [. . .]

MAY 12, FRIDAY.

I should like to have a glimpse of your way of thinking at present. I am sure we think about the same in basic facts but very probably after such a long separation we diverge in details. I am embittered about things of all nazi origin and connection, you try to find excuse for many European acts, as you must see the mistakes and blunders made on your side of the world. I, on my part idealize all, what is American, from such a space of time and distance.

I understand, that Hungary has to pay for the German occupation daily 3,000,000 Ps.

You know, the Horchlers are living at Pilsudsky út since February and their next door neighbour is Bö's sister, Teri. A few days ago she came up the stairs, met Péter the 15 years old nefew of Gizi, who said into her face: büdös zsidó![92] The janitor of the house was present, reproved the boy, went to the Horchlers, told them what happened and said: I had to reprove the boy as I have two sons myself and I don't want them to learn such manners. Was it not splendid of him? With little exception one can count on workmen only for reasonableness and decency.

Plans for the administration of liberated and conquered Europe are published in London today. I do not know what strategic plans allies have but at present it seems a bit farcical to "drink on the bearskin ahead"[93] as nothing is liberated and conquered yet.

5:45 p.m. American news brought a declaration of the united nations towards satellite countries and plans for the immediately post-war period. Second these plans General Eisenhower will be commander of the conquered Europe, but Chechoslovakia and the Balkans (that means us too, though we are not on the Balkans) will be not under Gen. Eisenhower's command. This means Soviet occupation. [. . .]

92. Stinking Jew! Pilsudsky út was in Budapest's 12th District, the same district where Mádi lived.

93. Meaning, don't celebrate prematurely.

Day by day there are many accidents in town, outside the town, everywhere. Yesterday a G. and a Hungarian military car escaped collision by a hairbreath, both stood motionless the next minute and the Hungarian driver, getting out, told the G.: *a golyó borotválja a pofádat*![94] Our news service—no doubt acting on G. orders—trying to get us accustomed to the idea of invasion, brings every day on leading place with thick capital letters something like these: Rommel about invasion (*Pest*, 1944, május 9), Europe is ready for every possible form of invasion (*Pest*, 1944, majus 10) Again: Göbbels about the invasion (*Pest*, 1944, May 12). Before one and a half years they stated that invasion is impossible, an absurd joke.

At 9:50 p.m. radio off the air. 10:25 p.m. sirens of Bpest sounding. I am ready, dressed, but stay in my flat. A very dark, cloudy night. G. soldiers everywhere, coming out and going into houses, especially into ours. Some very distant lightnings, no sound. Lights coming from the Transdanubian parts. From the shelter G. soldiers song: Es geht alles vorüber . . . [95] It would be pathetic, would it not be so silly. Smells too coming up, the sort of some dirty little saloon smells, alcohol, sweat, reak, tobacco. [. . .]

Midnight BBC news spoke about a new allied offensive in Italy, well, almost unbelievable after the "millimeter war" having lasted so long.

MAY 13, SATURDAY, 4:35 A.M.

I suppose, I have an enemy, a malicious enemy in the house, somebody rang my doorbell at half past three and this was not the first time. I think it is Lajtai, a rather hysteric neurotic young man, whom I seem to have offended unintentionally. [. . .]

The synthetic oil plants of Germany and Checkoslovakia were bombed the night. I often wondered before, why these have been untouched almost for two years? According to Ali, their synthetic oil production surpassed even the produce of the Ploesti oilfields.

SAME NIGHT.

I was free this weekend seen Mrs Stolcz and her mother, got lovely lilacs from their garden, I gave them in turn to Mamuci. Seen Bö, home at 6 p.m., Pubi was here later Mr Zoltán Németh, a neighbour from the house, whom I do not like, he is a worm. He brought me as present about 8 dk.s of coffee, which I would have preferred to buy. I shall have to buy some book for his wife. [. . .]

94. That was a close shave!

95. Everything passes (German).

MAY 14, SUNDAY.

There is a book of A. Huxley: Ways and means,[96] I believe. There are brilliant thoughts about paranoid morons, getting to power. I could read only a few pages of the book.

It was sickening to listen to our 9:40 p.m. news service, when at 9:50 it went off the air. I am greeting the coming alarm cheerfully. [. . .]

10:07 p.m. nuisance flights over Békés, Karcag. 10:22 p.m. probably nothing serious, as until now not only no alarm was given, but the alerts over Beszterce, Rahó were cancelled. May be there was a raid over Roumania and some of the planes were returning to the south (We got very-very sophisticated, as you see). 10:34. disturbing flights over Baja, Bácska. This is the way, normal raids (base Italy) used to begin.

MAY 15, MONDAY.

Nothing happened last night, but I dreamt about you, it was a vague picture of you, I knew, I have not seen you for years and I could not understand, what you had to tell me. It is only the second time in all these years I dreamt about you.

The evening Maria Pató came, at 8 p.m., I was lucky she left at 11 p.m.

MAY 16, TUESDAY.

Soon after coming home, Iván Bingert came too for an English lesson. He is progressing well. This winter he asked for some lessons, just after the G. occupation he said, he was too busy and has no time for English. Now he does not believe in his Germans. Of course, I do it out of friendship toward her [*sic*] mother and our furniture pieces are stored in their house. But opportunism seems to be inborn in this sváb-race.[97]

I shall have the vigil tonight from 4 a.m until 6 a.m. How silly it is.

The Gustav line in Italy[98] seems to be broken all right, but we are so impatient and tired of waiting.

11:30 p.m. We are living in a nightmare. Just now low moaning of a feminine voice was heard, from the street somewhere, a little later a scream. All still again. As we are deep in black out time, it takes a while to draw the blinds. Then I could hear the noise of a car starting, uphill. So it was the Gestapo,

96. Aldous Huxley, *Ends and Means (an Enquiry into the Nature of Ideals and into the Methods Employed for Their Realization)*, a book of essays published in 1937.

97. Ethnic Germans living in Hungary.

98. The Gustav line was the Axis defensive works across the Italian peninsula that halted Allied armies from December 1943 to June 1944.

taking somebody with them to their headquarters in Hotel Majestic on the Svábhegy.[99]

MAY 17, WED.

I have made, may be, a very valuable friendship here in the house. The shoemaker and his wife, people about 50–55, of very sound opinions. I have to tell you much about them. As to his wife's doctor and out of pure principle he gave me a pair of shoes on a really low price. I shall be saved for next winter, a shoe of leather soles!

We are simply told in ministerial speeches and newspaper articles, that *we* are going to build a Hungarian national-socialistic state. People, but especially the countryside are threatened and alerted day by day with the horrors of bolshevism.

MAY 18, THURSDAY.

The fortress of Monte Cassino[100] was evacuated by the Gs. The French General Juin[101] in an order of the day gave credit to his troups for good work (such praises mean always heavy losses). All seems to go well. [. . .]

I got a good advice for the very problematic case, could I ever get out to your country. To never get the homesickness, one has only to let send after you regularly the rightist papers. *Magyar Szó* is the gem of them all. [. . .]

A G. journalist, following Rommel on an inspecting tour round the Atlantic coast, announced today that above all technical defenses their faith is in the German troups! We have again leading articles and radio lectures about the *necessity* of an invasion, however the allies may shirk from it, but they, poor things, have to do it, absolutely, whether they like it or not.

It seems, something had happened to the Gestapo headquarters and offices up on the Svábhegy because since a few days they are moving down to the Pasarét and to our Németvölgyi ut[102] too. Many family houses were evacuated inhabitants and owners, not only Jews, gentiles too, among them Atzél, a councillor in the Home Office too.[103] All these people are told by the Germans to go and look for Jewish apartments. [. . .]

99. For the Gestapo headquarters location, see Braham, *The Politics of Genocide*, 1:396.

100. Monte Cassino was the key defensive position on the German line in Italy and the site of a battle (January–May 1944).

101. Alphonse Pierre Juin (1888–1967) was the commander of the French Expeditionary Forces in Italy (1943–44). Mádi's subsequent annotation about General Juin: "1969. A pseudonym, Apu said he was Count du Murielle."

102. The principal thoroughfare of Budapest's 12th District, where Mádi lived.

103. Elemér Atzél (1888–1954) was a pharmacist, doctor, and lawyer. He was head of the Health Department in the Ministry of the Interior (*MEK*).

I had to spend some hours with Erzsi, very hard to look at their indecision. I suppose it would be the same with me in similar circumstances, one is inclined to disbelieve the possibility of something drastic and hesitates to leave all her roots for good.

MAY 19, FRIDAY.

Two months since the G.s invaded the country. Since then it has been a continuous nightmare we are living in.

I had a busy day. At 3:30 p.m. I was with Tercsi néni, she had to see me. I was touched, she prepared coffee for me (though she hates it herself) and made Kuglupf.[104] She got a Jewish servant just today, it was about time, she is so exhausted, you remember many rooms, cooking, washing up, etc., etc. for four persons without modern equipment. [. . .]

MAY 20, SATURDAY.

BBC announces, allied troups have broken into the Hitler line in Italy. So I understand now the G. statement is yesterday's news: there is no such thing as a Hitler line.[105] [. . .]

SAME NIGHT.

All my days seem to be so busy now. We had not many patients at the office, so it was a rather dull and boring to sit out two and a half hours . . . Lunch at home, home-made, a very little rest and at 4:30 p.m. up to the Dutch family. On their balcony we had tea and a talk, at 6 p.m. I visited my patient, Mrs Láng, in bed with a tonsillitis since yesterday.

MAY 21, SUNDAY.

The afternoon I went to see Mici néni, Zsu was there too. She is quite a personality. You see, this is restlessness, I do not want to see people and still I go sometimes without having to do it. Again I can't stay for long, I have to move on again.

11:10 p.m. The Russian air-bus-service seems to be over us again. Disturbing flights over Miskolc are announced on the radio. I better continue with my reading Vinde's America.[106]

MAY 22, MONDAY.

Last night, about half past two a.m. the whole town was awoken by sharp AAC fire. Though no sirens were sounded, I began to dress, but as the affair was soon

104. Similar to a Bundt cake.

105. "Hitler Line Pierced," *NYT*, May 20, 1944.

106. Victor Vinde, *America at War* (1944).

over, I undressed again and went to bed. Of course, no regular sleep follows, it lasted a while until I could sleep and in the morning woke exhausted and indignant: I argued in my sleep with my father, I believe, over your education and told him how unhappy our childhood was under his thumb.

MAY 23, TUESDAY.

There lived in Bpest an Italian by birth, American by nationality, Introzzi, who married a Jewess. They missed the last opportunity to get out and now I hear, the man is in jail and badly beaten by the police. He is not given any food, so his wife has to carry food for him every day, though she is in the last days, expecting a baby. I understand, there were about thirty Americans still here, mostly Jews. They are interned. Of course, your government told them in time to leave, I remember well. May be their lives will be safe because of their citizenship but a bad treatment seems to be possible. I am told to go and see a neutral legation here is sure detention.

SAME NIGHT.

I left home at 11 a.m. and came back at 9 p.m., but it was a useful day. I am so busy, that the office hours are a comparative rest. Two letters sent for the papers of your Henfner grandparents, five minutes with Lacy, I lent them the Vinde book until Sat. next, the Kartals, the office of my attorney (he has disappeared in fact), Bö (she called me whether I won't see her as long as it is possible) and at 8 p.m. out to Hűvösvölgy to Edith F., with Klári's problem.

It is generally believed here, that it is dangerous to go to any neutral legation's building. Edith states that this is only the case with Turkey, the Swedish, Swiss, etc. (are there any more still?) can be entered without any danger.

I do not like the latest tone of G. news items about the "bestiality" of allied pilots, "chasing peasants and playing children with their machineguns." It seems to be a preparation for something.

Propaganda and foolishness: I heard a girl ticket collector on the streetcar complaining about a recent air raid–night alarm, after which she got home very tired and late. She finished her story with: this all is because of those damned Jews! She seems to believe the war a liberation war for Jews and that they are immune against air raids.[107]

Just the same as Jews are persecuted today by all the hate, propaganda can awake, the same would be possible with any other group for example civil servants, or peasants, or big estate owners. Against all of these groups heavy

107. See Braham, *The Politics of Genocide*, 1:486, 510, for the way that the Germans and Hungarian authorities explained the Allied air war as orchestrated by so-called world Jewry.

arguments could be launched, strong feelings stirred up, out of which some would be true and most of them just lies. This Jewish question shows some similarity with the coloured questions of some Southern states in U.S.A., according to Vinde.

MAY 24, WEDNESDAY.

10:30 p.m. Alarms raging over our radio. So it was the morning too, when the district of Vienna was raided.[108] Now Szamos, Kolozs (Transylvania) are mentioned, flights over Bpest too, just the same, I am going to bed, as last night I did not have much rest.

MAY 25, THURSDAY.

Yesterday Tercsi néni has shown me two relics of an American flying fortress[109]: a life belt, impregnated with some yellow dye (which makes them more visible on the watersurface) and a piece of the windshield. It is about 10 cm. thick, contains five different layers, three thick and two thin, no bullet can penetrate it. Only when the aircraft exploded, did the glass shield go to pieces.

There are several news items worth conserving for the future. The first is about Cassino. The second deals very carefully with a deportation train, a Jewish deportation train, from Nagykanizsa,[110] meant for the German frontier. I am told, the Vatican legation intervened with the minister of the interior, Jaross, because of these deportations. Jaross flatly denied it. Soon after the case the Nagykaniza train was due towards the German border, but it was returned again and it seems, during this delay (some days) the freight cars were sealed, people inside without food and drink water, so these deaths may have occurred.

MAY 26, FRIDAY.

Jews situation is more and more precarious every day. With the exception of Bpest they are herded into ghettos all over the country, into unbelievable crowded conditions—2 m floorspace/person—and many ghettos, especially those in the northeastern parts of the country, were emptied. These deportation trains go over the German border but no further, it is believed. G. Does not need any more workmen, as with the raids over industrial areas, thousands and thousands are left without work.[111] This all results in the recent fact that

108. More than six hundred US bombers of the Fifteenth Air Force attacked Austria this day (*CC*, May 24, 1944).

109. The B-17 bomber.

110. Nagykanizsa is a city in Zala County in southwestern Hungary.

111. Mádi's subsequent annotation: "1969. They needed workmen badly 1945."

even the most bourgeois Jews begin to hate the English (may be Americans too, but out of tact they do not say so before me), seeing no help coming from them. Russian sympathies on the contrary are rising.

SAME NIGHT.

The morning I had to get my marriage certificate from the Minor Franciscan Brothers' Church (Kapucincsok), it is a rage these days to have all the possible papers and to prove you are not Jewish. [. . .] After my office hours I had a talk with Bö. I had to shake her up, I hope, with full success. People here are just the same as the monkeys in Kipling's Jungle book, when Kaa hypnotizes them, before swallowing up the whole lot. [. . .]

A few weeks ago I heard about Kertay, whom you will remember from Maort days. He is a Jew, escaped from Kanizsa before they could put him into the ghetto and is working at present here, in Bpest. As all you Americans have known him, I suppose Dr. Papp won't send him back but whether he can do something for him when the Budapest ghetto round-up begins (they expect the new orders any day), I do not know.

According to tonight's BBC news it seems probable that Rome will be taken before Whitsunday[112] and then the Pope will be able to speak over the radio, what the Germans denied him in a rather rude way. But if allied progress continues at this rate (Sep. 943 beginning of the invasion of Italy–May. 944. Rome) we can wait another twenty years and I better knit Barbara's angora coat on your size.

MAY 27, SATURDAY.

There are rumours in town about Endre Lazló, secretary of state for Jewish affairs. He is a sadist. He used to go for inspection tours all around the country to see whether Jews are treated cruelly enough. Allegedly on one of his inspection tours somewhere on the south parts (Újvidék or Szabadka it is stated), a few days ago he was caught by Tito's partisans. Only, I am afraid there will be reprisals. Since yesterday many Jews are seized on the streets and taken to concentration camps again.

MAY 28, WHITSUNDAY.

I have to remind myself again, that you really exist and that it is not only a make believe about a Hilda, a Geo, a Barbara. . . . I was gardening in my lot on the balcony, nasturtiums and some of the antirrhinums are almost 20 cms

112. Whitsunday (Pentecost) was a floating holiday that took place on May 28 in 1944.

high and will be in bloom in ten days. Today's temperature and sunshine was perfect for them. Of course, you know, this is all a substitute for YOU and Barbara.

MAY 29, WHITMONDAY.

A few days ago BBC warned Hungarian listeners not to join groups called Eastern frontline association, Hung-G. association & those like. Last Saturday I have seen yellow leaflets on the streets calling people to join the Eastern frontline Brotherhood. Today I am told new leaflets appeared, very antisemitic. Preparing pogrom, I suppose, in a non-official way. In newspaper propaganda Jews are abused for living in luxury, now they can't have servants, they are ridiculed for their work. Their shops, jobs are taken from them "legally," but they again are attacked for not doing any work.

From about 10 p.m. the radio off the air. Alarms all over the country again. I am in bed peacefully, reading my latest Jalna volume, Wakefield's course.[113] Before midnight Bpest sirens were sounded, at 0:15 the affair is off. Are the allies so considerate these last weeks, because they are anxious for Jews wellbeing? Or have they simply more to do elsewhere? This morning it was the Vienna area's turn again. A Jewess, who hates the English, said recently: they (The Allies) don't move a little finger to save us, but at the end they will come with their statistics . . .

MAY 30, TUESDAY.

Perhaps I mentioned you before, how official propaganda almost persuaded our blitzed population to commit atrocities on the allied pilots. Today in a Berlin news item the same is reflected: they want the population to do what authorities do not dare, I hope, no use, as I told you before, blitzed people used to be rather meek and subdued, no bloodthirstiness can be observed, when they just escaped death.

At 10 p.m. our radio off the air, again. I am not even hanging on it, as I would miss the BBC news. The air raid warnings can be heard from the neighbouring apartments just the same, some people run their radios loud and they believe to be our benefactors too. 11 p.m. until now no raid but a group of G. soldiers (at least five of them) talking loudly before our house. During the intervals of air raid warnings, Bpest I. does not radiate anything. In these spaces we can clearly hear another station, Radio Sardegna, which gives all the time allied news in Italian, just now the "Voce di Londre."

113. Mazo de la Roche, *Wakefield's Course* (1941), set in Jalna, Ireland.

MAY 31. WEDNESDAY.

In today's *Maygar Szó* (the paper against home sickness) gives again a news item from Berlin, where the question of allied pilots bestiality is dwelt upon. It ends with the sentence: nobody should wonder, if in the near future new measures will be taken against these gangsters.[114]

JUNE 1, THURSDAY.

I have been very hungry as yesterday I forgot to shop for food and so I had no meal in the evening, neither breakfast. This morning, just tea. Hair dresser, at home Mrs. Láng, then I went to see Katinke (Marika's mother). I promised her last Saturday to call, but had no time so we agreed on today. I like to be with her and her mother, they are reasonable. Last summer she met your dear, dear uncle Imre at Balatonalmádi, where he told the company guests how he and his friends pledged thousand Ps for orphaned children, if and when New York will be raided . . . (not to New York children, of course). Again a proof, we were right in our judgement with regards these people. Walked home. Now it is dark, still a heavy airtraffic is going on above The Allies are approaching Rome.

JUNE 2, FRIDAY.

The day began with air raid alarms all over the country. Bpest sirens were sounded too, but nothing happened here. As I gather from different sources, Miskolc, Diósgyőr, Szolnok and Szeged got serious raids.[115] After my office hours I went out to the Bingerts as I promised Iván two days ago. We had lunch together, Jancsi is going into the publishers business, Iván had his English lesson, he learns very quickly but his pronunciation is relapsing again and again into the German. I made him listen to BBC news, even if he does not yet understand it, he can pick up lots of expressions.

JUNE 3, SATUR.

I heard on BBC that G. parachute troups made an attack on Tito's headquarters and almost captured Randolph Churchill.[116] This big heavy air traffic

114. "British Protest Slaying of 47 Escaping Air Officers," *NYT*, May 20, 1944. The murders were portrayed in the film *The Great Escape* (United Artists, 1963). Mádi's subsequent annotation: "June 25, 944. I see now this newspaper propaganda was for justification of the fact, they killed just these days fifty allied airmen, prisoners of war."

115. The Fifteenth Air Force sent four hundred heavy B-17 bombers against the cities listed (*CC*, June 2, 1944).

116. Operation Rösselsprung, May 25–27, 1944, in Bosnia. Randolph Churchill was the British prime minister's son; he led a mission in 1944 to work with Josip Broz Tito's partisan army in Yugoslavia.

above us was apparently a part of these raids on the mountains. We were told also, that American heavy aircraft landed in Russia to fight eastern Europe from there.[117]

Even now I do not believe for a second in spontaneous acts of revenge, but allied airmen will be killed on lonely spots by SS men. It will be stated, that the outraged population killed them [. . .]

This morning I got an offer from Ganz factory[118] for two hours in the morning, about 300 P salary monthly. But: it is out at Kőbanya, about the most dangerous quarters with regards to air raids. You know, I am not afraid of danger, but still I don't believe in risking my life seriously for dayly 10 Ps. Besides, as it is a war plant with military commander, I could not leave it until the end of the war. I think you would not like me to accept.

The fall of Rome is imminent, according to the evening news. The Alban hills were taken, there is nothing else as lowland further on the way to Rome. I am afraid we shall be told in a few days, that the Pope disgusted with allied barbarians took refuge with G. general command and Hitler, just as a favour, gave him the opportunity to go to Germany.

American pilots and heavy aircrafts arrival to Russia proves the impossibility of a Russia-German alliance, what pro-German elements like to spread. The Allies would not risk large amounts of their aircrafts had they no guarantees of Russia's reliability. Recently BBC mentioned an allied command in Russia, meant for a threat towards Roumania and Hungary. Quoting Anita Loos,[119] I almost had to smile. For us it is much more a hope, a promise, not a threat. Dénes writes on military postcard, they have chocolates and Spanish oranges in plenty. Chocolate we do not have since years and oranges since last year, but all these millions of G. soldiers have it in plenty. Not our young children, whose bones are in making, who will get rickets, all over Europe.

JUNE 4, SUNDAY.

I am told that the whole Weiss family, Ali, Erzie, Gabi, Juci, Marika, Jachi, Ali's brother & sisters, brothers in law, their children, The Mauthneurs, Kornfelds, Chorius, fourty and odd persons were taken by the Germans to Switzerland in sleeping cars, two or three days ago. In exchange for their lives (nothing else, but some small luggage could they have) Hungary's two biggest industrial

117. "Shuttle bombing" during the summer of 1944 involved US aircraft leaving from western airfields and landing in Soviet ones.

118. Ganz Művek (Ganz Works) of Budapest, manufacturers of railway rolling stock.

119. American author and screenwriter (1898–1981), author of *Gentlemen Prefer Blondes*.

companies, the Weiss Manfred works of Csepel and the Salgótarján mines were "bought" by the Herman Göring works.[120] This means all armament factories, aircraft plants, coal mines, canning industries, almost everything important in the country gone over into German hands. I am glad though, because of Ali. People, especially Jews are furious here. Other Jews can bid nothing like so high. Their leaving their flats is limited to dayly two hours.

Midnight BBC news announce the liberation of Rome.

JUNE 5, MONDAY.

Before my work some shopping, it is a treat, when you can get some chemicals against moths. After office hours I went to see Lacy. Both she and her brother are very depressed. Their younger brother[121] was called up for labour service. Later in the afternoon I made some cookies, baked in the kitchen of the Horchlers, then had to hurry home as Iván was due again for a lesson. We had to laugh a lot over Anita Loos' Gentlemen prefer blondes. On Iby's request I sent him home at 9:30, because of a possible air raid. Since 10 p.m. alarms on our radio from the eastern parts of the country.

JUNE 6, TUESDAY.

BBC announces at 9:30 a.m. that allied invasion has begun on the Normandy peninsula, between Cherbourg and Le Havre. I almost gave up hope these days, am trembling all over from excitement. If only it would be a success!

The afternoon. Very few G. soldiers can be seen on the streets, they are shut up in their quarters, I suppose, in order not to hear the news. Here the noon papers brought the news, without any trace of G. measures taken against the invasion.

This evening big, specially designed G. engineering trucks were racing towards Vienna road through the transversal road of Bpest. Api Fidy—allegedly—has stated before weeks, that only these early June days are suitable for the invasion because with full moon nearing is the tide the highest and invasion barges are 20 m's above the sea mines. I have seen Bö, Tercsi Néni and dined with Elko and Klári.

All these solemn speeches of general Eisenhower (I still do not understand him well, just the same, as I understand you, Geo darling, with difficulty) and Churchill seem to be a promise, they mean it really this time.

120. Braham, *The Politics of Genocide*, 1:514–18, explains the SS forced acquisition of the Manfred-Weiss Works; see also Kornfeld, *Reflections*, 146–89.

121. Lajos Lakos, who was Irén's brother and the father of Alfred Lakos.

JUNE 7, WEDNESDAY.

I am told that Márta had been caught for hiding Jewish property.[122] I shall hear more from Mamuci, may be. Stettinius[123] states that Portugal has stopped wolfram[124] supply towards Germany, guess, when? Yesterday! How well timed.

SAME NIGHT.

I just had a dish of vegetables, it cost me almost 7 p's and besides, I had to work hard preparing it. Today's papers printed G. statement, they are perfectly satisfied with the invasion. Showing off.

Elko, the optimist believes there will be no pogrom at the end of Jerry's rule. He thinks, at a concentric attack these "gentlemen" will get panicky and think only of saving their own lives. I am not so sure about it.

Until now the new, secret G. weapon turned out to be just tanks and machine guns. Jaross, Hung. Minister of the interior stated: the de-jewification (zsidótlanitós) of Hungary is not a mere program, but a fact (since there is no way out of the country for Jews, except Germany or German occupied territory, one can easily see what he is aiming at). Gestapo fellows are earning 35,000 p's for taking a married couple out of a countryside ghetto and putting them out down on the streets of Budapest. May be, they even report the case to our police, because checking of identifications is going on all the time on the streets. I have seen one this morning myself at Apponyi square.

Good omens in the present situation: 1) G.s are very vague in their statements about annihilations of different invading troups 2) even they have to state, that north of Rome the allies have broken G. lines. So much they did not confess since Stalingrad. 3) According to allied statements the ten and odd thousand invading aircrafts did not meet more then fifty G. fighters. Hurrah!

The G's state, the pope has barricaded himself in Vatican City, since they left Rome. How do they know, since they have left?

On June 6, when in our papers the fall of Rome was announced, a newsboy sold his paper shouting Hitler has saved Rome! Today an other screamed: All invasion troups thrown back into the sea! I overheard a girl on the street this

---

122. See Lévai, *Black Book*, 99, for penalties in cases where Gentiles helped shield Jewish property from state expropriation. Lévai estimates that the Hungarian police and the Gestapo received more than thirty-five thousand denunciations of citizens for violating the anti-Jewish decrees.

123. Edward Stettinius, US undersecretary of state (1944) and secretary of state (December 1944–45). See "Stettinius," in US Department of State, *Biographies of the Secretaries of State*, https://history.state.gov/departmenthistory/people/stettinius-edward-reilly.

124. Wolfram or tungsten was a rare metal used in strengthening the steel in armored vehicles during World War II, especially tanks.

noon, addressing her uncle (holding a fresh paper) What have *we invaded again*, uncle! This was not bad, I gave her a sympathetic glance.

JUNE 8, THURSDAY.

The dangerousness of the German masses lays not in the fact they are Nazi. They are Nazi because Hitler personified and incorporated too well all the German ideals, as the lust of power, domination, greed, cruelty.

JUNE 9, FRIDAY.

From this mornings news I see that G. resistance in France is stiffening. I hope, allies have got down their feet firmly. [. . .]

SAME NIGHT.

Rather full day. The morning I have seen Ilonka at her tobacco shop. She gave me one hundred cigarettes.

Coming home, we have air precaution exercises in the yard, up in my apartment three telephone calls and I had to hasten out again to the Kartals, where Emil lay in great pain. I left them after 10 p.m. Day by day my friends situation get more serious and weighs on me like a burden, still, I can not help really.

JUNE 10, SATURDAY.

Since 4:30 a.m. I can not sleep. Emil has to go this morning to Svábhegy, state-security-police station. The indictment against him is: occasional help in their household and listening to the janitor's radio. Anonymously reported. As they are very sure that the people in the house, they live in, are all reliable we have to believe that a former workman of their workshop, who seems to belong to some secret society, reported them. I hoped, they would disappear last night, but no, they still hope, it will be all right. Last night I had a talk with a young yellow-starred nurse on the firearms stations at Szalay utca.

Meanwhile drunken G. soldiers are making a lot of noise under our windows (it is 11 p.m.) I can hear with them the voice of the Gorrieris and Mrs. Lajtai, who all are living in this house. The radio off the air again. We had no raid for a considerable time, it is Roumania's turn now. It is announced, the oil refineries of Romano-Americana in Ploesti were raided today.[125]

JUNE 11, SUNDAY.

A few pages before I told you what I believe to be the main difficulty with the German people. In a future peace period it would be essential to give them a

125. Part of the attacks by 550 heavy bombers of the Fifteenth Air Force that day (*CC*, June 10, 1944).

new, effective, but harmless, sort of hobby, as surrogate for their world-power-complex. I think they would be unhappy and restive without their obligatory marching, parades, staccato songs, uniforms and megaphon speeches.

SAME NIGHT.

Márta is all right, she was denounced being of Jewish origin. According to the present law she is all right, nothing happened. We had a talk with Sanya, about you too. Your papers were discussed. I told her about Marika, how eager she is to help. Sanya has a message from Erzsi, Ali's wife. They are still in Austria, delayed we do not know exactly why.[126] So, after all, even they may get the fate of the others . . . Emil came home yesterday noon. He was denounced by one of their well paid, even spoiled workman, Károly Német of Érd, I want to remember him well. Even their former servant, Marika Sukori was indignant.

Radio off the air, I can hear it from the neighbours, air raid war news from the south and east part of the country. I hear, that a Russian offensive has began on the Carchan isthmus.[127]

JUNE 12, MONDAY.

German controlled papers begin to say more and be more interesting than BBC news. For example: BBC only mentions heavy fighting on the Cherbourg peninsula. German commentators on the contrary, say more. On the first few days of the invasion they proudly announced that allies did not reach their aim in occupying Cherbourg. In yesterday's paper Hallensleben[128] confessed to have been mistaken, as Cherbourg *is not* the chief aim for the allies, although fighting is going on there. After this I am confident that Cherbourg is going to be occupied in a short time. In Italy all G. organization seems to have collapsed, at last the pace of progress by allied troups is so astounding.

In today's papers new measures are announced about Jews' flats and living quarters.[129] Two of my ducklings rang me up, Erzsike is in hysterics, I can hear on her voice. Iván was still here, when Maria Pató came, I told her, she has better to avoid me in the near future. Iván left, Marika P. still here, when Marika Kanya arrived. She helped me to cook, offered her help again, left at

126. Baron Weiss's family was interned at Mauthausen concentration camps for some time before being allowed to leave Germany for Portugal. See Braham, *The Politics of Genocide*, 1:518; Szegedy-Maszák, *I Kiss Your Hands*, 155–56; Kornfeld, *Reflections*, 169–82.

127. A reference to the Kerch Isthmus of Crimea.

128. Martin Hallensleben, chief commentator for the Transocean News Service (German).

129. See the decree of June 17, 1944, Determination of the Buildings in the Capital District, as cited in Braham, *The Politics of Genocide*, 2:1196.

9:15 p.m.—well, I must not forget, Gizi was here, when Iván was alone here. They both agreed heartily, they are very antisemitic now! Holy opportunism!

JUNE 13, TUESDAY.

The night, from 12:45 a.m. until 2 a.m. people had to go down to the shelters again. Not me. Nothing happened here, may be at Győr or Vienna. From 4 a.m. until 6 a.m. I had air raid watch of the house. Sleepy and tired.

Germans want to fight the invasion troups *deep inside* the country (France). This is again to prepare for deep penetration. I had to see Lacy, Klári Forrai and Editke again. [. . .]

According to G. commentators there can't be left any space in English language papers, but for deep disillusionment and confessions of failure.

I begin to feel unwell with a sort of colitis, called here these days as Ukraine sickness. I am afraid it will weaken me, though I have so much to do just now.

JUNE 14, WEDNESDAY.

Pro-German elements state, the G's have thirty thousand planes on the western front and almost no men. This no men theory was quoted ever since Stalingrad, wherever they were regularly beaten. With regards the thirty thousand planes—New York papers, quoted in BBC put the question in headlines: where is the Luftwaffe?

At 4:45 a.m. I am up and can't sleep, but am better than last night, at least temporarily I had to get up and made coffee (out of twenty five coffeebeans!) You see, these are my newly acquired bad habits, which will disable me in future for family life.

At 11 a.m. a rather quick and noisy raid over Bpest, but other air raid warnings, over other parts of country too.[130] I was so absorbed on compiling a memorandum in Mrs. Forrai's behalf to the protecting power, I scarcely noticed sirens and all the usual paraphernalia, where the flack and detonations began, I had to hurry up with bath and getting dressed. At 11:20 a.m. all is quiet.

SAME NIGHT.

I was late for my office hours because of the raid. Going down the hill three big and dark columns of smoke rose, one east, one south and one westwards. [. . .] The raid seems to have been an exact, precision work, oil refineries struck at the Csepel area, the junction of the Bánhida power station hit at Kelenföld, but some oil storages too, because the fire was just the same black and powerful, as

130. The Fifteenth Air Force sent 560 heavy bombers to attack targets in Hungary (*CC*, June 14, 1944).

on the other places. [. . .] The AAC turned now inside the city, many splinters had fallen. Almost all the country had been alarmed.

Mrs Hermans, as a favour for me, did an errand on the Swedish legation this morning just after the raid. They say, I can go there without incurring any danger, so I have to go tomorrow morning. Elly was here the afternoon, before I had to see Bö, she believes, I have seen her apartment for the last time. I am very worried about her, she plans suicide. She delayed saying good bye, which is not like her, I felt unwell, but I could get hardly away, it was something in her looks, I did not like. I scolded her, letting down her husband and son, being not a good sport.

Mrs. Rakovszky, our former grocer's wife rang me up too, I have to meet her tomorrow afternoon at the cemetery. This is the place, where, as I hope, nobody is going to bother about a person with the yellow star and one without, being together. [. . .]

The whole town, even here, on the hillside is dirty with smoke, gathering storm clouds are dyed almost black with the burnt products of oil + phosphorus. It must be PhO_3 or PhO_5 (Trioxyde or pentoxyde) as it not only sticks on the skin but burns and itches too.

I understand, the Kecskemét[131] airport today bombed too. Some uncontrollable rumours: tomorrow all yellow starred males will be caught on the streets by the Gestapo.[132] Several industrial companies, who want to save their Jewish employees, told them. They won't be let out of the factories' premises and won't be able to see their families. Whether it will really save them? At any rate, one tells the warning to Jews, not to go on the streets tomorrow.

JUNE 15, THURSDAY.

The morning began with my visit to the Swedish Legation, where I spoke with a Miss Bruning or something like.[133] Much they can not do, I paid a telegram to England they are going to send. Sweden is the protecting power for Hungarians living in England, so, as long Elemér's British citizenship is not proved, he is their charge. It was good to be so near the old home. Rami gave me hundred cigarettes after two weeks, when he did not have any. At the Social Insurance Chief Med Office I heard officially about the fact, whispered in town yesterday, that our Ministry of War wants to protect Jewish war

131. A city about sixty miles southeast of Budapest.

132. See Braham, *The Politics of Genocide*, 2:735–37.

133. Mádi visited the Swedish Legation three weeks before Raoul Wallenberg arrived as first secretary with the task of issuing as many protective papers as possible. See Braham, *The Politics of Genocide*, 2:1212.

workers, clerks, etc. and does not let them leave the premises for their own protection. [. . .]

At 4 p.m. I had a rendezvous with young Mrs. Rakovszky at the cemetery we had a stimulating talk and I hope, I did help her a bit towards a decision. Fancy, her first name is Barbara! In town, before going to Farkasrét I met Gizi and Ily Várady (such a female! Talking all the time about Kállay's perfidy, the allies cruelty, etc.) on the streetcar we came with Elly Hermans, not by chance. I am advised to go to the shelter next time as people's imbecility does not believe that you are not afraid, but they believe, you have some special secret reason, mostly, you have a secret radio station or you give signals, sooner or later you will be reported and your apartment is searched. Now, I do not have any transmitter but this diary would be sufficient to hang me five times a week. So I better go down next time.

Three hundred thousand Chech Jews were gassed in Birkenau, March, 944, by the Germans.[134] (Lacy's mother!) The new super-fortress[135] raided Japan. But where are the new, secret G. weapons? What about the mysterious explosions, heard a few weeks ago allegedly on the southern English coasts?[136] Pro-German elements guessed, the English coastlines will be exploded, but until now nothing such happened. Turkey has stopped to let G. ships through the Dardanelles and Menernendsoglu, Turkish foreign minister resigned.[137]

---

134. Mádi shows a knowledge, as of June 15, 1944, about the gas chambers at Auschwitz-Birkenau. That date was two-thirds of the way through the mass deportation of Hungarian Jews to Auschwitz-Birkenau from Subcarpathia Hungary, Northern Transylvania, Northeastern Hungary, and other regions. In April the eyewitness *Auschwitz Protocols* were smuggled out of Auschwitz to Slovakia and then to Switzerland. See Miroslav Karny, "The History of the Vrba and Wetzler Auschwitz Reports," in *The Tragedy of the Jews of Slovakia*, ed. Dezider Tóth (Banská Bystrica, Slovakia, 2002), 221–42. In the week following Mádi's diary entry, leading statesmen, including President Roosevelt, Secretary of State Hull, Prime Minister Churchill, Foreign Minister Eden, and Pope Pius, received copies of the *Auschwitz Protocols*. Mádi conflated the murder of Hungarian Jewry in May and June 1944 with the earlier deportations from Germany's so-called Protectorate of Bohemia and Moravia and from Slovakia in 1942. See "The Holocaust in Bohemia and Moravia," US Holocaust Memorial Museum, https://encyclopedia.ushmm.org/content/en/article/the-holocaust-in-bohemia-and-moravia; also Ivan Kamenec, "The Deportation of Jewish Citizens from Slovakia in 1942," in Tóth, *The Tragedy*, 111–40.

135. Mádi's reference to the "superfortress" was the introduction of the new US B-29 intercontinental strategic bomber. See Craven and Cate, "The VLR Project," in *The Army Air Forces*, 5:3–32.

136. The Germans began launching the V-1 cruise missile against England on June 13, 1944.

137. Numan Menemencioğlu was the Turkish foreign minister (1942–44). The Dardanelles is the strait connecting the Aegean Sea to the Sea of Mamara and beyond to the Black Sea.

JUNE 16, FRIDAY.

This morning a long air raid alarm, nothing happened here. I used the opportunity to go down to the shelter and show myself to all present. New orders regarding Jewish houses. In every district several houses are designed for Jews, big, half a meter diameter yellow stars have to be put beside the entrance.[138] The inside will be overcrowded. All Jews are running to friends, looking for room. It is stated, they can take all their furniture with them (In five days, until June 21) but how, when a family gets one room in the best case?[139] Furniture left behind will be "disposed" later. Organized robbery.

A new G. explosive, by radio conducted plane seems to work in England. I do not see, how whatever it may be, could it seriously disturb invasion operations. I suppose, it is more an urgent question of prestige on Germany's part as they have promised retaliation in April, 943 already. Their propaganda will make as much as possible of the thing. [. . .]

Morrison[140] told the English people to go on with normal activities, in spite of the G. pilot less aircrafts. The effect must be serious, if going on has to be stressed. A new, even more terrible phase of the war seems to begin.

There are still funny stories here. I told you about Stefi Peregi, who, since she got Miss Dean's position at Maort (Osán) going with the evacuated departments to Balatonvilágos is very superior with poor Pató and bragged in her presence, how happy she is, the G's occupied the country. Now, today she desperately telegraphed her mother, to come immediately up to Bpest. They have put several pieces of their valuable furniture (and what else?) in Jewish apartments, in the house, they are living (Rákóczi ut 80, I suppose). The house has been assigned for a ghetto, they will have to move out but how they can get their furniture out of Jewish apartments, is very problematic. For Jews it is prohibited to sell or give away anything from their goods.

JUNE 17, SATURDAY.

The situation of the Jews seems to be almost hopeless, quo ad vitam.[141] In the country they have been rounded up weeks ago, separated entirely from the rest of the population, held under unbelievably filthy conditions and finally deported

---

138. See Braham, *The Politics of Genocide*, 2:735, for the legal decree of June 16 about yellow-star houses.

139. Mádi's subsequent annotation: "1969: Klari Forrai together her two teenage sons was squeezed into a room where they had hardly room to sit on the floor. There were 16 persons in that room."

140. Herbert Morrison (1888–1965), home minister in the wartime British coalition cabinet. See "Secret Robot Planes Hit England in Force," *NYT*, June 17, 1944.

141. More to life (Latin).

in trainloads to Germany. Several people have seen these trains, recently young Mrs. Székely, my right side neighbors too.[142]

It is Bpest's turn now. To leave Bpest is almost impossible for them. Could somebody still escape from here, with gentile documents, authorities check back, where from did he come and ascertains recently. To hide on the countryside is much more difficult as everybody used to know everybody. Now here in Bpest in a few days, they will be separated from us in assigned houses. In a short time orders will come, as I understand, that they may leave their rooms for only certain, very short-hours. Doctors, lawyers, and engineers may have one room for their special work out of the ghetto houses but they may not sleep there, no matter, how crowded their living quarters may be. This is not for gaining more room, but to have them in hand in special hours, especially at night, when anything may happen to them, without other kind of people being present or in the neighbourhood, no witnesses, who could testify later, what happened. Ration cards are changed this month, meant for identification purposes too.

As things are, I do not see any possibility of escape, no hiding here or outside the city, no papers and documents will be good enough. The only way of escape could be still (for Jews, who do not look Jewish) to walk on the streets, for days and weeks and months, if necessary, sleeping every night on different places (out of the ghetto), and having no papers. Even this is risky, as there are rumours that after the closing of the ghetto there will be a general searching of all Bpest houses, like it was in Sofia and Zagreb. Sure, Bpest, with its one and a quarter millions of population will be hard to search technically, but who knows, may be they will lock us up for a week.

SAME NIGHT.

Drunken G. soldiers creating noisy scenes on the street. It is almost 11 p.m. After my work I went to fetch a cotton dress from my little dressmaker (Jewish), for three days I was anxious to get my dress but hoped at the same time, they disappeared somehow. But no. Here they were as almost all of them, meagerly accepting their rather evident fates. The same with Erzri and Emil. The latter absolutely broken in spirit, after three days of looking for a place to live in the ghetto. The afternoon I went out to the cemetery, it is my late brother's birthday, he would be 54. I arranged the flowers there, planted various seedlings in

---

142. Between April 28 and July 8, 1944, the Hungarian Interior Ministry oversaw the deportation of more than 430,000 Jews to Auschwitz. An estimated 90 percent were murdered en route or upon arrival. See Braham, *The Politics of Genocide*, 2:607. Mádi's phrase "right-side neighbors" referred to those holding right-wing political beliefs, especially pro-Nazi and pro–Arrow Cross.

the empty middle side of the family plot, watered the whole surface and almost had the feeling, I have done something for him.

JUNE 18, SUNDAY.

At Erzsrike I met a distant relative of Emil, a young factory girl, who had an—in times before—unheard of adventure recently. She was walking on the street, Dob utca. A G. soldier, a Hungarian policeman and a Jewish girl came the opposite way and before she could even well notice the funny "ensemble," the policeman told her, to follow them so they went on, until eight more girls, were in the group, then they were headed into a school at Kazinczy utca, occupied by G. soldiers, and given all sort of work what would have been the responsibility of the G. soldiers cleaning, scrubbing, washing, ironing, sewing, mending, washing up dishes, etc. They got food, soup, vegetables and bread and got a room with straw sacks to sleep in. This lasted for two weeks. Then they were sent to some other place to do the same. All the time they were lost for their families, they were prisoners in the building, but had not been molested otherwise. This Sári escaped, when they were escorted to their new place of destination. Could you believe something atrocious like this?[143] Can you imagine, would it be, if it happen to us?

A new cruelty, Jews will be housed one room for a family.[144] Houses were assigned for them, but they have only three days, to move, so many Jews are left without a place to live, that they will be crowded 8–10 persons per rooms. They are resigned to anything. I am afraid, all hopes for escape are already late. Did I tell you that Serédy, prince-primate of Hungary,[145] in the name of the whole Roman catholic priesthood turned with a memorandum to the present government. So did the council of Hungarian protestant churches.[146] They both rose their protests against cruelty towards Jews. Today radio Bp broadcast a mass and an unknown priest used the strongest language against godless soldiers,

143. Mádi's subsequent annotation: "1969: Reminding of Kiev (Babi Yar)." Babi Yar was the site of a 1941 Nazi massacre of Jews from Kiev.

144. Braham, *The Politics of Genocide*, 2:735.

145. Jusztinián György Serédi (1884–1945), prince primate (cardinal) of the Hungarian Roman Catholic Church (*MEK*). Braham refers to the draft pastoral letter but also notes that Mádi's relative-in-law, Minister of Culture István Antal, put a stop to the issuing of the letter. See Braham, *The Politics of Genocide*, 2:1035, 1038. See also Lévai, *Black Book*, 207–11, for the suppression of the pastoral letter.

146. See Lévai, *Black Book*, 217, for the May protests by the bishop of the Reformed Church in Hungary, László Ravasz (1883–1975), against the Sztójay government's treatment of Hungarian Jews. Bishop Ravasz was able to secure the cooperation of the Evangelical (Lutheran) Church in Hungary in June for the issuing of another public letter. See Lévai, *Black Book*, 223–24.

godless policemen and godless civil servants. Apu believes, he will be arrested without delay.

G. propaganda tries to make the most out of the pilotless aircraft. Today papers came with the headlines: evacuation of London. A young man beside me at the streetcar stop bought a paper, then said loudly: It is a waste of money to buy a nazi paper.

I can not be sorry for our people, when they got a raid. Yesterday, at the grocer Kelecsészi several people were glorying in the new G. weapon's effect on London population. Beastly. They are talking like parrots.

It is 11:15 p.m. and again (in spite of the rain) drunken G. soldiers are singing before our entrance gate. They have some friends in this house and seem to accompany them home every night.

JUNE 19, MONDAY.

At 4 a.m. the janitor's wife rang me up. It is my turn again for night's watch vigil, but this time I did not know it ahead, I hope, I did not make a too stupid face to it.

The robots seem to do a lot of damage in England, as B.B.C. is weaker on the shortwaves then are the Russian, even German transmissions tonight.[147]

All signs seem to converge to the fact that in a few weeks all Jews will be put out of the way. Why have they to change their apartments until the 22nd June and report it only on the 25th July? On the 25th July there may be nobody left to report.

Out of the 36,000 houses of Budapest allegedly 2681 houses were assigned to Jews for the about 250,000 Jewish inhabitants of Bpest. Now, again allegedly, about 500 houses protest against being Jewish, and, of course their protests will be granted. There are small two-apartment family houses among them, so let us say, remains 2000 houses for 250,000 people (may be even more), that is 125 souls/house.[148] In our three storey house we had about thirty persons and it is a house with small, modern apartments, not so big apartments with one or two persons. Imagine, how crowded the Jewish houses will be, what hygiene surroundings there must reign with ten, twelve or even more persons for a bathroom or a lavatory.

---

147. See "Secret Robot Planes Hit England in Force," *NYT*, June 17, 1944. Home Secretary Morrison warned the British public that BBC broadcasts might be curtailed in an effort to jam German V-1 radio direction devices.

148. Braham, *The Politics of Genocide*, 2:734, recounts the numbers of apartments and families, pre-June 16, and the appeals of Gentiles to have their houses removed from the yellow-star designation.

I put a bunch of nasturtiums besides your photos. How terribly good, you are out of this filth. You could never be the same person, witnessing all these calculated cruelties.

Allies raid over Hamburg is a terror raid even today. But: robot devastation over London is justified retaliation.

JUNE 20, TUESDAY.

Lacy's sister in law[149] was arrested on the street Sunday afternoon. They do not even know, where she is. I tried to do something for her, just because of Lacy and Károly.

They are so desperate, though, looking at the case quite cinically. It is almost just the same, whether she is taken now or will be taken in two or three week's time. In our house was living an officer of the police corps (rendősforgalmagó), name Ubrizsy, whom I met once or twice at the shelter. He even used my telephone once. I know positively, he has a role in connection with Jewish arrests and I know too, he accepts presents (silk stockings for example) I know the intermediary too, Mrs. Flór. I went to see her, but she can't go to him, it would embarrass him (knowing too much about his affairs) and he told her to get lost the day before yesterday. In the meantime he disappeared from our house, this morning moved out of the house and the janitor must not tell, where is he going to live. Nürnberg u,[150] I found out, a Jewish apartment I guess.

After five days of silence my telephone is working again. As there was no big storm in this time, I believe, the pause was intentional. I have to take care.

A heavy rain is falling outside, and I still have to see the Stolczs and afterwards the Lakoses again, then at 7:30 p.m. to meet Marika Kanya at Monpti. Well, I must not forget about Mr. Ubriszy, he told poor Mrs. Flór, that by the 1 of August there will be no Jew left in Budapest.

I am so powerless, to do anything in the interest of my friends. The only thing decent people can do is a social boycott. At present the majority of people are so stupid and cruel, I shall stay almost isolated with my boycott, but I do not mind. Later there will be more and more, who will not want to have anything in common with criminals. I am tired, but I feel panicky again, like in the old days of Dec. 941–942. I can't see a normal end of this war. I fear chemical warfare. I fear terrible social reprisals after we witness the extermination of almost one million Jews.

149. Alfred's mother, who was deported to Auschwitz-Birkenau and murdered.

150. Nürnberg utca in the 14th District; it was renamed Ilka utca in 1951.

A new AAC battery seems to be installed in our neighbourhood, they do shooting practice and it makes such a noise, it will be impossible to stay upstairs during the next raid.

JUNE 21, WEDNESDAY.

It is 7:15 a.m., a rather unusual time for telephone calls and I woke just on Bö ringing me up. You know, how she used to play the superior—well, it was heartbreaking to hear her helpless voice. Her brother in law and wife committed suicide. I have to go and see her this afternoon.

I had to inquire Zsige Stolcy about some matter yesterday. He did not even know, what everything is all committed in the name of police. He was astonished to learn, women are arrested on the streets. I suppose, decent men are told, to go on with their routine and scoundrels selected for special Jewish work at newly installed offices, as Rökk Szilárd utca,[151] Rumbach utca, etc. Young, corrupted police officials are lords of life and death at such places. Zsiza (and several other people) are furious with the churches, who can or will not do anything to save those, who converted years ago to their faith, I suppose.

I understand an article appeared in a paper, signed by two Piarist fathers,[152] very aggressively abusing Jews—in these days! They will be remembered.

SAME NIGHT.

After a busy day I came home, to have my shoemaker waiting for me with the shoes he made out of Geo's Texan boots. You do not mind, Darling? Elly Hermans came with fresh strawberries from her sister's garden. [. . .]

At 9 p.m. Klári Bálint[153] came for the first time to me, she is living above me in the same house. A nice girl, we like each other. She has an eyewitness story. Today, at her doctor she met a lady who had to check the recording of Jewish properties in a certain house. They had to record everything, an inventory until the last handkerchief, they took away into their new place and again everything, they left behind in their old apartments. It was officially stated several times, these left things will be sealed down and checked by the janitor every day, whether it is untouched. Now this lady got the list of fine furnitures left in a Jewish house but before they could seal the place, G. soldiers came with a truck and took every piece away. On the truck with capital letters: Hungarian gift to blitzed Germans.

151. The building at 26 Rökk Szilárd utca, formerly the National Theological Institute, commanded by Pál Ubrizsi. See Braham, *The Politics of Genocide*, 2:773.

152. A Roman Catholic order established in the seventeenth century with a dedication to education.

153. She lived one floor up from Mádi in the 19 Margaréta utca apartment building.

Allegedly our Jews, called up for labour service, were told yesterday, that from now on they will be treated as prisoners of war. Can you make a sense of it? They are all Hungarian citizens.

JUNE 22, THURSDAY.

Sanya rang me up yesterday wishing to come here this morning. It was not she though, who came, but Marcsi Székely, because of you. It is all like a ghost story. We went away together, I ran to see Lacy, but found Károly at home. Nothing new about their sister in law. After my work—where I have to comfort my MD colleague, Dr. Timár I had to hurry up to Mr. Horváth, the furrier, for the storage of Bö's furcoat. The affair was a success, beyond hope.[154] After the transaction I met Hanna (dentist)[155] at Pick Ace, from there together to Alkotmány Utca. Erzsike & Co are already in their new place! Slum conditions and overcrowding. This house is owned by count George Károlyi. He sent an open postcard to the caretaker of the house, making a point out of the question, to be very nice and agreeable to Jews. He ends with the words: what are all our troubles compared with the misfortunes of our Jewish compatriots have to suffer, just because of some scoundrels!

We met with Hanna again, with the streetcar to Rami, I got some cigarettes, even for Hanna. Then we walked over the bridge and I dropped in to the Fidy's. At first only Éva was at home. She told me the visit of her cousin, Lacy, from Győr. He witnessed the ghetto happenings there.[156] All Jews, men and women were searched naked before military commissioner for jewels, women and girls even by midwifes. Then they were driven out of their houses, over the streets of the town, like cattle into an empty brick kiln, waiting for deportation. This cousin of Éva was rather antisemitic in feeling before, but not now. He is sick of what he has seen.

From Erzsi I hear, the 2000 Jews of Losonc are out already, their train had been seen at Kassa, by then they had already many dead.[157] The cars were sealed. Erzsi's mailman told her, terrible things are expected of them. I suppose, spying and playing the agent provocateurs. It is said, in Jewish houses the janitor

154. Mádi's subsequent annotation: "1969: After it was all over he said the G.s took it. A grey seal coat."

155. Hanna Szabó, who had her dentist's practice and home at 18 Ferenc körút in the 9th District on the Pest side of the Danube and near today's Petőfi Bridge (*Budapesti telefonkönyvek*).

156. See Braham, *The Politics of Genocide*, 2:621–23, for the making of the Győr ghetto and the subsequent deportation.

157. See Braham, *The Politics of Genocide*, 2:620. Losoncz/Lučenec is located in present-day Slovakia, but in 1944 it was under Hungarian control.

will be shortly replaced by policemen and csendörs.[158] Out of the 2800 Jewish houses as of today 600 were taken back. Among them the house Rákóczi ut 80, where the Peregi family is living. Pista Peregi made it, and they were the only gentile inhabitants of the house. Now all the Jewish families have to move out until tomorrow midnight, because of them. [. . .]

It will interest you, Geo, darling, that your former colleague, Kertai is still with Maort. It seems, he is needed at the Co, as he is still working here, is living in the office, may not go out on the streets and Dr. Papp sent a letter round to all officers,[159] to underline his wish to treat Kertai with utmost consideration. Was it not nice of him?

I am told, G's arrest Jewish labour service men on their way to their place of destination. First thing, their papers of identification are taken all away. Partly it may be, because they want their victims to be anonymous, partly, they want Jewish papers themselves, to save themselves in case of need.

JUNE 23, FRIDAY.

I have not seen any of my friends today, except Bö's sister Teri, whom I met accidentally. She was very unlike her usual self, always cheerful and confident before, but now quite desperate. They moved out of their house voluntarily two weeks ago, and since yesterday the house they moved has been taken off the list of Jewish houses, so they are homeless again.

I had to relax from the mental strain, but as you see, not so much success. But people—at least small people—see now the cruelty of this all. My two nurses, my hairdresser girl, the owner of the greenhouse I used to go, they all are deeply shocked by events and ask themselves: what if it happened to us?

New cases of suicides. Boys of the age of 16 and 17 are called up today for the Todt organization.[160] And our government sacrifices them too, after our soldiers. Only flowers are worth living for these days. After Ubrizsy moved out of our house, the Viktors are going next week into a Jewish villa at the Kissvábhegy.[161]

---

158. Gendarmes, the rural constabulary under the control of the Ministry of the Interior.

159. MAORT employees. Papp was placed in charge after the expulsion of the American managers in December 1941.

160. A German state construction company. The public story of the deportation of Hungarian Jews was that the Todt Organization requested one hundred thousand Jewish laborers to build aircraft in the German-controlled Protectorate of Bohemia and Moravia and that Regent Horthy approved that number. In reality, the Germans and Hungarians sought to deport seven hundred thousand Jews, expecting to kill 90 percent as unfit to work. See Bauer, *Jews for Sale*, 155–56.

161. Kissvábhegy was a fashionable hillside neighborhood in the 12th District.

Since yesterday Jewish doctors are prohibited to see other than Jewish patients.[162] I expect, from the Social Insurance work they will be driven out too, so my M.D. colleague, Dr. Timár. I am sorry for her, though these are only small details compared with the peril their life is in.

Almost 3 a.m. I have the watch until 4 a.m. again. Every 4–5 days we have our turn. How silly is it! We shall be tired out and sleepless when we shall need our strength best.

JUNE 24, SATURDAY.

By midnight today all Jews have to be in their ghetto houses. As it was probably the last chance, the morning I went to see Lacy, but did not find them at home. After my work I went to see Bö, as I promised her ahead. She was calm on the surface. God knows only, how did she feel inside you remember their apartment, how often did you play with Andris, when you were children! Now it looked devastated, she worked on the inventory, they are obliged to make in three copies up until the last handkerchief, the last stocking they had to report all their belongings, perfectly clear about the fact, they will be robbed of all. I wanted to say her a lot and I am afraid I said things, I did not want to say. She was brave, I wish I could be the same in a similar situation. I am very worried about her. So many suicides these days. She does not want to risk an escape, I am afraid. They are all nervously exhausted and perfectly broken in spirit.

I told you how simple, small people have their opinion about these things and behave splendidly. The Pravda family is among them even Béla, who, as I am told did not get to the SS after all. How it happened, I do not know. But other people again seem to be rather insensitive towards other people's suffering. Tonight I was asked to the Horchlers. I did not go for supper but only afterwards. We had a very cautious conversation, not to touch subjects painful for the other. Heinzi is living now with them and he is no genius, you know and very pro-German. They told me cheerfully, just like a practical joke, how two Jews hid in a flat (as subtenants) in their house and how they were found out by the police last night. How are people able to smile telling such tragedies, is a mistery before me.

Maria Pató came to me today with the news (she read it in her paper) that radio messages will be transmitted to the states from us. I told her never to mention the subject before anybody and not to try to send a message to her aunt, unless she does not want her to be black mailed. I remember well, how Jews out in the states have been blackmailed a year ago, on behalf of their near

162. Decree Concerning the Medical Practice of Jews, June 23, 1944. See Braham, *The Politics of Genocide*, 2:1197.

relations left behind on German occupied territory. With Jews it is about finished, it would be our turn now to help German finances with your dollars. So you will not get any message from me, but I doubt, whether anybody will. It would be only good to have a list in German hands with correct addresses.

JUNE 25, SUNDAY.

O dear, this would be the day of my silver wedding if not for our divorce, for the death of your daddy. Do you remember, when you were very much impressed by the ceremonies of the golden wedding of your Henfner grandparents and hoped for ours. When I told you, we can't celebrate it, because divorced, you said: well, we could celebrate the silver divorce! The day a quarter century ago was an ugly day, revolution, counterrevolution, shooting on the Danube embankment, bridges closed down, etc.

My neighbour in the opposite door flat, Benecze,[163] entered the Nazi party, as I have seen on a postcard, dropped by chances at my door. Again one reason more, to watch my movements. Last day, I brought home three pots of flowers from the greenhouse, they were rather heavy. Mrs. Benecze, made some excuse to come out of her hall and watched me closely and my parcels.

Through the Horchlers I can understand the G. mentality. They are the perfect type of citizen as far as obeying and fitting into new circumstances go. But they are dangerous with their acquiescing to the orders of any new regime, who has the upper hand. They would never take the side of the underdog. I inquired them yesterday about some former Jewish friends of theirs—they have no idea, what happened to them, though until now, there was opportunity enough to see them. But no more.

You see here the latest order: Jews may go out only between 2 p.m.–5 p.m., only for shopping etc. no visits, no walks.[164] Parks, they may not enter restaurants or espressos (only special Jewish ones, which we may not visit). Jews can not have any visitors or talk to anybody out of their windows. So this is perfect isolation. There is nothing else but to pray for them. To pray, they shall be able to die with equanimity, not to mind very much. And without further humiliations.

Against a terror system no organization is good enough. I deplore the lack of organization of the honest people, Bö feels the same with Jews. She states, the famous mutual help of Jews went to nothing in these days. There is nobody,

163. Ferenc Benecze, his wife, and their two small children lived on the first floor in a one-bedroom apartment at 19 Margaréta utca.

164. The decree limiting the hours Jews could be in public was an amendment to the original yellow-star decree of March 31. See Braham, *The Politics of Genocide*, 2:737.

or very few, who would not be suspected by present authorities, there is no place that could not be searched by them at any phase of the day or the night. There is no such thing as privacy these days.

Dédé sent me a front line postcard from June 16th. It is characteristic of military perspective: he writes, they can stay on their present place *for years*! Sure, they can, until the Russians decide to begin their offensive. [. . .]

I had some business with Tersci Néni this morning . . . Her brother, Ernö is not excepted from the Jewish law, as he married a Jewess. She can not see him anymore. She believes, after the Jews had been disposed of, mixed marriages will be the next. I hope, she is wrong. [. . .]

Perhaps you remember, the nice old girl at Majtenyi drugstore, who had been there since eternity. Tersci Néni tells me, she and all her family committed suicide last night, I hope only, they did all die and none of them will be brought back into this miserable life. One does hear it here and there, that the G's are disgusted with the turn of events here in Hungary. Of course, the economical destruction of the Jews does not help to maintain normal production. But without German invasion of Hungary these scoundrels, like Endre László etc. would never have come to power. No members of the government could be a minister of the cabinet, unless the G's approved of him.

Even deputy ministers, as was the case of Apu, had to be approved by them. So the first part of the responsibility lays with them. The second on us, because of the mean attitude of the middle class, especially the upper middle class.

For quite some time we had no raids over the country, though Roumania and Yougoslavia were raided several times. Are they more important at present or are the allies considering the dangerous spots, Jews on labour service are living in? In this case they are overdoing the thing, because some violent raids over living quarters would be a great help for Jews to disappear and to use the general disorder and confusion. In a few days it may be too late. Bö sent me Ortega's revolution of the masses.[165] He has remarkable things to say. Among others: the mass hates everything, what is different from himself. This will be dangerous for me, as I feel desperately different from people. Sometimes I almost wish I could be like them, it is so hard to be entirely alone. I shall miss Lacy and Bö very much.

THE NIGHT.

At a quarter to midnight the sirens were sounded and soon after a regular raid began. It did not last longer than 12–15 minutes but seemed to me very intense. All the time the AAC was strong, so no fighter was up on "our" side. After the raid Maria Pató, Mrs. Csabonyi and my self had taken a fresh breath out before

165. José Ortega y Gasset, *Revolt of the Masses*, translated into English in 1932.

the door, when a G. soldier came up, very much at home began shaking hands all around. I was so astonished at his impertinence, I gave my hand but I suppose, he noticed the unwillingness. I went up to my place immediately to wash my hands. This was the first time and I hope, the last, I had to shake hands with a Nazi (except Gerti and Rolf, but they are of the family).

JUNE 26, MONDAY.

I hear people to complain about the crackling noises in their radio too. Very probably those flimsy metal strips were dropped last night. To disturb radio location. 9:45 a.m.: The alarm is off.

SAME AFTERNOON.

Having been in town, I see, the night's raid was an efficient one. Eskü ut, Váci utca Piarista building, something in Parisi utca. Kerepési and Farkasréti graveyard (the Oti building opposite the Kerepési graveyard all windowless) Thököly ut, Váci ut, the quarters about western railway, Garay utca 14, Kispest, Csepel, the Andrássy ut quarters and *Hitler square*,[166] etc., etc. Small caliber exercises though. I hear that some G. headquarters was hit at the Rottenbiller utca. Serves them right. [. . .]

The afternoon there were again alarms on our radio, but here nothing. I hurt my foot in the cellar, where I had to look after my suitcase, put there for safety reasons. Just now a sharp glass splinter fell out of my hair. It must have got there the morning, when I walked by the Piarist building, at one point I had to close my eyes because of the dust coming from the ruins.

Did I tell you before, how I believe the Jews will be put out of the way? They are shut in their houses and may not go out except from 2 p.m. until 5 p.m., the gentiles (Christians) living still in some of these houses, will be moved out to some other quarters. Janitors will be replaced by policemen. The latest order: the police force is to be militarized, that is, may use their weapons freely or by gendarmes. Soon after having accomplished this, even the three going out hours will be taken from them and then day, but especially night raids (raszzia) will begin with "specially trained" men, that is sadists. As soon as the neighbouring houses, I mean, the gentiles will find out, that a Jewish house is emptied, we shall be told, they still had secret radio stations at planned communist revolutions or something like. This is how I imagined the trend of events.

Now, this morning in the city I heard three people talk on the Petőfi Sándor street about Jews. I stopped before the Barbetti shopwindow and listened. They

166. Kodály körönd in present-day Budapest.

went on with their talk. I understood, from a city house all Jews had been taken away the night, soon after the raid, because—now, listen—they remained on the upper floor of the house and made signals!

Elly Hermans tells me, the Jewish family opposite us, moved out Saturday. They were small people, some clerk or like. They moved out with only few pieces of furniture, one bed, a wardrobe, a small table. They put it on a sort of wheelbarrow and with the help of the owner of the wheelbarrow pushed it away themselves. Elly says, it was more sad then a funeral.

Jews will be responsible for the cleanliness of their rooms! They will be checked. Take into consideration the overcrowded conditions, they are forced into. Sure, among these Jews there are some scoundrels, worth all punishment, but so are scoundrels in great numbers among us, gentiles too. What if we would be made responsible (as probably, we shall be) for the misdeeds of these?

Vitebsk[167] taken by the Soviet troups and Cherbourg almost taken by the Americans. [. . .]

JUNE 27, TUESDAY.

11:07 a.m. Raid just finished over Bpest. Big smoke columns at north and east. We have seen lots of allied bombers and heard more then enough noise. Here is a splinter of our own flack, found just before the house.[168] There were several of them.

SAME AFTERNOON.

The alarm being off, street cars need to go after the elapse of twenty minutes. I went therefore at first to the hairdresser, to let comb my hair and so to the car stop. Heaps of people waiting, cars on the rails but no motion. I walked to the terminal of number 75 and sat there more then half an hour—in vain. Then I got out, stopped the first private car and told them, I am a physician and have to get to town. They took me (two young men and a girl) to the Danubia factory, somewhere far out Ibrahim utca, there one of the men and the girl got out and other took me to Madách ut.

Now it is clear, how a big city is lamed without its normal traffic. Private cars and taxis were taken almost all before, buses too, only streetcar remained. Their power plants can be found easily and here we are, with no possibility to

---

167. A city in Belarus. See "Soviet Push Grows: Vitebsk Escape Route Closing as Red Army Opens 2 New Drives," *NYT*, June 25, 1944.

168. Mádi pasted the flak shrapnel into the diary.

do the big distances, not to mention worn shoes. I am told, our Oti building or its neighbourhood is hit and Kőbánya badly. To the deep and spacious cellars of the Kőbánya beer factory were switched over the Csepel works' most important workshops after the first Csepel raid.

No M.D. at my office today. One was called up for military service, one, being a Jewess cannot leave the ghetto during our worktime and myself was unable to go there because of the distance. How silly it is! It is almost an hour I am at home now, and still dizzy with heat and fatigue. Well, I am no more twenty.

About 7:30 p.m. Maria Pató came (duration at least two hours each time). She heard of thousands of casualties from today's raid. Anyaföld, Kőbánya, Pestsztimre, etc. At the social insurance building patients have to be sent out before a raid, as there is no room for them in the shelters.

Cherbourg is taken by the allies, Orsa by the Russians.

Your friend Pocker[169] is an opportunist, as so many of the Sváb are. He did not feel grateful towards the Standard co, which gave him an exceptionally good job, when he said: Why should the Americans come back? We are all right without them. And he left poor Maria without a word, as soon the G's came in and the Jew hunting began, though he used to ring her up almost every day before and dated her whenever in town. Last time, being with the Apzingers, he pretended not even to recognise her!

JUNE 28, WEDNESDAY.

Going to Social Insurance I found the building unhurt but the Eastern Station half demolished and many damaged buildings around.[170] Patients were sent out from the Social Ins. Building when the raid came—it is stated, there is not enough room for them in the shelters—they went out the opposite graveyard, where hundreds of them were machine gunned. At Teleki Tér just the same. Many horses' cadavers are still there even today, near by a man lay, left behind by neglect, when the corpses were collected. Well, this is modern war. People begin to realize it just now.

Characteristic for people's nerves these days: my two nurses, who used to be the best of friends for years, today quarreled so violently, they kicked each other, spat on each other, rolled on the ground and the younger one fractured

169. Chief engineer at MAORT.

170. The Fifteenth Air Force sent more than three hundred heavy bombers to attack the marshaling yards of Budapest (*CC*, June 27, 1944). The yards were adjacent to the Eastern Station and near Mádi's place of employment at Oti.

the wrist of the old one, as x-ray picture has shown it, I had to separate them, scold both of them and hush up the whole affair, as far as it was possible. It all happened before the patients. You see, what complication life offers these days.

SAME NIGHT, 11:30 P.M.

A hectic air traffic. Every two–three minutes heavy motor noises nearing and slowly vanishing again. I spent the evening with the Hermanns. We listened to the news together. I shall have the night watch from midnight until 6 a.m. tonight but then hope to be free for about fifteen days.

JUNE 29, THURSDAY.

I promised Elko to have a walk this morning with him. We went up the Fortress hill. They are going back to Halas[171] on Monday, Klári a bit frightened, as helping one of her friends to disappear yesterday, this morning she was questioned by the police, whether she has some knowledge of the affair. You see, people are like this: her friend's family, who were left behind, stated at first question of authorities, that probably, the Rev. Mathé's wife knows about the disappearance.

At the last raid, when the grave yards on several places were hit, many leaflets were dropped. Among others, with the usual exhortation to break loose of Germany, there was the following text: remember your conscience![172]

The Russians have taken Mogilev and are about eighty km's from Minsk. Splendid how they work (if war at all can be splendid).

SAME EVENING.

I was out the afternoon at Farkasrét. Several small caliber bombs had been dropped there, I have seen the Jewish graveyard where crater beside crater is still to be seen. There are still broken bones scattered all about the place, a femur in two, vertebrae, etc. The craters diameter is almost 6–7 meters.

I do not know, did I tell you already, that even yesterday there was no water at the Social Insurance buildings, neither in the hospital, nor at the outpatients department. We had to wash our hands in a few drops of water, out of a bucket. And this by working mostly with bone tuberculosis cases. [. . .]

---

171. The village of Halasz, near Magyaróvár in Győr-Moson-Sopron County, downstream from Bratislava/Pozsony on the Danube.

172. "Tiszta a lelkiismereted?" (Is your conscience clear?). See the leaflet collection in the Hungarian language at https://www.psywar.org/.

JUNE 30, FRIDAY.

This morning I was woken at 8:30 a.m. again on alarms given by the radio. After the southern part of the country, Győr and Sopron were alerted, near the G. border, then Bpest. It is almost 10 a.m. but still nothing. Szolnok, Eger alerted. I am listening to BBC news.

On the street SS soldiers coming and going, one with a notebook in his hand, it seems, he is checking something on the street or houses. 10:15 heavy motor noises from the air, but no AAC. The noise is steady. 11:30 a.m. Meanwhile I was down in the foreground of the shelter, just to show myself to people in the house. All quiet, but the alert still on. [. . .]

I shall be late for Oti. The mailman got caught in our house, he gave me a postcard from my sister Margit. She is worried about my wellbeing, because they heard the disaster at the Oti. She quotes a card by Dénes, he writes: Maria must be worried about her friends. I think it is unfair of him to allude like that to the Jewish disaster. I wrote her on the instant, yes I am very worried for my friends, one has so few real friends these days.

Just before noon a second wave swept by near Bpest. One may count to the psychological effects of a raid, that the house keeping is at sixes and sevens. Housewives can not do their shopping, can not clean, have no time for cooking, washing, etc. Sick children are put together with the healthy for long hours into humid cellars. Here in our house there is a small boy with wooping cough, soon all the others will begin to cough too. [. . .]

After Oti (we had water today) I met in the city Marika Kanye by chance, she has information from the police, that from today on gentiles entering yellow star houses will be arrested. I was just on my way to Erzsike, whom I was to meet at first in a crowded corner of a market hall, but something might to have happened there, and yesterday she phoned, we shall meet in their staircase. Marika made me promise, not to enter the house, I promised, but seeing them waiting for me, I could not do it and entered. At first we talked in the dark back staircase, then I went up to their flat, as the dangerous thing is entering and leaving the house, so it was just the same. They are undecided, as before. Erzsike has the most sense of reality, she wants to escape, her mother not, for her it is of no importance. Emil again is optimistic beyond all measure, he believes, as he is forbidden to enter his own office in the opposite house, they will call him up for labour service (as far as that goes, may be he is right) and thus he hopes to be saved with all the family. I left them very sad. Told them to take refuge with me, what I told Bö and Lacy already.[173]

173. Mádi offered as early as June 1944 to shelter her friends in case of a ghettoization and deportation of the Jews of Budapest.

As soon as I got home, young Mrs. Székely, my next door neighbour came for med. advice then Maria Pató, again Mrs. Székely, Klári Bálint (all these from the same house, these are Légó[174] friendships) and Gabi Arnótly, a patient for a prescription. It was, believe it or not, 10 p.m. when at last I was left alone. At 10:30 p.m. alarms again.

JULY 1, SATUR.

Thirty thousand apartments have been taken from the Jews. Apart from the Jewish catastrophe, there is a shortage in flats among gentiles. Until now officially no indication, how they are going to distribute the empty ones, but blitzed G. families are arriving in vast numbers and occupy these richly furnished and equipped houses. Without any authorization. Just military force. [. . .]

A small event, so typical of the heroes, acting these days. A young man and a girl got on the street car yesterday, having a ticket of the day before. The ticket collector told them no and asked them, to buy new tickets. They did not. So the ticket collector told them to get off the car (as it was his duty). They refused this too and promised a beating. As the latter called a policeman and this asked to see their identification papers (Igazoltatás), they told the policeman, he will get into trouble. The bad thing is, it is possible, the police man will get into serious trouble, if the young terror man is influential enough.

I lunched out at Holub with Elko and Klári, as their guest. Elko came home with me, I gave him tea, then Gizi came. Elko is optimistic again believes firmly that the war will not last until fall. Gizi, when left alone with me, explained how Germany does not want anything else, but to be a big empire. We have seen this game twice already, what not wanting anything else means. A few months more, and they would cry out for their "Lebensraum" in America.

Tonight I had such a strange dream, the third time in the whole, in connexion with you. I have seen a small girl, with auburn locks and she ran to embrace me. As she embraced me, I felt such exquisite happiness that it was clear, she can not be anybody else, but Barbara, though somebody told me, it is not her but some other little girl, much like her.

JULY 2, SUNDAY.

Scarcely is the night's raid over, at 9 a.m. radio went off and gives alerts. Kanizsa, Pécs, Szeged, Földvár, Vezprém are alarmed, it will be Bpest next. It is 9:30 a.m., I am still without bath and breakfast, so hurry! 11:45 a.m. I am up from the shelter but the alarm is not yet off. It is quiet though. There were several waves over Bpest, big fires can be seen and even here, in our hillside the sun is

174. Air raid.

darkened. Something black like burned paper is floating down, but it is heavier than burnt paper, at closer inspection its structure seems to be like leather or human skin, entirely carbonized. Only an explosion could blow it so far. The smell of smoke is in the air.[175]

Maria Pató, who is the air defence commander of our house, will be in trouble in no time. She is terribly afraid of raids herself, poor thing. To hide this, she orders people about a lot especially does not let them out to breath fresh air, even when it is all quiet. Even on a far AAC she runs to the shelter and orders people to do the same. Now, other people have ears too. I told her twice already, to take care, not to be so imperative, but no use, she goes even further. Today I could hardly placate two people, who were ready to fly in her face.

Our radio repeated several times that by the morning's raid many explosive toys and utensils were dropped. I do not believe one word.

It was a regular raid over all the city, Angyalföld, Csepel, Illatos ut, many war plants and depots were hit and set on fire. Leaflets were dropped with maps of Budapest and arrows to all stations (Southern railway station near us too) on the one side and a text on the other, telling us to leave the vicinity of railways as they will be bombed relentlessly. A good advice but difficult to follow, as all, who are needed here, may not leave Bpest. [. . .]

Bö 'phoned the afternoon, we shall meet tomorrow morning, with Emil the afternoon. I am rather well off with coffee and tea these days but without them I don't think I could go on—the latest bon mot in town: How good for the Finns! They *too* will be defended now, like us.

It is 9:45 p.m., usual time for the evening news, when all radios in the street used to blast, now no sound can be heard. People are angry with their radio. I can not help being amused. People are deeply shocked, astonished. They never believed for a moment, this could happen to them. To other people—yes, but to us—no. They feel insulted. May be, only yesterday they wished England to be exploded and New York to be attacked by G bombers.

People feel that all the cruelty towards the Jews—well, serves them right or in the best case, very sad, but what can we do? Their own suffering or inconvenience is something monstrous. On the other hand Jews are relieved, hearing the sirens. Thank god, they say. During a raid no detectives and no gendarms come. We have peace as long as a raid lasts.

---

175. US and British air forces described only a "medium"-sized attack upon Hungary that day from bases in Italy. See "Text of Day's Communiques," *NYT*, July 2, 1944. By contrast, Zsuzsanna Ozsváth recalls a massive raid on Budapest on July 2 that she thinks was intended to cause Regent Horthy to halt the deportation trains to Auschwitz-Birkenau, a decision he made on July 7. See Ozsváth, *When the Danube Ran Red*, 124.

JULY 3, MONDAY.

To continue last night's reflexions, the best word for people's attitude towards the raids is: offended. Deeply offended but very much impressed. I hope, that when they will see, being offended does not help them, they will begin to reflect upon the situation, upon the worth of "G. help" of our "great ally," etc.

About 800,000 Jews were living in Hungary, whom we conserved until the G. occupation of our country. Considerable number have been interned and sent to labour camps. Large numbers—the male population from 18–48 years—were called up for labour service. All the time mysterious disappearances were heard. Now one hears talk about 50–100,000 hiding. I wonder, how many will be able to escape until the nightmare is over. I am afraid it will be but a small percentage. Recently a murder was discovered, it was committed by two waiters who hid two well to do Jewesses, with the promise to help them out to Sweden. For two days they were hidden in the headwaiters place, then they were murdered and robbed.

Klári M. states proudly, she has helped *ten* of her friends to escape. I believe, the statement is over optimistic. To hide someone is only the beginning of hardships. Control is sharp now, the only help in this direction are the blitzed regions, where control is almost impossible.[176] People disappear and appear to the surface, without ration cards etc.

EVENING.

Before my work I had to meet Bö. We met in the city, where radio alarms disturbed the routine of life. I hesitated, to go or not to go out, but decided after all to go out to the danger area and I was right, nothing came out of the alarms, at least, not for Bpest. [. . .]

I heard a tale from our clerk at Oti. She lives out of town, about Aszód, where some trouble developed yesterday. One aircraft was shot down and the people—excited by recent newspaper articles—rushed there, to get the "air gangsters" as our paper call allied airmen. One man got out of the plane, shouted in a foreign language, but people went on regardless. At last the pilot had to draw his revolver to protect himself—he was a German and the aircraft a G. fighter, shot down.

It is me, who has the night's watch from 10 p.m. until midnight. At 10:45 disturbing flights over Bácska—Baja are announced. So this is not in vain, I am up. [. . .]

---

176. The yellow-star house decree required janitors for each apartment house to take a census of the Jewish residents and keep a daily attendance roll. Braham, *The Politics of Genocide*, 2:737–38.

JULY 4, TUESDAY.

This is a national holyday for you and a holyday for us from raids, as it is raining.

The evening. After my work I was to see Pravdáné, begged them to go to the countryside for two weeks. They are close to the Eastern station and living there may prove rather unhealthy these days. Béla was there too I shook hands with him and told him, it is good he did not do as his plan was, else I would not shake hands with him.

JULY 5, WEDNESDAY.

The morning I had to get a book from Klári's (M) friend, but in vain. Just the same with Elko's sister in law, Frances. But I don't mind having seen her, she is a good girl and little Elko is about the age of Barbara. At Rami no cigarettes. [. . .]

JULY 6, THURSDAY.

Tercsi néni got a chicken for me yesterday, it was not even so very expensive (17.50 P), but it is months, I did not even see one. I had five green peas from Elly, bought some carrots and had fine food, have it even for tomorrow.

The morning I had several telephone calls, the first at 6:30 a.m. from Mr Gonczlik, the blitzed Mátyásföld friends, he wanted me to see his wife, she has high fever. Before going out your "twin," Marcsi Székely here. After Irmuska and my routine work I had to meet Erzsi at the Bazilika. They are converted catholics, as you know and we spent half an hour in church together. Different plans, too much hesitation and above all, still too much faith in events and people's conscience. Home Ancy, Elly and Mrs Székely, with milk. Tired out.

My flowers are lovely on the balcony. Cyklamen coloured antirrhinums. I shall put by some seeds for our garden in YOUR country. And how is Barbara?

Our male and female population is drafted anew. Out of four men, living in our house, three are enlisted to military service and have to join up in a few days. Young women are called up in large numbers. Men are taken even from war plants. Jews are taken too, by gendarmery, and others without the consent of our government.

JULY 7, FRIDAY

At 8:30 a.m. alarms, Bácska—Baja—Pécs—Földvár. Then, as it would be just Bpest's turn, it seems to have turned off to Győr—Sopron. Usually this means the Vienna area. Quick, as long as telephones may be used (only until the sirens are sounded and not until two hours after the raid) we cancelled our rendezvous with Hanna (Sz). 930 Bpest sirens sounded.

We do not see one single G. here around the house though they used to drop in several times. There are rumours, they are kept on alert? (katonai készültség) in town.

12:45 BPEST ALARM OFF.

I am told, that churches (r. kath. & protestants) are baptizing Jews now in great numbers. Whether it will be any help to them? It is not only looking for help on their part, they are deeply moved, having been taken in by the churches now, when they are treated like dirt.

9:45 p.m. alarms from the north. Rahó, Beszterce.

There is a tale in town, rather difficult to believe. Béla Aczél,[177] with several other labour service men was traveling, on way to Jászberény. At Hatvan a certain captain of the gendarmey, Zöldi, has seized and put them on a G. train, due to Katowitz.[178] Béla and the majority of them arrived there. Eleven out of these men, as none of their protests helped (they were under military obligation towards Hungary) jumped out of the moving train and escaped. Got to their place of destination, reported to the colonel, who learning what happened, praised them, let them have double rations and extra leave until September.

JULY 8, SATURDAY

9:35 a.m. radio off the air. Airdanger announced from Kanizsa—Pécs. 10:10 a.m. The raid seems to turn towards Austria—Sopron, Győr, Veszprém are alarmed. You hardly can imagine, how much these alarms do disturb everyday life. Shopping, various errands, rendez-vous have to be postponed day by day. Telephon calls can not be put through for hours. Not during actual alarm and not for two hours after.

SAME AFTERNOON.

I had to get my watch from Schober,[179] I had it there more than a week. He talked about the price of gold, which, according to him, is 42 P/gm, though the Zürich price of the pengö (100 P = 3 Fr. Swiss) it should be 100–112 P. . . .

---

177. He was married to an Englishwoman, Beatrice. They moved to England after the war. Béla was the brother of Aczél Benő, former editor of *Esti Kurir*.

178. Katowice was twenty-five miles from Auschwitz. Braham, *The Politics of Genocide*, 2:772–73, recounts the history of how the SS attempted to deport fifteen hundred Jews from Kistarca to Auschwitz on July 12, four days after Regent Horthy ordered an end to deportations. The attempt was foiled by Hungarian officials, but the Germans repeated the deportation on July 19. The transport reached Auschwitz, and the deportees were murdered.

179. Gyula Schober was a jeweler who worked at Vármegye utca no. 3, 4th District (*Budapesti telefonkönyvek*).

He has shown me two brilliant stones, beautiful specimens, one just under one carat, the other a bit smaller, which he can not sell for twelve thousand Ps, though at the beginning of March its price would have been twenty thousand. As I asked him, whether the origin of the stone is not dubious, he said no, it is all right, as he bought it a week ago from the wife of a high ranking G. officer, whom he knows personally.

JULY 9, SUNDAY.

Allied planes seem to have their Sunday stroll all over our country. [. . .] 12:10 p.m. Short waves on the radio give terrible crackling noises. Was the purpose of all these disturbing flights to disturb radio location? Is something going to happen in these hours? It is exactly a week, leaflets dropped promised raids over our railway stations.

Afternoon. Radio several times off the air. I am told, that Ali & Co,[180] at least, the majority of the fourty and odd members of the family are out at last in Lisbon but four out of them, Ali, one Mauthner boy and two others have to stay in Germany as hostages. They are staying as "Aryans," without stars, allegedly near Berchtesgaden.

Just before 10 p.m. radio off the air. Disturbing flights over Rahó—Beszterce—Naszód—Várad—Kolozs—Karcag are announced. It seems to be the regular Titobus.[181] I am told the morning's event was a big scale attack upon Ploesti.

It is stated, we are in war to defend our frontiers. Yesterday's G. communiqué announces Hungarian troups fighting at Baranowiczi.[182] It is a bit far from our frontiers.

Since last Friday rumours are in town, that Endre and Baky, both secretaries of state for the Home Office, would be out of the picture.

180. The Weiss family. Szegedy-Maszák describes the history of the family from March 19 until their arrival in Portugal on June 25 in *I Kiss Your Hands*, 113–61. She notes that news of the family's arrival in Portugal was published in the British press on June 29.

181. A reference to Soviet air supply of Yugoslav partisans fighting the Axis.

182. A city in present-day Belarus near the city of Brest.

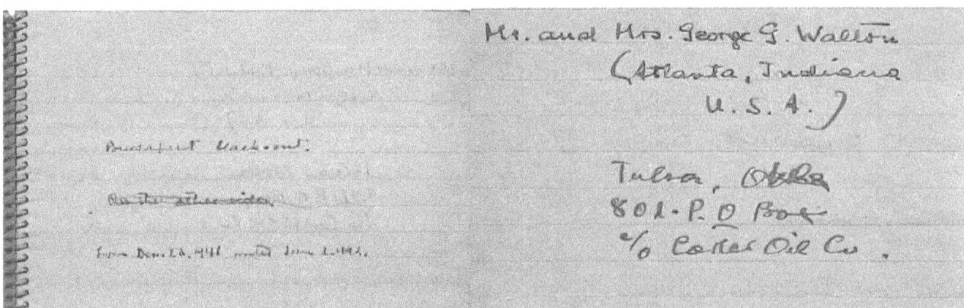

Mr. and Mrs. George G. Walton
(Atlanta, Indiana
U.S.A.)

Tulsa, Okla
801-P.O Box
c/o Carter Oil Co.

The opening page of the first volume of Mária Mádi's diaries, December 1941 (US Holocaust Memorial Museum)

Mária Mádi in Budapest, ca. 1941 (Walton family)

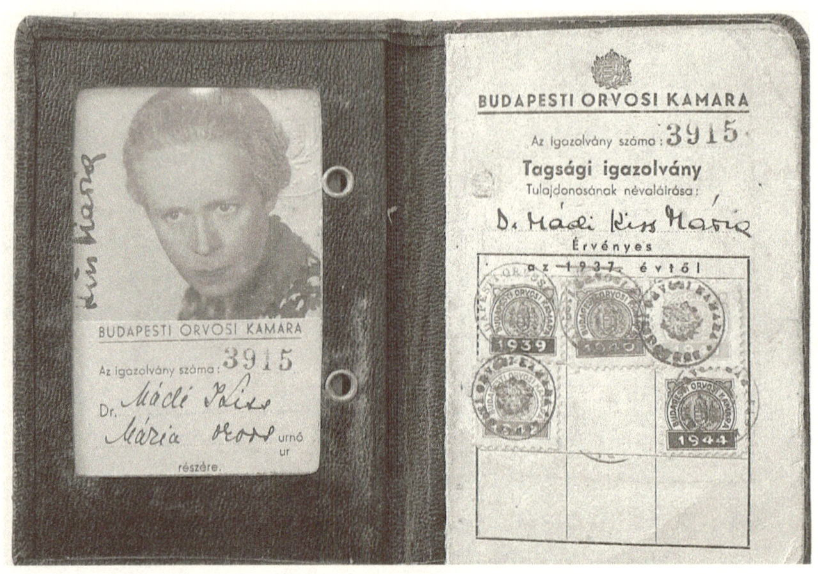

The diarist's membership book in the Budapest Physicians Association; stamps indicate annual dues paid (Walton family)

Daughter Hilda Walton, after her arrival in the US in the summer of 1941 (Walton family)

Mária Mádi with the family dog "Joe," ca. 1940 (Walton family)

Granddaughter Barbara ("Babu") Walton, ca. 1955 (Walton family)

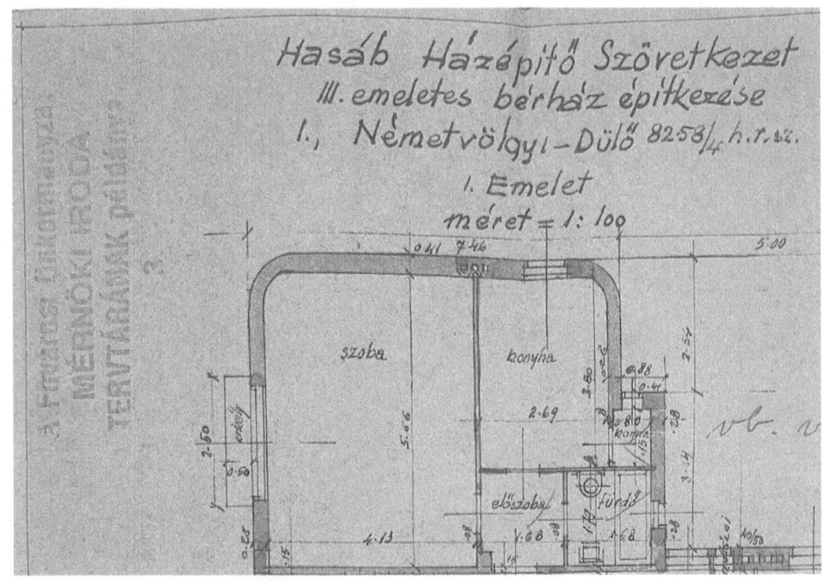

Floor plan for Mária Mádi's apartment at 19 Margaréta utca, Budapest (Budapest City Archives)

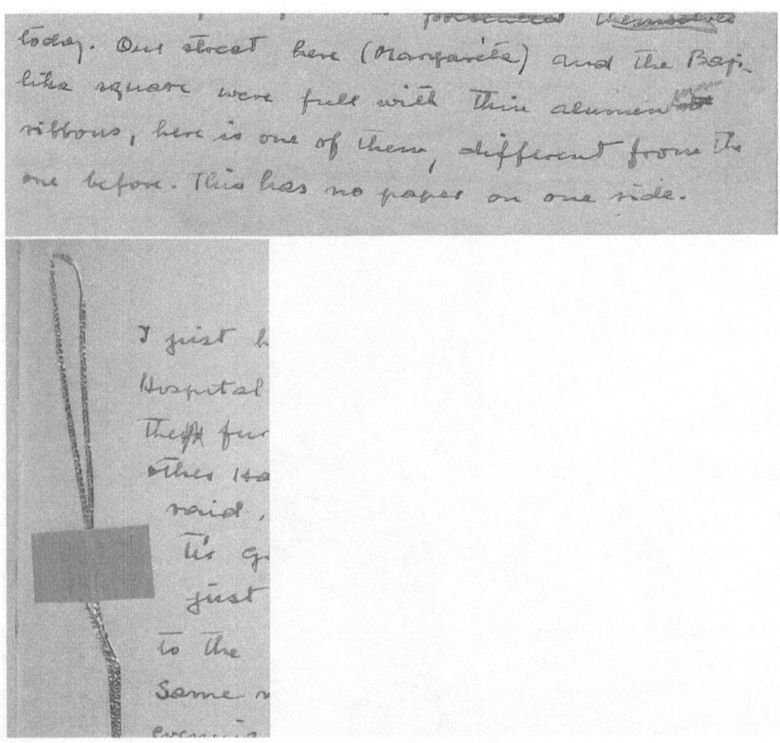

today. Our street here (Margaréta) and the Baj- [illegible] square were full with thin aluminium ribbons, here is one of them, different from the one before. This has no paper on one side.

"Aluminum ribbon" that Mária Mádi found on Margaréta utca, dropped by Allied aircraft over Budapest and designed to confuse Hungarian and German radar (US Holocaust Memorial Museum)

Alfred ("Frédi") Lakos with his parents, ca. 1943 (Lakos family)

Irén Lakos (*seated*) in Milan, ca. 1994 (Lakos family)

Mária Mádi in the United States, ca. 1950 (Walton family)

Mária Mádi's gravestone, Atlanta, Indiana (Ancestry.com)

CHAPTER 4

Hungary Tries to Leave the War, July–October 1944

At the beginning of July 1944, Mádi felt a brief optimism about the turn of events since the start of the German occupation of Hungary. On July 10 she expressed a hope that by Christmas she could have regular postal exchange with Hilda and perhaps even have a long-distance telephone conversation. However, during the rest of the summer and into the fall of 1944, Mádi's diary entries show an increasing pessimism about her fate, that of her friends and relatives, and that of her country.

After July 7 Mádi repeated at several points in her diary the news that Regent Horthy had stopped the deportation of Hungarian Jews to Nazi death camps in Poland. She attributed this decision to the moral authority of the Roman Catholic Church and the Reformed Church in Hungary. She was convinced that her Jewish friends who had converted to Christianity, such as Irén "Lacy" Lakos, were now saved from death, even as they suffered from civil discrimination and impoverishment. She reported the news that the king of Sweden's letter to the regent had also influenced the decision to stop the deportation trains.

Mádi wondered throughout July 1944 how long Hungary would cling to the Axis alliance. She followed the news of the rapid advance of the Red Army across Belarus, Ukraine, and Moldova into Poland and Romania, as well as the breakout of British, American, and Canadian forces in both France and Italy. The American-led air war on Hungary had slowed, and, more often than not, the ringing of the air raid sirens in Budapest indicated "disturbing" reconnaissance flights, not bombing runs. But most important to her way of seeing the world was the attempted assassination of Adolf Hitler by members of the German officer corps on July 20. She hoped that Hungary would be spared Soviet occupation if the Germans themselves toppled the Hitler regime and made peace. The doctor thought immediately of how the end of the war was close. "Dearest," she wrote in addressing Hilda, "I feel you come nearer to me." She even grudgingly admitted in an entry written for her son-in-law that perhaps Hungary was wrong to seize territories with German and Italian help back in 1938–41. The "circumstances . . . were unhealthy" was the euphemism she penned to George Walton on July 23 about the march of the Hungarian army into parts of Czechoslovakia, Romania, and Yugoslavia, even as she clung to the idea that Hungary was the victim of the Trianon Treaty.

The month of August 1944 was hot and dry in Central Europe, and the optimism Mádi felt in July began to fade. The damage to the country from earlier American bombing, as well as German requisitions of food and goods in Hungary, led to strains on the transport system, the food supply, and the medical system. Mádi wrote to Hilda in late July that she was down to her last bar of soap, with no prospect of procuring such a basic item. In September she lamented that she was subjected to the terrible body odor of so many unwashed, "perspiring and heated" Hungarians crowded on a tram. She proclaimed her country "a soapless society" and stated that "traveling on a streetcar these days is against all human dignity." Rather than taking a tram, she often walked long distances around Buda and across the Danube into Pest for work, shopping, and errands. Her new job at the Oti on the Pest side of the city put her in some danger because of its proximity to the Eastern Station railway terminus, a target for American bombers, but she approved of the sturdiness of the bomb shelter in the building. More of her days were spent shopping for food and other essentials not just for herself living alone but also for her Jewish friends. She made a point of obtaining specialties such as candy and cigarettes when they were available. These commodities were unavailable to Jewish persons in the few stores open to them.

Mádi also made trips to the consulates and legations of the neutral powers in Budapest on behalf of her Jewish friends seeking the protection of an external power. Diary entries for August 22 show that Mádi closely followed the news about the actions of diplomats from the neutral countries, especially Switzerland, that conveyed a foreign state interest in the rights of persons otherwise stripped of Hungarian citizenship. By early October, Mádi began to consider that she, too, even as a Christian, might need the protection of a foreign state if she was somehow detained by the Hungarian authorities. A pair of Jewish friends urged her to get a letter of protection from the Swiss government, which represented the interests of American citizens and property in wartime Hungary. The doctor reasoned that with a son-in-law and possibly a daughter who were American citizens (Hilda did indeed secure American citizenship in 1943) she might benefit from a Swiss letter of protection. However, she decided she did not need one, even as the thought nagged at her, and she worried, "Am I too optimistic?"

Readers of Mádi's diary entries may find map 3 helpful in following her travels by streetcar and on foot. She continued to live at 19 Margaréta utca, where just thirty meters away from her balcony the local 12th District Gestapo station had been established in a former primary school. She was also very aware of the Buda-side Gestapo headquarters at the Hotel Majestic, nearby on one of the city's hills, as well as its counterpart, the Hotel Astoria, which was on the Pest side. The map shows the location of the Swedish and Swiss legations, where Mádi went on behalf of Jewish friends to secure protective papers. The map also shows the location of the Lakos family apartment on Zichy Jenő utca, where young Alfred Lakos lived with his parents on the Pest side of the city. Finally, the map shows the outline of the Jewish ghetto that Hungarian authorities created later in the fall of 1944 and into which they forced as many as seventy thousand Jewish residents.

The diary entries in this chapter show that Mádi bemoaned the coarsening and degradation of the moral character of the Hungarian nation under German occupation. Her diary is filled with the accounts of daily inhuman actions suffered by Jews. On a Pest street corner, she observed seeing "a Jewess, passing a newspaper store, [who] just glanced on the papers. The newspaper vendor addressed her with such an obscene talk, I can not reproduce [it]." In the diary entry for May 12 (see chapter 3), during the occupation, she had described an incident in which a teenage boy insulted her friend Bö's sister with the phrase "büdös zsidó!" (stinking Jew!). Worse, the boy's parents saw nothing wrong with his taunting. Only the building janitor upbraided the boy. "Was it not splendid of him?" she wrote of the janitor and continued, "With little exception one can count on workmen only for reasonableness and decency."

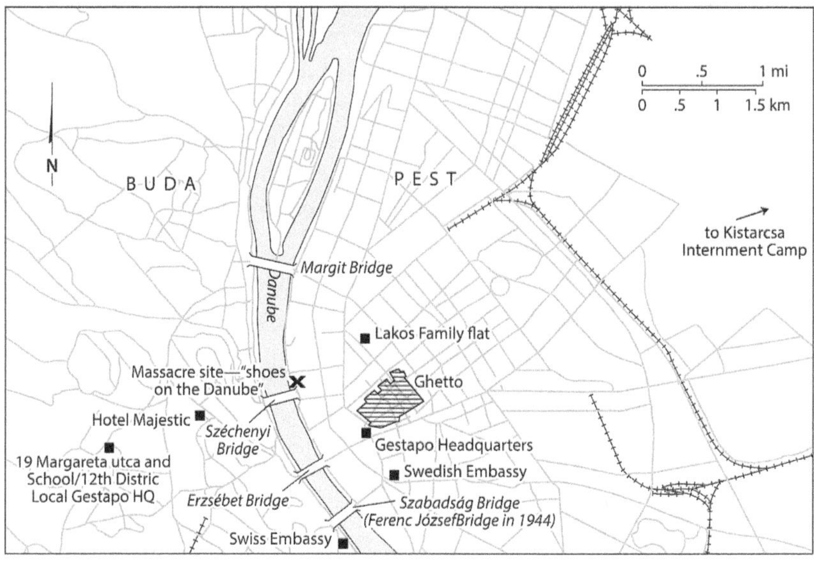

Map 3. Budapest during the Holocaust, 1944–1945 (Bill Nelson)

Another common emotion Mádi observed among Germans and Hungarians alike that summer of 1944 was greed, the desire of both the occupying power and the host citizenry to get their hands on a supposed vast treasure held by Jews. The doctor wrote often of the looting by the Germans and of observing truckloads of goods hauled away, ostensibly to relieve the German population suffering under Allied bombing. Hungarian civilians, too, including some of her neighbors at 19 Margaréta utca, hungered for the chance to get Jewish flats or Jewish possessions, including radios, carpets, furniture, gold, and jewels. The entries in chapter 4 return again and again to the theme of greed and looting as motives for the war against the Jews.

During the summer of 1944, Mádi wrote often about the disgraceful behavior of her countrymen toward Allied airmen who were shot down over Hungary. Radio Budapest broadcasts repeated outlandish stories about the American air force dropping booby-trapped toys to maim and kill Hungarian children. Budapest radio also picked up racist German propaganda about the Americans using "negro pilots" guided by "white women radio operators" to bomb and strafe Hungarian civilians. The official radio encouraged an "outraged population" of Hungarians to inflict summary justice upon captured pilots. The renewal of the American air war on Hungary in August brought new complaints from some of the doctor's acquaintances that the Jews were to blame for the air raids and that Hungary was the victim of "terror raids." Mádi condemned lynching prisoners of war as a crime that would bring both shame and retribution on her country. She heard of a lynching in her Budapest neighborhood and wrote about the moral depths to which her country had fallen under Nazi occupation. She also repeated a rumor about two Hungarian fighter pilots lynched as part of the "people's judgement" because they were too injured and dazed to speak when the mob found them in the wreckage of their planes. On July 30 she recorded that on the street outside her apartment windows she could "hear a woman's voice: Has my little girl gone too to lynch those gangsters? It is now I feel for the first time what terror is."

Mádi and the other residents of the apartment building at 19 Margaréta utca felt the effects of the aerial campaign against Hungary every day and night. Even when American, British, and Soviet aircraft did not bomb Budapest, they overflew the city, triggering alarms. Soon after the March 19 German occupation, the city's authorities organized civil defense procedures for every business and dwelling. The Margaréta utca building had a *légo* (air raid) commander, at first Mária Pató, who was a former coworker of George and Hilda Walton. Mádi sometimes complained in her diary about Pató's officiousness, even as she often hosted the woman at her apartment for tea and conversation. The residents of the apartment building were regularly thrown together in the makeshift basement bomb shelter. Mádi had had little to do with her neighbors for the first three years she lived in the building, but after the air raids began in the spring of 1944, she formed what she called "légó friendships." She became close to Elly Hermann, a Dutch national by marriage, and to Elly's mother, Albina Brunansky, to Klári Bálint, to the pregnant Mrs. Székely, to the Mikolay family, and to the Láng family. Others in the building were openly pro-German and suspicious of Mádi: the Janik family, the Gorrieri family, the Viktör family, the Lajtai family, and the Németh family. The diary entries for the summer and into the fall of 1944 give evidence about the political tensions within the building, especially when the residents were forced to sit together for hours in the basement shelter. Her pro-German neighbors cheered the V-1 and V-2 attacks on Great Britain and yearned for a German bombing of New York. By August 23 Mádi could only wish her neighbors more misery with "day and night alarms and sitting for hours in the shelter. . . . Serves them right."

It was obvious to Mádi by the end of the summer of 1944 that Germany had lost the war. She quoted conversations with German occupying troops who admitted their country's defeat. On September 7 she predicted that a German "collapse seems to be complete." A week later, she heard on the news that the American army was outside Aachen, Germany. However, many Hungarians in her circle refused to see the war news in the same light. She raged in her diary about the gullibility of Hungarians who believed German propaganda about new super weapons, including the V-1 and V-2 missiles, and, more fantastically, an antiaircraft "death ray" machine that would defend the skies against American bombers. Some neighbors were convinced that the Germans at the nearby barracks were constructing a death ray device to protect Budapest against war from the air, prompting Mádi to fume, "This egocentrism is fascinating in our people. Why do they not protect Berlin or the Rhineland this way?" One neighbor insisted that the steel and wood he saw deposited by Jewish labor battalions in front of the school barracks off Margaréta utca "are for the new weapon!" She ridiculed this neighbor's runaway imagination with the line that the death ray would "be used apparently for the first time in Europe just at Margaréta street corner!"

The most important war news at the end of August and into September was that onetime satellite allies of Germany, including Romania and Bulgaria, had abandoned the Axis and switched sides to fight alongside the Red Army against the Germans. Mádi noted that the Romanians had been promised that they would receive Northern Transylvania and that the Hungarian annexation of 1940 would be reversed. "I am sorry for it but it is perfectly logical," she wrote of the news, but she worried that the Romanian army would march on Hungary, as had happened in 1919. When Regent Horthy appointed a new government led by a former general, Géza Lakatos, Mádi hoped that the military experience of the new ministers would lead them to recognize that the Germans had lost the war and that it was time for Hungary to make peace with the Allies. On September 23 she noted that the Hungarian prime minister "awaits some offer from the allies, about Hungary's future. It is a bit late, to wait for an offer."

The diary entries at the end of September are a mix of hope and dread. Mádi hoped that the Hungarian state would find a way out of the war, that the Red Army would occupy Budapest in "a few days," and that the war would come to an end. She warned some pro-German women Hungarian acquaintances that they might expect what French women collaborators received in the summer of 1944: public humiliation by having their heads shaved as a mark of shame. However, some of the entries for the same weeks show a renewed fear of doom. The doctor noted on September 23 that during office visits at the Oti, "patients are asking more and more often for sedatives. Their nerves are shot." The food distribution system became more strained, and Mádi had depleted all her savings. When she heard British prime minister Winston Churchill speak of the war lasting another year, she wondered, "Prices are going up every day. What shall become of me? How shall I be able to survive these months?"

For Further Reading

Mádi's diary entries from July through mid-October 1944 reflect her efforts to help her Jewish friends acquire protective documents, as well as food, necessities, and other comforts, as Jews were severely restricted in their movement around Budapest. Theo Tschuy, *Dangerous Diplomacy: The Story of Carl Lutz, Rescuer of 62,000 Jews* (Grand Rapids, MI: Wm. B. Eerdmans, 2000), tells the story of how a Swiss diplomat issued papers to cover eight thousand families, who in turn claimed sixty-two thousand individuals under Swiss protection. Dr. Mádi wrote of the particular vulnerability of persons in mixed Jewish-Christian families because of the racial classification laws that the Hungarian government imposed. Marianne Szegedy-Maszák, *I Kiss Your Hands Many Times: Hearts, Souls, and Wars in Hungary* (New York: Spiegel & Grau, 2013), narrates the story of her family's mixed marriage and the deadly danger that her mother and father faced that summer. Rebecca Erbelding, *Rescue Board: The Untold Story of America's Efforts to Save the Jews of Europe* (New York: Penguin, 2019), details how a unit of the US Department of the Treasury swung into action in the summer of 1944 in an attempt to save Hungarian Jews.

~

JULY 10, MONDAY.

It should be a sad date for me, as I hoped so much—just personal lunacy—the war to end this day. Still I am hopeful. My next promise towards myself was: next Xmas we shall have letters, may be, cables. Not to mention telephon calls!

As soon as I got home, after having met Emil, Anny Pravda came here. She sat until 7 p.m., meantime Maria Pató called, O, dearest, whenever I shall be able to join you, promise me, I shall have a room, where I can be undisturbed for a month. [. . .]

At 8:30 p.m. Dr Németh came for a visit, ten minutes later Klári Bálint and an hour later Mrs Székely. All from the same house, I am living in. Alone at 10:30 p.m. Left alone for a short while with Klári, we had much to talk. She has seen her fiancé today, as she has strongly believed for months, against all probabilities.

May be, I told you already, I never used to listen to radio Bpest these days.

Alarms I can hear through other people's radios from the street and else I read several papers thoroughly. So I missed an interesting item, many people heard all Saturday afternoon repeated in short intervals. It was about a letter of Monsignore Angelo Rotta, Legate of the Vatican, addressed to all catholic priests of Hungary.[1] Our government forbade to read the letter in public, in the churches. It is believed, it was something about a veto regarding the persecution of the Jews.

Allegedly Jaross, the minister for the interior is no more at his post, Wesenmayer, G. minister in Hungary, recalled and a military dictatorship has the power in hand. This would be an unexpected turn of affairs, which would save Jews.

According to uncontrolable rumours, G. troups are going to leave our country in days. This I do not believe, or, if it is true, will not be a smooth affair.

11:45 p.m. Something unusual with the G.s in the next school building. They are singing loudly (are they all drunk?), so it will be impossible to sleep. Is it saying good bye?

Midnight. The G. chorus still the outstanding feature of our street. I suppose, they were told some splendid news about a new victory.

---

1. Monsignor Angelo Rotta, Vatican diplomat in Sofia, Bulgaria, and papal nuncio (ambassador) in Budapest before and during the war. The papal nuncio's actions in defense of Hungarian Jews began immediately after the German occupation in March, when he protested the anti-Jewish decrees to Premier Sztójay, and they continued regularly throughout April, May, and June 1944. See Lévai, *Black Book*, 91, 202. Nuncio Rotta issued fifteen thousand protection papers to Jews in Hungary in 1944. See "Budapest," in *Holocaust Encyclopedia*; Theo Tschuy, *Dangerous Diplomacy: The Story of Carl Lutz, Rescuer of 62,000 Hungarian Jews* (Grand Rapids, MI: Wm. B. Eerdmans, 2000), 164.

JULY 11, TUESDAY.

Last night it was 2:30 a.m. and our neighbours still singing loudly and one of them making continual attempts on Tannhäuser[2] pilgrims' choir on accordion. [. . .]

Thinking over various events and rumours, happened in the last days, the picture seems to be about the following: for about a week there must be known before the churches and authorities, that the Pope has the intention to put Hungary under ecclesiastic ban (egyházi átok) because of the Jewish persecution. The moment, to begin Jews' deportation from Bpest was fixed for July 8, Saturday. The Ministry for the Interior had the majority of gendarme troups some days ago concentrated to Budapest a certain part of them having been trained before in Germany, how to deal with Jews. Gendarmes were needed for the operations as military circles and War office were not in favor of the plan. Saturday came and second many facts, we can gather, it was not the Jews, deported from Bpest but the gendarme troups sent back to the countryside. It must be the Pope's intervention too, that during the last week the churches took in many newly converted Jews. Having altered the conditions inside the country (we do not know yet, who the originator of the changes is) the ecclesiastic veto was taken back, i.e. not read publicly. Wesenmayer's calling back may be the result of his failure in the country. He seems to have encouraged extremists and misunderstood it for general opinion, which was against them. [. . .]

The afternoon. In town I have seen G. armed soldiers in patrols. At Oti my yellow-starred M.D. colleague was dismissed today, on 'phone, telling her, she was lucky that no patient objected to her presence, until now, but from today on she better stay at home. Coming home I went to church and there met Erzsi and her mother. They love the quietness of these churches, they feel the peace, it means to be there. Today I am exceptionally tired, can't regenerate.

JULY 12, WEDNESDAY.

This afternoon I met Lacy, I miss her. It came to daylight, she had converted since 1938. Later I had to see Mrs Kárász, mother of Ilonka, Zsuzsa and Kati. I like her way of thinking, absolutely honest, we agreed on many points. Her daughter was called up for labour service and has she no luck, she may be sent to Rahó,[3] inspite her being in non-military employment.

Quite unexpectedly I met Lulu Sebestyén this afternoon. She told me there were scenes before the Teréz church at Nagymező utca. Many Jews are living

2. An opera by Richard Wagner (1845).

3. Today Rakhiv in Ukraine.

in the neighbourhood. Yesterday some organized gang appeared and made noise before the church and spat on the priest who tried to pacify them. No need to say, the hooligans had no yellow stars. In today's *Esti Ujság* I read an article in the same sense, christians complaining on Jews, because they "infest" the churches.

JULY 13, THURSDAY

A comparatively quiet day. The morning I met Elma and Lulu on the street, the afternoon Emil, instead of Erzsike. Later in the afternoon the two Mariannes, Horchler, Halasz, came here. They know about the same of the recent turn of affairs. There is talk about a letter, addressed to the regent by the Swedish king.[4] [. . .]

JULY 14, FRIDAY.

Same night. The morning we had alarm from 9:30 a.m. until 11:30 a.m. and a raid with some 500 bombers. It was again oil, Shell Fanto and something at the Gubacsi ut.[5] People do not even talk about it, we got accustomed to raids. [. . .]

The afternoon Lulu Sebestyén came to see me, she is a quiet person, good to be with. We went to the greenhouse together and got lovely flowers: phloxes, calendulas, marygolds, ox-eye-daisies and pink antirrhinums. Not to forget stock (viola) which have the most fragrant scent. Part of the flowers I gave to the Hermans, part I have here in my home. Lavenders I got too, to put into my closets and drawers against moths. I love the cool scent of them. It is so early Victorian, grandmother's times. [. . .]

Since 10 p.m. disturbing flights are announced from north and east. As I had four hours watch duty last night, I do not mind very much, am in bed and intend to have my sleep. One of our clerks at Oti (drafted for labour service) came back today, boys in their senior year of high school. They are digging trenches for a gigant [*sic*] airport in the vicinity of Kenderes the regent's estate.[6] Allegedly they were sent in order to save them from the G.s.

Jews, who were baptized recently, were told by their priests quite positively: there will be no further deportations.

JULY 15, SATUR.

Afternoon. The whole day long disturbing flights over the city. At 4 p.m. people saw clearly about fourteen bombers, flying at high altitude. No AAC, no bombs dropped. We hear there were leaflets dropped, promising a hot

4. Sent on June 30, 1944. See Braham, *The Politics of Genocide*, 2:714–15.
5. Csepel Island and the Gubacsi neighborhood opposite in the 9th District.
6. Birthplace of Regent Miklós Horthy and the site of his manor.

Sunday for tomorrow, but I do not believe in such forewarnings. It is people's phantasy working overtime.

My clerk tells me, she has seen this morning a large number of Jews arriving at the Eastern Station with a local, bundles, all. Police escort, I do not see, what can it mean?

People talk much about it, that in case of raids it would be much better if our AAC would not work. It makes the biggest noise, disturbs bombers to drop their load on unplanned objects and with shooting down about 2 percent of the aircrafts, does not deter them from future raids. And how much it costs and what organization it needs!

JULY 16, SUNDAY.

At home a 'phone from Marcsi, allegedly they are going to Madrid, Jenő as chief press agent (sajtófőnök? sajtóattaché?[7]) for our legation! But a stay in Spain would be rather convenient in these times, to be out of the war.

Since 9:45 p.m. alarms on our radio again. There is much talk these days about our impending national tragedy. I suppose, it is so but in a different interpretation. The consequence of present circumstances the nation will be impregnated with foreign elements (see illegitimate births) and involved into foreign interests (having done mergers between Hungarian and foreign companies, banks, etc.). Our middleclass has been mixed already with foreign blood (intermarriages), this is the explanation for its present behaviour. If in the future our lower strats[8] will consist in greater number out of this certain type of citizens, who's chief characteristic is, they like to march in parades and accept everything without criticism, we shall be really lost and the country nothing else, but a "Lebensraum"[9] for foreigners.

JULY 17, MONDAY.

My feet are swelling, they begin to be the feet of a "middle aged" person. Sorry for them, it was so pleasant to have slender feet. A continuous care is needed for my skin. Face, neck and hands. I do not mind wrinkles so much, but I know, how unpleasant it is to look at an unkempt person.

Eszter had a visit recently from Mrs Felsőbüky Henfner No IV,[10] the reason for her visit turned out to be curiosity. She was anxious to know, details about my emotional (non existent) life, whether I have a "friend" or not.

7. Embassy press attaché.

8. Social classes.

9. "Lebensraum" is a reference to the Nazi policy of conquest, native population transfer or murder, and resettlement by Germans.

10. Hilda's stepmother.

JULY 18, TUESDAY.

There are still honest men around. This afternoon, Elly Hermans was here, somebody rang the doorbell, I opened and a soldier stood before the door. After some explanations he turned out to be George Gyetvay, your cousin, whom we saw last in 1933, at the Jamboree. His peacetime work in forestry (conservation) now he is doing his military service. His way of thinking is all right and we understand each other quite well. Second all probabilities he will stay at Bp. until December and hopes(!) to see me weekly.

JULY 19, WEDNESDAY.

The southern flank of the eastern frontline seems to be nearing and the decisive fights in Normandy seem to be over. This summer is after all an eventful one.

We had some peaceful days since last Friday, but I hear this morning the Munich area was attacked. We used to have alarms, when these neighbouring regions are raided, but today nothing. I suppose, lost labour hours count heavily upon the balance and so notwithstanding the danger, we are not alarmed. On the countryside (where bells are the alarm signal) there must not be alarm, until bombs do actually fall, because the harvest must go on.

There are expressions, much used not long before, which seem to be entirely out of fashion now: axis, Lebensraum, Europe—fortress, Atlantic wall, not to mention Blitz-Krieg.

Looking everyday at the inside of my cigarette's case, inscribed "To Mami, May 14, 940, George" I have still the same sentiments towards YOU, as than. I am true, but being true is the virtue of age. Are you thinking still about me?

JULY 20, THURSDAY.

We listened to radio Bpest and there came the news of an attempt against Hitler's life. Several generals wounded, he too, allegedly only light burns and bruises. It must be something serious, else it would be held in secret. Very probably the building was damaged too and so the story could not be kept secret.

Reviewing the military situation all around, the Japanese political crisis and this above all (where only and exclusively G. high military factors could participate), I really suppose, the war is nearing its end. Dear! What splendid news it will be—stopping of hostilities!

Today's papers brought a detailed explanation by Seinderman (G. press chief) about Jew's situation in the Reich. According to his description it is so idyllic, I almost wish to be there. But why these explanations now? Before the motto was: extinction!

JULY 21, FRIDAY.

News are even more interesting this morning. There is talk about a new government being formed in Germany.

There are compensations in life. I am not yet old enough for my age. This morning, looking out of the balcony door, the sky was so deeply blue and so gloriously spacious, I had the feeling, on such a day one should fly, somewhere far away from earth. These thoughts are not suited for a grandmother.

SAME EVENING.

I had to meet Erzsike the morning. They hope to get out before long to her brother-in-law in Palestine, I believe, the plan is too romantic. 40,000 Jews should be exchanged for medicines and drugs with Turkey, via Constanza.[11]

During my office hours the Bpest sirens were sounded, I went for the first time down to the Oti shelter, which seems to be good. The afternoon with the Fidys. The evening here in our house I make people sign a circular, none of us insists upon continuous night attendance any more, so I hope we shall be free of this idiocy.

The situation in Germany seems to be critical, as really high military circles are involved in the attempt and even now some revolutionary signs can be observed. Dearest, I feel you come nearer to me.

JULY 22, SATURDAY.

The day begins without alerts but there are heavy detonations in the distances, one can't help feeling uneasy. Pista, Éva's fiancé has the story of the fertilizer plant, where yesterday a regular revolt of the working men took place. They are in the vicinity of the oil refineries, heavily damaged already. Their shelters are inadequate and are not repaired yet.

After several cool days today an extreme heat developed, ending in the afternoon in a violent storm, but not much rain. I did not mind the heat as I tried to imagine myself under Louisiana climate, where all would be well.

To show you, how "insignificant" the attempt on Hitler's life has been, here are some cuttings from today's Pest. The revolution was extinguished in six hours. Count Stauffenberg executed Thursday noon—but allegedly the affair happened but Thursday evening.

---

11. A variant on the "Blood for Trucks" proposal of the Hungarian Zionists to exchange US-made trucks for exit visas for Hungarian Jews. It was proposed in May 1944 and was rejected by the UK and the United States. See Bauer, *Jews for Sale*, 162–78; see also Braham, *The Politics of Genocide*, 2:941–51.

Met Bö and Lacy today. The evening Elly Hermans here. I must not forget to tell, I began to use my last nice cake of soap for today's bath. The one before the last I began on the 8 Sept. 943.

We had a comparatively long respite from raids. [. . .] Should the middle sector of the eastern frontline prove unsatisfactory for finishing the war, it will be our turn again. It is believed here in military circles, that the conference at Hitler's headquarters, where the attempt happened, was to decide about the use of gas.

JULY 23, SUNDAY.

Since early morning the Viktors are moving with a luxury car their belongings (kitchen utensils, suitcases, etc.) to their new place, a big Jewish house on the Kissváb hegy. There is no gasoline for medical car but this young army officer in the reserve can come and go with a requisitioned car ten twenty times.

I have told you long ago my opinion and defence about the Hungarian expansion in 1938 and on. I have to tell you that I had to review my ideas. I still state, that the peace treaties were neither good nor just.[12] But as much as we wished to restore at least parts of the old country, we should have to abstain from it. The circumstances, which made restoration possible, were unhealthy and the government should have had known that. [. . .]

I have told you already, that we have two hours watch/person every fifth day and everybody is tired of it. I told Maria Pató, our commander, what the situation is and asked her to get people's consent, that we do not want the watch continued. She did not want to do it, either out of laziness or because she is not very popular in the house, so I took the matter in my own hands.

JULY 24, MONDAY.

There is from early morning on a vehement air traffic over us, but from my flat I do not see the direction. Anyway, I believe them to be some loyal troups transferred in haste to some place, where they are needed.

Allegedly there is a terror wave in Germany. I am not very deeply concerned about it. These people—as long as things were going well—were the best of friends. They ought to settle their differences between themselves.

I should like to guess, whether our government is going to take any steps in face of a possible new situation, if yes, what steps? It would be time to think about them. [. . .]

12. A reference to the treaties of Versailles, Saint-Germain-en-Laye, and Trianon (1919–20), which the Allies presented to the representatives of Germany, Austria, and Hungary, respectively.

I suppose, the great purge in the highest ranks of the G. army will handicap their military ability. [. . .] . . . Though it may last some weeks or some months longer, but probably it will be better so. Clara pacta, boni amici.[13] A future can be built on clear bases. An unquestionable defeat will clear up future fairy tales.

JULY 25, TUESDAY.

The evening a silly dispute on the side of Maria Pató, she wants us to continue with night watch in spite of ourselves and authority. I did not argue but declined to have any more part of it. . . . People will be furious with her, I suppose, her so-called authority will go to pieces.

JULY 26, WEDNESDAY.

The new German total-war-mobilization will be a hard thing for occupied countries. All available men and women will be taken away for the Todt organization, God knows, where.

I told you, already, that 30,000 apartments were taken away from Jews. It is a big number and would be amply sufficient for housing the blitzed and other homeless families. Some other need must have arisen (refugees expected from somewhere?) because people are told, they have to wait for houses and other houses are requisitioned from the gentiles in great numbers. All the time the talk is about blitzed needs. [. . .]

You see, it is officially stated, that Germany does not need the Ukraine. She is self-supporting, her own farmers are able to provide her with all necessities.

The afternoon I met Lacy. There are news again about deportation of Jews to Poland. The evening Elko came to get me, we dined out, neighbourhood. After a quarter to ten the town became uninvitingly dark. We talked events over. He is optimist, as ever. Funny, he noticed the same in the latest Churchill speech (before the troups in Normandy):[14] "They are killing each other. I can't help."

Alarm on the radio. If the deportations are really renewed, I am afraid, raids will come again.

JULY 27, THURSDAY.

This morning a raid over Bpest. The eastern half of the sky is already darkened by smoke. Many time-bombs exploding still. People are impressed. I have to

13. Clear agreements make good friends (Latin).
14. "Churchill's Words Are Sifted," *NYT*, July 25, 1944.

go out to Oti, there I shall hear more about the objects. Is this raid—after a pause of 12 days—in connection with the renewed deportations?[15] The Kistarcsa interned and the Horthyliget[16] labour service men disappeared lately.

JULY 28, FRIDAY.

After my work I met Klári Bernauer, then Tercsi néni, who came home with me, she left at 7:30, soon after Éva with Pista came to get her. Then Elly Hermans and soon Marika Kánya arrived, the latter could not go home because of the alarms—streetcars were stopped and all streetlights too—and slept here. We listened to midnight news, they were excellent.

Marika has the news, that many Jewish girls try to save themselves by marrying foreigners. As there are not many available, prices are high. To marry a Swiss subject costs 250,000 Ps, a Sved or a Turk 150,000 P.s, a Japanese is not so expensive and a Chinese mere 25,000 Ps. In one case the girl was so beautiful, the Chinese took only 20,000 P. So that is that.

There are talks about the resignation of the regent, Bárdossy[17] as premier and Baky as minister of the interior. It would mean reaction again, may be, on a greater scale as before. But the churches still refuse to give the certificates to the newly converted. They promised, there will be no deportations.

After the declarations of a Polish National government in Cholm, the travel of Mikolaiczik[18] from London to Moscow is very interesting. There is much talk here how decently the Roumanian territories, occupied by Russian troups, were treated. [. . .]

From Göbbels radio speech very interesting details seem to come to daylight, as how these conspirator generals reacted on the military disasters in these later years. Beck[19] had sobbing fits, another disagreed so violently with their supreme command, that he was deprived of the right, to wear a uniform. Such details were never leaking out before.

---

15. Mádi raised a belief common in Hungary that summer that British and American bombing was tied to the treatment of the Jewish population; instead, bombing was directed at military targets and infrastructure. See Braham, *The Politics of Genocide*, 1:486. The USAAF rejected entreaties to bomb Auschwitz-Birkenau or any of the rail lines leading to the camp.

16. A suburb south of Budapest.

17. László Bárdossy (1890–1946), prime minister at the start of Hungarian involvement in the war (1941–42), indicted, tried, convicted, and executed for war crimes by the Budapest People's Tribunal (1946) (*MEK*).

18. Stanisław Mikołajczyk (1901–66), prime minister of the Polish government in exile in London.

19. General Ludwig Beck (1880–1944), chief of staff of the German army (1935–38), executed by the Nazis for his role in the July 20, 1944, bomb plot.

Alerts. Last night it was Ploesti for the fifth time. Elko was told by an oil expert, that until now neither Lispe nor Szőny, where the state built a refinery for Lispe oil, has been bombed.

With regards to people's reaction to radio and newspaper stuff, I would advice honest governments to prohibit all sorts of propaganda—except in business under penalty of death. There is no harm in spreading the belief, whether this or that shoe polish shines the brightest—but no further. [. . .]

Afternoon. Coming home from the office this afternoon for a few minutes it was as if you would sit beside me. A young girl, with about the same hair and a profile very like yours. She had a perfect complexion and soft features. But *en face* what a difference!

Since yesterday's raid my telephon has been out of order, though no damage was done in the neighbourhood. As Elko could not get my number, he came here the afternoon. I gave him tea and as I had to go out to Editke, he accompanied me. News rather surprising. There is talk about the Russians having broken through the lines this morning and would be inside the country already. I am afraid, very chaotic days are coming, since yesterday there is much talk about a "nyilas" government, etc. I am anxious for the safety of my friends.

G. soldiers, who have to salute now the nazi salute "Heil Hitler" on the streets, meeting each other, do it somehow hesitantly as they would be uneasy about it.

Elko has an interesting take from an engineer who on an official tour dined the night of July 20 at the Újvidék G. officers mess. The colonel was called away to their special radio set, came back after a while very pale, announcing, that Hitler is dead, that general Beck heads the government and is already in touch with the allies about peace terms, and there should be an end to all fighting. If this message went out to Újvidék, the same had reached all other occupying and fighting forces.

There are rumours about H's injuries: blinded and one leg thrown off by the explosion.

These are tonight's G. reports from *Magyarország*,[20] July 28, 944. The first about the Normandy situation, the second about the eastern frontline. The loss of five towns is announced, it is rather a shock for many people, who can not understand, why the G.s do not do something, to prevent such things?

JULY 29, SATURDAY.

At about the end of my hours at Oti, Bpest sirens were sounded, but no raid followed. I did not go down to the shelter, because I like to hear the motor

---

20. The newspaper of the Hungarian Nazi Party.

noises (a very strange sensation, the rhythmic work of several hundred motors high up at 6–8000 mtrs causes a vibration in the air, like the beat of one's pulse.) and goings on. [. . .]

I am told that since the raid of the day before yesterday the Weiss Manfred stocks do not have any value Göring owns the plants.[21]

The afternoon—it was idiotically hot—I had to go to the hairdresser. Afterwards Mrs Láng came up with a splendid, round "kalács."[22] She is all thanks because I healed her psoriasis.

Tonight's paper mentions that our troups have withdrawn at several places *into* the Carpathians, where one place—after the enemy's steady pursuance—has been broken through. All these with small type, inter alia, in an offhand manner. One can hardly notice it. [. . .]

JULY 30, SUNDAY.

Since 8 a.m. alarms on and off on the radio. [. . .]

10:30 a.m. Budapest sirens sounded. A few minutes buzzing like a disturbed beehive, then silence again. I am determined not to go down to the shelter. Rather a splinter, as to look at those stupid faces downstairs.

11:30 a.m. the air raid is over. [. . .] It seems an aircraft has been shot down, as people from the opposite yard has seen a parachuter caught at the Németvölgyi ut. Poor boy. I hope, he was not hurt and insulted by the mob. More may be found too, as Gorrieri just says down on the street (he is a chronic alcoholist).

I can hear a woman's voice: Has my little girl gone too to lynch those gangsters? It is now I feel for the first time what terror is. I can not go to help them.

Two men came just back from the school building and cheerfully brag, that two parachuters are in the school building under arrest and that the German soldiers, a Hungarian soldier, a girl and even the policeman have beaten them.[23] I feel terribly ashamed. A G. soldier heralds proudly now, that ten men were captured. I do not believe him, just boasting. [. . .]

The animosity, shown by people here in this case is about the same psychologically, as lynching in the southern states. Hate because other people (newspapers) says so. It has nothing to do with my sympathy towards you and your

21. Kornfeld, *Reflections*, 184, recounts how the family signed the corporate transfer papers at the SS headquarters in Vienna on June 25.

22. A Hungarian sweet bread.

23. On war crimes against downed Allied flyers, see "Flyer's Slayer Gets Life," *NYT*, September 28, 1945, 8. See also "Pilot Torturer Jailed," *NYT*, February 24, 1949, 13, about the case of András David.

country, which makes me indignant and unhappy about the affair. It is contrary to the rules of fair play, what has happened. Airmen should be fought in the air. Are they shot down, they have got just enough to "fight" them, when they are on the ground, helpless, prisoners, is a shame. The plans for this mob psychosis can be clearly traced down to the G. papers, official announcements (Sünderman)[24] and at the bottom, Göbbels' article in his paper.

The distribution of areas for military occupation is planned wisely, I believe now. Your countrymen and the English occupying forces would be no match for such mentality. You would be too lenient in punishments.

My former French teacher, Géza Laczko[25] wrote an article in yesterday's paper. He says with full right, that to call men in natural sciences as HOMO SAPIENS is very inadequate. Out of 200,000,000 inhabitants of the earth there are—in the best case—only 10 million Sapiens, so out of 200 men *one only* can be considered really intelligent, the others are stupid, "insipiens."

2 p.m. As I am sitting here behind the balcony curtain, still sick with disgust, again voices come up from the street. A woman's voice it is, one can hear, not an educated one (It was Mrs Székics, janitor's wife in the next house, No 17). She is violently arguing about the beatings. She says: to hit a soldier, who is without weapons and gave himself up as prisoner, is a shame . . . I am glad, after all the other opinion is heard too. There are still honest men and women here, even if not many.

The afternoon. From the opposite house atrocious G. records invade every corner. Some G. soldiers are visiting with a friendly family, they brought their own records, the family has the gramophone (before Noah's time), which is changing speed all the time. [. . .]

Allegedly, according to rumours, Rommel was seriously wounded in Normandy. He has lost one arm. [. . .] Regarding the coincidence of the exact date, one can not help suspecting, may be an attempt on Rommel's life was part of the Bendnerstrasse plan.[26] [. . .]

I have to return again on the terrible event in the morning. Elly Hermans is as sick of it as myself. People in the shelter cheered and were happy, when they heard the news, that an aircraft has been shot down and parachutists captured. Conclusion: *I do not want Barbara to learn Hungarian.* If ever I shall be

---

24. Helmut Sünderman, deputy chief of the German News Agency.

25. Laczkó Géza (1884–1953), member of the French language faculty at Eötvös Loránd Tudományegyetem (ELTE, Eötvös Loránd University) and member of the Magyar Tudományos Akadémia (MTA, Hungarian Academy of Sciences) (*MEK*).

26. Headquarters of the German army in Berlin and associated with the July 20 plotters. Rommel committed suicide in the face of Gestapo investigations of the July 20 plotters.

able to join you, I shall be careful, not to let know anybody, which country I come from.

JULY 31, MONDAY.

Almost unbelievable how low our people has sunk since the occupation of the country. Until then they were stupid but still sober (the tone of its papers), since then they are happy to see the sufferings of the Jews and the sufferings of defenseless prisoners. This all is a consequence of propaganda. Few people can stay independent enough of these influences. Only one should never mention before me the "Hungarian chivalry," which used to be a favorite tirade of our papers.

My shoemaker, who lived in Berlin from 1932 until 1941, tells me, as soon the nazis came into power, the first class quality, cheap margarine (contained 30 percent of Danish butter, 50 Pfennig per pound) disappeared. Then came the famous declaration: we do not want butter, we want guns! Soon they had an inferior quality of margarine for 90 Pf. per pound, and no more butter in it.

SAME NIGHT.

I had an active day. [. . .] Alarms on the radio. Frici, the brother of Gizi arrived today from Alag.[27] There he has seen a G. military train, black flags hanging from the windows, all soldiers drunk, all shouting: Pfuj, Hitler, pfuj Hitler (down H.).

AUGUST 1, TUESDAY.

There will be some separation of Jewish-Jews and baptized Jews in these days, but details are not known yet.[28] Whether the baptized will be able to get into their old houses, is not known yet. Erzsi's mother is going to return home tomorrow and as she states, their house is safe and no harm can become to them, I am going to see them tomorrow. Just as I was parted, next corner I have seen a scene, which frightened me. A Jewess, passing a newspaper store, just glanced on the papers. The newspaper vendor addressed her with such an obscene talk, I can not reproduce. It is an indicator, how these people are influenced in their underground party-clubs. God save us all, should they ever be let loose upon us.

---

27. Suburb north of Budapest.

28. See Braham, *The Politics of Genocide*, 1:462–67, for the legal distinction between "Jewish Jews" and baptized (Christian) Jews, dating from the beginning of the German occupation.

At Oti Bö called me, to meet . . . We sat on the stone steps on the lower Danube embankment and discussed recent events and eventualities. The afternoon Mrs Láng (again with a cake and flowers), Elly Hermans and Éva with Pista came. [. . .]

Mrs Láng told me, they and their friends in the neighbourhood were so sick with the lynchings on Sunday, they could not eat. But, thank God, there were a few people, who were disgusted, they heard a man coming down the street and saying it is a shame, to attack defenceless people.

In today's *Esti Ujság* Imrédy wrote an article: the country is in danger! I could not get the paper, it was all sold out by 4 p.m. I suppose, it is something like "Hannibal ante portas."[29] [. . .]

Though the expression: "Atlantic wall" is long forgotten, I still remember the lot of noise, our propaganda that was made around it. I believe, there never existed any real wall defense system but by a splendid system of roads and railway communications, the G.s hoped to be able to throw the best mechanized units on any place endangered in the shortest time.

There are rumours everywhere, in town about Hitler having died, as a result of the injuries. Allegedly the troups have to take the oath on Himmler's name already . . . Göbbels only second to him—just after the attempt, but since then only Göbbels can be heard.

AUGUST 2, WEDNESDAY.

I had to go out and order the birth certificates of the Forrai boys, after office I met Lacy. No trace of her sister in law. We sat near the Danube, sunshine, wind, it was almost like peace.

Today's papers speak quite openly about fighting *in* the Carpathians and Soviet troups having broken through several passes. Scores of refugees have been seen on the Miskolc and Aszód stations. The infamous gendarme captain, Zöldi, has been appointed as plenipotentiary at Újvidék.[30] Quem dii vult perdere, dementunt.[31]

AUG. 3, THURSDAY.

I hope, you are well, Dearest and nothing happened to you. [. . .]

---

29. Hannibal is before the gates (Latin), meaning there is danger ahead.

30. Márton Zöldi (1912–46), local commander in Újvidék / Novi Sad (1941), tried and convicted for war crimes by a Hungarian military court in 1943 but escaped to Germany. Captured by the Americans, returned to Hungary after March 1944, tried, convicted, and executed in 1946 at Újvidék / Novi Sad for war crimes (*MEK*).

31. Whom the gods wish to destroy, they first make mad (Latin).

According to Swiss opinion, if Germany had the wish to defend Hungary, they should have done it at the Carpathians. But no. It seems, they are going to "defend" it on the Danube line.

The morning I had to go to the Swedish consulate to see Miss Bruning, in Klári's[32] interest. Could not settle anything. She may go there *after* the 8th of August and than, perhaps, they can get on the list of Jews, who will be taken out to Sweden. On my question, whether it will not be too late they just shrugged their shoulders. Watch out how proud the Swedish will be after the war, how many lives they saved or tried to save . . .

Now a stream of yellow star men and women approached the Gyopár utca 8,[33] were sent to Minerva utca 1 (next house), stood there in line, for nothing. As I came out, I met Marika Milkó and her husband, without star but same purpose. Her first question was: have you news about Hilda? [. . .]

After Oti I met Klári, helped her to buy some candy for the boys and some cigarettes for herself, both things, they are prohibited to buy. Would you ever believe such cruelty? At home I had scarcely a quarter of an hour as the Léngs trapped me downstairs and I had to discuss with them political theories. I had to hurry up to Tercsi néni, she had some rice (1 kg = 26 P!) and butter for me. Éva, Pista and Api were there. Api tells us, there is definitely spread the propaganda the allies used gas on their Normandy break-through. So they expect now the use of gas on G. side.

He had the latest anecdote too. The war is finished, H. taken prisoner and condemned to die. As a last favour he asks for having a private interview with Roosevelt and Churchill. Granted. Being alone with them, he throws away his mustache and wig, saying: I am Jack Roberts of the Secret Service.[34] Your orders fulfilled, Germany is destroyed.

Churchill's yesterday speech is very promising as regards peace. His flying bomb statistics are a bit strange. According to him each bomb destroyed on the average not quite one person and not quite three houses. The number of persons seems to be small. I am still more sorry for the fighting losses in Normandy, where he says, losses were heavy, especially on American side.

I am told, that in two cases Hungarian pilots, shot down in air battle, were killed by the mob, as a result of the "people's judgement" propaganda.

32. Klári Forrai was a Jewish friend of Mádi.

33. The Svédország királyi követség (Royal Swedish Embassy) was at no. 8 Gyopár utca.

34. May be a reference to the Dashiell Hammett and Alex Raymond comic strip *Secret Agent X-9*.

Apparently they were dazed by the fall and could not speak immediately, the uniform is about the same.

AUG. 4, FRIDAY.

Tonight's news announce a purge in the G. army. Funny, after having depressed the revolt in six hours.

AUG. 5, SATURDAY.

Here Mr Schmalfuss (how can somebody be called Schmalfuss?)[35] states, the G. troups in Normandy broke away, the new line of defense is still a secret, as the enemy must not get knowledge of its whereabouts. [. . .]

12:15 the alarm here, in Bpest is off. In twenty minutes streetcars will go and I shall be off to Oti the office. No noon papers in their regular times today as work stood from about 9 a.m. on. People coming up from the shelters must be starving—one gets hungry at such periods—I am well fed and not tired, as I stayed up in my place.

Did I ever tell you how different animals react on raids? Dogs are crazy with fear. Birds—as long it can be heard—are singing undisturbed. Hens lay their eggs and announce the fact on the usual way amidst waves. Cats on the other hand are definitely contemptuous of human machinations and walk with deliberate, slow, unhurried steps on the street or lawn, when everybody is hiding. Horses I have not seen yet, nor cattle. Pigs, I am told, sense the danger, when noises are near.

Last year we had two expecting mothers in our house, thank God, their delivery was normal, without air raid accidents. This year we have again two, one recently arrived in the Viktor flat, both of them next door neighbours. If somebody thinks I am pleased with these expectant mothers, is very much mistaken. In connection with raids so may premature births happen! [. . .]

This morning two G. cars collided at Krisztina square[36] (one with Hamburg refugees), result: three dead. I could not see any phantasy in coming to Hungary, unless it is true, they are buying Jewish identification papers. They do not buy them from Jews, but from the G. Gestapo men, who took all papers as the first thing. What foresight!

I just heard a radio news item, according to which Bulgaria has asked for peace terms. If this is true, it looks very much like the situation in August–September 918.

35. Alex Schmalfuss, German News Agency reporter in France (1944). Schmalfuss in German means narrow foot.

36. Krisztina tér, in the 1st District, near the Castle.

AUGUST 8, TUESDAY.

The latest news seem to be remarkable, especially in France. The American drive towards Paris is promising.

Afternoon. All sorts of alerts the morning, the radio resumed its program just when I left my office, at 2:30 p.m. and at about 4 p.m., when I met Erzsike, it started again. I know, I should not work and have all these excitements, I have headaches, when I can hardly see. But who can help? After a painfully hot day the afternoon brought a distant storm and some rain. I took my analgetic and the freshness of the air will help perhaps to get well.

Erzsike tells me, twenty Jewish inhabited houses have been taken for Gestapo. Day before yesterday there had been fights around the Nyilas house and it was surrounded by police-cordon. The changes in the cabinet have been published today: Imrédy, Kunder[37] and Jaross dismissed, Bonczos[38] minister for the interior. Is it a turn for the left? Jews are forbidden to use public telephones, their own had been taken early in April. Nothing in the papers, just spread by mouth, by policemen warnings, etc.

Sztójay (before Stojkovics[39]), the present premier, has a so called niece a G. woman, keeping house for him. She questioned somebody not before long, as to the differences between the various right-side, political parties (nyilas, nazi, megujulás pártja,[40] stb[41]) "*nämlich der Döme kennt sich gar nicht aus*"[42] [. . .]

AUGUST 9, WEDNESDAY.

Early morning alerts now, at 10:30 a.m. renewed. It was between such a noise on the street, now, as serious alarms are East and West (Sopron—Zala on one side, Szeged—Békés—Szolnok on the other) everything is silent. Földvár is alerted just now, so it will be our turn soon. Hurry to take my bath.

SAME NIGHT.

Today's raid have been over Csepel, Budaörs airfield, Ferihegy and Tokod airfields, Almásfüzitő oil refinery and Győr. At 9:30 p.m. American news I heard something about Himmler being killed, but in the later German and other news there is no word about it. Was it just hallucination? or wishful thinking?

---

37. Antal Kunder (1900–1968), minister of trade and transport (1944) (*MEK*).

38. Miklós Bonczos (1897–1971), minister of the interior of the Lakatos government (August–October 1944), member of parliament, high secretary (*MEK*).

39. Sztójay went by the name Stojkovics when he was Serbian.

40. Party of Renewal.

41. Mádi uses stb for "satöbbi" in Hungarian, meaning "et cetera."

42. Because Döme does not know them all (German).

The afternoon I met Lacy. I am told, that, in spite of the Hungarian governments promise, that no more deportation of Jews will occur, a few days ago Gestapo men arrived at Sárvár, disarmed the Hungarian gendarmes and took fourteen hundred Jews away. Still no news about Rózsi, Lacy's sister in law.

AUGUST 10, THURSDAY.

Ilonka has a story. Her helper was in the big grocery at Eskü ut (Köztisztviselők)[43] where the cook of the Turkish legation was shopping. The cook told about all the fuss, they have, because they have to pack for departure (!). She said, Kállay is still with them, but "*we* are not going to take him!" (As no doubt, the Turkish minister confides everything to the cook, these are reliable informations).

Late last night G. soldiers were noisy again out on the street, this time not singing but some talking. Elly Hermans came to me this morning and said they had threatened us, because we slept in peace. They used obscene language.

AUG. 11, FRIDAY.

Chartres is in American hands, 75 km.s from Paris. I begin to feel relieved, their supply lines seem to be secured. Rommel would have backed out of the Normandy disaster, Kluge[44] apparently not. . . . Montgomery's speech to the allied troups in France is an index, I suppose, they mean to end it this time.[45]

AUG. 12, SATURDAY.

After office I met Bö on the stairs of the Danube embankment. It was hot, the aimless, cruel heat of the pavements and damp from perspiring humanity. We sat and talked, I know, they, all these friends of mine need these talks and it is a bit of hope, not all gentiles are against them.

At 7 p.m. I am alone at last. In these days I have your photos more often before me. As long as there was no hope, it was too painful to have them before me. Now hope begins to grow anew: sometime we may see each other. [. . .]

Rajniss,[46] the editor of the Esti Ujság, one of the dirtiest newspaper, is out of the editorship and is stated to have escaped to Germany. Very well. They are

43. Civil servants.

44. German field marshal Günther von Kluge (1882–1944).

45. "Montgomery Finds Enemy Is in a Bad Way," *NYT*, August 12, 1944.

46. Ferenc Rajniss (1893–1946), minister of education (1944–45), tried, convicted, and executed for war crimes (1946) (*MEK*).

rats, abandoning the sinking ship. But we must not forget, they caused the sinking of the ship.

At 11 p.m. Bpest sirens sounded, no raid followed and it was finished in half an hour. I have to grin over my fellow inhabitants of the house, who run down to the shelter on the first sound—I have spared myself this. Sure, I do dress up and prepare, but somehow I have a strong belief in my personal immunity.

AUG. 13, SUNDAY.

10:18 a.m. radio off the air. Alarms began at Veszprém. A sudden quietness subsides immediately on houses and streets. How beautiful it would be to live on the old hill and witness everything from there. Just listened to a recording of some parts of president Roosevelt's speech.[47] He believes war will be over by the end of the year. So do I hope.

Did I ever tell you what a big fashion illegitimization in these last months was? It is hard to understand what I am talking about, is it not? Now, take the case of Jóska Stolpa. He wished to marry Éva Láng, whose father was Jewish. It was a long legal process, until they proved the fact, that Eva's mother committed adultery and Éva is of illegitimate birth. Two Jewish girls were saved of all the perils of being Jewish, the Rainer girls, as they could prove, their father was born out of wedlock. Faludi (Kovács & Faludi Hunnia laboratory)[48] adopted an old servant as mother, allegedly he was smuggled into the family, without the knowledge of old Mrs Faludi, when her own child was born dead. He let himself be photographed with the old servant, bought her a house, etc., etc. The most absurd things.

SAME NIGHT.

I just came home from the Horchlers, where I was asked to spend the afternoon. [. . .] I can tolerate them only with utmost self control. They are my own sort of people, that is, gentiles, the same social class and about the same education. Our roots, customs, environment, circumstances are almost the same. In spite of these, it is hard to endure their absolutely primitive talk. For example: Elsa complains, how is it that American air force raids us, *because of the Jews*, and in the meantime antisemitism is growing in the States. As it is out of question to explain her anything, I could not refrain from saying, may be, they are coming to bomb the Jews. The same moment I felt a bit uncomfortable, that

47. "President on Air," *NYT*, August 13, 1944.
48. A film studio in Budapest.

she may feel offended by my joke. But no. She said, may be, yes, that ought to be so. You may imagine, how dumb one gets among people, speaking an entirely different language. [. . .]

The weather is a scourge in itself, stifling hot without a breeze to cool it down. It is almost 11 p.m. (our radio giving alerts again) and I am gasping for air in the tightly shut and darkened flat room.

AUGUST 14, MONDAY.

I am not going to mention alerts any more as they go on all day and all night. Yesterday as there was nothing special, somebody asked anxiously: what is the matter? Are they sick or what? [. . .]

There is talk in town, the war will be finished in the West in four days. I do not know, but it is not entirely impossible any more. Gizi tells me, Jancsi Bingert still believes in G. victory. It is a sort of "Wunschtraum" for him, he put all his eggs in one basket, apparently.

AUGUST 15, TUESDAY.

Our food supply lacks in certain materials the first absent material is protein, almost absent, until now we got 10 dks[49] per person and per week, now for three weeks nothing. No wonder, our G. soldiers here are so well fed, their trousers are tight on their hips. The second need is sweets. I often have an outspoken hunger for cakes and sweets. From the shoemaker, who is my patient, I got a bottle of honey the last week. I am four times a day on it, it has an attraction for me as never before.

I just hear about the landing at the south of France. This, together with the Normandy state of affairs, would make an end to the war in days, with any reasonable government. With the nazis I am not so sure about it as (when it is clear, they lost the war,) they have a few weeks in Berlin or at the Obersalzberg.[50] We often discussed, whether the allies' declaration about an unconditional surrender[51] was not going to lengthen the war. So it may be, but I suppose, it was pronounced because of ethics. These leaders of the nazi should not be spared and it must never be stated in later years they were deceived.

49. Decikilograms, that is, 0.10 kilo, or a little under a quarter of a pound of meat per person per week.

50. An early reference to a Nazi redoubt in the Alps.

51. Unconditional surrender of the Axis nations was first proposed at the January 1943 meeting between President Roosevelt and Prime Minister Churchill in Casablanca, Morocco. See *Foreign Relations of the United States* (Washington, DC: Government Printing Office, 1943), 4:837.

Károly, Lacy's brother was right of course, nothing helps against force as overwhelming force. The allies have superior equipment and superior armies, they can do the things. Their strategy in Normandy is splendid. But to sit and wait for this coming, here, for four years, was a long time, I can tell you. [. . .]

The last time Csepel was raided labour service Jews were not permitted into the shelter by a lieutenant, though there was room enough. When after the raid several dead (according to one source 22, and according to Jewish sources 80) were among them, the lieutenant announced, they have died for the country. His captain told him no, they were killed by you.

AUGUST 16, WEDNESDAY.

With the new landing in the South of France, allies seem to be going to cut off France (from the North to the South) from G. occupied Europe. If I were the allies, I would do another cut from Fiume to the Carpathians, across Hungary, that would cut off the Balkans and another cut from Holland to East Prussia, that would cut off all the Northern States. The possibilities for these actions are slim.

AUGUST 17, THURSDAY.

A busy day, with much headache. Met Klári Bernauer, yesterday Lacy. For every weekday I have one of these friends to meet.

Allies seem to hurry at a tremendous rate towards Paris. Do they believe, it will make an end? [. . .]

Still no mention of Göring. Sure, he hopes to get away by air. It is stated he is about the richest man in Europe. The Argentine is expected to be the hiding place for these nazi fortunes.

G. news could not hide the fact of the new allied landing, but they do not mention the most outstanding propaganda factor: French troups fighting on French soil.

AUGUST 18, FRIDAY.

Our papers quote today the latest Göbbels article: Germany does not make much of the fact, to evacuate whole countries, the stress will be laid upon new technical devices . . .

No more night watch here in tenant houses. It is officially announced. Poor Maria, what a blow for her, not to be able to order us around. Until now she used to type her order and paste it on the wall at the entrance. This morning the wall looked bleak, without orders. [. . .] . . .

The afternoon Ilonka Krasznay and Irmus were here. In vain, but I begin sometimes to clear up the real situation before them. Ilonka is more capable to understand it, so would be Irmus if not for the fact, a cabinet minister in the family. They like to drive in the ministerial car. It is impertinence, the way, Pista Antal tries to justify himself. He, as member of the present cabinet, is utmost responsible for all the cruelties committed against Jews and as I mentioned before, even for the invasion of the country. Now, according to Irmus, he dreamily observed (in family circle) about insulin: for this too we must be thankful to a Jew . . . Though I never in my life heard, that Banting[52] would have been a Jew (Pista tries to spread the information, that he is a friend of Jews, only circumstances forced him to act otherwise).

AUGUST 19, SATURDAY.

G. soldiers are buying canned food and are seen on the streets with enormous packages. It looks like, they are preparing for an end of their séjour[53] here. No wonder, when the Bulgarian premier declares in parliament, they are ruined and want peace. Here with us, Imrédy tries to get out of entanglements. After being dismissed as cabinet minister (without portfolio) yesterday his resignation from the leadership of the Brotherhood of the Eastern frontline was announced. This so called brotherhood is one of the darkest confederations for terror acts. His body-journalist, Rainiss, left the Esti Ujság editorial seat and is said to have shipped away.

The Allies tremendous air superiority may be measured by the fact, that during these days, when heavy bombardment is going on in France, partly from the same Italian bases, we used to be raided from, Ploesti was raided three times in the last twenty-four hours and here in Hungary almost the whole day and whole night alarms were going on. [. . .]

SAME NIGHT.

Almost the same routine. After office I met Bö, she is electrified by the news, which she predicted exactly three days ahead.

Allies eight miles from the Seine. Their armed cars around Versailles.

AUGUST 20, SUNDAY.

Five years ago—how happy we have been together. It is not so bad today. At 9:15 a.m. Bpest sirens were sounded, but almost everywhere in the country

52. Frederick Banting (1891–1941), coinventor of synthetic insulin to treat diabetes.

53. "Séjour" is French for "stay."

too. Kanizsa, Zala, Veszprém, Földvár, Győr, Sopron, Szeged, Szolnok, Békés, Ungvár, Nyírség all. [. . .]

9:47 a.m. it is beginning, apparently. All the time the noises get louder and stronger, the vibration of the air above, like the humming of gigantic bumblebees.

The United States and Great Britain promised to provide for Jews in neutral countries, emigrated from Hungary. But they can not help their getting out of the danger zone. [. . .]

11:05 a.m. Bpest alarm cleared and a few seconds later it was on again. People could not even get up to their places. Some belated cars running up the hill roads, they used to park up at Fodor utca,[54] where they believe to be more safe. Horses are freed out of harness, after raids many advertisements are in the paper for lost horses.

After stopping of hostilities it won't be more than six weeks—at most two months, may be even earlier and we shall have our air mail letters in six days.[55] [. . .]

No milk on Sundays, since the war. Why? Cows give milk just the same as on weekdays, work with them has to be done just the same, trains go, as on other days, so why can one not have peacetime organization in this small detail? On other days too, milk's quality is so poor, that we begin to believe that it is sour already in the udder.

G. protection was promised to Hungary, when we had to join them against Russia, when they occupied our country and on several other occasions, when something had to be squeezed out of the country's strength. We were raided several times at Győr, Horthyliget, etc., on behalf of aircraft factories. You would believe, we have at least plenty of aircrafts? Now, the country possesses 32, that is thirty-two fighters, not more. And G. help and protection? Nowhere.

On such Sundays as this mass is said in the afternoon. [. . .] When a raid begins in the morning, priests begin to have their breakfast, their luncheon early and after four hours after the lunch, in case the raid is over, they begin to read the mass.

Where are some of the well known G. commentators? Otto von Heydebreck's[56] name I did not see for a considerable time (His brother was killed ten

54. Fodor utca, in the 12th District, near Mádi's flat.

55. Mádi's subsequent annotation: "1969: P.S. May 8—I received the first letter some time in July. Only the help of the US Military Mission."

56. Otto von Heydebreck's brother Peter was a German Freikorps commander in the 1920s. He was killed during the Night of the Long Knives in 1934.

years ago, in the Röhm affair). And my favorite, Alec Schmalfuss? He seems to have disappeared with the lost battle of Normandy. Allies are over the Seine at Mantes. The Gestapo has caught Gördeler,[57] former Mayor of Leipzig, who was assigned as future head of a peace government in Germany. He will be killed, together with the Palombinis.[58]

AUGUST 21, MONDAY.

Since early morning alarms on the radio, Szolnok, Miskolc, Varád are in the foreground. Pécs—disturbing flights. [. . .]

SAME AFTERNOON.

This is an unexpectedly beautiful day. Somehow I could not sit quietly at the office so I left instructions and came home half an hour earlier than usual. Ten minutes before three p.m. Apu called me up, to see him as quick as possible. I guessed the reason and run on the instant. I was lucky to get a taxi at the Southern railway, produced my medical legitimization card and so he had to take me to Mihály utca. There I got your letters of Feb. 25 and June 13, with a slip of paper for the censor and seven photographs! Your letters are the most sweet ones I ever had, Geo's handwriting is there too! You may imagine, how I like the pictures and your looks and Babu's hairdo. I still have to digest it all, it will last a week until I really believe it.

There are interesting—good and bad—rumours. The G-s are more impertinent as ever, they wish to incorporate us as a protectorate for ever (!), they force the present government to deport Jews as quick as possible. On the other hand, Slovak diplomats have the news (and they used to have good informations from Chech sources) that the military occupation of Hungary would be effectuated not by Russian, but by Polish and Chech troups. This does not sound so dangerous.

AUGUST 22, TUESDAY.

We have reached the continuous raid period, apparently. At 9:30 a.m. Bpest sirens were sounded, for a change. We did not have them since midnight. The waves are branching off though, as already Sopron and Szeged are under alarm. I have such—may be ungrounded—confidence now, that, until our government does not begin deportations anew, there will be only strategic raids. For these our quarters are not concerned.

57. Carl Friedrich Goerdeler (1881–1945), executed for his part in the July 20, 1944, plot to assassinate Hitler.

58. A reference to an Italian general in the wars of 1848 against Austria.

I had to show off with the photos, so I dropped in to the Hermans last evening. The old lady, Mrs. Brunowsky, Elly's mother has observed the afternoon a huge gathering of G. soldiers and uniformed girls on the yard of the school building next. Some very striped, bestarved uniformed high official came, made a speech to them—apparently some explanation about the events—and then made them promise—a handshake with all of them in turn—to stand by the Führer. The old lady was prepared (by experience) for cheers, but none followed.

From Apu I got yesterday a box of Camels, he got from the Turkish minister. I try to believe, I am with you, when I smoke them.

The Swiss government turned to our government with a rather strange proposition. They wish every Jew, who claims to have some foreign citizenship be accepted as such, until the contrary is not proved by the nazi government. It would go too far, so I am afraid, it will not be accepted, but it clearly shows the danger Jews are in.[59]

After office I had to meet Erzsike. They try all sorts of things, besides Palestine their G. friend is out in Sweden now, to get affidavits for them. It is superfluous though, as America & England guaranteed the support of all immigrant Jews. The difficulty is getting out of the country.

AUGUST 23, WEDNESDAY.

The night Bpest sirens were sounded at 10:55 p.m., the alarm lasted until 0:45 a.m. I was rather unwell, so just lay on my bed at first full dressed, later, when it seemed probable, that no raid will follow here, undressed and in perfect peace. You may imagine, how tired people must be, day and night alarms and sitting for hours in the shelter seems to be a part of the daily routine. Serves them right.

The rate, American troups are invading the territory East of Paris, is marvelous. The end of the war is in sight, really, if they can keep up this pace.

This afternoon. Alerts all through the morning and noon. [. . .] The weather is hot again, but some slight breeze. After the routine I met Lacy, Wednesday is her turn. She is delighted with the photos. At Oti my former M.D. partner (there) came to see me. She has bad news from her husband. At the 15 July at 10 p.m. Ubrizry (a police officer, who lived in this house before) went out to their Csepel camp and took 32 men, all with the Dr title with him to Rökk Szilárd u. headquarters, where he is master of life and death. At dawn they were taken out to a station, put into G. wagons and sealed up. The train moved out but in a short time returned to the station (government orders) and they were

59. Tschuy, *Dangerous Diplomacy*, 163–67, explains the proposition from the Swiss government to respect foreign citizenship claims of Hungarian Jews.

taken out and sent with trucks to Kistarcsa camp. On the 19 G. SS men came, overwhelmed the Hungarian guards of the camp, put 1200 Jews on trucks and entrained them a few stations out of Bpest.

SAME NIGHT.

The Hermans and Apu had been here for a coffee and we celebrated for Barbara with a white cake and three candles. [. . .] He had to hurry home before 10 p.m. to listen to BBC news, as a neighbour used to come to him to listen too. Apu asked him, does this neighbour have no radio set? Yes, he has, but G. officers are living in his house and they do not want to have BBC news in the same house, they are living in, but are very eager to have them from somebody else. Is it not a farce?

At 11 p.m. I hear that Roumania made peace with Russia.[60] So they could be the first of the Balkan states. Maniu comes, I suppose. Bulgaria will be free to make peace now and Russian or Chech forces will be free to invade Hungary or to cut up Balkan G. forces. [. . .] I do not believe, they could fight in Roumania so very probably a terrible rush to, or over Hungary will begin already tonight, passenger trains will be stopped shortly in Hungary and strategic bombardment will follow all over the railway lines. [. . .]

A quick withdrawal of G. troups could save our Jews from deportation.

In detailed midnight news I just hear, Roumania has got back Northern Transsylvania from the allies (I am sorry for it but it is perfectly logical) and so I suppose, they will have to work for it. It depends, on what G. force is at present in Roumania, how soon the Roumanians will move into Hungary. Is the Hungarian government sleeping? Or is there some agreement in preparation? It should have been agreed before, of course.

AUGUST 24, THURSDAY.

Barbara three years old! I suppose, she feels very important and you celebrate in a large scale.

AUGUST 15 [*SIC*], FRIDAY.

Yesterday after the morning's alarm I got in time to the office. After work I met Klári Bernauer. They—deprived from their radio and isolated in Jewish houses and having only a few hours to go out—are perfectly informed, even "overinformed," as often rumours are spread among them, which prove to be false.

---

60. On August 23, 1944, King Michael I dismissed the pro-Axis government and signed an armistice with the USSR, switching sides to the Allies. "Break in Balkans: King Proclaims Nation's Surrender and Wish to Help Allies," *NYT*, August 24, 1944.

It was a very hot and stifling day. The afternoon I lay on my sofa, rather exhausted. The evening I spent an hour with Klári Bálint coming home at 10 p.m., Mrs Székely came to see me, stayd almost until midnight. These two are happy too about recent events. [. . .]

A G. diplomat used to order his shoes from Mr. Láng. He was here lately, said, things are very grave. He said too, that Roumania is going to take Transsylvania from Hungary, it serves the Hungarians right, as they had their mind always on robbery. Now, anybody else may reproach us with that, but a German?

It is so hot, so exhaustingly hot, I have seen a nun on the street—with short sleeves!

AUGUST 26, SATURDAY.

I was unhappy since yesterday evening, as I could not find my fountain pen. I looked ten times in my purse, in vain. Tonight, as I reached in for my cigarette box, I touched it in one of its inside pockets. It is as if dshins[61] would have their play with us.

I had to accept another medical assignment today for indefinite length of time, daily four hours plus. I do not know how I shall manage with my energies, but I guess, I shall have to, else they could transfer me out to the countryside. Laboratory work at II. Kapás utca.[62] [. . .]

AUGUST 27, SUNDAY.

Should Hungary turn against Germany—much too late of course—people even here, the pro G. elements I mean—will reproach her of breaking the alliance. It would never be forgotten, that with the occupation of the country all alliance has ceased to exist. One is not allied with the oppressor.

12:50 p.m. Bpest sirens the second time sounded. I use my time wisely, two dresses ironed, some sewing etc. Other people sit patiently in the cellar, though no sound could be heard until now. [. . .]

I read in the obituary column the name of Mike Gervay, you remember, he used to be in your dancing class. Poor boy. Frontline, of course.

Our news service is splendid: Churchill has been at the Vatican on Wednesday, it was announced today. The taking of Paris is not yet admitted, though it happened Tuesday night.

I am told, that since a few weeks the Kunder children are out in Tirol. Kunder is one of the recently dismissed cabinet ministers, who, with Imrédy, followed the most subservient pro-G. policy. He knew well, to what danger

61. Genies or spirits.

62. In the Castle District of Buda.

they lead the country and therefore sent his children out in time. The most attractive feature for these people in Austria is, the promise of the allies, Austria will be occupied by American and English troups.

I know, how ridiculous it is, to give early Victorian advices, still I have to tell you this. I have seen many people, men and women alike, who, middle aged, got deplorably provincial in their way of thinking, though they were smart in earlier years. Your aunt Margit, Ibola and many others. The big danger is a happy, married life, when these people cease to think independently of their husbands or wives and an economically secure life when they trust papers and the whole world around, as just suited to their tastes and needs. You are in both dangers. Please, never believe anybody, not even me, but always think it over yourself, with your own sound judgement. This is the way, as I have noticed, George used to do thinking, but you have to do it yourself and then discuss it with him. Always depend on yourself. The second: never stay, where you are, contented with your achievements. You may be proud of them, but go on all the time improving yourself. Reading, discussion, observing people, their reactions, etc. It is more fun, to live like that. [. . .]

The most fun about observing our G. origine, G. feeling compatriots is, their eagerness to identify themselves with the nazi cause. If only they could see a bit ahead, how decent G. people will disclaim all identity with the present gang, as soon they will be free to state it. But sure, the imperialistic, pan-German claims are common with all G.s. Not long before Gizi said to me, poor Gs, why does the world not let them be, they do not want anything, but to work in peace!

Every afternoon these military funerals! From Farkasrét the band returning at the Németvölgyi ut, next to us. On their return they play cheerful marches and melodies. Almost every afternoon the same. Every time a young life put into the earth, without any sense. And how few can be taken so far home! The majority is buried on the spot, if they can be found at all. [. . .]

AUGUST 28, MONDAY.

It is 9 p.m. and I just got back from my work. I am so exhausted, I do not see, how can I do it on the long run. Yesterday weather began to turn to fall, one could be a bit cold, but today was again very hot. The morning a tel. call from Erzsike, Emil is in hospital, later Pravádné came and we sat through an alarm here in my flat. [. . .] To all this comes a new anxiety for my friends, I understand there is military readiness in town (készültség) and four thousand gendarmes are again in Bpest. I am not able to do anything but I am at the end of my nerves.

With regards the Balkan situation, I believe Bulgaria was more honest, declaring her intention of breaking with Germany ahead, but on the other hand Roumania was smarter, doing the turn in a moment and taking Germany by surprise. The best of all her moves was the detention of the so called G. diplomats, who are nothing else but Gestapo. In an invaded country there can be no talk of diplomats (by the invader) so they are not entitled to extraterritorial privileges.

The contrary here: Hungary still holds out on G. side. Sure, it is invaded. Gestapo men took wagon loads of dissenting politicians out of the country these days, into G. concentration camps.

AUGUST 29, TUESDAY.

9:45 a.m. Bpest sirens sounded. [. . .]

I suppose, the Transsylvanian railways and military centers are raided. According to this morning's BBC news the Russians entered Transsylvania at the Ojtoj pass. A colleague who is called up for military service and traveled to Kassa a few days ago, returned yesterday with the news, they are off for Nagyvárad.[63] I suppose, we are going "to show the Russians." With all our immense military strength! With all our 32 fighters! Sure, the obituary column grows every day.

12:02 p.m. Hardly did I reach the streetcar station when the sirens were started again. I had to return home [. . .] Here I am again my place having a cup of Ovomaltine,[64] a bread and butter with green paprika. Raids are announced all over the country, especially the Eastern parts. Arad and Torda are announced, though they belong to Roumania. They are apparently in G. hands now. [. . .]

I believe, almost all our provincial cities will be raided to ruins, but this will be the only means to show people (even to leading politicians) how absurd this G. "alliance" has been. The continuous sparing of Bpest can be no chance, but some agreement. Bpest will be raided by retreating Germans, but on the example of Paris I believe, they do not have anything left but incendiaries.

SAME NIGHT.

At 9:15 p.m. alarms begin anew on the radio. I had much to do today, the heat is inhuman, two hours ago on the Halászbástya one could hardly take breath. I came home at 8:30 p.m.—in this house everybody sees everything—and half an hour later somebody rang my bell. I do not open any more my door. What do these people believe, when do I my cooking, my eating, my bath, not to mention my rest? [. . .]

---

63. Nagyvárad/Oradea, a city in Northern Transylvania in present-day Romania but under Hungarian control in 1944.

64. A Swiss, powdered malt-chocolate drink to be mixed with milk (or water, in Mádi's case).

AUGUST 30, WEDNESDAY.

At 10 a.m. Bpest sirens sounded. [. . .] I started to answer my correspondence, neglected for a considerable time. 11:05 a.m. alarms cleared. Off to work.

SAME NIGHT.

After Oti I met Lacy. She realizes the danger, they are in, I told her again to dash to my place the moment, she senses danger coming. I would not know, what to do without her and Bö and Károly and Emil, they are the most sensible of all my friends. A telephon talk with Hanna, evening: walk on the hillside with Elly.

I have to tell you, that on athletic competitions girls still do not have better result in high jump then you did: 145 cm s.[65] On the 27th August, last Sunday, I have noticed this and spoke about it with Marci too. I supposed, Barbara will be one for high jump!

AUGUST 31, THURSDAY.

With regards the pro-G policy, followed by our politicians—at least, those the G.s have left us—I often had doubts, may be, after all, they know something, I do not know. Some fact, which would give a justification of their policy. But now it turns out, their political farsightedness was about the level of a provincial vote-getter (kortes).

The new Hungarian government—born after several days of labor—with Lakatos (a general) as premier, two other generals, Csatay for war and Hennyey for foreign affairs, does not say much. There are new and better sounding names, Iván Rakovszky for education and Vladár (a judge) for justice (Pista Antal out this time, I suppose, for ever). I do not know anything about them. My only hope is, that soldiers used to know first, when they are beaten or in a hopeless position. A civilian, who does not understand strategy, would order to go on (see Hitler).

SAME NIGHT.

It is too much of the heat, I had to go to Rami this morning and after Oti to Klári B, as she is not well, I had to climb five floors as the elevator did not work. Two days ago, during alarm, down in their shelter an air defense district commander appeared with a policeman and told them, they must not be disturbed by rumours, as the police is on permanent attendance and whenever

65. 145 cm = 4′9″. Hilda Felsőbüky, before her marriage to George Walton, had been a star high jumper in Hungarian women's track and field, competing at matches for the Veres Palné Gimnasium of Budapest. Ibolya Csák of Hungary won the 1936 gold medal at the Berlin Olympics in the high jump with a leap of 160 cm (5′3″).

they notice some "suspicious move," they should report immediately to the next police station.

About the new cabinet. Lakatos, it is stated, is the choice of the regent. Vladár, the minister for justice was head of the section, which prepares new laws (törvényelőkészítő osztály) and resigned when given the task, to prepare the Jewish stuff. So he can't be a scoundrel. [. . .]

This August was a cruel month to stay in a city, working. Still, I do not mind, if the weather on the channel side is favourable for operations, to finish this business as soon as possible. These last minutes seem infinitely long.

SEPT. 1, FRIDAY.

Russian troups are in Bucharest. Chechs and Slovaks are allegedly fighting the invading G. troups. According to latest news Slovakia, except the Eastern and Western ends, are in partizan hands.

Bulgarian diplomats have arrived to Cairo, to sign the armistice terms. So our's is the honour, to be the last ally of Germany in these parts. How long? Slovak regular troups—about four divisions—were disarmed half a year ago, out of safety reasons by the G.s. How did they get arms now? I suppose, the fact that allied troups let maquis[66] French enter almost every town ahead, means, they let them settle their little accounts with collaborators. Allies do not want to partake in killing French. But these four years of occupation were too long, there were too many collaborators so the dangers of civil war too big.

According to the recently published allied armistice terms, Roumania has to give 1,400,000 workmen and 100,000 skilled men to reconstruct devastated territories in Russia. It will be about the same number, Hungary will have to give, I suppose. . . . Besides, I am convinced, workmen and engineers alike will be eager to work for Russia, they will be well paid and well-treated.[67]

In these last days heat, more and more G. officers can be seen in town, wearing British khaki uniforms. They are from the happy Africa days, I supposed, readjusted to G. fashion. [. . .]

No doubt, these will be the most interesting weeks of the war, only one has to survive them.

At 11:15 Bpest sirens sounded again. There is no possibility of work or a date to keep. My meeting with Iván is off. Bácska alarmed this morning at least for the third time, may be, it is the fourth. This second raid over Bpest costs the Hermans four P extra expense. They used to take much luggage down the shelter and hire a boy in the house to take it down for them. Each up and down two P-s. They could have eaten it.

66. The French underground resistance to German occupation.

67. Mádi's subsequent annotation: "1969. I was wrong."

I have read something in yesterday's paper, which, in spite of all, sounds true. The officially fixed price of the dollar in France is 50 Francs but the black market price should be 400 Frs. [. . .] All obscure origined fortunes try to convert themselves into dollars, where no dangers await them and they could stay anonymous.

SAME NIGHT.

Emil came home from the hospital (housed in the Baár Madas girls' school building),[68] so I went to see them. It is a terrible sight, to see them closed in their houses, crowded. They were just at the table, at least ten people. I fled in two minutes.

It is tonight, I need your letter most! I feel forlorn and good for nothing. Oti has lied after all with regards salary, they pay much less, then promised and the second office hours, I tried to do too, is too much for me. I simply can not do it. I have spent heaps of money since the spring and spent on nothing else, but eating. At the age of fourty six I am not able to support myself. To do it, I ought to work from morning to evening and this I can not do any more. Into the darkest hour of self-depreciation comes your letter, which assures me, that you both love me still, though if anybody, you must know me with all my faults and short comings. I am well aware, that from the distance I look better than I am, but am confident again, that even from a short distance, you will put up somehow with me.

SEPT. 2, SATURDAY.

Last night BBC mentioned some rumours—unconfirmed—about Hungarian peace tentatives in Turkey. The whole course taken by Hungary was of course mistaken, but even so, it would be high time not to go on with these mistakes. All our countryside towns, where G. communication lines go, are already in pieces. Who is defending them? Who is going to build them up from the ruins? Surely not us, for a long time and not our "great allies."

SAME NIGHT.

Still very hot, it is full moon and the air stifling. Black out at 9 p.m. is a torture. [. . .]

There was no alarm over the country the whole day; the night will be safe because of the full moon. Are they temporarily done with their task or is the pause intentionally because of peace-tentatives? Allegedly Kánya would be out

68. Baár Madas was the Reformed Church in Hungary high school in Budapest for girls, founded in 1907.

in Ankara for this purpose, but how he got out, I can not see. News are good and many, Lille, Charleville, Nancy, Ventimiglia, Pisa, gothic line-break, Guirgin, etc. After my work I met Bö, she wanted to see your photos for the second time.

SEPTEMBER 3, SUNDAY.

Hilda day. At 10:10 a.m. alarms beginning. Mamuci called up this morning. News splendid: allied troups half across Belgium, Finland pleaded for peace.

The latest: what is the nazi ideal? Blond, as Hitler, well shaped as Göbbels, slim as Göring and Adolf must be his name.

Yesterday, as we sat with Bö on the lower Danube embankment, I noticed the G. barrack (laktanya?) ship was under steam. It never was before. They seem to be ready to depart.

SAME NIGHT.

The afternoon Klári Bálint called me up (from the floor above me) whether she could come. She is a self-made, very efficient woman, we had a long talk, she said, it helped her. As soon as she left, at half past eight, Elly Hermans rang the bell and stayed an hour. The first believed, I am going to eat later, the second believed, I had supper earlier, but as it is not so important, I cooked my meal at about 10 p.m., had a hot bath, had to finish some washing and now, at 11:15 p.m. am in bed.

SEPT. 4, MONDAY.

Bruxelles[69] is occupied, allies heading towards Antwerp. Here alarms on the radio again. Finland and Russia stopped hostilities this morning. Dearest, what do you think about all this? [. . .]

No more excess heat. The evening is nice cool. From now on I hope we shall be able to enjoy sunshine and its warmth.

BBC tonight mentioned some rumours, that the Hitler gang tries to get out to Madrid. If it is true, so there must be strong revolutionary signs inside Germany and if no, the foreign workers—17 millions—ought to have a leading part in it.

SEPT. 5, TUESDAY.

The latest orders here about raids, everybody has to go on with work on the first sign of alarm which signs air danger. Pray, so why signal it at all? Psychologically it is impossible (in case you are afraid) to know, danger is coming and not to prepare for it. [. . .]

69. The French spelling of the city of Brussels.

In town many people have heard about a film photographed by G.s and allegedly played in Swiss and Swedish movies. In the worst terror days in June–July, how Jews were kicked into the railway cars by Hungarian gendarmes, how they arrived on the G. frontier, many dead among them and how nicely they were treated by G.s there, given food, etc. The G. gas chambers are omitted.[70] I hope, nobody will forget, that such cruelties happened everywhere the G.s set foot, nowhere did they happen, before they set foot and that cabinets, after the invasion of a country were chosen by them.

Middlewaves[71] begin to be interesting again. Until now you could go over twenty-four and odd stations and get the same G. rubbish. Now Sofia, Bucharest, Paris, Rome, Bruxelles, Luxembourg are different.

The Russian drive over Roumania leads over places you have been: Ploesti, Sinaia, Brassó. Do you remember your Brassó stay?

10:55 a.m. an unmistakable raid swept over Bpest, fires were started, people, looking out to the street, believe the bombings were around the Eastern station. Smoke shadows the sunshine. There was a critical moment during the raid, at least for me, I did not take warnings seriously, as for a long while nothing happened here at Bpest and I began to bath belated. As I was sitting in the tub, AAC grew very strong and splinters fell on the street. I finished my bath in a hurry, you may imagine!

SAME AFTERNOON.

The new bridge south[72] of Franz Jozsef seems to be hit at several places and much else, but we do not know details, only see the fires. No more, then four patients showed up today. [. . .]

I just hear from Hanna Sz that the Radium Hospital was hit, the entrance hall is in ruins, the furniture out on the square, other Hanna managed to get there after the raid. This is the second time, the Bakáts tér got bombs and Municipality is still just talking about evacuating them to the St. John's Hospital.

SAME NIGHT.

Home after an evening out with Elko. We met on the fortress hill and had a look round over the fires still burning then dined at Kriszt. I was definitely hungry and even after dinner I was not absolutely satisfied. As he got up at 3 a.m. this morning, I persuaded Elko not to see me home and returned alone, that is, crammed into a crowd on the streetcar with many G. soldiers and soldier-girls

---

70. See Braham, *The Politics of Genocide*, 2:610–12.

71. Medium-wave radio broadcasts. In the United States, these are the AM frequencies.

72. This refers to present-day Petőfi Bridge.

(they call them Blitzmädel). The soldiers were very young, 16-17-18, the oldest among them could not be more than twenty. Very deep tan, the British origin tropical shirts and capias.[73] They were dead tired, sleeping on their feet, coming from Eastern station (I believe several day's travel from Greece)—going to Southern station, that means Austria—Staiermark.

SEPT. 6, WEDNESDAY.

New rumours about Jewish deportations (only from Bpest) allegedly beginning on Friday. I hope, they are just rumours, according to Apu no technical possibilities exist for removing three hundred thousand men and women. But this labour-service announcement is hard enough for them. From 14–70 years! No such obligation exists for non Jewish persons.

The Óbuda gas works was damaged, many people could not cook their meals today.

Russia has declared war on Bulgaria. Why not before? They were not so touchy these three years. Is it a common trick, to get nearer the Dardanelles? This is the version, Elko is believing in and that at this junction Great Britain will turn against Russia and us here saved by allies. It is a sort of "Wünschtraüm" and I do not believe it.

Rumours have a reshuffle of the Hungarian government would be in way, with Arnóthy-Jungerth as premier.[74] [. . .]

Again there are news of Croatian unrest. Everything in boiling state. On Budapest streets every morning printed messages appear. Peace! Down with the Germans! Russian troups are at Turnu Severin, on the Yougoslav border.

Canadian troups are before Calais and Americans have entered the G. Reich.

SEPT. 7, THURSDAY.

I just hear that black out precautions will be at an end in ten days in England! How splendid, even for me, because it means a rapid end of the war and total defeat of our common enemy. I was prepared, that the drive towards Germany will have a respite at this phase, but so it seems no, they will be able to go on.

G. soldiers, questioned by people here about victory, confide: we are lost . . . Collapse seems to be complete. [. . .]

No raid today. After Oti I met Klári Bernauer, got some cigarettes for her and some candy for the boys. They are not allowed to buy such things. Coming

73. Mádi is referring to a kepi, a military hat with a flat top and wide brim.

74. Mihály Jungerth-Arnóthy (1883–1957), deputy foreign minister in the Sztójay government who brought the protests of foreign governments about the deportations to the cabinet and to the Crown Council in late June 1944 (*MEK*).

home, I met Ancy on the streetcar. By the way, traveling on a streetcar these days is against all human dignity. A soapless society crowded together in incredible numbers, perspiring, heated bodies in close contact for miles and quarters of hours. In black out time, waiting at a station I first smell some bodies, then two or three people emerge from the darkness. [. . .]

Two days ago, Baky, the other secretary of state was dismissed, today Endre. *Requiescant in pace.* Two monsters.

SEPT. 8, FRIDAY.

The morning, at 8 a.m. an old woman came with a letter from Bö.

I am told, Hungarian troups are in the southern part of Transsylvania, Arad and Temesvár. In face of the general situation, it seems insane.

SAME NIGHT.

I wrote a letter to Editke and took it out to their house myself, then went in for a few minutes to the Horchlers. They are again (at least for the seventh time) hoping in G. peace offers. Gizi is very careful now, accompanies me home, as she never used before. Iby was to see her lately, she does not want to see me apparently, as my theories proved to be right and their theories proved wrong.

Gizi was at the station two days ago, but it is unbelievable there. Hundreds of people are sitting between the rails, waiting for hours in vain. A train, due for Szombathely, which used to start from Eastern station at 8 p.m. started Tuesday from Southern station after midnight. Instead of third class cars cattle cars are used and even these, full with people until the stairs and tops. Almost everybody, who traveled these days, had adventures of bombing. [. . .]

Do Russian troups really intend to invade Hungary? There was time enough for that and they still crowd the border. If I understood well this morning BBC news, for cooperating with Russian, Roumanian and Tito's forces there is an allied force on the Adriatic. This—to have American and English troups here—would be our big hope. I am sure though, that people here will be deeply offended. They will say: we never had any quarrel with the Americans! England ought to know our being in German alliance was just forced upon us!

SEPT. 9, SATURDAY.

Tito announces the whole Balkan's railway system destroyed, well, if it is like the Hungarian railway system, so I can see no escape for our much beloved allies. But: I should be more happy if all these allied strategic moves would cause us to be *cut off from* Germany, instead to *encircle us, together* with them. The Allies do not see any difference between us and them.

The drafting of Jews for work has begun at the Pozsonyi ut houses, as Bö told me today. [. . .]

Here is something about drafting non Jewish elements for work, it's conditions seem to be not so cruel as with Jews (difference of age, having to go out of town and God knows, what else) but still, it is a sinister thing, we used to be told, can happen only under bolshevism. I am a bit anxious, what is going to happen to me, may be, they will not accept my three hours daily work as sufficient. I am hungry too, a hunger for proteins and chocolates and good food in general.

Kolozsvári Borcsa Mihály,[75] press chief of the government, who gave orders to destroy Jewish literature, is dismissed. Hlatky,[76] whom you may remember from the radio, steps in his place.

SEPT. 10, SUNDAY.

Apu told me, two days ago, Friday, we had been on the point of slipping out of the war, somehow it came to nothing. Details I could not get. He is very depressed, myself not, though it would mean more for me. With regards our government I am prepared for the worst.

I heard a story about Peter Heim, former chief of detectives.[77] He had collected big sums out of Jewish property, then, when they wanted to put him under arrest, produced a G. passport and went off to Germany. Such people, Heim and Endre, Baky, Ubrizsy and others like them, have been the lords of life and death over us for months.

We went for a walk with Elly Hermans the late afternoon, up to the Fortress hill. I like to have a look-round from time to time and to see the incredibly soft colours of the fall. Air is transparent as crystal and one can see far away, over the blue mist of the hills. Elly has the same experience as myself with friends. They begin to hate me, because they were wrong in their pro-Germanism.

SEPT. 11, MONDAY.

As my Oti nurse, Sister Anna told me today: She was out yesterday to see the Palatine museum at Hűvösvölgy and met several G. soldiers there. As she is of

75. Mihály Kolosváry-Borcsa (1896–1946), journalist and head of the Hungarian News Agency foreign press bureau (March–September 1944), indicted, tried, convicted, and executed by the Budapest People's Tribunal (1946) (*MEK*).

76. Endre Hlatky (1895–1957), director of Hungarian State Radio during the war (*MEK*).

77. Mádi is referring to Péter Hain (1895–1946), detective inspector of police, government counselor, and head of the Political Department of the Police Headquarters in Budapest. He was indicted, tried, convicted, and executed by the Budapest People's Tribunal (1946) (*MEK*).

G. origin herself, they began to talk and the G.s confided in her, they are very embittered and fed up with eternal fighting and being told lies. From Elly H. I gather, G. women and children are sent home from Hungary. It is evident, even to the G.s that our getting out of the business is just a question of days. Even sister Anna realizes it, though she too, like many others, felt her G. blood very much in times of G. successes. [. . .]

My balcony garden begins to be lovely again, after the blazing sunshine and heat and wind. The September weather is something on the flowers' nerves too.

SAME NIGHT.

A very good jazz music, with French words, is coming from Paris. Among others the three little pigs. What splendid cheerful years have been those of the pigs and Lambeth walk.

It is your wedding's fifth anniversary. Unbelievable, what everything happened between then and today. Events for the worse here, changes you would have never believed possible.

One can see how G.s are going home. Enormous knapsacks, parcels in the hands, sacks, bottles, boxes, whatever imaginable. Their coming was an imposing march, tanks, armed cars, lorries, cars. Now 8–10 soldiers flocked together on streetcar stations, camping before Southern station, waiting for a train. What happened to their equipment? Down, somewhere on the Balkans, destroyed or in Tito's hands. Only cars they still have, at least some of the officers of SS or Gestapo. No honest man has a car here these days, just G.s, politicians and collaborators.

For a pair of sandals the janitor's wife got two chickens for me. One of them I sent to Mamuci, where I used to lunch so often and where, just yesterday, all the time during lunch, we talked about how hungry we are. The other, Janikné[78] roasted for me quite well, so I am well fed tonight after several days of actual hunger. From my sister Margit there came a box of eggs this morning, 70 fill/piece,[79] here they are 1.30–1.40 P.s.

Coming home from the church on the Elisabeth bridge, we have seen refugees on a horse cart. Various house hold utensils and several people on it.[80] Rather sad to see homeless people but I could not oppress the thought: may be they committed cruelties and they are afraid of consequences. Here I could

78. Mrs. Janik.

79. One hundred filler = one pengö.

80. Szegedy-Maszák writes that the Countess Dessewffy noted in her diary that Budapest was flooded with refugees from Transylvania who were fleeing both the Romanian and Soviet armies in the fall of 1944. See *I Kiss Your Hands*, 167–68.

point out several people, who, if given the chance, would take to flight, because of their bad conscience.

SEPT. 12, TUESDAY.

New restrictions are imposed upon postal traffic. No picture cards, no papers or letters in parcels, letters utmost half a sheet, etc. a nice censorship inside the country. What a deep breath I shall take, when all this is at an end! But never more am I going to place myself under such a system of bullying.

Do you remember Szőzi, the former fiancée of Jencike? She is not doing any particular work and has a friend, apparently some nazi agitator. We talked about the new labour control identity cards and I hinted to her, they are to find out, who is living out of secret propaganda subsidies. She got red in the face and was speechless for a time and looked very frightened. I told her, just casually, how in France women, who went with G. soldiers, had their scalps shaved. She did not like the idea, I can tell you.

SEPT. 13, WEDNESDAY.

The morning Pravdáné came, to do my washing but as soon as she arrived, Bpest sirens were sounded and in short intervals three Bpest alarms followed with just a short raid. [. . .]

After my Oti hours I met Lacy, did some shopping for her—they can't buy in shops after 3 p.m., food not after 1 p.m.—then run out to see Marica Stolcz's baby. She is a nice little thing and Marica very happy with her. Coming home I went out to see the cemetery, found the plot neglected, worked a little with weeds (a rather hopeless task) then came home. You must not believe, I am just lazy, but such simple things exhaust me. Sometimes I feel very healthy and elastic, but then, beyond a certain limit I am finished, and the limit is much narrower than it used to be before. This is age and poor nutrition.

Our sugar ration cards (women's only) are held back for this month, allegedly until the 18 of Sept. What about households, where are no male members?

G. soldiers are going out of the country, no doubt. Meanwhile, they are not permitted to stay out after blackout time. But today two G. so called ladies made a scene on the streetcar, because an old lady had a basket in her hand. [. . .] I stared at them fiercely and comforted the old lady rather pointedly. After this the G. females went deep into the car, as far as possible from me.

Trains are passing the new Horthy Miklós bridge, in the middle of inhabited quarters, since the last Tuesday's raid. The locomotives make noise under Hanna's windows, Ferenc körút.[81] A shame to endanger people like that.

81. Hanna Szabő, Mádi's dentist friend.

The latest nazi propaganda here (exclusively for Hungarian use, I suppose) is the good old death ray theory. It is stated, no plane can get over the Transdanubian region, because those famous death-ray apparatuses are working near Pápa. This egocentrism is fascinating in our people. Why do they not protect Berlin or the Rhineland this way?

Some people have such horror of the coming occupation, I can not help asking, what have they done? There must be some reason for their terror.

The Roumanian armistice is signed, Le Havre has fallen to the allies. Csikszereda, Kézdivásárhely, and Székelyudvarhely in Russian hands.[82] No weapons, no clothing, no boots, not even shovels and axes available here. Are we going to ask for armistice, when Russian troups are at Soroksár?[83]

10:15 p.m. The raid was prolongued and came in several waves (after the fifth wave I gave up counting) so against my best judgment I went down the shelter's foreground and am up just now, stealing up quietly in the dark as poor Maria Pató orders people furiously around. As we had recently almost but daytime raids, when she is out, she missed this pleasure for a long time and has to enjoy herself tonight. [. . .]

SEPT. 14, THURSDAY.

I woke on the explosions of antiaircraft guns, allegedly these new ones more powerful than the Bofors, they should go up to 12,000 mts.[84]

I could get Hanna's telephon, they are all right and Tercsi néni too, though the big market hall next to them was hit.

At 14 hours air danger sirens were sounded and all patients dispersed in minutes. I did not want to stay near the Eastern station in case of alarm so departed via Tisza Kálmán tér. No alarm followed, so I went to see damages. The corner opposite Astoria[85] was hit (Rákóczi ut & Muzeum krt sarok) all buildings around are without window panes. The National Museum building inside burnt until the morning, but looking at it, one does not see any damage. The garden around it is roped off . . . Then I had to see Klári Bernauer at her place. The street full with furniture and trucks. G.s going away. I am sure, they came without furniture. After my visit to Klári I remembered Apponyi tér and went there. The building of the Kmac[86] had incendiaries. At Ferenciek tere the corner of Curia utca is burnt out and only the steel beams are visible. [. . .]

82. Cities in Northern Transylvania under Hungarian control (1940–44).

83. South suburban Budapest in 1944. Today part of the city as the 23rd District.

84. Meters, about 39,000 feet.

85. The Astoria Hotel (established in 1914) was the Gestapo headquarters in Pest in 1944 (see map 3).

86. Királyi Magyar Automobil-Club (Royal Hungarian Auto Club).

I went up to Elly Hermans at 8:30 p.m. as I have promised I took a pot of tea with me but scarcely had I poured Bpest sirens were sounded. Elly is rather sensitive with raids, they went down to the shelter and myself back home. Today's experiences: no heavy bombs were dropped, except of fire and small damage (fragmentation on the top floors) almost nothing else was hurt.

11:45 p.m. up from the shelter. Mrs Székely's labour seems to begin. The raid was prolongued and thorough. In the direction of Újpest very big fires, it looks like a crazy sunset. There were moments when the house shook under our feet.

0:30 A.M., THE 15 SEPT., FRIDAY.

Mrs. Székely's pains come in 7–8 minutes, her husband away on labour service (I supposed only, she does not say so). I believe I shall have to go with her to the Sanatorium as no taxis and no ambulance is available, not to mention that telephons can not be used.

At 5 a.m. my doorbell rang, Mrs Székely, who spent the few hours in quiet sleep, was there, water began to go away from her. As she has a rather narrow pelvis, I let her lie down and called the ambulance, but got them only after 6 a.m. We went together to the Red Cross hospital and I left the poor little thing there, but comforted, I am sure. I walked home, the morning sun was rather cool. [. . .]

The night down the shelter, one can not help listening to people's talk. Astounding, I call it. Mrs. Gorrieri confided in her neighbour, the war will be over in three days with G. victory! How does she imagine it? I could not question her, because then I could not hold my opinion and these people are dangerous. They used to go with G. soldiers. I can see her with a shaved head.

American troups are fighting at the outskirts of Aachen. There is much talk about the Siegfried line.[87] I do not believe, it can be anything else but some fortifications, hastily prepared, as the G.s always prepared for the offensive and new [*sic*] perfectly well, the French are not going to attack them.

SAME NIGHT.

[. . .] Váci utca (Angolkisasszonyok area) Molnár u, Veres Pálné u, Magyar u, the Boulevards so densely hit, it is impossible to enumerate it. Bakáts tér a heap of ruins, locomotives do not go any more on the Horthy Miklós bridge, it is hit again. At present I can not tell you any more as at 8:15 p.m. air danger signal was given here and judging by the alarms all over the country, in no time we shall run down to the shelter. A hit was last night not far from us at Böszörményi ut.

87. The Siegfried Line was the German defensive works from the Swiss border to the Netherlands, opposite the French Maginot Line. It was constructed in the 1930s.

Since a few days mysterious messages on our radio, only in G. language. They used to be as follows: Krokodil, gross, Lichtbild, and about twenty other words like this, all seemingly without sense. Are they the same, as French messages used to be on BBC during the occupation of France?

On our streetcars tumultuous scenes. People, so called "ladies" pushing ferociously with elbows and even kicks. Disgusting. I hate, sometimes even fear to travel. The line of No 6, which used to go round the boulevards, is recently broken at the Margit bridge, at the Rákóczi ut crossing and at Ferenc körút.

SEPT. 16, SATURDAY.

Poor little Mrs Székely still in labour. I just called her sanitarium, Dr Lekoczky-Semmelweiss[88] is with her, I hope, they will deliver her. It is almost two days, she has been in labour. Narrow pelvis grade too.

After office I met Bö, the evening Hanna. They both advice me to get a Swiss protection letter, though I do not see the reason, why (am I too optimistic?) and I do not believe, I could get one, just because Geo is an American citizen. Your citizenship I do not know Hildukáim. Was it three years after your setting foot on States soil or is it five years?

There is talk, that much stronger G. forces are in our country, as at the invasion's time. Allegedly the regent is not acting any more but a regent's council (Count Gyula Károlyi, Zsige Perényi and a third one are acting for him).[89]

There are signs for some secret arming of the nyilas party by G.s.

SEPT. 17, SUNDAY.

The morning I called Red Cross sanitorium and learned with relief, that to Mrs Székely a son was born and both are well. A short time after Emil called me, they got the grant, being exceptioned (kivételezés, nem számít zsidónak)[90] are very happy, must not wear the yellow star any more, may be can return to some better house to live (their old one is occupied already) and wants to come to see me. We fixed his coming on 10:30 a.m. but at 10:10 a.m. Bpest sirens were sounded, as well as almost in the whole country. Waves are announced from the South, so this time they ought to be Americans and they won't drop their bombs over the city, I hope.

Yesterday, I got a Bpest mailed letter from Gerti. Her husband was apparently here, going to Yougoslavia as a journalist . . . Gerti's letter is all invitation,

88. Kálmán Lehoczky-Semmelweis (1889–1967), physician (*MEK*).

89. Mádi's subsequent annotation: "1969. General Nagy Vilmos."

90. Privileged, not counted as Jewish.

in case I should need a place to live in at Vienna, but I suppose, she wants to be invited, in case she could leave Vienna and come to Hungary. Even the last year she seemed to be afraid turning of the tide. [. . .]

More and more people stay up in their apartments. I can hear the Bencze family across the hall with two small children.

Some parachutes seen by some people on the street. I hope, this time they will be treated with more consideration. A "commander" is living out her hidden power complex. Ordering people back to the shelters.

New wave is announced on the radio. Miskolc is alarmed for the fourth time this morning.

Apart from strategic reasons, these raids aim to soften people, which is done to perfection. It is a special nazi lie, raids stiffen people's resistance. They are soft and impressed. Very young people have fun out of it, not out of raids, but the way different people behave during it. My med. clerk, Erzsi Jónás tells me, what fun they have on the train, travelling a 50 km distance in *five* hours. But they are in crowds and all about twenty of age. [. . .]

After the last two Russian raids, when bombs were dropped all over the city, our papers wrote: outspoken terror raid over the capital. What has been the raids before? They always write about "terror" raids.

1:35 p.m. still heavy explosions. The sky a heavy grey, like in November. If we are so brave, to risk all, this danger and damage, why could we not risk it against Germany?

I am scribbling with these experiences. The greyness is so thorough, all shadows disappeared, the next house could be a big poster, no depth can be seen. [. . .]

8:30 p.m. the country was up to her ears in alarms and raids. It is coming from the North this time.

Mamuci is afraid to see the end of the war. I suppose, she did not mind very much, as long they were rather well off and—this is the chief thing—in an exceptional position. They had Swiss money, coffee, textiles (all from Apu's travels), she could go to the Slovak Tátra,[91] the children were safe until recently, that was all right. Sure, this is human, all too human nature: we do not mind other people's troubles. So many people have not the insight, that war, however advantageous to their purposes, can not go on infinitely.

Mr. Láng believes that forced labor in Russia, promised to 1,500,000 Roumanians, is but Nazi humbug. I do not think so. How could Russia reorganize all devastated territories without many millions of workmen? [. . .]

91. The High Tatra Mountains in northern Slovakia, part of the Carpathian Range.

SEPT. 18, MONDAY.

Emil came after a telephon call soon after 10 a.m. and a short while later Bpest sirens were sounded. We sat out a four hours raid together, here in my apartment. He never before could do this, in their Jewish house and with limited hours to go out. Now he came without the star, feeling a free man. I am very glad, they are out of danger or let us hope, they are out of danger. One family's worry less for me.

SAME NIGHT.

It was not only too late but impossible too as for two and a half hours no streetcars were going, even then only certain lines and very scarce. Our No 75 and 59 is nowhere. A bomber was hit somewhere not far from us. I could hear the crash and apparently this dismayed the line. You can not imagine, how the whole life of the city is paralyzed.

No traffic, no shopping, no postal service, no telephone, no work done and much damage. Myself could not get over to the other side of the Danube, could not post a package to Magyaróvár, could not mail money to your aunt Marguerite, could not go to Ilonka for cigarettes, could not do any shopping for food. The noon papers were not on the streets by 5 p.m., when already the evening paper *Magyarország* used to appear.

Hanna tells me, the Danube RR station, under the new bridge was hit, no train is to disturb them for a while now. Today's raid was heavy and for an American raid, very long. Until now your people used to come, raid and go within almost one hour, it is the Russian custom to come in small numbers, then others come and whole affair lasts for hours.

People are exhausted, exasperated, but still believe, the only remedy is, to hold out by the G-s. Again I can tell you, what I have told you already several times, there is no hope, where the bulk of the population is so dumb.

The second reason, why I believe the future of this country (or people?) hopeless, is the fact, we had a constitution almost a thousand years old, we had been very proud of and used to accentuate the likeness with the British constitution (See Magna Carta—Arany bulla,[92] almost the same date). Our institutions have been rather feudal, voting system, agrarian reform, etc. but on the whole it was not so bad, you could say your opinion in public without any danger. After all these preliminaries comes a few months of nazi propaganda and all our constitutional rights were swept away, like a building on the sand without the least resistance or even resentment by the great majority of the population. [. . .]

92. The Golden Bull of 1222 was an edict issued by King András II of Hungary.

There is an old lady in our home—Mrs Mikolay by name—and this morning, as Elly H. had a talk with her in the shelter, she did not know yet, that France is lost by the G.s. You see, it was never in the headlines. She said, in spite of this, Germany is going to win the war

About the scheme of yesterday's air landings[93] I have heard the plans two years ago, when I have staid at Magyaróvár on Dénes' radio, from an American station.

11:30 p.m. I am up in my flat. The alarm is not yet off but the raid—several waves—seems to be finished. It was a rather heavy raid, but, considering the concentration over certain targets—Újpest was the main one—I suppose, it was American or English. [. . .]

SEPT. 19, TUESDAY.

Irmus called me up just now and tells me, their house was hit on the night of the 13 and the next flat is in ruins. She has heard, that the Oti building I am working in, got air pressure[94] as the opposite fire station got hit. [. . .] . . . It is incalculable, how air pressure works.

2:10 p.m. Just got home from town. I have seen Ilonka, she left her flat to live with her daughter, as all around their house so much damage was done and her windows broken (I can see Budapest the winter with paper instead of window panes). Opposite our Oti building the fire station was hit all right, this side of the Oti building in ruins, but my rooms are in order. [. . .] Back from Oti already in town we had the air danger signal and hardly reached I home, the sirens were sounded. Cooking a bouillon soup with eggs.

On the streetcars you can meet more and more bombed out people, with small bundles of their left belongings. They are in a hysteric euphory, talking all the way to strangers, how they got hit, how many bombs fell directly around them, etc. They are dirty, neglected and shaken. Well, this is what they wished for, with the G. alliance.

I am sick for real coffee. The last time a quarter of a kg was offered for 200 Ps and I refused, because I could not afford it. But now I feel I could renounce eating, only to have coffee.

Klári Bálint was here the evening. At 8:30 p.m. the airdanger signal was sounded and a quarter latter Bpest sirens. I quietly sat and read Illyés's[95] book on Soviet Russia—a very reliable work—when the raid began to be too violent,

93. The airborne troop operations in Belgium, especially at Arnheim, the "bridge too far," written about by Cornelius Ryan in his book of that title (1974).

94. A reference to the blast or shock wave from high-explosive munitions.

95. Gyula Illyés (1902–83), Hungarian poet and author (*MEK*).

even for my taste. Two bombs fell rather close, the sound they gave, was like a bobsleigh gliding on a very hard frozen ground. So I went down in a hurry.

At 10:30 p.m. I had enough of downstairs and as comparative quietness reigned, came upstairs again.

Klári B. has some information about twenty one persons, among them the regent, the former cabinet members etc. being on the list of war criminals and because of this, allegedly, our government has taken up again wholeheartedly the pro G. line

During a lull in the raid I was left for a while alone with Mr Csabonyi (a fellow tenant) who put very anxious questions, what do I think about the developments ahead of us. I took care, not to say too much.

SEPT. 20, WEDNESDAY.

11:45 a.m. air danger signal over Bpest, the Southern parts all under alarms and raids. Mothers shouting for their children, who are missing on the yards or the street. The alarm helps me to eat in fairly normal hours. No raid yet (12:45 p.m.) and my paprikás krumpli[96] is nearly ready.

There is general talk in town about Sztójay, who hidden in an ambulance car, allegedly fled to the G. border. Recently the same is said about Bonczos, the present minister for the interior. They ought to be among the twenty-one list.

Our people down the shelter are very sure about the new, secret G. weapon (Even Göbbels does not talk any more about it). I mentioned before that the G. soldiers in the next school building seem to plan new buildings here, on the empty yard. Many heavy beams were carried here by Jewish labour service men. [. . .] Mr Lajtai knows for certain, these beams are for the new weapon! To be used apparently for the first time in Europe just at Margaréta street corner! It is not nice, to be the center of our universe!

2:00 p.m. A wave passed over us, rather noisy affair. I went down after several near hits, it is believed the Southern station is burning. May be, it is so, but I suppose, it was farther away. [. . .]

Very little bread, no potatoes and no onions in town. This all shows a tendency towards the end. No salt. Yesterday we did not get any milk on rations.

6:10 p.m. returned from town, still no streetcars. Except the military, police, etc cars everybody walking. These distances, with such footwear! And parcels besides. Home, but hungry. Southern station is not in function, I do not know why, but people arriving by trains are coming from the direction of the railway tunnel. The population looks rather depressed. But we are holding out! At

96. A dish made with boiled potatoes with onions and pepper.

the sacrifice of thousands a day in human lives, we protect those twenty-one persons. [. . .]

Dearest, today I feel very homesick for you and decent life. The city and town are ghastly.

9:25 p.m. alarm over Bpest. 10:08 p.m. the alarm is off here, without raid. I feel miserably, but it's nothing, but nerves. Overstrained. I prepared for death, without any particular reason.

SEPT. 21, THURSDAY.

Two telephon calls the morning, *légó* all over the country, Veszprém, Szeged, Várad, Eger, Miskolc, Szolnok, Győr, etc.

11:45 a.m. Bpest sirens sounded. We were expecting it though. Reading Huxley's Point counter point,[97] for the second time, after so many years. You had been about ten or twelve years old, when I first read it, it did not make much impression on me but Bö strongly recommended it this time and lent it.

12:30 p.m. More and more children back in Bpest, in spite of evacuation plans. [. . .] Families are more afraid of the war coming, then of air raids.

The sunshine is not so brilliant as it was these last days, but still, it is a nice day. I know, I shall be ferociously hungry but until now I could not eat anything, just had two cups of "decoctum" tea (that is, leaves already used once, boiled for a few minutes).

12:52 p.m. Bpest alarm off. Nothing happened. No noise, no planes. The *légó* commander of the opposite Municipality house orders people to stay where they are and announces she is going up to the top floor and look for timed bombs! Nothing but idiocy and power complex. And these commanders can not be contradicted, just as you can not resist a policeman.

Ancy Pravda tells me, on Tuesday a mass demonstration was held and dispersed by the police, at Vérmező. [. . .] Demonstration's cause: no bread. We want peace.

SEPT. 22, FRIDAY.

Nothing happened here last night, about midnight I went to sleep and slept until the morning peacefully. The morning a telephon call from Emil, we agreed to meet at Monpti (He had not been to an espresso since April, with yellow stars they are not let to enter them). I sold some broken gold pieces for them at our Schober, 48.45 gm = 4270.50, that is 90P/gm, but 1.8 gm were less worth, only 6 carats gold, so he paid the gram with 40P. They have (Emil & Co) no money at all, as part of their money and values were hit at Mátyásföld, part

97. Aldous Huxley, *Point Counterpoint* (1928 novel).

they were with a friend, who, since a big raid last week, disappeared and there is cause for anxiety.

Coming from Oti, I have seen a big G. lorry full with Persian rugs, via Eastern Station. So it is true, what I am told, they are collecting Persian rugs out of closed Jewish flats and taking them out of the country.

From Emil's office last week his two typewriters were taken, by a certain Dezső Foizt, some finance official, a Hungarian lieutenant and two levente.[98] Not even a paper note was left behind.

At 6:20 p.m. Bonczos, the minister for the interior made a speech on the radio. All staged like a popular show military marches before and after, a stentorian voice. Just a fiery csárdás[99] was omitted. I am sorry, but these people have nothing to say for me and I am not impressed at the least by their speeches. Cold blooded swindle.

SEPT. 23, SATURDAY.

Tallin (Reval) is taken by the Russian army and Arad in Hungary. The gothic line seems to be broken at last in Italy.

There is a passage in Lakatos's speech, mentioned in BBC news, which was suppressed in our papers. Second them, Lakatos awaits some offer from the allies, about Hungary's future. It is a bit late, to wait for an offer, in a hopeless position, when all neighbours stepped out of the G. alliance and only this country sticking to them.

A surprise: at the night's air attack over Kassel in central Germany, some rays are mentioned by BBC, as acting instead of fighters. So the death-ray-stories would be not entirely bluff, after all.

Oti patients are asking more and more often for sedatives. Their nerves are shot.

It is 10:30 a.m., still cloudy after yesterday's rain so no alarms are yet on the radio. Smells of cooking lunches creep in from the opposite house (or next flat?), offensive, crude smells and the singing of G. soldiers from the next school building is too much audible in my flat. Why have I to suffer all these? Their choir is not at all musical, I can tell you. [. . .]

SAME NIGHT.

The rays, mentioned the morning, can't be very dangerous as 9 bombers and one fighter were lost out of a force at least 500.

98. Levente was a military service organization for Hungarian teenage boys in the 1930s.

99. A Hungarian folk dance.

SEPT. 24, SUNDAY.

No raid last night, though the weather cleared up and no raid this morning. It is almost a peacetime Sunday noon, except for the G. soldiers on the streets.

SEPT. 25, MONDAY.

No raid. The rain was pouring all night, the day cold and grey and very windy. I am still going bare legs, what I have in stockings, won't be enough for the winter.

At the office, Dr Krompaczky[100] turned up, after an absence of five months. He was on military duty, Kassa, epidemic hospital, mostly typhus.[101] Got all his knowledge from Soviet sources. They have the most experience in it.

Saturday night I dreamt about my mother, she was with old Fáni néni at the Fő utca flat,[102] I had to leave them but before leaving, persuaded them to go down to the shelter. [. . .] Of course, there is nothing premonitory in this dream, only I suppose, I am too much preoccupied with death these days.

Refugees are pouring into the inner parts of the country. After the expected Northern Carpathian drive the offensive before Békéscsaba and Makó is surely a surprise. But propaganda is flourishing. Several people told me yesterday and today, the lull in air raids means that the G. rocket planes destroy allied planes by the hundreds, so no more raid is possible over the country. Besides, the G.s have frozen 80,000 Russians in an encircling operation. Are you astonished that anything may happen to people with so much credulousness?

On the other hand, I do not like BBC's silence when things are going wrong. The difficulties of the Arnheim glider transported troups were mentioned but today, they announced, that Temesvár[103] was taken by Russian troups but never mentioned, G. troups marched in the town before. Etc. etc. Allies do not need these camouflage silences, so why do it?

These last minutes of the war are hopelessly slow. I am sick with impatience, expectation, hopes and hopelessness. I suppose, after this stress, I shall be fit but for the lunatic asylum.

---

100. István Krompecher (1905–1983), physician and physiologist and a member of the Hungarian Academy of Sciences (MTA) (*MEK*).

101. Mádi's subsequent annotation: "1969: Protective serum (Wenzel) against typhus costs 300P/person."

102. The pre-1920 Mádi family residence in the Castle District.

103. "Arnheim" refers to the failed Allied Operation Market Garden, the attempt to cross into the Netherlands in September 1944. "Temesvár" (Timișoara in present-day Romania) was another Soviet advance in the fall of 1944.

SEPT. 26, THURSDAY.

After yesterday's bad weather it is a lovely day. A bit windy but sunshine is splendid. It is twenty six years today, my brother died.[104]

This morning I met Jancsi Bingert, in uniform. He plans to send his family away to the Transdanubian. Sunday night, when I met Hanna, she told me the same about Charlie. He is full of hysterics and wants Hanna to go away too. What harm could happen to her in a big city, she a dentist and half Jewish origin?

Second BBC a crowd yesterday forced his way into the palace (which palace? Royal palace or Prime minister's palace?) here and made a demonstration for peace. Rumours here know about an attempted sabotage action in MOM (Optical factory) near us. They were found out and put into prison. No raid, since four days in succession. Are there some parleys? Or do allies just wait until some of the damages are repaired? Dear, I am tired of this eternal having to wait.

SEPT. 27, WEDNESDAY.

After office I met Lacy. We had a splendid sunshine on the stone stairs of the lower Danube embankment . . . We both find things going very slowly, too slowly for our taste and needs for them, every day is a new danger. G.s want to deport them at any case.

From my clerk I heard an "eyewitness" story how the "death-rays" are operated. A woman from Pápa stated to her on the train, that the G.s have big cauldrons, they take them out to fields and are cooking something in it, before and during the raid.[105] Planes flying above, are falling down. Questioned nearer, she confessed not to have seen it distinctly but from a considerable distance. As for the falling down of planes I very much doubt, they had the courage, to watch the raid.

I give daily a healthy dose of ultraviolette rays on the skin of my legs as I want to go without stockings as long as possible. The irradiation causes a good circulation and a certain amount of hyperaemy,[106] so I am not cold, besides, the following pigmentation (tan) is like the colour of a stocking.

I am told by Lacy that a Jewish and a not Jewish house, opposite the school building, where a bomb was dropped on G. soldiers, was evacuated and people taken away by the G.s, nobody knows where.

---

104. Mádi's brother died in service in the Austro-Hungarian army in 1918.

105. The raid on Pápa, a city in western Hungary.

106. Hyperemia is an excess of blood in the vessels supplying an organ or other part of the body.

A second item is, it was announced yesterday at Isaszeg (about thirty kms from Bpest) that all strangers have to leave the place. Many evacuees from Bpest stayed there. They interpreted the announcement so, that there will be no more raids, they can return to their homes. Of course, the cause is, there begins a digging of fortifications around Bpest—Germany is going to defend Bpest!—and Isaszeg is one of the places. Jewish labour servicemen are taken there too, as Lacy's brother.

SEPT. 28, THURSDAY

Three fourths of the Arnheim glider troups sacrificed—why and how could it happened?

Authorities made a big effort to provide bread in plenty. They know, how dangerous such a shortage may be.

A patient has news from Transsylvania, that three villages at the Parajd region, had been extinguished, everybody killed—not by the Russians but by the Roumanians. May be, it is just a tale but it is perfectly possible too. The results of our minorities policy used to be suffered by people, who are entirely innocent in it.

Churchill said today he can not guarantee the end of the war in this year. So I began to believe it since a few days. But it is terrible. Since March this year I have lived up more than 6000 P.s, mostly eaten. Prices are going up every day. What shall become of me? How shall I be able to survive these months?

Hungary was mentioned in a rather friendly way by Churchill, as if everything would be only caused by the G. invasion.[107] He hopes, as soon the opportunity will be given, Hungary will fight wholehearted against her destructor. I wish I could be so sure about it.

SEPT. 29, FRIDAY.

At stations passenger trains are pushed out of the way for hours, to let G. military trains pass. But even G. trains have to stay at places, my clerk has seen yesterday 2 p.m. a G. train on their station, and this morning found it on the same spot.

After Oti I went to see Bö, the first time in her ghetto flat, I am glad, she is comfortable there and has a splendid view over the Danube and the isle. Her friend, Éva was there too, we had coffee. They have information, allegedly five years Russian military occupation lays ahead of us.

107. "Prime Minister Churchill on Military and Political Situation," *NYT*, September 29, 1944.

SEPT. 30, SATURDAY.

Wonderful, the way how Germany is defending our country! Fighting is going on in the middle of our territory.

I had a busy day. The morning, with much difficulty, I could get Mici Ormos on the 'phone. My neighour asked her as a family doctor to little Laci. Then I hurried to the post-office, were [*sic*] I could mail—after two weeks pause—the empty egg-box to Margit. At 11 a.m. I had to meet Hanna Sz. at Coffein-bar, a new espresso, opposite the Hotel Pannonia.

After Oti I had to go to the Toperczer's flat, as Tullia sent message the morning, she is here for only this day. [. . .] It is disgusting the way, they are hurrying to save themselves. Kőszegszerdahely is a place near the G. border, they have taken two rooms there and are traveling with as much belonging as possible, tonight. No talk to save the country this time. Hanna has taken six weeks sick leave. Mayor Farkas (Ákos) told them, the whole municipality administration of Makó was hanged or killed elsewhere, so you may imagine their fright. May be, I am over-confident, but I still refuse to be frightened by the Russian troups. I felt sick though listening to them and was glad to have an excuse to leave in a quarter of an hour.

By the way, their Zsuja, who married into an estate and who was exempted from military service on behalf of the estate, was the first to think about taking refuge. These people, who were always the loudest in speech, the country must be defended against bolshevism, do not think for a moment, that military duty (or nemzetőrség) national guard duty is meant for them too. Their children are the pretext. What about other people's children? Just today's paper gives the news, that orphaned children in consequence of war, raids, will get monthly 30–50 Ps from the state! It is not enough to starve.

Coming home, tumultuous scenes on the overcrowded streetcars and at Southern station. Crowds of Hungarian and G. soldiers getting on and off, due for the station and elsewhere, the whole square was full with people swarming like an angry beehive. At 3:30 p.m. a telephon call from Erzsike, they are coming tomorrow afternoon, to sort out warm clothing from their trunk. Emil was drafted this afternoon for labour service, he hopes to get at least delay as his kidneys are affected. But it is so on the whole line, Klári wants to exempt her two sons, Bö herself, Lacy too (but she has Frédi[108] to look after, who's mother disappeared). It is perfectly understandable with the yellow star tribe as they can not stand behind a system, which has the intention to kill them. It

108. Alfred "Frédi" Lakos (1937–2021). His mother had been caught in a roundup and deported to Auschwitz-Birkenau, where she was murdered.

is not so natural though with Zsuja & the other Toperczers, with Charlie, with the Beck & Horchler males, who enjoyed very much being gentiles and Hungarians or even Germans and who are not willing now to fight for their own ideas. [. . .]

This afternoon I went to see Tercsi néni, she feels very lonely as she 'phoned me the beginning of the week, to "spare for her a little time." I could not go before, even today for a short time as I dread being out at blackout time (7:45 p.m.) and traveling by streetcar is something terrible these days.

Coming home I went to see the baby next door. They are very pleased with Dr Ormos. Ida told me that the whole afternoon G. officers (three of them) and a soldier were burning documents on the school yard.

At Tercsi néni I met Api, he is still believing in big German reserves and in the new G. rocket plane's superiority, which, second him, can open fire from 2 kms. He states, that Russians treat prisoners of war very decently, are doing about the same with the civilian population, as the G.s, that is, they come with ready lists, pick their people but otherwise their troups are very well under control.

OCTOBER 1, SUNDAY.

Shops in the city—whole streets—look so devastated, that those still existing, have to put out signs: Opened—or: We are here or We are working!

SAME AFTERNOON.

Lunch with Apu, Mamuci and Peter. Second official reports every place, given up by the G.s, is entirely devastated by them in this country. Szászrégen, a charming little town is wiped out, nothing remained of its houses, streets, etc. Allegedly they do the same with their own, Aachen is the same. Lines of fortifications are built all across the Buda hills. The park below our old home, the hillside, all are prepared to "defend" the capital until the last. I do not see, how it will be possible to survive it. It is a policy of madmen. Young and not so young officers are made (here!) to take an oath on Hitler's name. It is a sort of conspiracy.

There is talk about a new, entirely right side, so called government, with Peter Heim as police minister. Members of the present cabinet do not sleep at home these days in fear of arrest. Apu does not feel secure, I invited him to come for the night to my flat, I could go over to Mamuci quite well. But I do not believe, he would be picked out, he never had to do anything with politics. There were foreign office difficulties recently with the G.s (their inferiority complex!) they wished the foreign minister to make a speech on occasion of the three-part-pact, when Ribbentrop, Musso, Sigemicu, Tiso,[109] and the Croat resp. made announcements. They were more than offended as they could not extract it out of us.

The official reports about the Makó executions is that only the vice mayor and the police chief were hanged. We know perfectly well, what kind of people were picked for such posts these days, so I am sure, they well deserved it. Even this was not done under Russian occupation but before they came into the town by inhabitants of Makó.

This afternoon, after a message from Emil, there is danger in coming so I must not expect them, Mr Láng, later, after him Mrs Láng came up with a plate of goose liver and goose töpörtyű.[110] Their generosity is touching. Recently he made a repair of the soles of one pair of shoes (the black market price is 80–100 P for it, outside of black market it does not exist) for 12 Ps. He is going to be drafted on the 15th Oct and I am afraid will be taken too.

Knitting an angora lumberjack[111] for Barbara.

OCT. 2, MONDAY.

We are back from Summer time and have blackout at 6:30 p.m. It is terrible as the streets are so dark, one does not venture out.

I have seen Ilonka (she had a postcard from your little brother Gábor, he believes, he will be at the Franciscans at Esztergom, this year). After Oti I went to see Károly, Lacy's brother.

Home, a postcard from Ibolya (they are told, their telephon won't function until the war is over), the card came in four days, from Bpest to Bpest. A letter from Margit in which she sends a copy from Dénes's recent card. It sounds very misterious, probably he was a prisoner for a time or he is leading a sort of partisan life. With him everything is possible.

OCT. 3, TUESDAY.

Since yesterday no passenger trains. It came as a surprise, so many people are trapped far from their homes, no refugees can come any more, as it is going to last for 8–9 days, it is believed.

---

109. Ribbentrop was the German foreign minister. "Musso" refers to Benito Mussolini, who in 1944 was the head of the Italian Salò Republic. "Sigemicu" is Mamoru Shigemitsu, foreign minister of Japan. "Tiso" is Monsignor Jozef Tiso, president of the Slovak Republic. See "Ribbentrop Utters Axis' Desperation; 'Fight to the Last' Speech by Nazi Foreign Minister Keys Tripartite Pact Talks," *NYT*, September 27, 1944.

110. Crackling goose skin.

111. Mádi's subsequent annotation: "1969. Cardigan."

The afternoon. I do not like to tell you disagreeable news, but still, this is a chronicle of my days spent here, so it is to be told too. You know I am working at the Oti since April 28, acting for a colleague, called up for military service. Two months later my other colleague there, a Jewess, was dismissed and I had the whole outpatients service alone, until a few days ago, when the military colleague showed up. But there is still the vacant place of the Jewess. With her I have cleared before, I do not hurt her interests in staying there, at present she could not return anyway, later, when Jewish restrictions will be annulled, she will have her rights just the same. So you see, I was correct and Oti needed me badly, as there was a shortage in physicians.

It is cold, a bad weather instead of a promising sunshine in the morning. [. . .] In intervals I am brushing the floor with unusual fervour, to get warm.

Miklós Majthényi, president of the Oti, is a pronouncedly right-side man, this was a reason, why I did not like to ask his help and why I did not go to him before, though he could have helped me on other occasions. But unlike other right-side men, he is an honest one. Very simple in manner, with a marvelous memory (he remembered me at the first words on the phone, though we met last time when you have been at Zsámbék!).

Brrr! I was called to the shoemaker's wife after blackout time, they are living in the same house but their door gives to the yard. I could hardly find my way around the corner with rain beating and wind lashing into my face.

I often wonder these days, shall I begin a general practice or not? The reason I do not like it, is no reason any more but I have no raincoat and only an umbrella with a hole on it. Besides, I suppose, there would be more extra taxes then income.

Feeding, eating just out of necessity, is not an agreable or cheerful business. There are no hearty meals, you can not enjoy it. As Sunday I had the goose liver from Mrs Láng, so yesterday I have not been so hungry and decided to have rather nothing then just potatoes. Today again I had to eat, breakfast I have not every day, as there is no but tea, the luncheon is forgotten most days, coming home I drink an Ovomaltine with water and two cups of "decoctum" tea. In spite of scarceness, I do not like to eat potatoes and am more eager for coffee then food. Until now food, every sort almost, was available in town but on fancy prices. One goose 200 Ps and over. 1 kg of grapes 15 Ps, butter 55 Ps, crackers 20–30 Ps, 1 dk of pepper 8 Ps, etc., etc.

Today I heard a nurse who works in peacetime at the Oti (almost 200 Ps monthly), is now on the frontline, was wounded several times, and came to ask for the difference to be paid to her, between her Oti pay and her military pay. So out at the frontlines, in life danger, she is not even getting so much, as she used to get here.

OCT. 4, WEDNESDAY.

I had to go to Oti, Barla Szabó, med. chief of Oti.[112] I am to stay at present on my place . . . Well, it means a prolongation of two months, I shall see, what I am going to do then. At present circumstances it is a long time.

With Lacy I walked near their flat, as I had to see the Kartals, not having met Emil. I took a warm robe for Erzsi's mother, they need it already. At home, after some shopping (1/2 kg of Ovomaltine + 1/2 kg of grapes = 14.23 P) I went for the second time to Mrs Láng, prescribed, promised to see her tomorrow again.

Here in my flat, Pubi called up and was here in half an hour. Left at 9 p.m. we had a very hearty talk. The boy is honest, well meaning sees things with practical realism, I wish, there would be more of his sort. He is out at the AAC at Rákospalota, got twice bad hits, at day and night raids. All their officers and men are all right, they listen to BBC and Moscow with the military radio, the rank and file call BBC Bpest III. His only wish is to get out for two or three years to some decent country, then intends to return home. He is the sort, I would not be ashamed of.

10:15 p.m. Alarm in here. Planes coming the North and South. 11:15 p.m. alarm off.

OCT. 5, THURSDAY.

The temporary boom in bread has broken down, yesterday again people were standing in lines in several districts.

At Oti today they promised me something better, but it still has to be found. I am rather fatalistic, so if I can find out a fairly good thing—possibly better paid—on our side of the Danube, I am going to accept.

OCT. 6, FRIDAY.

8:05 p.m. just got home after an exhausting day. I am transferred to the ENT outpatient department. Place, hours almost the same. Have seen Bö and Mici néni.

A large amount of our population has occasion to remember in these days, what they have done to the Jews. It is often mentioned: they had to go the summer, we have to go now!

Landings in Greece and Albania would be so promising, if only it would be nearer.

10:04 airdanger signal over Bpest.

---

112. József Barla-Szabó (1911–91), specialist in surgery at Rokus General Hospital, Budapest (*MEK*).

Second our papers 20,000 persons are indicted in France because of collaboration with the G.s, in Bulgaria 4000. With regards the resp-populations this is 1:2,000 in France and 1:1000 in Bulgaria. In France the Maquis have disposed of a lot before. Considering, that under an occupation the population majority seem to acquiesce, it is not a big percentage.

OCT. 7, SATUR.

At Oti from 12:40 until 3:30 p.m. we sat in the shelters, a terrible crowd in scores of rooms. Nothing has happened at Bpest, as is stated, though we did hear a lot of noises. Chief targets seemed to be Győr and thereabouts. We agreed with the Kartals they would come to me this afternoon, but the long *légó* upset all plans.

At the Uránia G. picture house a bomb was thrown yesterday evening, at the same time, after black out, an explosion destroyed the Gömbös statue at the Dőbrentei square,[113] the symbol of axis friendship. I had a good time, seeing its pieces on the street.

The night. Dinner with the Horchlers. Hányi just off for Igrici, near Miskolc, where his family is still hesitating, to come back or not to come back. He traveled in sports suit, with a knapsack and may be on way for two or three days. Last time he had to sleep at Hatvan in a public park. We—during dinner—avoided politics and had a nice time. They are such faithful friends.

You remember maybe Gizi's chief in office (a Dutch name by origin) Van Royen.[114] With Lacy we noticed for a long time, he may be the nazi influence upon Gizi. He is the sort of man, who, having his 6–8000 monthly income, does not mind nazis and war and Jewish persecution, etc.

OCT. 8, SUNDAY.

The Russian troups invaded the Trianon frontiers[115] 60 kms, they are at Gyoma, Körösladány, Szeghalom, Orosháza, Békés. Splendid to be defended by the G.s! In these last days they hoarded big amounts of food into the caves of the Buda hills, truck loads of flour, vegetables, canned food, poultry, etc. No canned food in town any more. I decided to sell my traveling whool plaid (got it as a present from Rhoda) for two geese, if possible, but as long as passenger fares are stopped, nothing is possible.

---

113. Gyula Gömbös (1886–1936), prime minister of Hungary (1932–36) (*MEK*). Dőbrentei Square was on the Buda side of the Danube, adjacent to the Erzsébet Bridge (see map 2).

114. Gyula Van Royen, an attorney in Budapest.

115. For the Trianon frontiers, see map 1, which shows the borders of present-day Hungary.

Some refugees come on rather false pretenses. Toncsi, Gizi's friend, who lived at Nagyszőllős and had nothing, left now a house, vineyards, big amounts of wine, could take with a military truck five rooms furniture and 50,000 Ps, she complains, she had to leave there her *life's* work, and it is because her husband helped the Jews (in June) they had to fly (now!). Some help.

Emil called up this morning, they will come at 4:30 p.m., in case no *légó* sets up all plans again.

10:50 a.m. alarm over Bácska. The sunshine is coming out with strength. Here we are.

SAME NIGHT.

There seemed to be many raids over the Eastern and Northern parts, but none over Bpest. The weather was lovely, I went in a cotton dress and barelegged. Sunshine, lovely colors, the air so smooth. On the hill we had a good talk, Apu being with me more communicative, than ever. Generally it is believed the Russian troups will be here in a few days, I personally do not think, it will happen so quick, though a quick action would mean luck for the capital. It could not be robbed so thoroughly by its "allies."

I am told, the government turned to all trade unions with the question, would they back the government against the G.s if armed. The trade unions declined, saying, they do not go with rifles against tanks. There is some reason in it, one has to admit.

CHAPTER 5

Arrow Cross Coup and Nazi Terror, October–November 1944

Mádi was a self-described member of the Hungarian "landed gentry," a social class that she heard an October 1944 BBC commentator blame for the country's thirty-year run of catastrophe since 1914. She responded to the broadcast in her diary, stating that "the pro G. elements have been the industrials and lower middle class" and not her fellow gentry. She wrote this two days before leaders of that same "lower middle class" toppled the Horthy regency, established a Fascist regime, and vowed to continue the war on the side of Germany. In almost unimaginable ways, the catastrophe of 1944 was about to get far worse for the residents of Budapest in the days after she replied to the BBC broadcast.

Chapter 5 contains Mádi's observations of the Arrow Cross seizure of power in Hungary and the subsequent terror unleashed on the civilian population, even as the Red Army advanced toward the city. By the end of the summer, Regent Horthy had wished to surrender Hungary to the Allies, but before doing so, as a matter of personal and national honor, he felt the need to inform his German allies of his intention. The Germans showed no appreciation for Horthy's sense of honor and instead arranged a coup d'état on October 15, 1944. They imposed a government led by the leader of the Arrow Cross Party, Ferenc Szálasi, who abolished the regency and proclaimed himself führer. Mádi gleaned from the news that the Germans and their Hungarian allies had decided to mount an active defense of Hungary as a battle space, mainly to protect Vienna from the Red Army. Unlike the German surrender of Paris and Rome earlier in the summer, Budapest would not be ceded to the Allies as an open city but instead would be defended in yet another Eastern Front "cauldron" battle.

Before the combined German-Hungarian armies could turn Budapest into what Mádi heard them call a "reverse Stalingrad," the Arrow Cross launched a war at home against its domestic enemies. Mádi recorded her observation on the day of the coup: "We are in a revolution." Given the advances of the Soviet army, deportation of the Budapest Jews to Auschwitz-Birkenau was a logistical impossibility. Far from being saved, however, Budapest Jews were subjected to new dangers. The Szálasi regime soon abolished the designation of yellow-star houses and instead directed Jews to relocate to ghettos, the largest of which was in the Erzsébetváros neighborhood of the city. Jews caught outside the ghetto were subject to summary execution. Mádi reported on public murders of Jews in the most prominent parts of the city, including the Castle District of Buda and the fashionable Andrássy Boulevard of Pest.

Mádi wrote about Arrow Cross gunmen who imposed a lockdown on her 19 Margaréta utca building from 5:00 p.m. until 7:00 a.m. She could see the immediate danger to her Jewish friends and invited them to come to her apartment for sanctuary. On October 17, Lacy came and, to Mádi's surprise, brought her seven-year-old nephew, Alfred (known as Frédi), as well. Frédi's mother had been caught in an Arrow Cross roundup, deported to Auschwitz-Birkenau, and murdered. His father had been drafted into a Jewish labor battalion, and so Aunt Lacy stepped in to care for the boy. Mádi's friend Bö also sought refuge in the one-bedroom flat.

Mádi expected that she would need to shield her friends for only a short time, because by mid-October the Red Army had reached the Great Hungarian Plain and was bearing down on the capital. Mádi heard of plans to compel physicians to attend six weeks of lectures to prepare them for the battlefield medicine that was expected from house-to-house fighting in Hungary. She scoffed at the timetable, as if "Russian troups will wait outside politely" so that Hungarian army specialists could "finish their lectures." She expected Budapest to fall to Soviet forces within a week, and then the city's Jews would be saved. However, it took the Red Army not merely one week of fighting but another sixteen weeks to liberate the city from Nazi and Arrow Cross control. Some of the delay was due to a pause by the Red Army to resupply and refit after the battles in eastern Hungary, and some was due to the stiffening of German resistance. Mádi's 12th District neighborhood was one of the last conquered by the Red Army in early February 1945.

The gallery of photographs for this book of Mádi and her family includes a reproduction of part of the blueprints that the builders of the 19 Margaréta utca building supplied to the Budapest Municipal Committee to obtain a construction permit. The blueprint gives the outline of the doctor's flat, showing what appears at first glance to be a five-room apartment. There was an entryway or hallway (*előszoba*), a pantry (*kamra*), a kitchen (*konyha*), a bathroom (*furdő*), and a living room (*szoba*) that doubled as a bedroom. The flat also had a small window balcony (*erkély*) that looked over the backyard and toward the rear of the elementary school that the Gestapo occupied after March 1944. The door to the flat opened onto the building's central staircase. The dimensions of the flat were given in meters, about 7.5 meters by 5.5 meters, that is, under 450 square feet. Although five rooms were listed on the blueprint, the flat was a studio apartment.

Mádi's diaries tell the story of how she protected Lacy and Frédi (and Bö for a while) in the most dangerous of circumstances. Upon taking power, the Arrow Cross conducted a head count of the population in Budapest apartment buildings, looking for Jews living outside yellow-star houses. The doctor was able to hide her guests when the building janitor knocked on her door to make his tally. He recorded just one person living in the flat, the doctor. Despite the danger, Mádi decided the day after Lacy and Frédi arrived to share the news with her friends in the building, commenting, "Elly [Herman], Mrs Láng, Mrs Székely, Klári Bálint all behaving splendidly towards Lacy and her nephew." A few days later, she commented of her circle of neighbors in the building, "All these nice people (not nazi minded) in the house were charming with my people as soon they were here and overwhelmed us with food presents, which is most precious in these days, when even on ration cards you can't get what you ought to get." Mr. Láng, the shoemaker neighbor in the building, and his wife even took young Frédi on a walk outside without being questioned or detained.

Mádi showed great personal courage in shielding her friends, but, as she acknowledged, she needed the additional help of "not nazi minded" neighbors. She felt keenly that the actual Nazis in the building were observing her, and she feared their denunciations. Mária Pató and the Lángs were arrested by Arrow Cross police, Mádi suspected, on a complaint from the Gorrieris and the Janciks. "Darkest middle ages . . . These are the hours of personal revenge," she wrote. The Arrow Cross takeover brought forth the basest impulses among her neighbors, including denunciations to seize other people's property or apartments. "I am rather astonished," she wrote on November 3, "I am not gossiped about and not reported for allied sympathies. May be, Elly is right, these cowards want to have a med doctor in the house, for their own use."

In December the Arrow Cross again required the building janitor to take another census, this time to catch Jews outside the Erzsébetváros ghetto. Mádi hid Lacy and Frédi behind a full-length mirror, and they escaped the janitor's inspection. The building had several pro-Nazi residents, so neither Lacy nor Frédi could leave the apartment for fear of being spotted and reported to the Arrow Cross. Even stepping onto the apartment balcony was risky. Across the backyard stood the neighborhood school that had been taken over by the SS and the Arrow Cross. A sighting of Frédi, who was not on the head count for the flat, would have triggered a knock on the door and the execution in the schoolyard of Mádi, Lacy, Frédi, and Bö.

During air raid alerts over the city, residents, at least non-Jewish ones, were required to take shelter in their building basements. Mádi had to leave her guests in the apartment and take shelter in the basement with the other residents, where she was subject to yet another head count. Finally, she decided in

December to defy the mandatory shelter decree and remain in her flat with her friends during raids. Frédi's father, Lajos, managed to reach Mádi on the phone one day to ask if she, Lacy, and the boy were safe. "I told him everything is OK," the doctor wrote. "We are here and intend to stay here. Most people from our house are sitting hours and hours in the shelter, I do not indulge in such folly." Instead, for the rest of the siege she and some anti-Nazi friends in the building waited out air raids in her flat.

Over the course of four months of Arrow Cross rule, Mádi's days were reduced to a basic struggle for survival. She tried to work at her job; to keep food, water, electricity, and heat in her flat; and to stay safe from bullets and shell fragments. She had not been paid by her National Social Security Administration employer since July but kept going to work anyway out of duty to her patients and to gather scraps of information from fellow staff and patients.

Her world shrank to the streets of the 12th District of Budapest, then further to her 19 Margaréta utca building, and finally to her one-bedroom flat. Her diaries from October 15, 1944, through February 8, 1945, are an unfolding account of how she, Lacy, Frédi, and for a while Bö experienced the Battle of Budapest. On November 10 Bö Tárnocsy took her chances with the Arrow Cross gunmen and slipped out of Mádi's flat to seek other shelter, making use of Mádi's own identification papers for protection against police stops. In December Mádi was able to find some cyanide for Bö in case her friend had to choose the method of her death. Then all contact was severed between the two friends until March, when Mádi learned with pleasure that Bö had survived in the Pest ghetto.

Mádi witnessed the roundup and forced march of some of the more than forty thousand Jewish women from Budapest who were sent in November and December to dig antitank ditches to defend Vienna. "I felt my eyes hot with tears and resentment," she wrote of the cruel treatment that Arrow Cross guards inflicted upon hundreds of Jewish women she saw at the November 10 roundup while she was taking a ferry across the Danube, but to her further shame, "people on the ferry did not have any sympathy with them." Her sister Margit, who lived near Magyaróvár, by the former Hungarian-Austrian frontier, "saw on the Vienna highway rows of Jewish cadavers." Others in her circle of friends were oblivious to Jewish suffering, prompting Mádi to record on November 15 that her friends "would still hope for G. victory, as the best solution. I can't help being disgusted with these friends."

After the Arrow Cross coup, Mádi continued to serve on the Oti medical staff. Indeed, on November 9 she was named chief of the ENT (Ear-Nose-Throat) Department. Later that month, the Arrow Cross regime ordered Oti's top administrators to flee west to Austria with what was left of the government, yet another order she ignored. However, she did not make it to what she called "office hours" most days, with December 23 her last day on the job, just as the Soviet army was about to close the circle around Budapest, trapping a combined German-Hungarian army and somewhere around one million civilians inside the ring.

For Further Reading

Mádi regarded the members of the Arrow Cross in Budapest as uncultured, semiliterate opportunists engaged in an often-drunken orgy of violence. Scholars of the Arrow Cross Party, both before the October coup and after, have tried to put its history into a wider perspective of other Fascist movements in and outside Europe, and readers may wish to consult the work of Phillip Morgan, *Fascism in Europe, 1919–1945* (London: Routledge, 2002). Morgan places Hungarian Fascism among the "second wave" of European movements and finds that the Arrow Cross appealed to more than just the hooligans decried by Mádi. The doctor was attuned to both men and women in her apartment building who held pro-Nazi views, including some of the women at 19 Margaréta utca. On the history of women in the Arrow Cross, see Andrea Pető, *The Women of the Arrow Cross Party: Invisible Hungarian Perpetrators in the Second World War* (London: Palgrave Macmillan, 2020). A memoir of how one Jewish family managed to evade the Arrow Cross terror in Budapest is found in Tivadar Soros, *Masquerade: Dancing around Death in Nazi-Occupied Hungary*, translated by Paul Soros (London: Canongate Books, 2000). Mádi does not record any meetings or dealings with the Swedish diplomat Raoul Wallenberg; however, readers may learn more about Wallenberg's heroism as an ordinary person facing extraordinary evil in the book by Paul A. Levine, *Raoul Wallenberg in Budapest: Myth, History and Holocaust* (London: Vallentine, Mitchell, 2010).

~

OCT. 9, MONDAY.

I am told, that the passenger traffic's suspension was caused by the nyilas plans for a "putsch." The government's intention was, knowing about the plans, to have nyilas workmen far from Bpest. The head of the putsch—beside Szálasi[1]—was Bárdossy, who apparently has entirely lost his head because of wounded vanity, since his dismission from the premiership.

9:50 a.m. Alarms over Kolozs and Nyirség.

Hennyey,[2] the foreign minister of the Lakatos government who is a follower and personal friend of the regent, states, that the old man is still the most

1. Ferenc Szálasi (1897–1946), the Nyilas Party leader who seized power in an October 1944 putsch as the self-proclaimed "leader of the nation." He was indicted, tried, convicted, and executed for war crimes by the Budapest People's Tribunal (1946) (*MEK*).

2. Hennyey Gusztáv (1888–1977), Hungarian foreign minister (1944) (*MEK*).

consciencious and politically most farsighted of the whole lot. He really feels responsibility to sacrifice hundreds of thousands of Hungarian lives, while for Csatay and the others it is nothing but raw material. But, being 76 years old, the last person, who talks to him, has the most chance. On the 7th–8th Sept. we had been on the verge to get out of the war, but somebody, I do not know, who, dissuaded him and so the last historic moment was missed.

SAME NIGHT.

No raid over Bpest today, but alarms over several other places. At Oti laryngology a lot of work.

No meat (beaf, veal, pork or mutton) in restaurants, where people like us used to eat. On rations no meat since two weeks. All is for the G.s.

Today I returned rather late, as I had to see my dentist and returning the streetcars kept stopping all the time, they could simply not go on with so many people hanging all on the stairs. After many delays I got home and soon Mr Láng was here for a check up examination, but he talked about a lot of actual things and was here almost until 9 p.m. Meantime Elly Herman came, but seeing I am not alone, left from the door. It is a bit too much for me anyhow, yesterday the Kartals and Erzsi's mother, the same time Elly, but she came the evening a second time, then Klári Bálint dropped in. To be alone, I have to be rude sometimes and not open the door.

This morning I got a postcard from your aunt Margit. Their naïvity is almost touching. She does not understand, why their Bpest friends (Rittenberger, etc.) seem to be so pessimistic in their letters. They, the Magyaróvár people, are cheerful and know from informations from the soldiers on leave, that G. parachutists have occupied (does she mean: reoccupied?) the Carpathian passes, the Russian troups are in a cauldron here and nearing their inverted Stalingrad! [. . .] With regards the Russians, if in a cauldron, they are moving rather freely, considering, they announce today the occupation of Karcag, Hajdúböszörmény, Kaba, Zenta, Obecse, etc. (Tiszafüred, our Ida cook's home).

OCTOBER 10, TUESDAY.

In the county Sopron so many refugees[3] have fled, that a *bed* for a month costs 1000P, an egg 8–10 P. [. . .]

Neutrals expect a climax in the near future as the Jewish girls, who were accepted by the Swedish legation in their care a few months before (but left to stay at home) were hurriedly collected yesterday into Swedish houses.

3. Mádi's subsequent annotation: "1969. These are Nyilas."

The G.s seem to be rather cruel with their best servants. Pista Antal, who did everything for them in matter of propaganda, has to stay, where he is, at Kircell, in his well known villa. I happen to know, he had plans of taking refuge, apparently he can not. Or, does he expect, to turn over to the red side?

The vitality of the old man Churchill is splendid. I just hear on BBC's morning news, he is in Moscow, hardly back from Quebec.

There is a story about a lady in Tusnád (Transylvania), mother in law of a gentleman in the foreign office, which demonstrates, in war so much depends on luck and not all troups are behaving the same way. This lady remained in her house at Tusnád, when Russian troups came in. A R. army major was lodged in her house, who spoke French. They used to lunch and dine together. She told him frankly, how we were frightened by propaganda and what a surprise their correct behaviour was and asked his advice, to stay on or to go to Bpest. The major told her, his soldiers were all right but he does not know, what troups will follow, so she better takes refuge. He gave two men, who helped her with all her luggage across some secret place on the border and here she is in Bpest. [. . .]

SAME AFTERNOON.

Quite exceptionally I had nothing to do after my Oti hours, so, instead of luncheon, I went up the Gellért hill, just the same as years before, towards our old place. [. . .] Somebody was scrubbing the veranda stairs. G. speech could be heard. The orchard, as much as I could see, does not mind a bit, whether it is us, or the G.s. or anybody else, who is admiring its multicoloured beauty. Nor the view on the Danube curve. It looked just the same, as in 1938 or 39. I went up, seeing it again, I hoped everything would be settled but no, nothing is settled. [. . .]

Anyway, back in my flat . . . I am positive, the place never belonged and never will belong to anybody as much it belonged to us and nobody can be so happy there, as we have been, when undisturbed.

According to today's papers we are defending the country already at Szolnok. What a splendid thing this G. alliance! But I am told, Russian troups are at Kecskemét. If this is true, Elko won't be able to come up to Bpest any more. I wonder, whether they are going to stay there, at Halas. Morally, it would be compulsory to stay, as is the case with rom. cath. priests.[4]

This month's flour rations, the last three potatoe rations (6 kg) and some other necessary foodstuff are no more available. I am a bit anxious for the

4. Mádi refers here to the directive of the cardinal primate of Hungary to Roman Catholic priests and nuns to stay at their assignments with their parishioners and not to flee the Red Army, even if the clergy had to suffer death, in other words, "martyrdom."

apparently coming siege of the city, for I do not see I could hold out ten days, not to mention the period after.

OCT. 11, WEDNESDAY.

The city looks very ill at ease. People discussing news on a low voice, looking round cautiously every instant, then go on whispering.

At Oti a new colleague turned out today, a refugee from Szeged. They all fled *on orders*.

This cutting from today's Pest is the latest. There is no more talk about defending Hungary. They are going to defend Austria. CLIPPING: Felhívás sáncmunkára Ostmark lakosságához.[5]

On the streetcars today G. soldiers traveled from Eastern to Southern station, they are coming from Szolnok. The Kecskemét labour service camp was dissolved, leaders were the first to flee.

Almost no food to get. No bread, flour, not even Ovomaltine, which is because of its price a luxury. I am worried, at best I can hold out until for a week, not more. And the example of Warsaw shows, the Russians are not always in a hurry.[6] Oti did not send my cheques for the last two months, so at present I am out of money too. It is a scandalous neglect, the work I did from the 16 of July on is not yet paid, and will be never paid, may be, if a sudden overturn comes.

I have spent an hour with the Hermans this evening. Elly has a paper (to be posted on her door, when the occupation actually happened) from the Swedish legation, stating her Dutch citizenship in Russian and Roumanian language.

They have observed the G. soldiers in the next school to have slaughtered a pig two days before ago and to take carloads of different objects away, at present the building is almost empty, not more, then six or seven soldiers stay there. They hope and made the conclusion, the G.s are getting out of Bpest. On the other side they observed, that rifles and some smaller things, hidden in rocks (probably handgrenades) are smuggled into the opposite house by Hungarian soldiers. I suppose, this ought to be the Hitler oath and the nyilas-arming I mentioned before. A danger for us. [. . .]

Kolozsvár and Debrecen, besides Szeged taken simultaneously by the Russians today.

5. "Calling for Work on Behalf of the Austrian Homeland."

6. The Red Army reached the outskirts of Warsaw in early August 1944 but did not fully capture the city until January 1945.

OCT. 12, THURSDAY.

Some action seems to be planned by the average people of these parts. With early black-out no noises used to be on the street after 9–10 p.m., last night many people came down from the hill side (may be only from the next school building) at quarter to midnight. They came in formation, but no soldiers, spoke Hungarian and mostly men. Restaurants close at 11 p.m., so they did not come from any of them. None of the usual cheery talks, you hear after some drinks. As most of these people around, feel nazi, I am afraid there is prepared some program like action may be, they are trained by the G.s.

SAME NIGHT.

At 2 p.m. alarm over Bpest, which found me at the Eastern station. I did not like the idea to stay just there, in case of a raid, so walked towards home. Nothing happened over Bpest, so I sat on a bench at the hill side, on the transversal road. Three G.s came and crowded me off the bench, without even saying: excuse. This is their charm.

Before and after noon swarms of G. lorries trucks streaming westwards through Bpest. I wish, they would go away for ever.

Elko turned up tonight, they have fled from Halas, he seems to be rather shaken. He has noticed some episodes on their trip, which, as he says, mean unmistakable revolution. [. . .]

Eisenhower announced the probability of a sixth winter campaign.

OCT. 13, FRIDAY.

9:41 a.m. Bpest alarmed. It is nice of them, to come so early, so I am not caught at Oti or Eastern Station. [. . .]

1:20 p.m. Bpest alarm off. It is late for Oti, for Ilonka, Rami, etc.

During the alarm the postman brought me a belated cheque from Oti (426P), which was due at the middle of September. I can pay some debts at least now.

SAME NIGHT.

I had to see Bö and Klári. [. . .] At Bö a second alarm caught me, I had to go down to the shelter with them. Luckily it did not last very long, about half an hour. Last night house searching was conducted at many Jewish and non Jewish houses, in the VI and VII districts. In Jewish houses they (Hung. Police officers, detectives and gendarms) were looking for money (over 3000Ps), jewels and labour service men. In non Jewish houses for soldiers, deserters. No atrocities. A police officer found in a Jewish flat gold coins (érmepénz) in a cigarettes-case, covered them up with a newspaper and did not say a word about it.

I am told, all our bridges are undermined. I should not like to be left stranded on the other side.

Coming home I switched on the radio on the African service of the BBC. Old man Wickham Steed[7] gave a commentary on the situation to be expected in near future in Europe. He must be a bit senile, as he stated, the Hungarian gentry was the cause of the Monarchy's dismemberment and caused the unlucky Trianon Treaty. Well, this is much, even for me. I am one of this gentry, I know and acknowledge very many faults of them and am really not so keen about their survival. But to state, they had something to do, but suffer and loose by the treaties and by the dissolution of the Monarchy, well, that is too thick. Even now, in this war, the landed gentry was much more anti-G. The pro G. elements have been the industrials and lower middle class.

The fall of Kolozsvár and Szeged were admitted in today's papers.

7:55 p.m. Airdanger signal over Bpest. The third time today. [. . .]

Athens is taken by Greek partisans. There could not be much G. resistance. Aix la Chapelle 85 percent destroyed. It is a lunacy, what G. leaders are doing with cities.

Churchill arranged marvelously the day's difficult problems: Bulgarians are going out of Yougoslavia and Greece, London-Polish leaders are invited to Moscow. [. . .]

Second BBC the Hungarian government had asked for armistice terms.

9 p.m. Bpest alarm off. No raid.

OCTOBER 14, SATURDAY.

At 10:05 a.m. alarms begin over Kanizsa, Zala, Szeged (The latest means only the district, as the town is no more in our hands). Yesterday's main target was Székesfehérvár.

According to BBC's last night and this morning news, our government has asked for armistice terms. It was not commented unsympathetically. As it was several times repeated, there may be something in it. I did not trust our government with even so much sense, I was prepared, "we" shall fight on after Germany has laid down the arms. Or at least, when Bpest lays in ruins.

We do not know yet, what the G troups are going to do at this turn of the affairs. What amount of destruction will follow.

10:15 a.m. Airdanger over Bpest. Alarm over Sopron. This looks like Austrian objects.

I had been up with the Hermans' two evenings: they, especially the old lady (Mrs Brunowsky) are desperate, because of Lily and family. They are wild with

7. Henry Wickham Steed (1871–1956), former Vienna correspondent and later editor for *The Times* (London).

terror before the Russians, plan suicide combined with shooting invaders, in the meantime plan to fly to Austria (blackmarket, that is the only possible way to enter Austria, price 100,000P/person), leave everything, house, 300 acres of orchard *here*, factory, all behind, because the idiot, their son, a lieutenant instills fear into them. I suppose, this will quiet down, I remember well Apu and Lajoska, who planned to kill their families and now are sitting quietly, waiting to see.

I am told by the Hermans, down the shelter a terrible noise all the time, as all children are back in town again. Young Mrs Németh is back too, is quite crazy and exalted, repeats that she came to die with her husband. [. . .]

I am told by the refugee M.D. colleague in Oti, that when all took refuge from the Szeged hospital (on orders), four nuns remained there. Considering the wild rumours in currency, this is heroism.

The prince-primate's call to all priests, to stay on their posts, even in face of martyrdom, I believe, you will agree with me in the hope, no Russian general will make the mistake, to hurt any priest. Other question, what the mob will do to some of them in the interval, before the Russians come in. Some of the priests are unfortunately corpulent, which is a source of suspicion with hungry people, they are living too well.

11:05 a.m. Bpest alarmed. Just the moment, I was off for Oti.

Elko and Klári were looked for by the Gestapo twice, about two weeks ago. At their Bpest flat it was told, they are at Halas, but nothing followed there. Now they are not living in their own flat. It seems, no official warrant was given out against them, but some personal act of hate, some enemy, who had a Gestapo friend. [. . .]

SAME AFTERNOON.

Soon I was off for the office. No streetcars were available for a long time and when available, they were slow as a snail. At 2 p.m., at the end of my workhours I was still at Apponyi square, progressing with a speed ½ m/min. [. . .]

Yesterday Bonczos, the minister for the interior was dismissed and Baron Péter Schell[8] came in his place, the husband of Kati Teleki. Today there is talk in town, that Horthy would have fled to Germany and a Szálasi (nyilas) government has the power. If true, the joke can not last long. G.s would never consent to a Szálasi régime, if everything would not be lost here already.

At Nikáczy one kg of grapes 18 P and apples 13 P today. Shopwindows—except fruit—empty.

According to tonight's BBC news, the Times recent article expects the Hungarian government's answer on Russian armistice terms any hour. So it ought

8. Péter Schell (1898–1974), minister of the interior spokesman (*MEK*).

to be serious, the Times being government organ. But if the nyilas party has the power in hand, the answer will be: we fight on.

I did not switch on Bpest radio since March 19, day of the G. invasion. In a short time it will be interesting again.

9 p.m. I was just thinking about you, my dearest, when somebody rang the bell and George Gyetvay stood before my door. Just in time, to prevent cozying. He is here again apparently likes me, as I like him. Elly came in the meantime to put through a call from my flat, they have met before. The $ price (for banknotes) today = 120 P, as I am told.

Gyurka tells me that general Bakay[9] was arrested by the G.s. a few days ago. Reason: by the last "putsch" attempt he ordered to arrest some of the "nyilas" officers at Szombathely. This proves the supposition: the G.s are flirting *now* with the nyilas, their enemies since the occupation and using them for their purposes.

BBC's late night news announce, that Bonczos, former minister for the interior, has been taken to Germany. He suppressed last week the nyilas putsch. So that is the reason, why Schell came in his place.

Since the third day it is with persistence, BBC mentions the Hungarian armistice.[10] The latest about it, Turkish news agencies report a Hungarian armistice delegation to be on their way to Moscow. Recently since the rather friendly Churchill remark, even commentators speak in a more friendly way about us. Yesterday somebody said on the radio, though the Hungarian nation can not be freed from all responsibility, the country is in a very difficult position. This is more, in my experiences than we deserve.

OCT. 15, SUNDAY.

One of the funny things, Dr Szivér told me yesterday, was, that our War office is going to organize lectures for M.D.s about the special treatment of burns, gas, etc., all in connexion with streetfighting. I put the question, when is it going to begin and how long to last, she said, about the end of Oct, lasting for six weeks. Well! This I call optimism. They believe, Russian troups will wait outside politely, until they finish their lectures.[11]

---

9. Szilárd Bakay (1892–1946), a lieutenant general in the Royal Hungarian Army. He was arrested by the Germans (1944) and then arrested by the Soviets (1946), tried and convicted in Soviet court for war crimes in Ukraine, and executed (1946) (*MEK*). Mádi's subsequent annotation: "Army Corps Commander at Bpest."

10. See "Hungarian Truce Expected Hourly: Armistice Held Contingent on Exit from Adjacent Lands and Arrest of Germans," *NYT*, October 15, 1944.

11. Mádi's subsequent annotation: "1969. P.S. They did."

SAME NIGHT.

As I started for the hill this noon, going on the street, I heard the radio, giving a proclamation, by the regent to the people of Hungary, in which he announced to have asked for armistice terms and explained, why he had to abandon G. alliance. It was all very correct. I am told, at 12 o'clock Veesenmayer was received by the regent, when he told him the facts, at 1 p.m. The proclamation was read in the radio and a few minutes later our soldiers began to march on the hill (Gellért) and form lines. The street was very quiet, but civilians could go undisturbed. I reached the hill safely. G. soldiers knew the news already, sat and stood around their houses. [. . .]

As the radio repeated several times the proclamation and telephon calls could be put through, radio and telephon centrals ought to be in Hungarian hands. Since about 3 p.m no more telephon and since about 5 p.m. a proclamation in the radio from Veres, head of the Gen. Staff,[12] that fight is going on, I suppose, these buildings went over into nazi hands. Veres is known to be a nazi. I am told, 18,000 soldiers are in the area of Bpest, it seems, many of them turned out to be unreliable and attached to the G.s. I am told about a colonel, the neighbour of Gizi, who went away with the motto: we shall fight on!

Coming home with Apu, at 5:03 p.m. we found our housegate shut, the janitor standing before, putting the fierce question: where is the gentleman going? I told him, he is my guest, we came up, made a tea and discussed what to do. He was going to stay the night, I meant to go to some neighbour, but because of the janitor Apu decided to go somewhere else. I accompanied him, feeling rather anxious for his safety, as his person is precious now. About this all sometime later.

Returning for the second time home, I asked the janitor, what is it all about. He told me, the afternoon a gendarm captain with five men came round, ordered, that from 5 p.m. until 7 a.m. the housegates must be closed, no stranger may enter the houses, especially no Jews. These gendarms, their barracks behind our house and next to the G. occupied schoolbuilding are fraternizing with the G.s, put up machineguns on the roof, dug trenches, so we have every hope of close fighting.

I am very worried for my friends, Bö, Lacy, etc. This night may prove fatal for them.

---

12. General Lajos Veress (1889–1976), commander of the Hungarian Second Army, was arrested by the Arrow Cross on October 16, 1944. He was repatriated to Hungary (1945), indicted, tried, convicted, and imprisoned by the Budapest People's Tribunal. He was released (1956) and resettled in the United States (*MEK*).

We are in a revolution. Much depends on how far or how near are allied troups.

Our nazis in the house are pale and trembling. The Némeths took two suitcases out of the house hastily. I went to see the Hermans, then to Mrs Székely, where I found Klári Bálint and Maria Pató. I am told, the Gorrieris disappeared three days ago. The janitor says, all houses will be searched tonight. [. . .]

9:43 p.m. shooting at the next corner. Senseless. Hungarian radio giving some lengthy text, but with blinds down, I can not hear from outside and my radio is no good on medium waves.

10 p.m. I was asked by my neighbour, to go over. The lengthy speech on the radio was a proclamation by the Szálasi government (who seem to have seized the radio building) to go on by the side of our great allies, etc. etc., Horthy having sold out the nation. Afterwards the Eastern frontline brotherhood called up all members to report at once.

I am not sure, how far they are. I do not believe, they could get into the fortress or the Royal castle. May be, they have only the radio and telephon center, nothing else. I hope, in two days Szálasi will give his proclamations from Sopron or Vienna.

10:20 p.m. a big explosion. Meantime BBC mentions recent Bpest developments. London called all Hung. military forces to march on Bpest, to relieve it from G. domination. [. . .]

OCT. 16, MONDAY.

The night nothing but occasional shots and the steps of the guard on our street.

At 6 a.m. sharp the siege of Bpest began. Machine-guns, AAC (used on the surface, as no aircraft is present at yet).

I have a holyday-ish feeling. No work or going anywhere will be possible today. The adventure, we felt to come for a long time, has begun.

At 7 a.m. mostly quiet. Shots ceased, only occasionally here or there one. People cautiously venturing out on the streets. No streetcars, as I can hear.

8:45 a.m. I hear somebody out the street, one can not go over the bridges to the Pest side.

Veron, the English speaking servant of the Horchlers told me last night, when I met her on the street, there are women organizations, shooting squadrons, against the Russian troups. This is the good old G. prescription, to involve civilian population.

I do not believe in the success of the Szálasi program (that is nazi propaganda), to fight on. After five years of war, with empty stomachs, always that fellow will be right, who proclaims peace. People, who are making most noise about fighting on, mean, that other people should fight on, not themselves.

Something was said on the radio, about Jews being interned. Now a speech by Szálasi. Alarms signalled between. Everybody called up, to return to work. Without streetcars and bridges, I should like to know, how?

Two G. soldiers with rifles and steel helmets going up and down our street.

After 11 a.m. I left for Oti. I could get down to the Southern station by train, from there nothing, you had to walk. I went through the tunnel, strongly guarded by lots of G. machinegun soldiers. At the Buda side of the Chain-bridge[13] one could pass only with ID papers, first by Hungarian after by G. soldiers. Round the Fortress hill everywhere G. guns, armed cars, machine-guns and fully armed soldiers. At the Pest side of the Chainbridge I have seen blood at three different places. At one place, beside the blood, in a heap the belongings of a soldier were on the pavement. Going over to Apponyi square, I have not seen other open shops as Borhegyi and Molnár és Moser.[14] Grocer's shops are sold out almost entirely, there is nothing left in there but surrogates.

LEAFLET: *Honvédek!*[15]

Here is a leaflet, I found on the street this morning. You will see on the absence of "accents" (French) on the second big letters, it was printed in Germany, or with types got from Germany.

The present situation does not mean at all a preponderance of the arrow-cross party. It means only, Gs have the power in hand and they use the nyilas as camouflage.[16]

According to a latest radio order, Jews, all, exceptioned, etc. have to wear the yellow star again, else they will be deported. But just the same, they are arrested on the streets, stars or no stars. Shooting was going on at the Oti quarters area and Népszínház u. at 2 p.m., later at 4 p.m. [. . .]

On BBC I have heard the full text of Horthy's proclamation.[17] It is all right what he said, only too late. It should have been done much earlier, months ago.

---

13. The Chain Bridge, so called because of the iron chains from which the bridge is suspended, is also known as the Széchenyi Bridge (see map 2). It was built in the 1840s.

14. Perfumer and fashion emporium in Budapest.

15. "Patriots!" The leaflet is reproduced in Lévai, *Black Book*, 74–75. The accent appears in the word *Honvédek* at the top of the leaflet but not in its second appearance.

16. Late on the night of October 15, after the Germans had kidnapped his son, Regent Horthy placed himself and his country under formal German protection. The next day, the Germans forced Horthy to resign and turn over responsibility for the civil government to the Arrow Cross.

17. Regent Horthy's statement in Hungarian ("A kiugrási kísérlet") is available at http://www.rubicon.hu/magyar/oldalak/1944_oktober_15_a_kiugrasi_kiserlet/. An English translation ("Regent Horthy's Radio Proclamation") can be found at http://www.hungarianhistory.com/lib/montgo/montgo20.htm.

On radio Bpest Szálasi orders all foreign office officials to report tomorrow at 8:30 a.m. in the foreign office. So apparently they have the Fortress hill or part of it in their hands. [. . .]

At about 9 p.m. a new proclamation was read into the radio in the name of the regent, taking back all he proclaimed yesterday. It is either he was captured by the G.s. and forced to retract it or rather do I believe the proclamation to be apocriphous [*sic*], not made by him.

10:10 p.m. I hear on BBC that regent Horthy has resigned. So the taking back was really forced upon him and he is in G. hands. If they could not prepare this armistice action better, why in heaven's name did he not resign seven months ago?

OCT. 17, TUESDAY.

10 a.m. distant cannon shots.

BBC announces, the resignation of our regent is very doubtful. Shooting continues. [. . .]

SAME NIGHT.

I got two tel. messages this morning, one from Erzsi's family. Promised to go there about 2 p.m. Going to Oti, I heard already from the Boulevard, until the Eastern Station explosions, not so far off. At Eastern station all streetcars motionless at the Fiumei ut, people came rushing from the Oti direction, one could not go near it. Many people standing around and discussing news. I listened to some of them, all spoke about alleged Jewish resistance, hand grenades thrown by them, etc. This is again a well known G. prescription, why should they throw hand grenades just now, with the odds mostly against them? [. . .] . . . It seems, this morning the deportation of the Jews began and where they did not open the gates, G.s and nyilas worked with hand grenades and even armed cars. A regular pogrom,[18] followed by a mighty wave of propaganda: people are all shocked by the Jewish behaviour. [. . .]

Going to the Alkotmány u, I found out, Erzsi, her mother and husband, together with all other Jewish inhabitants of the house were already taken away, at about 10 a.m.

No news from Bö either. I had to see Ilus and arranged things with her. On my way home I have seen several groups of Jews, herded by nyilas soldiers. Was late at home, only at 4 p.m., found guests waiting for me. About this day I have to tell you so much, some time later.[19]

---

18. Lévai, *Black Book*, 342, wrote, "Szalasi's reign begins with a pogrom."

19. Mádi's subsequent annotation: "1969. Lacy and Frédi arrived."

Second BBC, the commander of the first H. army has gone over to the Russians.

OCT. 18, WEDNESDAY.

The morning we slept until 9 a.m., a good thing, considering the poor accommodation possibilities. Two telephon calls. [. . .] At Ilonka I got cigarettes and matches. After Oti I had to go to see Pravdáné. I lunched with her, it is touching the way, they care for me. They bought a goose and her husband insisted upon her inviting me for the liver! She spoke so excitedly over the phone though, I was very much afraid to find some uninvited guests in their flat. But nothing of the sort.

Mrs Láng did some shopping for us, Elko came, later Gyurka Gyetvay. My other two guests in the bathroom meantime. We had a hearty discussion, Gyurka is all right, I can tell you. Elko told us some details about last Sunday. We had breakfast at Hotel Hungaria when explosions and shots were heard in the neighbourhood. Young Miki Horthy was kidnapped by the Gestapo.[20] This hastened the break out of events, the streets leading to the Fortress hill were hastily undermined, Miki H. is under arrest at the Svábhegy Gestapo headquarters, his father very probably taken away by the G.s.

At Halas a labour service train was ahead of a Gestapo train, it was in their way, destroyed the six wagons with the labour service men (coming from the Bor mines, Yougoslavia)[21] only four of them escaped. Hand grenades, machine-guns, etc. The old tale was told to the people of Halas. Gestapo has saved Halas, as these labour service men came armed against the town of Halas.

Tonight's Magyarország has the news, the regent and premier Lakatos[22] has given themselves into G. "protection."

Elly, Mrs Láng, Mrs Székely, Klári Bálint[23] all behaving splendidly towards Lacy and her nephew.

OCT. 19, THURSDAY.

The noon papers brought a new order about all Jews, whether foreign citizens, or married to non Jews, or exceptioned. They had to go into Jewish houses

20. Miklós Horthy Jr. (1907–93), younger son of the regent, was imprisoned by the Germans until May 1945. He was liberated by the US Army and resettled in Portugal after the war.

21. The Hungarian government sent labor service Jews to German-occupied Serbia to work in copper mines starting in 1943. Braham, *The Politics of Genocide*, 2:1208. The miners were returned to Hungary in 1944 and murdered.

22. Géza Lakatos (1890–1967), prime minister (August–October 1944) (*MEK*).

23. All neighbors in the 19 Margaréta utca building.

until 8 p m. tonight.[24] Think of Tercsi néni etc. what a terrible situation for them, who have since long years lost all contact with Jews. Besides, Jewish houses are so full, it is hardly believable, more persons could be put into those flats—19 persons for example in a three room flat. At 6:30 p.m. the radio says, the order is suspended, for the time being. Do you notice the system? Besides, many army officers are intermarried.

One of my friends was arrested two days ago. A neighbour went after him, when he was on his way towards a safe refuge.

The afternoon I had to see Mrs Németh, Mrs Láng and after the hairdresser Lujzi Horchler. [. . .] . . . At the hairdresser I met Elza Beck, Gizi's sister I managed not to give her my hand.

At Moktár,[25] as Gizi tells me, tomorrow all clerks have to sign a statement, then take an oath on the new régime. All, who do not sign the paper, will be interned. I do not know, what am I going to do, if at Oti something similar is expected from us.[26]

OCT. 20, FRIDAY.

A busy day. Mrs Mogain, Tercsi néni, an attempt to see Mamuci, here Elly, the Lángs, several tel. calls.

Going up to Mamuci at Hegyalja ut, I had to turn around half-way, as about two–three hundred Hung. soldiers lined up there on the terrace-like streets and entered the houses full armed, rifles, machine guns and some other two–three men carried devices. [. . .] . . . One BBC news in G. language this after noon mentioned street fighting in Bpest between Horthy troups and G. SS men. No other news repeated this item but sure, from time to time we can hear shots outside.

Lacy had heard by a misfortune tonight the news about her brother. You can imagine her terrible state of mind. We know the address, where he is at present and Mr Láng believes it to be the headquarters of the G. "death head" legion. God help us.

Tonight's news are heartening about the landing on the central Philippines, the fall of Aachen, Belgrade and Debrecen. But you see, in the meantime tragedies are happening, which can't be remedied.

OCT. 22, SUNDAY.

I had a very busy day yesterday and had no opportunity to scribble my usual notes. The morning at about 10 an alarm on Bpest was announced, lasted until

24. Szegedy-Maszák, *I Kiss Your Hands*, 169; Lévai, *Black Book*, 345.

25. Hungarian National Central Savings Bank (*Budapesti telefonkönyvek*).

26. See Szegedy-Maszák, *I Kiss Your Hands*, 170, for the oaths demanded of employees at the Foreign Ministry.

noon and afterwards the streetcars were so full, I was still at Apponyi tér at 2 p.m. No Oti for me that day. I went to the family, Marika lives with, yesterday she was missing and knowing her courage, I felt anxious for her [. . .]. I had to see Ilus at Sándor street, there are developments to be awaited. The second alarm got me there, I left and walked over to the Gellért hill. In town one can walk after alarm for about twenty minutes, then streets empty almost entirely and *légó* commanders do not permit people on the streets any more. Pure hysterics, as in these last weeks no bomber came near Bpest, this is the Transdanubian towns' turn now, Székesfehérvár, Szombathely, Győr, where, as I am told, there is no trace left, there was a railway station before.

At home Elly's sister called up with a message for her mother and Klári Bálint wished to speak to me, so I had to go up to both, fetched Klári down to make friends with my guests. All these nice people (not nazi minded) in the house were charming with my people as soon they were here and overwhelmed us with food presents, which is most precious in these days, when even on ration cards you can't get what you ought to get. These friends from the house told me, yesterday's alarm in the shelter was such a noisy business they could not hear when a bomb would have dropped upon the house. Our "nyilas" ladies were quarelling, they used to get extra foodstuff poultry especially, from the party and the day before one family got and the others did not. [. . .] I am so wicked, I was delighted with these developments.

Another funny spot amidst the squalor, we are living in. At the foreign office all doors of the high officials have to stay ajar, a young "nyilas" guard walking up and down before them, just as in a prison. Before every door, when passing it, the guard puts in his bayonet, saying: work! go on with your work! (dolgozni!). Is it not sweet? Apu, I am told, put all old farciculs (akta)[27] on his desk and turns a page whenever the guard passes by.

One kg of grapes 24 P. A farce. The yeast (élesztő), only on black market prices.

I am still not finished with yesterday after noon. Klári was still here, when Mr Láng came and stayed until 8:30 p.m. We were exhausted. Before, in the staircase M. Pató asked me to meet her at Ida, so after I had a cup of soup, I went over, Maria and Kántás and Kertai are dismissed without any notice from Maort, without any compensation. Apczinzer going about with the nyilas armband. [. . .]

No Jewish houses can be entered since Monday morning, no Jewish house can be left by Jews since the same time. In some places, where the janitor is hostile, they are out of reserves and have to starve. I am told, the Kartals are

27. File.

back but Emil missing. Jewish men are taken for labour service from the age of 16 until 60.[28] Women left at home for the while, but without protection. No news from Bö or Klári, I wrote them postcards, but do not know, whether post mail is delivered in these houses, probably not.

Still not finished with yesterday. After Waldbauers I dropped in to Katinka Stolcz, I have lent her a book and it would be dangerous for her, to have it in her house.

The evening finished for me by seeing the Hermans. Coming home, I found everything prepared, bed, cushion, blankets, it is my friend, who works all day. This morning we gave the child over to the Lángs, who are going to take him on an excursion. He is so keen for a walk, which we could not risk. Let us hope there will be no discovery this time, until now the business seems to go safely. [. . .]

At the Foreign Office at 9 a.m. officials have to be in, else they are marked (at 9:03 a.m.) for misbehaviour. All had to take the oath, all were searched going in and coming out at 3 p.m., doors shut in the interval. Paperbaskets and stoves were searched for wastepaper and ashes. Baron Kemény[29] and "brother" Berce, the chief of the most important section, have never seen the inside of a foreign office before . . . Officials are supervised by machine guns and automatic pistols, an old detective, who has his post inside the building for ten years, was taken his revolver away. All these things are like a farce only it is difficult to find your place in it. One of the gentlemen made an attempt of suicide, dayly one or two are put under arrest.

Posters appeared today on the streets, Jews have to report on labour service from 16–60 of age, Jewesses from 16–40. They have to take with them blankets, warm clothing, pots, saucepans, food for three days. For a week they could do no shopping though. In the Tisza Kálmán tér district, where whole houses were evacuated on Monday's battle day, they were robbed entirely, one, two, three times in succession. [. . .]

OCT. 23, MONDAY.

At Szt István krt 5 I had the following story today: the janitor's son in law, a nyilas himself, had three nyilas friends with him and last Monday morning

28. On October 20 the Arrow Cross rounded up all Jewish men between age sixteen and sixty to dig trenches to defend the capital against the advancing Red Army. See Lévai, *Black Book*, 348–49, 352.

29. Gábor Kemény (1910–1946), minister of foreign affairs in Szálasi's Government of National Unity. He was indicted, tried, convicted, and executed by the Budapest People's Tribunal for war crimes (1946) (*MEK*).

ordered all Jews (Zsidók) down, into the cellar and turned the key on them. There they were left with short interruptions until Thursday night, when the nyilas party told their man to let them up into their flats. I suppose, you ask me, why did not somebody report the case to the police?

Coming home this afternoon from my work (Oti, Vilma, Klári) I got a message from Erzsike to do something for her. I immediately went out again, rain, darkness, fighting for streetcars, etc., at the end could not find the place (a convent) in the black out and had to return home at about 7 p.m. I was exhausted and almost in hysterics. It is terrible, both black out on the streets and streetcars and people's revolutionary rudeness. Tomorrow I have to begin again, though I know ahead, it will be useless. E. wrote a letter to a nun at Sacré Coeur, but they will not be able—even in case if willing—to help them.

OCT. 24, TUESDAY.

These days are so rapidly rushing by, in spite of all we have to suffer. [. . .] The Sacré Coeur convent has given up one aisle of its building to the Swedish Red Cross.[30] Scores of ill fitting people are crowded inside. It is difficult to gain admission. [. . .] This can not be done either, they are full with children and refugees, two sleeping on one mattress. Oti finished, I went with the answer to Mrs Novák then to the city, to get a box of Ovomaltine from Molnár & Moser, I bought yesterday. The last ones for a long time, I am afraid. Coming home I met Gizi and we came home together.

In today's papers lots of draftings (calling up?) are announced, from 1896 until 1926 born years (évjáratok). Mr Láng has to go. Iván has to go. Gizi told me, Iván called her up the morning, from the University, reading the papers, whether she could find work for him at the Optical works (Heinzi) as war-plant workers are temporarily left at their places exempted. Considering Iván's pro G. sympathies, I was very much astonished, why is he not eager to fight for his friends? A different thing, theory and practice.

My friend, here with me is absolutely tactful. We do not disturb each other in the least. But with the poor child it is more difficult, I can hardly stand him. He gets on my nerves.

OCT. 25, WEDNESDAY.

The whole town looks so revolutionary, so full of expecting some sudden change, though most people do not know, what sort. Streetcars are entered on both sides, in spite of all protests of the ticket collector. So many stray dogs on

30. See Lévai, *Black Book*, 355–56, for the work of Raoul Wallenberg in issuing safe-conduct passes and the Arrow Cross government's willingness, initially, to accept them.

the streets. Forlorn, poor, hungry, lost creatures, lost by refugees from villages, may be, from Transylvania and they look round bewildered on the platforms, squares, streets.

This morning I got a message from Bö, had to meet a friend of hers in the city. At Oti the news were spread everywhere, by everybody, that a revolution has broken out in Russia and Stalin killed. It is nonsense, of course and so I told them. Would there be a real basis for the news, the newspapers and radios would be full with them. At Oti I got a telephon message from Erzsi. They are out of their house and I had to see them in the afternoon. With this friend Ernő Szabadhegyi we helped them out from an other yellow star house and by now they are on their way out of town, I hope.

Nothing to be had on our ration cards but new orders announce death penalty on spreading of non-official news, on hiding Jews, on leaving your workplace, etc. etc. [. . .]

The afternoon, going back to the other side of the town, on Margit körút, I have seen about three–four hundred Russian prisoners of war. They were guarded by gendarms. At first sight I took them for H. soldiers, the colour and shape of their uniforms is about the same. The type of the men was very much alike to our peasants too, middle statured, stocky, with prominent cheekbones, hair blondish-brown. There were some very Asiatic types too, but not many. They were looking fierce and angry, no wonder, as some of them went bare foot. Shoes are precious with the G.s. These prisoners of war were meant as a sort of triumph-march, I suppose, but behind them G. cars and trucks came, a retreat from the Miskolc region, then refugees on Russian vehicles.

Yesterday's papers announce, 16–17 years old boys will be used here to fight tanks. They are not even drafted, it will be just "levente" duty.

OCT. 27, FRIDAY.

Much business done yesterday for Erzsike, Ernő, Lacy. The evening a telephon message from Károly, he is safe out, with his younger brother at Csepel. He was meant though for Svábhegy-Gestapo. How he got out, we do not know yet. Maria Pató was arrested last night by four nyilas-civilians and a policeman. They said, her papers were not in order. At first she was left here, then, after half an hour they returned (I suppose, without the policeman) and took her away. A few minutes later an alarm was signalled and a prolongued Russian raid followed. We sat in my flat, but the affair was rather close, lasted for about two hours.

SAME EVENING.

[. . .] Especially at Oti we all were desperately cold, sitting there for hours without heating in a half demolished building. I had to see Ernő Szabadhegyi, after yesterday's transactions, got a new note from Erzsike. Went to look up Maria Pató's aunt at Havas utca but did not find her at home. From my young neighbour I heard this afternoon, that Mr and Mrs Láng are missing, on their door the same arrow cross sign as on M. Pató's door. We do not know, when did it happened, but Lacy heard two shots very near this noon. I am very worried about them but do not even know, how to begin to help them. Darkest middle ages.

I suppose, you will never believe, all these things could really happen.

Elko was here, his Klári is working for the International Red Cross as press agent. From different sides but references about Russian occupants behaviour towards the inhabitants. They organize local authorities everywhere, put at the head of it some popular, well known man, an M.D. or even a local leading priest or at Szeged Prof. Szentgyörgyi[31] (of the Nobel prize).

A telephon call from Klári Bálint, Elly and Mrs Székely here. The janitor has told Ida, that the Långs were arrested last night, the same time as Pató. These are the hours of personal revenge, I suspect the Gorrieris and the janitor family behind these reports. Very probably the Gorrieris have a friend, who would like to have Pató's flat. And these three people may vanish for ever.

Last night's hits were many fold, I know about Corvin department store, which is burned out (G. Co, serves them right), opposite Rókus hospital the Szövetkezeti bolt (another store). People on the streetcar said: it was meant for the hospital!

OCT. 28, SATURDAY.

Here we are in the flat, nothing happened. Elko called up the early morning, whether we are still here. We were prepared for house searching, it was so with Pató and the Långs and the latter were my patients, came often here. I suppose now, that no more poultry is distributed among the nyilas party members, they are paid with the fulfilling of personal revenges. Two days before a general round up of "suspicious" elements, yesterday house searches and arrests. Our people were taken away by foot, I am afraid, not far, just to the next building, the gendarmery. The night, at 1:30 a.m. I heard shots from there. Very probably, these revenge actions are at an end for the present and we may be safe for the while.

The more I am attached to my Jewish friends, there is a certain Jewish type I hate, and the best joke is, this seven years old child is just the worst type, whom I try hard to save. No bad quality, we used to know as Jewish qualities, is missing.

31. Albert Szent-Györgyi (1893–1986), chemist, member of the Hungarian Academy of Sciences (MTA), and Nobel Prize winner (1937) (*MEK*).

SAME NIGHT.

Almost 1:30 a.m. we were having a talk with Lacy. These times are weighing heavily upon her. Her mother, her sister in law, now her brother's case is a bit too much even for her.

OCT. 29, SUNDAY.

The evening and today the morning and even in the noon hours alarms over Bpest, but no raid followed . . . After the first alarm was over, I set out for the hill, on my usual Sunday program to the Sebes. Apu is cheering up, as he hopes to be kicked out from the F.O.[32] On the way I met a couple of soldiers, rank and file, one of whom, with broad, peasant accent said: "I hear all the time, we have beaten the Russians back, we have shot out so and so many tanks, and still . . . I have to laugh!" No more. The others laughed too. This is the effect of G. communiqués even on simple people.

For deputy foreign secretary, our military attaché from the Stockholm legation was appointed but he declined the offer and rather stays out in Sweden. So a colonel from the War office was put on the post as deputy. His first act in office was to take his son out of military service, as "the leader has announced, all wishes of old party members has to be granted." The son is out of military service and sent out to Berlin as member of the legation.

The evacuation of Bpest is prepared. It will be compulsory, at first the Pest side, then Buda, somewhere into Germany. With all refugees, the inhabitants of Budapest are estimated to be about 2–3 million. Such a mass can not be evacuated on trains or cars. I am not going to go and in case of need, I shall hide.

8:30 p.m. until now four alarms have passed, no raid. Miskolc, Szolnok seems to be raided. Lacy says, I am radiant, when the alarm is sounded and she may be right: something is happening at least. The Russian drive did stop since three–four days, after Szeged and Baja they announce far places like Ungvár and Palánka or they do not announce anything.

OCT. 30, MONDAY.

At 10:08 a.m. the second alarm over Bpest.

SAME NIGHT.

The morning a telephon call from Klári (F), I had to see her the afternoon, they hope again for Swiss visa, without any real ground of course. And it is me, who should produce all these wonders miracles. Well, I shall write to Editke and she will tell me if there is anything to be done. [. . .]

32. The Hungarian Foreign Office, or Ministry of Foreign Affairs.

Last night the Németh s were here at my door, but I was very sleepy, as I told them, so I could send them away. They went to see Elly, made inquiries of all sort, hoped, she will take care of their baby after the war, etc., etc. They are the real sort of snoopers, so I have to ask them for Friday, will send my friends over to my neighbour, and arranged with Elly to come too, so they should not be able to observe me and the flat closely.

Tonight the janitor was here to register the amount of hot water used this month. I had to show him therefore into the bathroom, but put my friends—before opening the door—behind the big mirror. It was a splendid joke, like hide and seek.

The Némeths (and other people's, like them) conception of the present situation is the following: there is no danger of defeat here for the G.s. as those poor Russians, who have never known any sort of decent life, nor private property, seeing the life of the cultured Roumania and Hungary, will be no more able to return to their old way of living and therefore a revolution will sweep away bolshevism, Stalin, etc. In the meantime they are afraid of Russian invasion, occupation, violence, etc. Advice Elly to take refuge into the Swedish legation, so that Mrs Németh's father could have the Hermans flat. [. . .]

OCT. 31, TUESDAY.

The evening, at about 7 p.m. some bombs dropped, without any alarm signs, at the big Oti building at the corner of József u and József krt, at Tisza Kálmán tér, Rigó utca, etc. Today the morning began with an alarm at 8 a.m. Short, nothing happened.

SAME NIGHT.

The day passed as usual, alarms, alarms off and on, some stray planes flying low over the houses, people paying no heed to any of them. Mailed a letter to Editke, have seen Ilonka, after Oti some shopping with big results: one bread, five bottles of Yestor meet [*sic*] extract, 10 small boxes of Ovomaltine, four packets of Darling cigarettes, one packet (10 boxes) of matches. Well, grapes too, 1 kg of blue grapes 12 P. It used to be 40–60 fillérs. After coming home I gathered some eggs, margarine, sugar and milk powder, went over to Lujzi, as she is going to bake a kuglupf for me. I had luck to start in time as I met Gizi before the housegate, coming to me. At present circumstances she would be rather inconvenient here.

Coming back, I found Elko before the house, he came for tea. Still here, Mrs Láng came, they were released this afternoon, having been arrested for one day at Győri ut 1, a nyilas house and for five days at the Svábhegy, Mirabella house at a police headquarters (Heim Péter's detachement). They suffered cold, hunger, crowdedness, fourty–fifty people in a small room, titled people among them, mostly not knowing, what are they there for. One believed, he had said something before his grocer. The Làngs have been reported by all probabilities by the servant of the Németh s, she told on them and the Némeths told the Lajtais and Lajtais reported them as communists and spies. In spite of all these they were released today by the police, not being any proof against them. They have made several friends, countess Bethlen[33] was there too. Their daily food was two or three times a day two decilitres of thin soup with a very small piece of bread. Several times they were questioned about the Hermans.

NOV. 1, WEDNESDAY.

Klári Bálint called for a few minutes, then Gizi came for me to go out to Ibola, to talk over this furniture business, whether our few pieces of furniture can stay there or not. [. . .] Jancsi all the time not at home.

People are seized by a collective hysteria. Jancsi, who seems to have gone over to the German group (Bund) and is going to take refuge in Germany, wants them, Iby and Iván to go with him, but Nami can not go, as she is not registered with the G.s. They would have just sitting places on a G. truck. Imagine their life there! Iby has some common sense left and Iván does not want to fight for Germany (neither for Hungary, I suppose) so they declined Jancsi's plan at this time. I told them, they are right and that it would be a folly to go out of their life into insecurity. They begin to believe now, Germany would not be such a safe place after all. But they still look on me as extremist, pessimist and what not else, because I prophesied some of these things.

NOV. 2, THURSDAY.

The morning began with alarm at 8 a.m. [. . .] The morning followed with alternate alarms, so I could do nothing, what I should have done, instead wandered to and fro, to the Fortress hillside, back to Southern station, to Oti, to the Marosys (not at home), to Mrs Kárász (invited her and Mádyka to Coffein bar for a coffee), to Mrs Fidy, to Rami, but at Francis Joseph bridge and Gellért square such a chaos reigned, the place jammed by G. vehicles, cars, horsecarts, etc. A retreat—in chaos.

Yesterday's Russian news were Kecskemét, Lajosmizse and Dunavecse, the picture here is in full accord with events. No streetcars were able to move until the Buda side of Elisabeth bridge, I had to walk in rain and mud, on the pavement cavalry were retreating, sometimes in pace and sometimes in (ügetés).[34] It was twilight, so I was not able to distinguish, whether these cavalry was H. or G.

33. Margit Bethlen (1882–1970), writer and journalist (*MEK*).

34. Trotting.

It is stated, the Swiss legation has left Bpest[35] this morning—I can hardly believe it—after having given 10,000 protecting papers to Jews, who happened to hear about it and who could stay in lines before the Vadász u. building.

The distance between Budapest and the Russian troups is 40 kms today, guns can be heard already. Ankara announces that foreign legations and consulates were asked to leave the town. That ought to have but one meaning, the G.s intent to "defend" that is to destroy the city.

NOV. 3, FRIDAY.

During the night hours all the town heard the cannonade, allegedly not very far, at the outskirts of Budapest. Today Soroksár, Pestszentlőrinc, Üllő are mentioned by all people. [. . .]

The morning disturbing single planes dropped bombs on the Tattersall,[36] machine gunned the area, while the G. trucks were busy carrying away all possible stuff: kitchen furniture, nursery objects, even boards, then again carloads of vegetables. Our shops tell us, they won't have any more supplies, just some apples, cauliflowers, carrots, nothing else to have. The bread situation has deteriorated, no potatoes since weeks.

SAME NIGHT.

I had guests for tea this afternoon, Mrs Németh, the nyilas spy in our house and Elly to help me. My friends I slipped over to the next flat for the time and all went splendidly, they returned unobserved, I hope.[37] Károly called me up the evening, they are well out at Csepel, though as Klári Bálint describes the situation there this afternoon, it is everything, but peaceful. I am going to meet Károly or Lacy tomorrow afternoon, if it will be still possible to cross the Danube. Today people have shown me the red string on the Elisabeth bridge, which leads to the explosives. It may happen in any hour, the G's blow up the bridges. Several people state, the night the Russians have been at the outskirts of Bpest.

Today's papers bring the new orders about all Jewish properties going over into the possession of the State, that is, I suppose, to nyilas robbery.[38] There are rumours, Jews will be evacuated from the Buda side to the Pest side. I am afraid, they will be herded out before the Russian lines, it is the plan of the nyilas program, to annihilate all Jews.

---

35. The Swiss Legation, headed by Carl Lutz, did not leave Budapest. See Tschuy, *Dangerous Diplomacy*, 186.

36. The National Riding Academy stables, located near Keleti train station (see map 2).

37. The maneuver was to protect Lacy and Fredi.

38. See Lévai, *Black Book*, 350–51.

Taking in consideration, how the Lángs, poor silly Pató and even Elly are persecuted and being held under suspicion in our house, I am rather astonished, I am not gossiped about and not reported for allied sympathies. May be, Elly is right, these cowards want to have a med doctor in the house, for their own use.

Wondering about the pros and contras of this war, I suppose, I am right to state, that in such a case nobody is right, but the course, taken by the allies is the right one, though very cruel and slow. The course taken by the G.s is cruel and not right, so it has to be eliminated by all means.

NOV. 4, SATURDAY.

I have told you before, I suppose, that since the G. invasion of the country, I do not listen to radio Bpest. This morning BBC Italian news service announced, Bpest has announced last night Russian troups in the outskirts of the town. Pity, I did not hear it, as Moscow did not announce anything more but a town occupied 17 kms away from Bpest.

SAME NIGHT.

The morning I crossed the Danube over the Marguerite bridge, at 2 p.m. it was detonated, nobody knows, by whom, but certainly in the face of retreating G. forces.[39] I had to walk with several thousand other people over the chain bridge. Some other damage must have happened too, as on other lines too there were scarcely any streetcars. I was late for shopping—food shops closing at 5 p.m. and I am afraid, we shall be without bread for the siege of the town. It looks like, it would be actually here Russian troups are announced at Újpest and at Pesterzsébet, that is, the North and South of the Pest side.

The town looks more empty then before and very disorganized. Communist fighting is mentioned at the Futó utca. A G. hospital is evacuated from the Szilágyi Erzsébet girl school. Everybody is scandalized by the rate, the G.s are robbing not only public but private property. It is not possible to hide it any more.

On Jewish houses, where gentiles are living mixed, white crosses are painted on the doors, near the yellow star. Some paint the crosses even on their window panes. [. . .]

Second BBC the Szálasi gang has fled this afternoon, after having taken the regency oath this noon. [. . .]

---

39. The bridge was destroyed on November 4, 1944. An estimated six hundred civilians and forty German soldiers died in the explosion. See Szegedy-Maszák, *I Kiss Your Hands*, 170.

NOV. 5, SUNDAY.

The morning began with Mrs Láng coming at an unholy early hour, but bringing a fat goose (ca 4.5 kg, price 152 P). She prepared it for us, came and went several times, then, as she was off, Irka's Ilus and Bözsi came, we called our Csepel friends Karolyi up, Elko 'phoned, later he came to take me for a walk and so I landed at last with the Sebes. Last night they got a small Russian bomb near their house, at a curve of Somlói ut.

Meanwhile I hear your election result, Pres. Roosevelt seems to be elected for the fourth time. Did you vote too, dearest?

The Margaret bridge is much worse off as I believed yesterday. Three arcs of the Pest side are in the water, three double streetcars are lost, full with people. Imre Waldbauer,[40] the violinist was there too and as he put it, he is one of the four people, who escaped. It is stated, it was just a sillyness of the G.s, the undermining went off somehow in consequence of the streetcar traffic, therefore all traffic was prohibited on the other bridges.

I have to confess I hesitate a good deal, whether to cross the bridges tomorrow or not to cross.

A few hundred heavily armed G. soldiers arrived into the next school this afternoon. I hope, we shall not be evacuated from our flats, as people around the Ludovica military academy[41] are evacuated today, the place will be used second all probabilities as a fortress.

NOV. 6, MONDAY.

I was over to Pest, in spite of good resolutions. The situation was calm enough, so I did not want to be a coward and stay away from work. No gunshots since two days, the Russians seem to have retreated from the outskirts of Budapest and BBC announces strengthening G. defence. The scoundrels. The town is absolutely mad, all inside out and sloppy. Girls, anaemic proletarian women, without the least charm, dirty, unkempt, neglected, wearing not elegant slacks, as ladies used to in days before, but shabby man's trousers and nobody is paying the least attention to their clothing. The remaining bridges (two railway bridges hit earlier by air raids, the Marguerite bridge blown by clever G.s on Saturday) are full all the time with stagnating traffic, consisting chiefly of G. booty.

My usual hairdresser could not wash my hairs as he is alone in his shop, instead of with four helpers, as he used to be.

Ilonka gave me twenty packages of cigarettes today, so I hope to be insured until the beginning of December.

---

40. Waldbauer Imre (1892–1953), violinist (*MEK*).

41. The Ludovica Military Academy was located in the 8th District.

Pesterzsébet and Csepel are said to be evacuated today. If the G. mean to defend the town, this compulsory evacuation will threaten us too. At Kecskemét people were told, the cellars will be searched and people, who are found hiding, shot. You see, except nazi scoundrels, normal people do not want to take refuge. The deviltry of the G. method is, they make people to take refuge, then enlist men into the SS, women into warwork and so everybody is involved into co-guiltyness against the allies. Hungarian soldiers get behivó[42] directly to Berlin or Graz.

Dearest, I wish so much to be with you. But nobody else, just you (all three).

NOV. 7, TUESDAY.

Ida, Mrs Csernos called me up the morning, she wanted to meet me. Ernő I called up in vain, his office did not answer, I suppose, he dare not leave his Pécel house in fear, he could not return. So I am cut off from my friends there. I met Ida at Monpto, but no coffee there, went to Rami, no cigarettes there, went to Stühmer,[43] no candies there. Among others no bread in town and, as no hope, to get our sugar rations any more, black market price of one kg of sugar has risen to 100 P.s. [. . .]

Confusion is growing everywhere. I have talked to refugees on the streetcar, who intend to go on from Bpest, if possible, to Germany. Let them go, if they are so silly. Many soldiers and labour service men are hiding, we have some near us. It is splendid joke, our secret meetings in the different flats, among our numerous nyilas neighbours. If they only know! It happened, that I heard in the streetcar the news, that the gendarms will be evacuated tomorrow. This is lucky for us, so I hope, we shall not be evacuated from our flats.

The afternoon Elly came here, then Ida, then we went for a walk with Elly. When we returned over the Svábhegy side, it was after black out time and the hillside looking towards Southeast, we have heard the guns and seen the lights flaring up. [. . .] Here, in the flat we scarcely hear any noises, so, that one of our hiding men[44] can hardly stand the quietness with his nerves rattled by Csepel raids.

Coming home, my friends' former housekeeper came with some food, then I had to go up to Klári. We had a lively talk, at 8 p.m. back again. Irmus called me up, they have the Antals still in their flat, but they are crazy with nervousness

42. Mádi's subsequent annotation: "1969. Draft cards."

43. Chocolate factory in Budapest. It made specialty candies for Gerbaud's Café.

44. Apparently, Frédi's father and Lacy's brother were temporarily staying with Mádi in hiding.

and since Sunday sleep all (Lajoska, Margit and five children) in the cellar, this noon they lunched there. I wonder, what are they going to do, when the real siege of Budapest begins.

At Klári I met János Fóti,[45] a former journalist of the *Pesti Hirlap*. He is in hiding too, I do not know, where, but has had already some adventures.

NOV. 8, WEDNESDAY.

It is a day of surprises, I can tell you. The morning white posters everywhere, announcing, that all men (this time not the Jews) from the age of 16 until 50 have to report the following three days at 7 a.m. at Vác, from where they will be directed towards Tata and Vál. Families, who are capable of marching 16–20 kms daily, may go with them. No luggage but winter clothing is advisable, as the march may last two or three weeks. This means deportation to Germany.

Jewesses from the age of 14 until 40 and seamstresses have to go into designed Buda houses from the Pest side. This seems to be in accordance with my theory, the Jewish population left behind in the Pest Jewish houses, will be annihilated by the nyilas and G.s. or herded before the Russian tanks. Men from the age of 16 until 60 are already out of these houses, now capable women are taken out.

Factories are surrounded by surprise by the G.s and workmen put into trucks and taken out of the country. I hope, many nyilas are among them, their worst punishment will be this pleasure trip to Germany.

I met Marika Kánya this morning, we have said goodbye for a while, she living on the other side of the Danube. The G. and military traffic has subsided to such a grade, I do not venture any more over the other side.[46] About fifty small boats are prepared on the Danube embankment, I suppose, for the case, when the Chain and Elisabeth bridges will be blown up too.

In today's papers house commanders and janitors are obliged to search all flats for hiding Jews. The child with us here is difficult and his naughtiness may mean death for us all. I have to confess, I am a bit nervous.

According to some rumours the number of the victims of the Marguerite bridge explosion is six hundred. Bö, who is with us since this afternoon, was at home in her ghetto flat, opposite the place, says, it was a terrific explosion, all their window panes went, they could hear at the same moment the shrieks of drowning people. [. . .]

---

45. János Fóthy (1899–1979), journalist and art critic (*MEK*).

46. This diary entry suggests that Mádi stopped working at Oti. That is not so; she continued to work there occasionally until the Germans blew up all the remaining Danube bridges in January 1945.

Today the Russians seem to be withdrawn and G defence strengthening. It could last for weeks.

NOV. 9, THURSDAY.

Money is nothing, only barter. Fuel for honey, food for wood, clothing or shoes for wood. One hundred kgs of wood is over hundred P these days. [. . .]

It is over 10 p.m. and still no house searching. I suppose, both commander and janitor are so sure of their knowledge of the house, they do not even doubt, everything is in order. Bö is still nervous but a bit better then yesterday.[47] I wish, she would stay with us quietly, but she plans all the time to go away. After three weeks of terrible nervous strain in a yellow star house, she can't help being restless and very much down.

We had several visitors this afternoon: Elly, then Gizi and Hanna (Sz.) These two were not meant to meet my friends, so they were again hidden behind the big looking glass, for half an hour. Later, when they left, Gyurka Gyetvay came to say goodbye and brought me a lighter, which has been out of sale for months: This was nice of him and he was taken into our confidence. He looked flabberghasted when three persons marched out from behind the mirror.

Irka[48] is splendid, doing all our work and all the time cheerful, at least outward. Her brothers had got Swiss and Swedish passports, we hope, they will be safe from deportation.

NOV. 10, FRIDAY.

By yesterday I am again the chief at my former office, where Dr Fábry succeeded me. The chief is again at military service, while Gabi Fábry disappeared a week before. As her husband is an army officer, very probably they went hastily out of town. You see, it is not so bad after all, to feel fatalistic. I wished to stay there, and I am there again, but with a lot of more experience in ENT. They, the Oti I mean, are in terrible need of M.D.s. The big problem is, how long shall I be able to cross the bridge. [. . .]

To get a streetcar is almost impossible, besides the weather was abominable. Cold, wind, rain. Because of the wind I could not hold an umbrella and was drenched to the skin together with my furcoat. I had to cross the Danube at the Marguerite bridge (it looks like that):[49]

---

47. Bö made a fourth person living in the one-bedroom apartment (with no living room, just a kitchen, dining room, bedroom, and bathroom): Mádi, Lacy, Bö, and Frédi.

48. Nickname for Irén, that is, Lacy.

49. Mádi made a sketch of the damaged bridge. See "I Am Going to Be a Witness: Maria Madi's Diary," 12:79, https://www.ushmm.org/collections/the-museums-collections/curators-corner/i-am-going-to-be-a-witness-maria-madis-diary.

below the former bridge two ferryboats are going at irregular times, an open wooden bridge fastened on four pontoon ships, we had to stay in the slop, exposed to rain and wind, at least until twenty minutes. Not the least shelter on the deck. Meantime several hundred labour service Jewesses were herded by police men up the Buda embankment, somewhere towards Óbuda. I felt my eyes hot with tears and resentment but people on the ferry did not have any sympathy with them, a brand new leather coated and booted nyilas said, they are only there to kick into them, then looked round, whether anybody dares to contradict him. I boiled inside. Got home late and very cold, all wet. We planned with Elly to go up to her sister to get a big pot of home made jelly, which she sells, but as a Viennese schoolfriend sat with Elly, we did not go and it was a relief for me. Elly has heard yesterday in the grocery as the grocer read loud ahead a new order, second which no more milk will be available in future, but Mondays and Thursdays, 4 decilitres, only for infants. [. . .]

In yesterday's papers the news were announced, that Beregffy (what a name!)[50] the war minister visited the *first* frontlines—at Soroksár, You will appreciate the savour of it, *Hildukáim*. As if the first American frontlines would be at Coney island.

Bö has left us this morning. She is so restless, I could not hold her back any more. I am afraid, she will do something inconsiderate.

NOV. 11, SATURDAY.

The same story told by refugees from everywhere, the last that was told at the next grocery (full with shopping people) from Pestszenterzsébet, at the outskirts of Bpest. A woman retailed[51] they were given fifteen minutes by the G.s, to evacuate, she could hardly take her bedclothes and some underwear, but the same time the G. soldiers began to plunder their homes and put their furniture on lorries. They had to witness all, without word.

Klári Bálint has seen before last night, the Lajtai family leave the house with much luggage on a luxurious car. The Lajtais were the chief nyilas in our house, they reported three people,[52] who were arrested. He became secretary of one of the cabinet ministers and she went after him, very probably to Sopron or Vienna. These are splendid news for us, we only hope, the other nyilas will follow them.

---

50. Károly Beregfy (1888–1946), minister of war, indicted, tried, convicted, and executed for war crimes by the Budapest People's Tribunal (1946) (*MEK*).

51. Mádi used "retailed" as a synonym for "related" or "told."

52. Maria Pató and Mr. and Mrs. Láng were the three neighbors at 19 Margaréta utca denounced to the police.

SAME NIGHT.

Last night I had a telephon call from Emil's attorney and I had to meet him this morning. Street communication is undescribable, so it lasted a considerable time until I got to Apponyi tér. We recognized each other, though never met before. He had a card from Emil for me, second which I had to consult Mrs Grónay. She was not in her shop, so after my Oti hours (had there quartz and Sollent irradiations myself as help against bitter cold in the rooms)[53] I went to her flat and accomplished my task. I have to pay the attorney for Emil, he has freed or going to free Emil's brother, as Swiss citizen from labour service, Pünkösdfürdő.[54]

The Russians have cut the Miskolc railway line, Northeast of Bpest and they are over the Danube, between Baja and Apotni, marching towards Pécs.

NOV. 12, SUNDAY.

Just after 10 a.m. we went off with Elly to the house of her sister Lily, to get a jar of jelly I would buy from her. A big pot of good quality, costs only 25P. The walk was agreeable but you know me, to get off so early on a Sunday morning, I was a bit unhappy. Coming home, Bö's sister in law came to get a toothbrush for her. I gave my papers too.[55] Then I had to be off for the usual Sunday lunch. Apu could escape deportation, which was due yesterday, but he got transferred to the Ministry of Justice, for a while he is safe, in case he should have to submerge, his friends will look for him at my address. He had his friend Henrik Siebenlist for lunch too, a high judge, who was kicked out the Foreign Office too. We talked over many possibilities, but I can tell you, these men are looking for advice just the same as I do.

NOV. 14, TUESDAY.

Yesterday's morning paper announces, that party members' evacuation is compulsory, in contrast with other people, who's evacuation is only optional—yet. I suppose, the G.s won't let us stay here peacefully, as almost everybody is waiting for the Russian troups as liberators. Who would have thought such a thing

---

53. Mádi used the radiology equipment to warm the medical rooms.

54. A mineral water spa bath on the Buda side of the city. It opened in 1935.

55. In addition to shielding Lacy and Frédi Lakos and, for a while, Bö, Mádi lent her identification papers to Bö, and she lent Hilda's identification papers to another Jewish woman. Braham estimates that about twenty-five thousand Jews in Budapest were living with false papers. Another one hundred thousand or so were living with protection papers from one of the neutral legations such as Switzerland, Sweden, Portugal, and the Vatican. Braham, *The Politics of Genocide*, 2:999–1003.

even a year before? I can not hope though the G.s would pull out without taking a considerable part of the population with them. This can be done only at an expense of utmost misery, the population of Bpest having swollen over two millions with the refugees. Except the guilty, nobody has a wish to leave the town whatever may come. People say, they would rather die in their own surroundings as on the highway, leading to Germany.

We did not have telephon communications from 9:30 a.m. until late afternoon since about ten days. There is nothing what could not be done to us.

The robbing of the country is without any parallel. G. trucks are full with geese, with pigs just slaughtered, still bleeding, cattle is driven over the streets of the city.

SAME NIGHT.

I had to see Károly, Irén's brother at a Swiss Red Cross house this afternoon, after my Oti work. They are living in comparative comfort, no heating of course and food supply from outside. Károly told parts of his adventures, he was arrested twice, the second time for asking for a Swiss passport and escaped only by a lucky chance. But, he says, compared with the adventures of his fellow lodgers, his are nothing. He has pointed out an old man to me in the room, who, on labour service, got into Russian hands with some other labour service men. They hoped for the best and reported as Jews before the Russian army officer, who happened to be a Jew himself. This got into a terrible rage, said, they should see what the Polish Jews have done in interest of the allies. In spite of their pitiful begging, sent them back to the G. lines, saying, they were not Jews, but Hungarians. So these poor people are condemned to death here, for being Jews and not Hungarians, again rejected by their only hope, the Russian "liberators," for not being Jews, but Hungarians. They hardly escaped shooting by the G.s. and the Russians have taken their wristwatches just the same, as they used to take from other Hungarian prisoners. [. . .]

There are some who believe that I eat early, they come about 8 p.m. and stay late. Others believe that I eat late, so they come early and used to stay until the other sort is ringing the bell. An outsider, Mrs Németh has tried to penetrate my premises this afternoon but I remained firm and not understanding and said Good bye to her before the door.

NOV. 15, WEDNESDAY.

The day was disgusting with rain in torrents, traffic tumults and late as I was for home, with almost incessant visitors from 5 p.m. until 9:30 p.m. The noon rather strong bombardment was heard from the East, it was generally believed, the Zugló outskirts were shot at, where our furniture is stored.[56] No streetcars were going further than Eastern station during the noon hours . . . Ilus was here the morning, brought us a duck, which is a help these days.

I suppose, I told you my last meeting with Ily. Today I got a letter from her, through Gizi, she is sorry, she writes, to have seen green light in my eyes last time, but she is sure it is only because I am separated from you. She seems to have heard nothing about hundred thousands of Jews having tortured and killed together with non Jews, who are not in agreement with present governments. Today, when I was exhausted and unhappy in the terrible weather, though well clad and in streetcars mostly, thousands of Jewesses, separated from their children, robbed by nyilas from their warm clothing, are driven on the highways on foot at about Komárom, on their way to Vienna.[57] It is impossible that Ily or Gizi should have no word for it and they would still hope for G. victory, as the best solution. I can't help being disgusted with these friends.

G. spread rumours of the day: revolution in White Russia, a new *Greek* liberation army on his way towards Budapest, to fight on G. side. The last proclamation to the man population of Pest (age 16–50) seems to be without results, as today men from 21 until 32 are called up compulsorily and from 33 until 50 voluntarily for war service, out of town. They are promised 20Ps per day. Our soldiers don't get more as 20 fillérs per day.

NOV. 16, THURSDAY.

A brilliant morning, blue skies, sunshine and not really cold . . . After 2 p.m. at my Oti work, we got some light bombs in the neighbourhood, police headquarters at Mosonyi u (your driver certificate you got there) at the Eastern station, Thököly ut, etc. Streetcars almost impossible, from noon on until after dark I had to walk almost all the time, without much result. Ernő did not come into town, shopping: nothing to buy, no cigarettes at Rami, etc, etc.

A yellow star-patient told me, Swiss and Swedish cared for Jews are packed tight into some houses, all other Jews and Jewesses are evacuated and sent to Germany.[58] No more yellow starred homes will remain. Today I am told, the

56. Mádi had stored the family furniture at her friend Mamuci's estate in suburban Budapest in 1941.

57. Twenty-five thousand Jewish women were forced to work on digging trenches and antitank traps to defend Vienna. See Braham, *The Politics of Genocide*, 2:838–43; Lévai, *Black Book*, 371–74.

58. On November 18 the Arrow Cross government ordered nonprotected Jews (an estimated sixty-three thousand) to move into the compact ghetto surrounding the Dohany Street synagogue. At the same time, the government commanded eleven thousand Gentiles to leave the ghetto. See Lévai, *Black Book*, 375.

Pope's nunciate has given some papers too, but all these are closed down now and as I hear, many of them are not respected by the nyilas. Nyilas houses distribute clothing of all sort among their party members, all looted from Jewish houses and shops. Many of our simple people, nurses, char women are disgusted by these cruelties.

I have seen two G. soldiers on the streetcar, travelling from the Eastern station to the Buda side of the Elisabeth bridge. They were haggard, ash grey, emaciated, as if after a very heavy wound or sickness, not yet properly recovered. They were with full war equipment. This must be the new drafting system, men not by far able for military service.

The Russians announce the capture of Gyömrő, Vámosgyörk and Rákoskeresztúr,[59] but for us it is too slow. G.s and nyilas have leisure for all sorts of measures. It is like a slow motion picture.

NOV. 17, FRIDAY.

I went to town like a camel, full with parcels, but could deliver none. Ernő did not come into town, apparently and Mr Gonszlék I could not meet because of two alarms. I sat through the two alarms at the Oti shelters, rather tedious affair. At Oti center many of its officials are absent I am told, they had to evacuate, compulsorily, as nyilas party members. Serves them right!

I met Marguerite yesterday, Kuri[60] is hiding, she is worried too, not to be taken by the G.s as hostage. Their estate and castle was taken yesterday by the so called G. legation, so Hédervár[61] is condemned to death and ruin. She too has seen on the Vienna highway rows of Jewish cadavers. Frici Horchler sen. has seen yesterday on the Andrássy ut many Jewesses driven somewhere, an old Jewess could not go fast enough and was shot there, on the Andrássy ut!

This afternoon from the streetcar I have seen many Jews and Jewesses driven from Döbrentei tér towards Döbrentei utca. Men went ahead as I could see, in overcoats, with armed nyilas guards.

Women and children went behind, with unarmed nyilas guards, youngsters. No age was respected, old women and children of about 5 years were on the road, in thin clothing in the cold wind. You know, Jews used to be better off with clothing, so they were robbed of their warm things. Most of them wore some knitted sweaters or just a dress, as one used to sit in a room, I have seen many of them, crying bitterly. No one in the streetcar raised a word of protest or horror.

59. The eastern suburbs of Budapest.

60. Mádi's brother-in-law, Count Viczay.

61. The Viczay family castle today is an artists' hotel. See "Hédervár," Wikipedia, https://en.wikipedia.org/wiki/H%C3%A9derv%C3%A1r.

The town got some bombardment from the air and from the ground too. I can not be sorry for these people.

From Elly I hear, Mr Arnold, the Dutch consul has been arrested by the nyilas and released by a high police officer with aid of a trick. A Dutch Jewish couple disappeared, the nyilas having not respected their foreign citizenship and a very rich Dutch family, the man a former director of Philips, disappeared (reason: conspiration with Croatian partisans!) apparently to Germany as the man sent a postcard to Mr Arnold from Hegyeshalom. [. . .] . . . Many cases are heard of Swiss or Swedish protection papers being thrown into pieces. These legations seem to do nothing about those violations of international law. A convent was overrun by the nyilas too, all protected and the nuns arrested in the presence of the police. The Nunciature seems to have intervened, so the nuns were released a week later.

NOV. 18, SATURDAY.

The morning I had to travel out to Kőbánya, to see Mr Gonszlek.[62] It was possible, that I could not return but no, the Russians are not in such a hurry. On my way out I have seen from the streetcar hundreds and hundreds of cattle, driven towards the city. They were drooping from fatigue. They are destined for Germany, may be, the Hortobágy, cattle, beautiful oxen with large horns. The country is robbed entirely and systematically.

At Oti Pravdáné was waiting for me, with lovely goose liver, her husband sent me. Her daughter Anni with all fellow workers at the Optical factory, was told a few days ago, that they better be in readiness with warm clothing, as in a few days they will be deported with all factory equipment to Germany.

Pravdáné has seen two Jewesses dead on the pavement of Garay utca yesterday. They were shot, because they were not able to follow the others.

The nyilas party, the national socialist party and the Eastern frontline brotherhood have done a merger today (fuzionáltak), I hope, they all will have to clear out of the country, soon. It will be a nice place without these scoundrels.

Yesterday I met at Pilsudszky road a G. civilian motorist, he asked me on Hungarian, where Rege ut is. It is here in the hill, but I shook my head and answered: I never heard of it, have no idea. These are our small compensations at present.

Yesterday's papers announced, that for these three days (and how many more?) no milk will be available even for small babies. There was no other milk for a long while, now not even these small amounts (4 deci daily). Cows are slaughtered by the relocating Gs so no wonder, there will be none, not for

62. Mádi's attorney, who was representing her in a real estate transaction.

three days but for months to come. Dearest, how happy I am, you are out of all these!

Elko called me up tonight, he almost succumbed to a Russian bomb at hotel Gellért yesterday noon, when the restaurant corner of Gundel was hit. He was just going there to lunch. It was but disturbing flight, soon an alarm followed, so he did not look round to see Rami, whether his shop was damaged or not. I am anxious for Rami too, but for my cigarettes supply also. This is our daily life, you see.

Pravdáné has seen some machine gunning today at a row, waiting for bread at Király utca.[63] I do not know whether you will be able to believe me, but we got accustomed to this hazardous sort of life. I even could make the boy in my flat get used to all this shooting and bombing noises. He was terribly afraid at first but then I told him it is nothing and that Russian guns are a lazy pack and do not work enough. When no noise was to be heard I complained bitterly, when shooting began, I expressed joy, so he does the same now. It is so much more easy this way.

NOV. 19, SUNDAY.

Rev. Péter[64] states, about ten Swedish protected houses were overrun by the nyilas in the past days. Apu was taken back by the Foreign Office, he has to go on there and is ordered to leave the town and country with them. Hostages are collected throughout the country and Budapest. István Antal is among them, I am told.

The day was involved into deep mist and fog, I came home early, had visitors from the house, then made a sort of crackers with the Hermans, in their oven (25 dkg of flour, 20 dkg butter, 10 dkg sugar and two egg yolks) but got so tired, I had to lay down on their sofa. I feel my heart, am exhausted, though in bed since a few hours here at home. Lacy spoils me with all her kindness . . .

NOV. 20, MONDAY.

At the Pest side of the city no current,[65] we could not work at the office. I had to go after my salary, due to me since the end of August. With regards to the perfect dissolution we are heading, may be I can induce them to pay it at once this time. Other employees have paid three–four month's salaries ahead. Prices

63. One of the main streets of the Jewish quarter, later, the Jewish ghetto.

64. Péter Zoltán (1901–1969), Reformed Church pastor, college professor, and head of the Reform Collegium of the University of Debrecen (*MEK*).

65. Meaning no electricity.

are unbelievably high, *one* small celery costs five Ps, small apples 10–15 Ps per kg. In the shops almost no foodstuff, in restaurants nothing to eat. [. . .]

NOV. 21, TUESDAY.

At Oti I could not get my money but the working localities were terribly cold, and I got out after two and a half hours virtually frozen. Out at the street an Atlantic wind was breaking just in, stormy but so cheerfully springlike. It was—for a few minutes—unbelievable, that the city and many of the inhabitants are doomed. I am told by three different sources, that the outer end of Baross utca and the Ludovika region of Üllői ut are under artillery fire since Sunday.

NOV. 22, WEDNESDAY.

For weeks we could not get any meat, last night Tercsi néni called me up, to tell, she has something for me. As it is prohibited to buy at blackmarket prices and else you can't have anything, she just told me, there is "a döglött állat"[66] and something else. There was some talk before of a goose, so I was prepared to find this. The morning Ilus, the former housekeeper of Lacy and Károly came here, she brought a duck. Now, as there are not so many opportunities, I accepted this too and the two kg-s of pork, offered by Mrs Láng, just the same. At Tercsi néni it turned out, the something was a chicken (27.50P) and fifteen eggs (2.40P apiece), the goose will be for tomorrow or after tomorrow. The pork we got for 25P per kg, rather cheap, as I heard about 40P prices too. Coming home, I had to supply some vegetables (every day they may be the last), spinach and red cabbage 10P per kg, small apples 24–25P per kg. Mrs Láng got one litre of milk for us 2P, that is very cheap, as almost non existing luxury. Now we have to preserve our meat supplies, as very probably there will not be any more for weeks. We have fat and liver preserved too, some dry bread no potatoes. With some reliable people in the house we intend to cook together, when severely under siege. Some of them have potatoes, we have fat, another has a small stove (all we either have gas or electricity, which will not last long).

My Oti work does not pay, because I have to cross the bridges, twice every day, it is rather dangerous and the situation of the building is dangerous too, rather exposed to bombardment, as it is between two railway stations. The only value of this work is the information gotten from different patients. I am told by them, that at Gödöllő the forced evacuation was announced yesterday. Sunday night and since then too Russian tanks came into town to until

66. The dead animal.

the Ludovica, then retreated. At Rákoskeresztúr the battle is raging. People go to the frontlines with streetcars.

I am told, the day before yesterday about fifty Hungarian generals were arrested by the G.s. It seems probable, they have planned something, but of course too late. I do not see any merit in recognising facts, when the game is lost. Just the same with the regent. I am told, before three years he tried to justify his pro G policy with the words Pity, but we have to put our stakes on the winning horse! There is no use for politicians who's insight of world economics is so limited.

It is not a unique story, we have heard from Ilus this morning. A young Jewess, Anna Prúhler by name, whose husband was killed in labour service two years ago, was separated from her three year old daughter and sent towards Vienna, with many hundred other Jewesses. She herself 25 years old, her father, with whom she lived, was taken for labour service too. She escaped on the way somehow, is hiding somewhere. Whether she knows something about her little Kati, we do not know. Can you believe and imagine such horrors?

NOV. 23, THURSDAY.

Casualities begin to happen within the city. The Ludovica Military Academy region seems to be especially exposed. Lujzi told me today, a friend of them, Laci Friedrich with four members of his family were walking home Saturday night on the Üllői ut, when a shell hit, all died.

This morning we heard a series of terrible noises close to our house, we believed, this part of the town was shelled, but it turned out, a couple of G. soldiers were practicing with rifles at the school yard. May be they are members of the new Volkssturm, who are just learning to handle their weapons.

From Lujzi I hear, Peter Beck is out at Reichenberg (Sudetenland) since three weeks or at least he was due there, but no news came from him. Elza and Móki left two weeks ago for Vienna (we are Germans—Elza used to stress the fact), today a card arrived from her, she never saw Vienna, is sent towards Berlin, she wrote the card at Budweiss (Moravia), is travelling in a cold freight car. She is very tired. Such are life's small compensations.

At Oti I got today (at last) the money due to me, 845 Ps, 200 less, then I believed but except a few opportunities to buy food, there is nothing I could buy for the money. [. . .] I look at the illustrated advertisements of Sunday Evening Post, the chocolate bonbons, they offered—well, may be next year I shall have some.

Márta (Waldbauer) called me up this afternoon, she wished to send an unknown young man to me, I gave him a date, just for Márta's sake, but as he was one and a quarter hours late, I did not answer the doorbell. I hate people intruding upon one's privacy, and added unpunctuality. [. . .]

NOV. 24, FRIDAY.

I had to meet Márta's young man this morning. A complete stranger, about the same swindler type, as Márta's husband. Did not want anything else, but to have your papers![67] I told him, I can not give them.

At Oti I am informed, M.D.s were called up to report for work in Germany. Well, they can wait for me to report. A charwoman has heard about my former colleague Dr Timár. She was deported to Germany, along with other Jewesses, no luggage nothing with them. No special treatment as a physician.

This morning the Lakihegy relay-station was hit, no more 200 KW power station for Hungary. I do not mind a bit as so much damage was done by radio propaganda these last years.

At Monpti I was told, this is the last day for coffee. All coffee reserves are taken for the "soldiers," that means, for G purposes.

Elko was here the afternoon, pessimistic about the Russian drive towards Bpest. He believes, they are exhausted and can not fight any more. I do not think so. On the Western front (Strasbourg was taken today) he is all hope and believes in a complete G. breakdown before Xmas. This again I think is his usual over optimism.

Today the silence around us is depressing. Hungary is scarcely mentioned in news' bulletin. No cannon fire heard. Terrible, getting on our nerves. My vagus[68] is acting up.

NOV. 25, SATURDAY.

The cannonade is strong today, but, as I am told, it was yesterday too, only not audible at our quarters. Api Fidy, who is commander of the Budaörs airport, states, the situation yesterday was so critical, they believed, the Russians will walk into the city. Well, they did not.

NOV. 26, SUNDAY.

It is your birthday, Dearest, and the twenty fourth! Since your last photo I slowly realized, that you have grown up to a responsible person, with duties, a husband and a baby to care for and fully aware of this fact. At the Sebes lunch we drank to your health.

---

67. An encounter with the black market for identification papers. For one family's experience in obtaining false documents, see the memoir of Tivadar Soros, *Masquerade: Dancing around Death in Nazi-Occupied Hungary*, trans. Paul Soros (London: Canongate Books, 2000).

68. The vagus nerve is one of the cranial nerves.

The robbing of the country and individuals is without parallel, everybody is bursting with fury and tales about the G. looting. Serves them right, should I like to say, if it would not mean extreme poverty. I can visualize the war's end now but have no phantasy enough to see how we are going to survive the period, when the G.s will be out and until the allies can supply us with some food, instruments for agriculture, seeds, cattle, sheep, etc, as nothing on earth will be left here.

The Turkish and Dhingis Khan[69] devastation was nothing compared with these up to date G. organized methods. War plants—machinery and workmen—are taken to Germany, day by day. Military units just the same. The infantry unit at Komárom (about 800 men) are to be transferred to Dresden.

NOV. 27, MONDAY.

M. Pató took a lodger into her one-room-flat, in fear it would be taken from her. My flat is the same size, but I do not think it possible, one could take a one room flat from one person. So many flats are empty, since the prominent nyilas families had to leave. Sure they all pretend, they are not away and some relative comes to air the flat regularly but after all, everybody knows.

My sister Margit wrote a letter in which she states, thirty thousand people were massacred at Újvidék by the Tito troupes (total inhabitants 68,000) and that according to the refugees the horrors, committed by the Russians are tenfold of what our newspapers tell us. You must not forget, she gets her information from the refugees constantly streaming over their town and refugees, sobered out of their first fright, try to justify themselves by telling the most horrid tales, probably not witnessed. I refuse to believe these. I can believe though that men in military service age are collected by the Russians and they will have to fight on, until the Austrian border, against the G s, as Roumanians and Bulgarians had to fight on.[70]

There are rumours, that after the first army headed by Dálnoki Miklós Béla[71] and after general Vörös,[72] last Saturday a hussar regiment went over to the Russians.

NOV. 28, TUESDAY.

Elly comes with the news, the G.s are pulling out of the next school building. Their kitchen is emptied, no chair, no stray piece of wood is left, on the front

69. Mádi is referring to the Ottoman occupation of Buda (1526–1688) and the sack of Hungary by Genghis Khan (1240–42).

70. Mádi's subsequent annotation: "1969: I was naïve. They took prisoners from the streets—anybody."

71. Béla Miklós de Dálnoki (1890–1948), prime minister, defected to the Soviets after October 16, 1944 (*MEK*).

72. János Vörös (1891–1968), minister of defense (*MEK*).

side trucks are loaded with bedsteads, matresses, cushions, knapsacks, steel helmets and everything available. Apparently the Russian move imperils them, let us hope, they will pull out as quick as possible.

Us, the public, is reproached by our papers, that we do not take seriously the horror stories, told us daily about Soviet cruelties. It is stated with horror, that even learned men, university professors, doctors, etc. do not believe in these!

At Oti an evacuation order was published today: those, who do not evacuate, will loose their jobs. Unprecedented now these about two thousand active nyilas deliver the country's population to the G's devilish scorched earth plan.

The janitor was here tonight, to see about the meter (vízmérő), he came a day earlier, as we expected, so I could not let him in. The child was just noisy and undisciplined, I hope, Janik[73] did not notice anything and caught suspicion, it would cost our lives, all three of us.

Medical men and women were called up a few days ago, to register for going to Germany. It is not compulsory—yet. I am told, railway men were called up for going to Germany or Checkoslovakia, if they do not go, they will loose their right for retirement benefits. My hairdresser's wife and the hairdresser girl, Magda are called up compulsorily for streetcar ticket collector work. Another help at my hairdressers and his daughter, apprentice at the same place, living at Cinkota, can not come into town any more, are digging trenches outside the city.

Garbage has not been collected for days, it lays before the doors and gates in big baskets.

My sister Marguerite writes me, their flat is requisitioned for G.s and refugees, out of four rooms they have but one left for themselves. Caravans of Jews and refugees stream across the town incessantly, the early morning they bury their dead, then have to go on. Refugees are inventing such horrors, they begin to think about taking refuge themselves. This is pathological.

The Jónás family (my former clerk's family) are entirely separated. The parents out at Hévizgyörk, where heavy fighting is going on since 8–10 days. The boy, born in 1926, was called up for labour service a few weeks ago dug trenches and will be deported by boat to Germany, if he is not able to get away. Capital punishment for this. The girl will be deported to Germany, as according to the latest order, university courses ought to be transferred to Germany.

NOV. 29, WEDNESDAY.

The morning Dénes called me up, he is in town for a day, laying with his battery near Zsámbék. I could not have him in, so arranged to meet him for a

73. István Janik was the janitor at 19 Margaréta utca.

short time. He seems to be sobered out of his Germans, does not advise me to evacuate.

It seems improbable that in the afterwar periods, for a good many years, any form of settled life would be possible. On territories, where the G.s have devastated before evacuation, no houses, flats, furniture, livestock, machinery, traffic possibilities remained. At Kígyó utca and Duna utca, streets of the inner most city, booby traps are being built. The railings of the Danube embankment are wired, very probably for explosives . . . I am told, the Palace hotel at Lillafüred, the Kékes hotel at the Royal castle at Gödöllő were all dynamited after looted by the G.s. The Royal castle (a state property) was said to belong to the "traitor" Horthy.

SAME NIGHT.

Dédé called me up again and I could not refuse to let him come here. I had to hide Lacy and Frédi behind the big looking glass and was determined to let them stick it out there, when Dédé began his visit with the confession "you were perfectly right in everything, the G.s are the most detestable elements, I had several quarrels and even fights with them." He had to chase once a couple of G.s out of his own bed and of the sleeping place of his men with an automatic. G. heroism goes until the point, as long they are outnumbering the other side. Of course I took Lacy out of her hiding place and we spent a very pleasant evening. I am so happy, Dédé has come over to my side! He has found out by himself all the G. lies, their primitiveness, brutality, all. He has very healthy plans, only misses some positive clues in Bp. III. messages.[74]

NOV. 30, THURSDAY.

Last night's news announced the surprise capture of Pécs (it could not be evacuated and looted!) Bátaszék, Baja, today the fall of Eger. We are beginning to hope. Today I have seen columns of motorized heavy artillery retreat to the Buda side. Few were going in the opposite direction. Should they begin to pull out already?

Dédé had a story about the usual G swindle-methods . . . When Lacy questioned Dedé, how is it with this always mentioned strong G. resistance, Dédé laconically answered, look here, I am strongly resisting since Marosludas,—it is about the Eastern end of Transsylvania—and here I am at Zsámbék.[75]

---

74. Mádi called the BBC Hungarian Service "Bpest III," after the state stations Radio Budapest I and II.

75. Located twenty miles west of Budapest.

CHAPTER 6

The Battle of Budapest, December 1944–February 1945

The siege of Budapest is chronicled in chapter 6. Readers may consult map 4 to see how the siege lines tightened around the city between December and February. Soviet units had reached the outskirts of the city in late October, but rather than press ahead, they instead drove north and south to draw a net around the capital. That net was closed by Christmas of 1944, and most of the fighting for the next several weeks was on the Pest side. The Germans had inadvertently dynamited the Margít Bridge across the Danube in November. By mid-January they deliberately blew up the remaining bridges and retreated to Buda. The battle for Buda began after January 16, and it took Soviet troops almost three weeks of street fighting to reach Margaréta utca.

Remarkably, Mádi kept writing every day during the siege, stopping only when she experienced angina-like chest pain and treated herself with digitalis. When the electricity in the apartment building failed, Mádi wrote by candlelight, but even that was limited by the supply of candles. On January 2 she wrote, "I should like to tell you so much, amusing details, but our candle is short, so we are going to sit in the dark (it is only 6 p.m.)." A few days later, exhausted by sleeplessness, dirt, hunger, and cold, she addressed Hilda directly, "May be you have noticed, since the middle of October the charm of telling you all is gone for me." Nonetheless, she carried on witnessing by writing. During a session with her diary at the end of January, she wrote, "We are attacked incessantly by Russian light planes," and then dryly added, "One gets used to all these."

The week of Christmas 1944, the electricity to the 19 Margaréta utca building was cut, the result of a stray Russian shell that damaged the district power plant substation. With no electricity to power her radio, Mádi was cut off from the BBC, Voice of America, and Radio Kossuth broadcasts. She could learn some things from the Arrow Cross newspapers, at least by reading between the lines, but even those publications soon ceased printing. The telephone stopped working by the end of December, and Mádi was further cut off from the outside world.

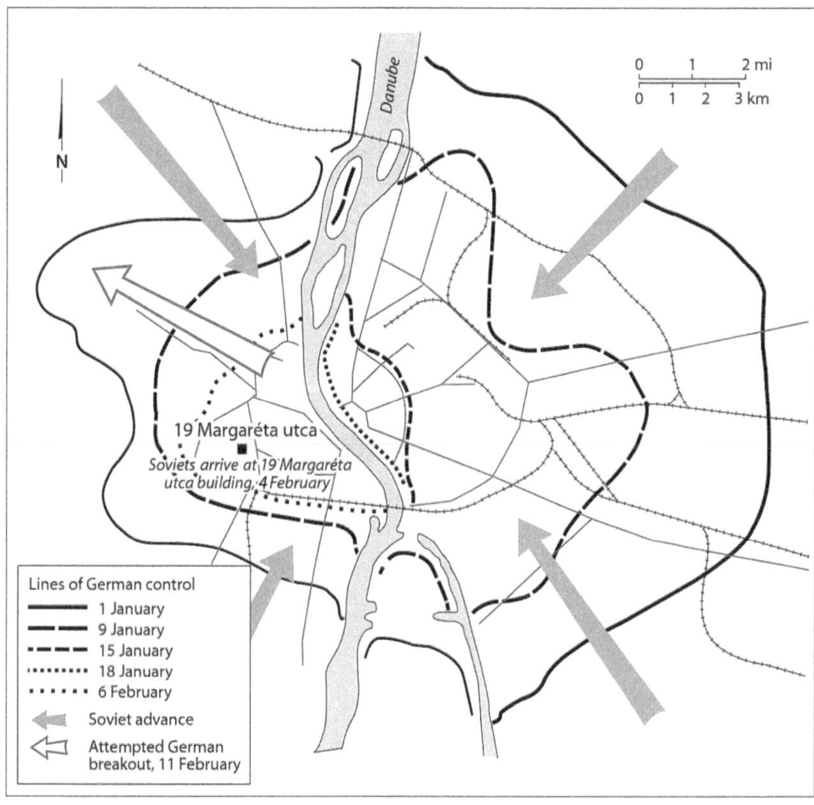

Map 4. Budapest during the siege, December 1944–February 1945 (Bill Nelson)

The last paycheck Mádi received from Oti had arrived on November 23. The paycheck, 845 pengö (about $175 in prewar exchange, perhaps a fifth of that value by the end of 1944), was the last money she had to buy food and other necessities. She had a ration card for one adult female that gave her access to bread, meat, fruit, and vegetables; however, all four foodstuffs were often unavailable. Mádi faced a bigger challenge because she had to stretch her ration card to feed two adult women and one child. During the siege, the doctor and her friends somehow found enough food to maintain life. Hungarian money became useless; only barter sufficed. The anti-German collection of families in the building shared their food and the cooking duties. When one flat had gas sufficient to run a stove, that family cooked for the others.

What sustained the residents of 19 Margaréta utca was a set of rural connections that brought in food when the city stores failed. As Mádi noted, "If you have somebody in the country side to supply with eggs (there amidst the agricultural population it is more easy to get some) you can get a package, under two kgs." Mádi's older sister, Marguerite, countess of Viczay, was that somebody in the countryside for the doctor and her flatmates. The countess used the Hungarian post office to send a weekly package of eggs from her estate on the Danube River. In turn, Mádi sent her sister books in English by return parcel post. Another source of food was the former Mádi family servant, Pravdánéne, who provided potatoes and the occasional goose. Childhood friends of Hilda who were serving in the Hungarian armed forces stopped by the Margaréta utca flat and left army rations for the doctor whenever they could.

Within the 19 Margaréta utca building, several of Mádi's neighbors proved resourceful in acquiring food. Mr. and Mrs. Láng had country connections and were able to save up and share home-canned vegetables and meats. Mária Pató, George Walton's onetime colleague, sometimes contributed to collective cooking in the building. Elly Herman had food sources in the countryside, too. As the siege continued, the women in the building relied upon one another. Mádi had earlier in the autumn revealed to some of her neighbors that she was protecting Lacy and Frédi. To her surprise, she learned that another neighbor, Klári Balint, was similarly protecting a pair of Jews in her flat two flights above Mádi's.

Midway through the siege, Mádi found herself witnessing work horses slaughtered on the street and sold or bartered to civilians. She wrote on January 10, 1945, "I hope, the siege won't last so long, that I should be sorry for not buying any of it. I did not feel tempted by it the least." By January 28, however, she penned the words, "I ate horse meat. I can not say I care for it but well prepared, it is not repugnant." A week later she bartered her services as an obstetrician to a woman in childbirth in return for some cigarettes and "one plate of horse gyulyás [goulash] stew."

As the food supply for Mádi, Lacy, and Frédi grew more tenuous, so, too, did the water supply to 19 Margaréta utca. A December 27 diary entry reads: "A stray Soviet shell struck the district water works and severed the flow to the building. Workmen made temporary repairs." Then on December 31 she wrote: "The taps began to whistle. . . . Lacy is just scrubbing the boy, who screams as a jackal." Mádi contrasted the loss of water with the loss of electricity: "I feel a millionaire with plenty of fresh water supplies. . . . The absence of the electric current, including the radio, is not so hard as not to have water." The restoration of water to the building was short-lived. Mádi and some of her housemates had to work like "camels" to find a source of water in the neighborhood. A few days later, she wrote, "The afternoon Klári B, Elly, Mr. Láng and myself went . . . to get water. Bullets whistled around air attacks, going on not far away, but I got five liters of drinking water." Mádi, Lacy, and Frédi got their last baths around January 19. On the twenty-ninth, she wrote, "We all are losing weight, wrinkles, some dirt accentuates it even more, as it is more than ten days, we did not get any water." The water shortage became so severe toward the end of the siege that the residents of Mádi's flat were reduced to gathering snow from outside the building and bringing it inside to melt. The shoemaker, Mr. Láng, risked his life one day to provide snow for the circle of neighbors who depended on him, including Mádi, Lacy, and Alfred.

The last week of the Battle of Budapest, at least in the 12th District, Mádi and her guests lived without electricity, with little food or water, and without heat. All the windows in her flat were blown out by exploding artillery fire. She hung rugs and Hilda's remaining clothes in the window frames to keep out the cold and snow and to protect against bullets and shell splinters. She and her flatmates, Lacy and Frédi, waited for the Red Army, hoping for an end to the nightmare but resigned to death should it come from a stray bomb, shell, or bullet. Sleep was difficult, and throughout January, the doctor confided to her diary that she took an occasional opiate medication for sleep, and she administered the same to her flatmate, Lacy. The situation in the building worsened when a squad of ten German soldiers occupied the building, some camping in the hallway but five occupying the flat across from Mádi's. "This may be our end," she wrote matter-of-factly. The presence of German troops in the building was certain to bring Soviet firepower on the structure. Mádi, Lacy, and Frédi ignored the order from the German troops to evacuate their apartment and move into the basement shelter. Instead, they took to their beds, pulled up the covers to keep out cold and splinters from explosives, and waited for death.

For Further Reading

The military history of the Battle of Budapest is told by Krisztián Ungváry, *The Siege of Budapest: One Hundred Days in World War II*, translated by Ladislaus Löb (New Haven, CT: Yale University Press, 2006), and map 4 in this volume of the Red Army encirclement of the city follows the narrative in Ungváry's book. Mádi's neighborhood in the 12th District of Budapest had a strong Arrow Cross presence, alongside the German soldiers. In recent years, scholars have uncovered the violent history of the last few weeks of Arrow Cross rule in that district, including the massacres committed by Fascist paramilitary groups just a few blocks from the doctor's apartment on Margaréta utca. Lázsló Csösz and Laura Csonka, with the support of the European Holocaust Research Infrastructure initiative, have produced a digital collection of documents and eyewitness accounts of the Arrow Cross murder of Jews in the 12th District: "Murdered on the Verge of Survival: Massacres in the Last Days of the Siege of Budapest, 1945," https://blog.ehri-project.eu/2017/02/08.

~

DEC. 1, FRIDAY.

After my Oti work I went to see a woman, who has news about Lacy's brothers, then to see Klári Forrai at the Scotch mission house. The school building is under Swiss protection, the value of this protection is rather problematic. There are about 180 Jewish persons, sheltered, they have to work and to pay, and *not* leave the premises. The other side of the building is occupied by H. soldiers. [. . .]

From Monday on we are going to have blackout from 4 p.m. until 7:30 a.m. It is paralysing.

DEC. 2, SATURDAY.

Soviet troops have occupied Kaposvár, Bonyhád, Dombóvár, Szekszárd and Paks.[1] The drive seems promising, just the same as the Eastern drive seemed at the end of October—but here we are still with Gs and nyilas rule. They have time plenty enough to form a ghetto here, at Budapest, under the most terrible conditions. The stories I have from Klári Forrai, Klári Bálint, the Lángs, etc. are beyond any imagination. I can not force myself to tell them all. Booby traps are prepared right and left of Police headquarters, in the Vigyázó Ferenc and the Zrinyi utca. It is believed, the quarters around the bridges will be evacuated in 500 m-s radius. Almost all espressos in the city will be closed in this case. Today at Mignon I met Lóránd Toldy, he is more dumb as ever. They went to live in a Jewish flat, are going over to Garas utca now. He does not know whether we medical doctors will be forced to leave or not, though he is head of the Mabi Health Insurance Services[2] (since March, of course).

The next nazi move with regards the ghetto will be—I suppose—they will detect secret weapons within the ghetto and then all Jews will disappear so, as no Swedish or Swiss legation will have the right, to protest against their execution or deportation. The district is already encircled by a wall, no gentiles may stay there or ever enter the premises and no office, not even a police station may be left inside. They will be entirely at the mercy of the nyilas and nazi and without eyewitnesses.

---

1. Cities south and southwest of Budapest that were part of the Soviet encirclement drive to surround the capital.

2. Magánalkalmazottak Biztosító Intézete (MABI, Private Employees Insurance Institute).

DEC. 3, SUNDAY.

It would be the birthday of my mother—the seventy ninth. Many telephon calls the morning, at noon Elko came with a plan of his new book and a chapter almost ready. We discussed it from different points. We walked up the hill to Mihály utca, said good bye. Apu got half a years leave from the Foreign Office on pretense of nervous breakdown. He is really very close to it.

This is what happens: when the Russians make an attempt to cross the Danube, a telephon message by the G. observer goes to the Gellért hill SS people, they have four or five tiger tanks, go out with them to the spot, some shooting is done and as generally the Russians are there but with small forces, they retire, finding resistance and the affair is finished. This is war, rather like a joke.[3]

DEC. 4, MONDAY. BARBARA'S DAY!

I had to meet Pali this morning. In spite of traffic difficulties, we met in time at Mignon. Several of their officers were arrested by the new nyilas regime, some killed (a young count Széchenyi among others) in the Gestapo style. The nyilas are faithfully assisted by the gendarms even now.

At Oti we have to clear out at 1:30 p.m. as at 2 p.m., "night duty" begins, as black out is at 4 p.m. from today on.

Patients say, the Russian troups are at Ercsi and they have occupied Siófok. May be, this is so at any rate, they are nearing Bpest and the Austrian border simultaneously. Here disorder and chaos is growing by every day. The police and their families are evacuated, military persons and their families are going to be evacuated in the next days, from the Balaton area refugees are streaming back to Budapest and meanwhile the army is busy quarrelling with the nyilas party members.

About the impertinence of the latter here is a tale: a surgeon went to St John's hospital, to do his daily routine work there, when at the gate a nyilas youngster (about 16) with an enormous rifle stood in his way, asking for ID papers in an insolent way (per *Apuská*).[4] With much difficulty the surgeon got inside, to his

3. Lévai wrote in 1946 that "the regular siege of Budapest by the Russians began on December 8th, with regular artillery shelling of the city" (*Black Book*, 381). Krisztián Ungváry dates the Battle of Budapest as starting on December 26, 1944 (*The Siege of Budapest: One Hundred Days in World War II*, trans. Ladislaus Löb [New Haven, CT: Yale University Press, 2006], 111), but Mádi wrote of the earlier encirclement of the capital from late October onward. On December 1 the Germans ordered Budapest to become a "Festung" and hold out in a "cauldron" to the last man and last bullet (Ungváry, *Siege*, 43). The armies fought in Pest until January 17 and then on the Buda side of the Danube until February 11.

4. Mádi's subsequent annotation: "1969: Daddy-O."

own ward. Ten minutes later a shot was heard, then swearing and a colonel appeared with the nyilas guard, both wounded, the colonel having the boy at his collar. The young hero was playing with his rifle, shot his own foot, but the bullet skidded on the stone pavement and injured the colonel too. This got furious about the affair, slapped the boy and took him to surgery. Our surgeon, recognizing the former guard, asked: now, young man, would you let me in now? Jaj, bácsi kérem, ne tessék haragudni[5] wailed the nyilas. [. . .]

Elly's nephew, a second lieutenant of an infantry regiment, who all were transferred to Dresden, Germany, were deported in sealed wagons, as the boy's father has seen himself at the RR station.

My heart acted up today several times. It is not pure hysteria, as I get it riding on a streetcar and among heaps of work too.

Elly's brother in law, vitéz Szemlaky, a Serb-born pensioned off army officer (Gazdasági hivatal)[6] laid down his vitéz[7] title, out of fear, I suppose. These are the opportunists, who are Hungarian and vitéz, when all is going well and are the first to abandon the sinking ship.

DEC. 5, TUESDAY.

The streets seemed to be less crowded then before, but may be, I am mistaken. Horse cadavers, but human cadavers too are almost everyday affair, horses from exhaustion and men—well, nyilas terror. Policemen, three of them were shot a few days ago at the Oti area—a communist riot, it was said. But why did they shoot the policemen? [. . .]

The face, whole appearance of the city is changed, for the worse. Before the entrance of Gellért a big gun, the Danube embankments are camouflaged two meters high with corn stalks and leaves, behind them the chestnut trees are dug out and concrete stands for big guns placed behind the corn, pointing to the Danube, ready, I suppose, for the Russian Danube flotilla. These all are hasty preparations, booby traps at Vámház körút, etc., everywhere near the bridges, on the Pest side, while the Russian troups are strong on the right side of the Danube.

5. Mádi's subsequent annotation: "1969. Please mister, don't be angry."

6. Mádi's subsequent annotation: "1969. Ordnance."

7. Vitézi Rend was the veterans society established by Regent Horthy in 1920. It was disbanded after World War II by the Hungarian Republic. For a Vitézi Rend leaflet, see Ungváry, *Siege*, 100. The United States denounced Vitézi Rend as a Nazi-controlled organization, and membership in it was deemed grounds for denial of a visa to enter the United States. See US Department of State, "Ineligibility Based on Human Rights Violations," *Foreign Affairs Manual* (2017), https://fam.state.gov/fam/09FAM/09FAM030207.html.

Before Oti I had to see Ilonka, they had no other cigarettes or tobacco, but the inferior sorts and very little besides. After Oti I had to return a book to Tercsi néni, on my walk through Veres Pálné utca I went up to Anikó Kalmár's place, found the whole family together, have shown your recent photos, a big alarm came, we remained in the flat and I asked Anikó to get some candy from the Stühmer factory for me. She was sweet and promised. I am so starved for sweets, I simply had to do this.

At home the afternoon we had a busy day. A patient, Mrs Borbás came and I had to make an incision on her finger. Her daughter and her cousin János Fóti came too. The latter is the author of the libretto of the *Pozsonyi majális*.[8] Mrs Székely came to cut the hair of Frédi, two months neglected, Mr Láng came in matter of his documents and Elko, who read a paper, written by a protestant minister, who stayed two days long under Russian occupation of his village, Új kécske. The statement is interesting, the cruelties chiefly committed by the Roumanian soldiers and many of the population were helped and sheltered by the Russians. One Russian officer asked him in his study, whether his Bible is the Károli translation. It turned out, he left the University as a linguist when the war began. Most of these Russian officers were considerate and humane. Horthy's name was very popular with them, as his declaration promised the shortening of the war and going home for them.

The death of Gyuri Faragó, the pianist, is announced today.[9] Pity, he was a fine musician.

DEC. 7, THURSDAY.

The Russians seem to have crossed the Danube anew at Ercsi and other places, South of Budapest. Funny, it is not mentioned by Moscow, only announced by the G.s, in our papers. According to patients' tales Soviet troups are inside Vác, this would shortly mean a coming North of Budapest too.

General sentiment in town—except G.s and nyilas—is very pro-Russian, people are hoping for their arrival like for a picnic, though everything will not be so pleasant, I suppose, as the country must be practically empty of food and all. This the Russians will not supply to us, not to mention telephon wires, etc.,

8. *Pozsonyi majális* was a ballet by Ludovit Rajter (1906–2000). (Pozsony was also known as Bratislava and as Pressburg.)

9. See Ozsváth, *When the Danube Ran Red*, 83. Faragó was a practicing Catholic, but because he had a Jewish ancestor, he was dismissed from his faculty position at the Liszt Academy of Music. He made a living as a piano teacher and included the young Zsuzsanna Ozsváth among his students.

all robbed systematically by our great allies. The G.s announce to have raided and hit the railway bridge at Dunaföldvár.

This afternoon the following persons (guests and patients) here: Hanna (as dentist, for Frédi), Mrs Láng, Mrs Hermans, Mrs Borbás, Pal Szenezy, again Mrs Borbás, Jancsi Fóti.

DEC. 8, FRIDAY.

The dawn and the whole morning a very intense cannonade was heard not so far away. Russian troups seem to have reached Nagytétény on the South side. According to other rumours, Russian troups have crossed the Danube at Visegrád. Let us hope, it is true. The stories in spite of all official terror-propaganda about Russian cruelties, are not at all bad. According to a Dunaharaszti tale, one night, when under Russian occupation, two R. soldiers knocked at a housedoor and asked for drinks the family was glad to give them two bottles of wine and they peacefully departed. Two days later, when G.s have been again in the village, again knocking was heard the late night. The two R. soldiers returned the two empty bottles.

Apu called me up the morning with the news, young Pali is at home for a few days, asking me for lunch. I suppose he "slipped on oil" (olajra lépett) as it is said in these days. His unit was deported to Germany.

DEC. 9, SATUR.

Since 3 a.m. big explosions. It sounded, as all important buildings would lay in ruins. [. . .]

Meanwhile a story, yet unfinished. The Gorrieris used to have almost every night G soldiers in their flat and they drink heavily. Some nights ago Pató from the next flat heard the drunken voice of a G. repeating several times the following words: Now, look here: clothes, underwear, your papers, Sunday at 11! I suppose, they are going to leave town with help of their G. friends. [. . .]

University professor Géza Zemplén,[10] the physicist, was arrested, when he objected to the deportations of the Universities. The professors were called to Rajniss,[11] who promised them everything fine in Germany, in order to have the authority's consent. Zemplén, who has a collection of orders about G University professors, read them loud before all and questioned Rajniss, whether the

10. Géza Zemplén (1883–1956), chemist and member of the Hungarian Academy of Sciences (MTA) (*MEK*).

11. Ferenc Rajniss (1893–1946), minister of religion and public education in Szálasi's government. He was indicted, tried, convicted, and executed by the Budapest People's Tribunal in 1946 for war crimes (*MEK*).

Hungarian professors will be deported for pure pleasure: do you believe, we are invited to Germany for a pleasure trip? Then and there he was arrested.

SAME AFTERNOON.

Alarms the whole morning. Our bridges are still there, night's explosions were allegedly hits from nuisance raiders. Along the upper Danube embankment there are trenches. During the second alarm I spent the time with Lujzi Horchler. Hanyi and his family went away yesterday at first to Sopron-Lövő, then to Salzburg, on a covered truck. Four small children! Elza and her children are near Reichenberg, they have plenty of milk, butter and sugar. This is the reason why our infants and young mothers have none. No sugar, milk or butter even or rations here. Bibi, Elza's husband, who acted as G spy here, was taken away by the G.s on a refugee train last Wednesday. This, I hope, has the meaning, G.s are going to give up Bpest.

I have seen Anikó Kalmár today for the second time, she could acquire for me some candies, but the Stühmer factory is taken by the nyilas, with all its contents (Képlet lefoglalás)[12] so no more sweets for us.

I feel sometimes so queer, very weak, I suppose, mostly malnutrition. It would be nice to have healthy food in plenty. What would I give for a glass of good milk!

SAME NIGHT.

The town is shelled constantly. Some uneasiness is showing all over the city, as if something would be in preparation. I hope all scoundrels will pull out of town, as Russian troups threaten to encircle Bpest soon. The Rókus hospital got a hit, almost killing the Fidys (Béla bácsi and Tercsi néni), Pali, the brother of Tercsi néni, committed suicide. Pista, Éva's husband was in a streetcar, which got hit this morning, but he is unhurt. This is too much for a family for a day.

DEC. 10, SUNDAY.

The town seems empty, especially of G.s. I went to Rókus hospital to see Béla Fidy and have seen Tercsi home, Mária utca, where she is living at present. I did not go up to the flat, as on the way I have seen concrete triangles built on the pavement of Elisabeth bridge, so this seems to be a phase of the last act. [. . .]

As I went out of this house, I met the Gorrieris, they are still here. I wonder, how many of our nyilas and nazis are going to stay? The best place for them would be Germany.

---

12. Along with its formulas.

DEC. 11, MONDAY.

Still over the other side of the Danube. Most shops closed for the time being, even Ilonka not in her shop. [. . .] The town is shelled all the time. There are some rumours about a Russian ultimatum to the G. military forces to pull out, so they could and would be willing to spare the capital. It is generally believed, the G.s have rejected the offer.[13] What is it to them, if Bpest is going to be destroyed? Tonight artillery fire and air activity is growing. The baker Ruzicska's house and workshop[14] were destroyed by a shell yesterday morning at Pálya utca, he and his wife dead.

New orders of all kind on posters, a new drafting, a new evacuation order, no more extraterritorial rights for neutral possessed buildings (this will be against protected Jews). At Tisza Kálmán tér I have seen several Jewesses, escorted by many armed nyilas, so as escape seemed absolutely impossible. Even now, when the Russian troups are said to be at Újpest, they have time enough for this.

I am rather tired of all this long drawn out expectation . . . Bread I can not get since Saturday, we are almost out of it and today I have tried to consume a three weeks old dry breadpiece. Not so bad, but we shall be short of vegetable too, though we have still some tinned meat and fats. No potatoes either. No milk in town, not to mention butter or other milk products.

On the next side you will see the calling up of all taxis for military service, that is for going to Germany, with drivers, drives with clothing they do not possess, with food for three days, which they do not possess either. Characteristic of stingy G [. . .] . . . Tonight a mighty air raid was made over Budafok, as I am told. May be, these unfortunate taxis were already on their way for Vienna.

DEC. 12, TUESDAY.

The morning alarm, distant hits, I suppose, roads and railways, retreating G.s and nyilas refugees. During the alarm we have seen a police patrol go house searching into the opposite house. We are prepared for this. No sign in my flat, that more people are living here. Elly's brother in law were here this morning to tell her, no streetcars are going. So this will be the first time, I have to give up my work and I suppose, I better go into obscurity for the present.[15]

13. Ungváry, *Siege*, 116–23, discusses the Soviet attempt to get the Germans to surrender Budapest.

14. Edo Ruzicska, baker. His house was at 9 Költő utca, 12th District, and his bakery at 11 Palya utca, 11th District (*Budapesti telefonkönyvek*).

15. This was about the time that Mádi stopped working at Oti and became instead a general practice physician in her 12th District neighborhood.

BBC 10 o'clock European news just announce, Russian troups are approaching Újpest, many H. soldiers have gone over to the Russians and that G. rearguard are fighting the last phases of the battle of Bpest.[16] BBC says the G.s are in such a haste, they leave behind heavy equipment and their wounded. Of all these we do not know—yet—anything.

SAME AFTERNOON.

I had to go over to Lujzi, to get some potatoes, as we are out of food. They have plenty of it and offered weeks ago to lend some, if I needed. She told me her sister Teri (Mrs Aurél Telkes)[17] has fled from the Balaton to Körmend, her husband, a leading nyilas, has left Bpest to join her and they are going to Germany. They do not intend to stay there but have visa to Switzerland! He has made some important transaction in favour of somebody, very probably, on the Swiss legation, who, in turn gave him the visa and foreign money he ought to have too. I can see how they will act the innocent victims of nazi and nyilas persecution in Switzerland.

DEC. 13, WEDNESDAY.

I had to see the Sebes, as Peter is ill. He has scarlet fever, but I am told, many of the 16–17 years old boys have it these days.[18] The red paper on their door will be a great help to all of the family. At Oti we got an alarm, afterward I had to see Bözsi Tárnosky. She is living with my papers in a gentile house, has gone over terrible things, suicide, Jewish hospital, hiding, taking refuge, etc. She sobbed, as she told me some details.

General Beregffy (former Berger) called up the population of Bpest to resist until the last drop of our blood. He—meanwhile—is staying at Sopron. People shrug their shoulders only. The news of tonight are rather disheartening. The battle around Bpest may last still a considerable time.

Officially announced, that garbage will not be collected in the future. I have seen the garbage wagons and heavy horses draw westward out of Budapest.

DEC. 14, THURSDAY.

A poster on the streets about a new "voluntary" evacuation of the Bpest population. It is fixed for the 19 and 20 Dec. Another poster about papers, that

---

16. Mádi's subsequent annotation: "1969. Last phase! It took until the middle of February '45!"

17. Aurél Telkes, financial services inspector (1944) (*Budapesti telefonkönyvek*); for the marriage of Terezia "Teri" Horchler to Aurél Telkes, see Family Search database, accessed April 21, 2021, https://www.familysearch.org/tree/person/sources/LKND-468.

18. Budapest experienced an epidemic of scarlet fever in December. See Lévai, *Black Book*, 391.

must be posted every house door. Number of rooms is to be stated, number of persons living there, age, name, name of parents, profession or job, etc.

Your uncle Béla came to see me at my Oti rooms. He is desperate about Pali, he is out at the front line, but has left things at sixes and sevens here.[19] Remind me to tell about it some time. Uncle Béla has the intention to go away to Szenc because of the state of affairs. I dissuaded him as well as I could. He promised to get some poison for Bö.

So difficult to understand the Russians. Sometimes they seem to force the siege seriously, then again they slack off and we do not even hear the shells. I perfectly understand, the occupation of Bpest is not urgent for them but for us it would be. Nazi and nyilas scoundrels have so much time left!

I went over to the Horchlers this afternoon, Lujzi made some cake for me out of my own materials. Gizi sold me one kg. of lard on a ridiculously cheap price: 5.60? She does not say, I was right, but this lard seems to be a confession without words!

A new order: all male and female persons from the age of 13 until 70 are liable for honvédelmi (military) service. Persons from 13 until 18 at home, others even out of the country. The Swiss legation—according to my Jewish friends—is behaving abominally, headed by their minister, Mr Jaeger,[20] who seems to be a perfect nazi. The Swedish legation and Swedish Red Cross on the contrary behave splendidly. They are present at every railway deportation of Jews, they go to Hegyeshalom, the border station before Vienna and select the Jews with Swedish visa out of the masses to be deported, they quarrel with the G.s and nyilas, they protest every day.[21] Today Moscow announces that the nyilas government demanded the Swedish Red Cross and missions leave the country at once.

DEC. 15, FRIDAY.

I had to see Lacy's two brothers at a Swedish house. They are living rather comfortably at present, I have my own fears, they will not be left there for long. I went up to see the Sebes, especially Pali jun. as he won't stay long at home. Mamuci accompanied me when I left. At home I had not yet time to

19. Mádi's subsequent annotation: "1969. An illegitimate child."

20. Maximilian Jaeger (1884–1959) was the Swiss minister to Hungary (1938–44). "Jaeger, Maximilian," in *Diplomatic Document of Switzerland*, accessed April 21, 2021, https://dodis.ch/p569.

21. See Lévai, *Black Book*, 379, for the rescue of some Jews from deportation at the Hegyeshalom railway station on the border between Hungary and the German Reich. Mádi's mention of the "Swedish legation" is a reference to the work of Raoul Wallenberg and his colleagues.

eat my luncheon (at 5 p.m.) when Zsófi Victor came to see me about Klári Forrai. Zsófi is a teacher at the Scotch Mission School and did wonders in the interest of about two hundred Jews. They were taken away last Tuesday by the police to the ghetto, Klári with her sons in an entirely furnitureless room with thirty other persons. No food, no pots or pans, no bed, not even a rug, to cover themselves. Zsófi was still here—we could not think of any sound plan, as my papers are not available for Klári, there are no papers Bö has them for the boys and without such they can not walk out of the ghetto, besides, they do not know, where to go. Klári alone I could have here, but two boys impossible, considering our present number, and they will not part, very naturally.

Well, Zsófi still here, Klári Bálint came with our electric plate boiler (forraló) which one of her guests repaired for us. In a few minutes Elly came. Klári and Zsófi went. Again my doorbell rang, the house légo-commander, Mrs Csabonyi[22] came about the papers we have to hang on our doors. My friends—Lacy and Frédi—disappeared on the sound of the bell behind the mirror, so the formal controle of my flat is over and she never suspects, there are more people living here. I only hope we shall be so lucky the next time, a check is coming. It will be coming, according to all probabilities.

Mrs Csabonyi still here, Elly's mother came, Csabonyi left and we had a cosy evening. I am rather exhausted though, with Bö, Klári, Marci, Gabi, Károly and Laci (Frédi's father) weighing heavily upon my conscience. I do not see much hope for them. Erzsi & family ought to be out of Bpest with friends but the place seems not yet to be occupied by the Russians and what of a forced evacuation? For them it is mortal danger. Sometimes I think I should not have mixed myself in other people's fates as it is so little, one is able to do and so terrible, to remain passive.

Russian guns are almost inaudible, eagerly we counted five distant explosions just now, but I have to confess, this is not the way, a "Blitzkrieg" is made. I can see the allies in Berlin, Vienna, everywhere, but we shall have still to sit here, with this nazi and nyilas pack on us.

Some details from our daily life these days: the bank safes were opened all, with or without the presence of the proprietor. Except silver (because its weight) all gold, platinum and jewels were taken away to Germany.

The newly equipped Otba hospital (and very probably many more) are left empty, as all equipment, even beds and linen are already in Germany.

The price of a Swiss fr. is four hundred Pengö,[23] 10 dkg of tea 300 P, 27 dkg of raw coffee 300 P.

22. Mrs. Csabonyi was a fellow resident at 19 Margaréta utca.

23. One Swiss franc was about twenty-three cents in December 1944; alternately, $1USD = 1,710 pengö in 1944.

Mamu heard about a friend of Lajos Kreybig,[24] who, as very pro-nazi, went out to Germany, that at the G border all furniture and most clothing was taken away from them and jewels, valuables had to be "deposited, for safety's sake."

Thirty Hungarian officers were housed in one single room, got to eat once daily, members of a family were separated even in work and were insulted by the G population as: you traitors, you dogs, why did you come here to eat, etc.

DEC. 16, SATURDAY.

In town the G. traffic seems to flare up again. Several rumours the G.s have reoccupied Vác and even Cegléd. This affair—I mean the siege of Budapest—seems to be a long one. How much more suffering in this time!

DEC. 17, SUNDAY.

In old peacetime years this used to be the so called golden Sunday, with all shops open, people busy shopping, streetlights shining, tremendous traffic, etc. Well, the only traffic today—except some overcrowded streetcars, suitable for the Epsilons of Huxley's Brave new world[25]—are the military trucks running all over the big thoroughfares. No shops, but they do not open even on weekdays.

Almost everybody is in danger. Not only Jews (the ghetto was closed yesterday noon, as Elko states it) but all gentile youths, older men, girls and women. They have to report for labour service or to fight, digging trenches around Bpest or to go against the Russians—without arms. Elko and Klári are living at the house of the Jávors, Jávor arrested by the G.s, his wife disappeared somewhere. The house was searched yesterday, because they got some kind of protection from the international Red Cross. At the Sebes, Apu is so depressed, he wishes to commit suicide with the whole family, they resisting bravely. The afternoon I had to see Papa W. on behalf of Klári Bernauer, may be, he can get papers for them. At home (Sunday, our hot water and wash day) Mrs Láng appeared, then Hanna came to check up Frédi's teeth, then Pali jun. [. . .] Your second alterego—who, by the way, is a violinist—is liable for labour service too, with Hilda Felsőbüky's papers.[26] I advised her to contract scarlet fever, if she can not hide at some safe place. It is such a complete turmoil, would be ridiculous if not so dangerous.

---

24. Lajos Kreybig (1879–1956), chemist, agronomist, and member of the Hungarian Academy of Sciences (MTA) (*MEK*).

25. Aldous Huxley, *Brave New World* (1932).

26. Another Jewish person Mádi helped shield by lending her Hilda's identification papers.

Meanwhile I can see you, shopping and preparing for Xmas. Even if a small town, Shreveport ought to be shining, with splendid shop windows, sales may be, the best clothing, stockings, finery, dolls, jewels, all. I am so happy you are living on the other hemisphere.

Elko lent me today a Dorothy Sayers, a thriller's persiflage, I am told. This will help to forget the world around me, I hope.

DEC. 19, TUESDAY.

The news of a mighty G. offensive between Aix and Luxembourg[27] are sad enough for us. In spite of the air bombardments, in spite of the sixth year of war, they are still in a position to launch a powerful offensive! You will agree with me, there is no other means of protection for the world, but to extirpate[28] them. I am afraid, no peace-treaty will be able to accomplish this task, may be they themselves, as long as they are going to fight, will decimate themselves, but surely, not sufficiently.

Starvation is threatening us here in the city. If the Russians—no hunger for them—delay the capture of Bpest until four–six weeks, it will be too late for us. [. . .] In the ghetto people were starving even the last week. There is a long row of freightcars at the Budaörs railway station, since weeks, full with Jewish labour service men, they are starving too, the sealed wagons are opened but every third day. To Bö I could give some cyanide, I got from Uncle Béla, he prepared for himself. I could not bear the misery, in case she would be detected, to go through on the highways. [. . .]

Did I tell you, all skis were requisitioned here by the G.s? No skating either this year. [. . .]

Elko bought 500 very bad cigarettes for me (Király and Princessas) on black market price: 375 P. I hope to be able to exchange it for food. It's normal price would be about 50 P.

DECEMBER 20, WEDNESDAY.

It was a busy day. Thanks to a rather good digitalis preparation my heart was O.K. Coming home, I have tried the hairdresser, for the second day in vain, let us hope, tomorrow I shall have more luck. . . . The evening I had to go over to the Horchlers. They asked me for Xmas eve, which I had to refuse because of my friends with me, but promised to see them the afternoon. They are very lonely, nobody from their family, except Frici, here.

27. German offensive in the Ardennes Forest, December 1944.

28. Mádi's subsequent annotation: "1969: terminate."

One small Xmas tree (stolen tops of the fir and pine trees from the parks) today 120 P. There is no import—of course—in Xmas trees, but all G. trucks have at least one of them. They can't be else, but stolen. G. barbarism shows in the fact, that all big trees in the Pest suburbs were cut. [. . .]

By Ancy I am told, five corpses were hanging at Szabadság tér (Liberty square—what farce!) this morning. This terror is called by present propagandists as bloodless revolution. It is a favourite G. propaganda here, they did not intend things to happen this or that way. Now, this ought to be made clear, nothing happens here without or against the G.s. [. . .]

Mrs Láng got some cabbage and cauliflower for us, 31 P, a bargain. May be, we shall hold out two days longer.

DECEMBER 21, THURSDAY.

The town is ghastly today, even the stationery shops are closed. Florists (one pot of azalea 400 P and one small artificial Xmas tree 4–500 P) chemists and a basket shop open. In the basket shop nothing but dog baskets. I could pick up some toys for Frédi—in a drugstore. No books available. [. . .] Magda, my hairdresser told me about a body in their street up the way to Svábhegy, laying there until the evening last night, hands bound together, shot, a yellow star on him. I suppose the man was not even a Jew, the star was put on him just as an "explanation" for the murder. Nobody dares to ask questions in a Jewish case. [. . .]

I woke this dawn at quarter to five, this is 10:45 p.m. with you. I suppose you talked about me, didn't you, dearest?

DEC. 22, FRIDAY.

I have not been able to attend to my work as an alarm came just when I was on my way to Oti. So I dropped in to Kogirt[29] (boobytrap before it on the Piarista utca) and after the alarm had a moderate luncheon for 18 Ps. From Rami I got 25 gms of tobacco, from Ilonka 100 Symphonie cigarettes, so this is not so bad for today. I had a look at the recently blown up nyilas book shop (former Bárd) at Kossuth Lajos utca.[30] After the explosion ten Jews have been brought to the spot and shot, the bodies left there for a day.[31] . . . On the thoroughfare

29. Kogart was a restaurant on the fashionable Andrássy út.

30. Kossuth Lajos utca is the main east–west arterial avenue on the Pest side of the Danube, commencing at the Erzsebét Bridge (see map 2).

31. The German policy on retribution for Germans killed by partisans was at first one hundred Hungarian Jews for every German slain. The policy was later changed to ten Jews per German. See Braham, *The Politics of Genocide*, 1:485.

of Buda side of Elisabeth bridge booby-traps are prepared today—it seems, as if the main G. forces were out of Bpest already.

Frédi, the seven years old boy here gets terribly affectionate sometimes, is more easy to take in hands as before, but in spite of all, gets terribly on my nerves sometimes. Lacy never. She is so tactful, we can tolerate each other very well, since Oct 19. And that is much to say in such a tiny flat and in perfect seclusion.[32]

DEC. 23, SATUR.

Cold, little fuel, no food in the shops, that is what we are going to have this Xmas. I did work at Oti today (for a Jewish patient we gave out a treatment card carefully ante-dated on a false name) but most of the time was occupied by an alarm. This Jewish patient, who used to come before with the yellow star and who is well known by many other patients, is not reported by any of our other patients, many of whom had been great nyilas.

The afternoon I had to see a patient, had my hair combed at the hairdressers (no electricity for about ten minutes), Elly came to telephon from here, got a tel. call from Irmus and Tercsi néni, both like to talk at length. [. . .] After all these I was out and my pains around the heart began anew. My Lanaclarin[33] helped though, but I feel a bit shaky after these attacks.

One of my nurses was forcibly evacuated from her little house at Pestszentimre. Now the Russians are out of the village, she has tried to get back but every house was undermined and blown up on the people, who, resisting evacuation, have gone back when the G. soldiers left the place. [. . .]

Dearest, are you still there? Is there still another world of peace and light and plenty? Today's prices: 1 kg of fresh mushrooms—90 P, one kg of spinach 44 P, one egg 8 P, one kg of dry mushrooms 140 P, one kg of pork 70 P. Fruit is only for children's rations, but only theoretically, in practice none is available, the same with rationed meat.

DEC. 24, SUNDAY.

Frédi was taken the morning by Ilus, to see his father. I would not take the responsibility myself, there is danger on the streets, but it was the wish of the

32. On December 23 the Arrow Cross government issued a new decree ordering all Jews in hiding to report to the ghettos. Lévai, *Black Book*, 395, estimates that there were as many as ten thousand Jews being hidden by Gentile protectors, including Mádi.

33. Lanaclarin was a cardiac glycoside treatment popular in the 1930s. See Siftár Endre, ed., "Tájékoztató: A Gyógyszerkészítmények Rendelésére," accessed April 21, 2021, https://adoc.pub/gyogyszertar-udafest-vii-peterfy-sacldor-u-13-felofoo-221-2t.html.

family, so all right, there is more peace at home. At noon an alarm was sounded, Elko just managed to get there (no streetcars on our side of the Danube, may be, they were stolen) and after the alarm we went for a walk, myself bound for Klári Forrai, about whom I got a message this morning, they are out from the ghetto. I had to go over the pontoon bridge (a substitute for the exploded side of the Marguerite bridge, on the lower embankment have seen a lot of blood and signs of a body having been dragged to the water. Nobody has paid any attention to it. At Klári in a Swedish Red Cross house at least sixteen people in a small garçon flat,[34] I left some food and cigarettes, heard with amusement they come out from the ghetto in an undertakers' lorry as corpses. Had to walk back, at Rózsadomb and Városmajor three close shaves (shells exploding very near). [. . .]

At home I put on my evening dress, Lacy prepared a comparatively good dinner and we felt fine with the news of Székesfehérvár and Bicske taken by the Russian troups. The Bpest-Vienna railway line cut and the city itself almost entirely encircled. The whole day long Russian planes over the capital, after 8 p.m. a very near explosion, I heard the glass fragments on the pavement. At 8:30 p.m. prolonged explosions, I am afraid one or more bridges exploded. We have still electricity and water supply.

Ancy had a tale about G. officers, who went to the house of a count Nemes, told all men to go into a corner and pillaged the house for silverware. One of the guests could somehow slip out called a G. general living near, who shot one of the G. officers on the spot and chased the others out. People are no more surprised on such things.

Last Xmas I hoped very much for a letter from you (under normal circumstances) for this day. Well, if only we could get rid of these scoundrels and treated decently by the Russians, I would not mind so much having to wait for your letter. I know you are with me tonight (3:30 p.m. with you), are you not, Dearest? We have a Xmas night very much in style tonight, constant air attacks (without syrens being sounded, I suppose, they have been stolen too since the noon) and explosions.

Second BBC news Hungary has an elected national assembly and a government, headed by Gen. Miklos. We have to see, what it is going to be, but it can not be so mean, as these people at present. Russians have shown a distinct self-restraint in waiting so long with political consequences. G.s would have formed a pro-nazi government after occupying a single village, see Horia Sima[35] and Cancoff in Vienna. [. . .]

34. A studio apartment.

35. Horia Sima (1907–93) was a Romanian Iron Guard leader. "Horia Sima," in *Biographical Dictionary of the Extreme Right*, ed. Phillip Rees (New York: Simon & Schuster, 1990).

I have listened to president Roosevelt's Xmas message the night, I suppose, you did too.

DEC. 25, MONDAY (XMAS DAY).

The shelling of the city stopped about 1 a.m. and began at 6 a.m. anew, heavily. The Láng's shopwindow went into pieces yesterday about 8 p.m. nothing else in the neighbourhood. This morning Mamuci called me up and I promised to lunch with them, but I could not, it looked too dangerous even for me. At about 2 p.m. shells ceased to burst on our streets, an hour later they began again but no more so intensively. [. . .]

The new Hung Miklós government's[36] program is very remarkable with respect to the fact, that private property will come into its right with help of the bolshevists.

The early afternoon our Frédi was bought back to us as the Swedish houses are in danger. Allegedly all people at the Finnish legation were attacked by the nyilas, again from a Swedish Red Cross hospital. Jewish children were taken away in feverish state by the nyilas. It was rumoured, that because of these events the Swedish government has severed diplomatic relations with the nyilas government here. So Lacy's brothers felt danger in the air (they are in a Swedish house) and sent Frédi away with Ilus, she had him for a night and took him back to us this afternoon. The poor child is again naughty, terrible manners, impertinent with Lacy, etc, etc. [. . .]

Tonight's Moscow communiqué states the capture of Torbágy, Budakeszi, Zsámbék, Solymár, Leányvár, Piliscsaba, Tinnye, so Budapest is surrounded and even the Vienna road cut. I do not think, there are G. forces left inside the circle, may be demolition squads, who hastily try to exchange uniforms for civilian clothes. So do some of our policeman, I am told.

DEC. 26, TUESDAY.

This is a cheerful Xmas at last. Russian troups seem to come slowly down from the Svábhegy, a lot of guns a few H. or G. guns were firing close to our house, but they are silenced now or retreated further down, towards the Southern station. This area may be cleared till the night. At dawn, from 4 a.m. on very heavy explosions were audible, I slept exhausted and did not mind all the fuss, but had to awake on every detonation, speculating, what would it be? Then bored my head deeper into the pillows and slept on. A tel. call from Károly this morning, whether things are not dangerous here. I told him everything is OK,

---

36. The Debrecen Provisional Government assembled on December 22, under General Béla Miklós.

we are here and intend to stay here. Most people from our house are sitting hours and hours in the shelter, I do not indulge in such folly.

The first point in the program of the new Miklós government is to ask for armistice. I can see my first letters from you about the middle of January. Hurrah![37] [. . .]

12:45 p.m. sirens for alarm sounded . . . I do not see why raid a city, almost in their hands already.

SAME NIGHT.

The alarm did not last long, but gunfire went on the whole afternoon, mixed sometimes with machine guns and rifle fire. We are only guessing, but it would be possible, that Russian troups have already bypassed our street and may be fighting about the foot of the hill near Southern station. [. . .][38]

This afternoon I had to go down to the cellar to get some firewood . . . Well, I would never imagine the disorder, filth and stupidity of people living in this house, who, as it turned out, have been sleeping for several nights in the cellar, shelter or what-not. I felt sick as I came upstairs. Pubi just called me up, he is all right and sure, they can not be deported any more. The gap open (I suppose it is between Esztergom and Leányvár) is no more then ten kms.

DEC. 27, WEDNESDAY.

Still no Russian soldiers on our street. Hardly anybody venturing out from these houses. From the morning on rifle and machine gun fire alternately. Last night we were told by BBC that Esztergom was occupied and the last gap of escape closed. The Western suburbs of Bpest, that is Pesthidegkút, Hűvösvölgy and Lipótmező occupied. The Russians have turned the G. plan inside out they were expected from the East side and all preparations were made according to that.

Since 9:30 a.m. there is no more electricity, no radio and I am told, no gas either. Explosions were so heavy that about 10 a.m. the Hermanses came running down, to find shelter in our first story flat. They left reassured in an hour the shooting subsided for a while.

We had food prepared for today, so I had to warm it only up at Elly's. Mrs Láng came to offer her help before 2 p.m., just when the radio began to work again. So we hastily are cooking some beans for two days ahead, in case the

37. Mádi's subsequent annotation: "1969. How optimistic!"

38. The Red Army was still on the Pest side of the Danube, not the Buda side.

current would fail us tomorrow. Elko called me up now, they are in the middle of a battle, near the Fillér utca! He fears a long fight.[39] [. . .]

At 8:45 p.m. an attack seems to be launched but see we can not anything. There is snow and frost on the twigs, rather cold not only outside but inside the flat too.

We hastily began to cook when the current worked, got so far as to boil thoroughly the beans, but none further. Elly and her mother can be expected any moment, they will be afraid in their second floor flat.

DEC. 28, THURSDAY.

The situation seems to be unchanged the past two days, in the next house a G. observation post seems to work, so this region gets plenty of shells. Elko could call me up this morning, they too are in the same situation, a battle raging around them, but nothing seems to move forward. The G.s do not care for us, they defend the city until the last ruins.

People in this house use the siege as an excuse for not washing. Women unkempt, not properly dressed go up and down the staircase, nobody ventures out the street. The janitor does not clean the staircase any more. I am told, there are a few people on the streets at the Pest side, almost none at the Buda side, communication over the Elisabeth bridge until 5 p.m. There are the few nyilas newspapers left, but not enough people to buy them. No shops open, no bread since Saturday. We have still some, may be for two or three days and some more in dried slices.

The cannonade began before 8 p.m. again, I hope, they will be able to accomplish something more. The windows of Elly and Ida, at the back side are out since this afternoon, only the outer panes. No current tonight, though we had for an hour the early afternoon.

DEC. 29, FRIDAY.

It is the fifth day, we can't set foot on the street. No water on the faucets since the night. Shooting goes on, went on all night, heavy guns and machineguns too. The night a heavy explosion was heard, this morning Hanna called me up (I can not call people, but some lines can call me) and told me, that the Southern railway bridge was blown up. Pubi phoned, Elko and the father of Frédi in the course of the day. Pali jun. turned up the afternoon, came to get Mr Láng, I went out with him to the shop of the Làngs, I felt rather unimpressed by the shooting on the street.

---

39. Mádi's subsequent annotation: "1969. The very first time he was right in his predictions."

With dusk an air attack began, which seems to last for a considerable while. Pali runs a considerable risk in coming here. No current since last noon and no water supply since the morning. The candle abominable, I have to stop.

DEC. 30, SATURDAY.

It is apparently no use, if you are not afraid of the battle around you, the heart rate quickens on every exciting noise . . . There is a certain limit one can take. I should like to stay in bed today if only visitors would let me. No water, no electric current, no radio and we have to stay behind blinds, in the dark.

From 10:30 a.m. until noon we had shelling. I am fed up with it. No damage in my flat until now. Elly & mother came down during the attacks, Elly upset, trembling and sobbing, I had to give a sedative to her. No possibility for cooking today. The shelling continues even after noon, but not so intense. Almost dark in the room, we have to use the blinds all the time and our candle is dwindling.

DEC. 31, SUNDAY.

Yesterday we had the worst day until now and the night concluded in a hit on the next house balcony, when we lost one of the big panes of the balcony door. The weather is a bit warmer, so we can do somehow with the blinds down. With water the situation was hard, I just felt convinced, we can't hold out more then two or three days, even not washing. Then the taps began to whistle and soon after we got water down at the basement, later even in the flats, so I risked to scrub the tub and we seem to get it full with clean, fresh water. Irka (Lacy) is just scrubbing the boy, who screams as a jackal. [. . .] . . .

I feel a millionaire with plenty of fresh water supplies. Klári Bálint organized a bread-baking for us both, I gave her the flour, the potatoes, salt, etc. her fiancé worked the dough and at Mikolays it was baked in the gas oven. So we have bread too, about one kg. During the whole fuss around the water—people all running up and down the stairs with bottles, pots, etc.—an alarm is on, nobody cares for the explosions, when such a precious thing is at stake. The absence of the electric current, including the radio, is not so hard as not to have water.

1945—JAN. 1, MONDAY.

Another hideous year finished, *requiescat in pace.*[40] We do not notice very much, sitting most of the day behind the blinds. A big attack is going on North and East of us, may be fortress hill, may be the Pest side of the city. We get plenty

40. Rest in peace.

of shells and air attacks (bombs and machinegunning), here too. My broken balcony doorpane is covered with the old Persian rug, it is almost better against cold, as it was with glass. Another rug is at the lower part, it belongs to Bö, I hope, she won't mind.

Cooking is organized at various places, we have no means of cooking, as there is no current (neither water, since the night). Sometimes we cook on the gas of the Székelys sometimes on the stove of the Hermanses, a bread was baked by the Mikolays. On the ground floor there is gas pressure, on the second floor almost nothing. [. . .]

Mr Székely, my neighbour is home from labour service,[41] he could not come into the house unnoticed, but as nobody dares to leave the premises, he is not reported—yet. Last night he sent me four leaflets, fresh from the Russian planes, telling us, how G. military authorities refused to give up the city and therefore they will be responsible for the death of several thousand citizens. They are perfectly right only the fact is little consolation for us, sitting here, the eighth day of the serious siege. [. . .]

Money is not accepted in these days. On the one hand you can't set your feet on the street, no shops open, no traffic, etc. On the other hand, the janitor does not accept the rent this month, he will not have much money on him. Cooking (gas) is done by Mrs Székely in exchange for cigarettes (though she will pay it in money). Mrs Láng gives things (bread, oil, sugar) for firewood. They have no fuel, neither window panes.

JAN. 2, TUESDAY.

We are still in the flat, the cold is not extreme, as from the staircase side I lined the entrance door with stripes of your white felt trousers (Roumania, fancy dress ball). I hope, you don't mind. The windows of the staircase are broken too, and we feel the cold from that side more, than from our own balcony. Persian rugs are good insulators as I always fancied reading about Dsengis khan.

Shooting goes on the whole day and air raids (most Russian fighters) are frequent. Lacy does our cooking in the next flat's kitchen, no window and at least four families cooking on the three-ring gas oven, almost continuously. We do not have tea for our breakfast since yesterday, just a slice of bread the morning. The battle does not seem to move forward, no news from the world outside.

You seem to be unreal, your way of normal living absurd. I wonder, if we shall be able to last until the end of the siege. I should like to tell you so much, amusing details, but our candle is short, so we are going to sit in the dark (it is only 6 p.m.).

41. Mádi's subsequent annotation: "1969. Illegally, of course."

JAN. 3, WEDNESDAY.

Several fires around, the gendarmery next us[42] got a hit too. Three people ventured out of the house today and all say, our place is comparatively peaceful and undamaged. Allegedly the Horthy körtér[43] is in ruins. The waste of materials is terrible. Mr Szücs from our house (something in the Szücs factory) came home, telling that all the food storage of the factory (!) was pillaged by soldiers, several hundreds of kgs of flour, meat, bacon, honey sticking on the sacks, peacetime soap, etc. By this pillage he was swindled out (!) of 50 kg s of meat, due to him. Cows were slaughtered on the premises. All this terrible amount of food was hoarded up in this simple factory, in other factories it was just the same, while others of the population, for example humble M.D.s, like myself, could get nothing, not even rations. Allegedly, Beregffy, the so called war secretary of the nyilas, spoke yesterday on the radio, declaring, that all bakers have to go on baking. [. . .]

JAN. 4, THURSDAY.

I could not sleep much the night, because of my anginal pain[44] so I slept rather late the morning (there is not much to do and the room is cold). At 11 a.m. I had to help the Hermanses with their gasoline stove. An air raid followed shortly as we began cooking in their second floor kitchen, I could see the fortress hill bombed and afterwards several points burning. Some people were out from the house the morning and came home triumphantly, the relief army is here, Székesfehérvár and Bicske are again in "our" hands and tomorrow Bpest will be relieved from the siege. With Lacy and Elly we think this is so typically nazi propaganda, we are not really worried.

The afternoon we heard a shop opened, with Klári Bálint and Maria Pató we went there but found it closed, two men were before the house door and told us there was nothing else but Igmándi water.[45]

As I was already out, I ventured up to the Horchlers, they are well, told them my story with Lacy (only now), they seemed to be happy about it and sent us a pot of jelly and potatoes we needed badly. They know about a well somewhere in the new military hospital, I have to go there tomorrow, as we are almost out of drinking water. [. . .]

Would be the situation not so serious for us, we could laugh at the few shots fired tonight. Is this a siege? Are they going to take the city at this rate? March

42. A reference to the school across the backyard from 19 Margáreta utca.

43. Móricz Zsigmond körtér (square) in present-day Budapest.

44. Chest pain due to constricted blood flow to the heart.

45. Mádi's subsequent annotation: "1969. A laxative."

will be here, when so, and nothing changed, except that we shall be starved to death, long before. [. . .]

We are scarcely washed, badly nourished, cold and hopeless. Honest men, like Mr Láng, go together with other not so honest (Németh, Mikolay) to get some coal from the school, left behind (by wonder) by the G.s. 50 kg coales[46] were carried away in a few hours. I did not see a newspaper since the 23 Dec., no telephon calls the fourth day, no mail since two weeks. The worst is, no hope for relief. [. . .]

JAN. 5, FRIDAY.

It is the twelvth day of the siege. Most of the night I lay awake, pondering chiefly about our water supplies. The morning I got up early and went out to find water somewhere. Shelling increased from yesterday, so I felt uneasy about staying out any longer and as the addresses given for a well seemed vague, I did not want to drag Elly and Klári with me, into uncertain adventures. Down at Gömbös Gyula ut[47] I found three houses, where they had water in the flats. Many people gathered with bottles, buckets and pots. The flat-owners took in the big containers and put it out before the door and we had to fill them there. I came home triumphantly but a bit shaken because of the whistling of bullets. [. . .] . . . Elly was afraid but behaved bravely, Klári too. Almost no men on the streets, they are afraid of being seized for digging themselves. Women and children do all the work you can see.

The shelling goes on, a battle of tanks seems to be going on, may be, at Kelenföld, Elly believes at Újpest.[48] [. . .]

JAN. 6, SATURDAY.

The night and the morning were so noisy, we did not go to get water and we had luck, as at about noon our water supply began to function again, after a pause of several days, I do not even remember, how long. We washed ourselves and everything, we could, took fresh reserves here in the evening and we still have water.

Small items: Elly came radiant this morning. She has washed herself, in spite of all. Mr Mikolay does not show himself in the house since the siege.

46. Mádi's subsequent annotation: "1969. 100 lbs."

47. Alkátos utca in the 12th District of present-day Budapest. Mádi walked about six blocks in search of water.

48. Kelenföld is a neighborhood on the southern edge of the Buda side; Újpest is a neighborhood on the northern end of the Pest side. In the absence of radio or newspapers, Mádi and her neighbors depended on rumors to follow the street fighting.

Allegedly he is sitting the whole day in the lavatory in a steel helmet on his head. [. . .]

JAN. 7, SUNDAY.

It is only the date what reminds me of Sunday. Our life is the same as always, since these fourteen days, sitting in the flat, seeing people from the same house and speculating, how long food is going to last. We are short of bread, we own hardly two slices and it has to last until Tuesday noon, when the new bread, Klári is baking will be ready.

I had a thorough wash this morning. I feel better.

May be you have noticed, since the middle of October the charm of telling you all is gone for me. I am never alone, the child is all the time talking, irritating, making noises and trouble. I hardly would give you the facts most outstanding. This is now an exceptionally peaceful moment, Frédi still in bed allegedly reading, Lacy in the anteroom, brushing clothes, the shelling goes on somewhere far. [. . .]

We are longing to hear one morning foreign commands on the street, Russian uniforms and G. pack chased out. The day before yesterday, when we made our excursion for water, I have seen four G. soldiers, they are like doomed men. Hollow eyes, yellow in colour, emaciated, though they have plenty to eat. They know, I suppose, they are caught in a trap and so I hope too.

Since last night the water supply has stopped. We have reserves for about a week. My fuel will not last longer than the same period and the weather is cold, no window pane on one side. Fuel the Russians will not give us neither window panes, may be not even food. This is a competition, who will be able to hold out the longer: G.s with ammunition or the population with food. I was never much good at competitions. [. . .]

Klári B. came with the news, police officers go round the houses, looking for hiding men.

Ancy had two visitors yesterday from the Gellért hill, they say, the houses there are looking rather sad, no window panes, because a truck with anti-tank weapons was hit at the Szirtes ut and Milály utca corner. They went to see the town too, G.s. retreated to downtown and consequently the city lays in ruins. The Krisztina square and quarters too.

Mrs Láng brought twelve pancakes, filled with apricot jam, she made from our own materials. This our luncheon, we are rather hungry.

JAN. 8, MONDAY.

Klári has the news, the Municipality press (Fővárosi nyomda) at the town hall is destroyed by the G.-s, all letter types mixed, workshops used as horse stables. This does not serve any strategic purposes, just sheer destruction.

Elly was attacked by Dr Németh yesterday to empty her fuel cellar in "common interest," so as the people of the house shall be able to cook there, to distribute her woods[49] between all other cellars, to take all her values downstairs compulsorily, but he, Németh, can not take any responsibility. I advised Elly to refuse flatly. These people (he as vice commander in the house) are intoxicated with the sense of power but they won't dare to use force.

There is an order, allegedly spread by megaphons on the streets and squares, according to which in every house people have to pool food. I hope, in our house it will not be made, as Mr Bencze, the commander has the most food and he will be not keen on sharing with us, who have almost nothing. For me and Klári[50] it would be disastrous to give up our small food stores and to get meals for one person while we are three persons in both flats.

SAME NIGHT.

Pali jun. was here the afternoon, with growing beard. He has seen a good part of the city, everywhere human and horse cadavers on the streets, horse flesh is taken away by people. [. . .] . . . the G's Xmas offensive has been entirely stopped and reversed, since about the day we do not have news. A G. relief army exists somewhere at Komárom and it seems the Russians have taken out considerable forces of the siege, to beat them.[51] [. . .] This accounts for the two quiet days here . . . Pubi is still with Charlie, he even promised to get us some bread, fat, sugar and flour out of their liquidated headquarters that would be a marvellous help. I am not hungry today, since there is no more gas in the house, we are cooking in our stove, we had tomatoe soup and beans but monotony of our food begins to get on our nerves and appetite. I never felt so anxious for Pubi before, I suppose, he means for me the memories of your childhood, the absurd idea, that like he, you could be involved in these abnormal and terrible affairs.

JAN. 9, TUESDAY.

Almost deadly silence, except a big explosion the night. Lacy did not sleep at all, as last night we have heard rumours about the Swedish protected houses, where her brothers were housed, among many others, allegedly these houses were evacuated, the Swedish visas destroyed and people taken to the ghetto. I am afraid, this is very probable.

---

49. When the coal supply ran out for the central heating plant at the 19 Margáreta utca building, the residents were reduced to finding firewood to burn in the woodstoves in their flats.

50. Klári Balint was also shielding two Jews in her flat at 19 Margaréta utca.

51. See Ungváry, *Siege*, 188–200. The battle of Komárom on the left (north) bank of the Danube between Budapest and Bratislava lasted from January 6 to January 22.

Myself could hardly sleep either, Frédi was very noisy and restless all the time. I am only afraid, after the occupation of the town, when they will not be in danger any more, they will not be able to go home, as, may be, there will not be any home for them. With Lacy I could live for months peacefully but the boy is a nuisance.

The morning Gizi was here to see Lacy for the first time, it is three days, I told her. She brought a bottle of (green) beans preserves, which will be handy. I hope, their friendship is restored. When Gizi returned home I accompanied her to have a bit of fresh air. At Pilsudsky road two horse cadavers were cut into pieces, the poor wounded beasts were shot on the spot this morning and people already gathered around to buy the meat. I hope, the siege won't last so long, that I should be sorry for not buying any of it. I did not feel tempted by it the least.

Since Dec. 23 we did not get any bread on our rations, there is some talk today, ration cards were collected, may be, we shall get 90 dkgs (on 10 day's rations).[52] [. . .]

From Pubi I heard, the Debrecen government was recognized by allied powers and by Sweden.[53]

The evening. We had a discussion with Mr Bencze, the recent commander in the house. Elly has to shovel snow tomorrow morning but I told them, she is starving, she can not do it, until we don't get our bread supply. I got some bread for her from the Benczes, so she will do it all right. These people around us have plenty of supplies so they do not care for our bread rations.

I had to lay in bed late afternoon, my heart is acting up angina like pain. Patients are accumulating, Mrs Borbás here the afternoon, I am asked to see Dr Németh, which I have to do tomorrow, by daylight. I shall have to do it for food and fuel, if possible.

JAN. 10, WED.

There is talk about the civilian evacuation of this area. This would be the most terrible thing, that could happen to us. The Gellért hill was mentioned too, but Pali jun. being here this afternoon, says, there is no truth in it, at least not until 10 a.m. this morning, when he left home. Charlie and Pali sent us (Pali on skis) a lot of food, flour, fat, beans, marmalade, canned food, coffee dry preserves, cigarettes, sugar, crackers. It seems about a week for us, if only evacuation

52. For Mádi, December 23, the end of rations, marked the beginning of the siege. "90 dkgs" of bread was about two pounds, to last for ten days.

53. The Soviets oversaw the meeting of a constituent assembly in Debrecen on December 21, 1944. Five political parties in opposition to the Nazis and Arrow Cross made up the interim government.

does not rob us from all, we have. Two patients today, from the pharmacist I could get some medicine too. [. . .]

JAN. 11, THURSDAY.

Pali had the story about all Swedes here, not only Jews under Swedish protection but members of the Legation staff too (with exception of the minister, who took refuge into the Vatican's Legation Nunciature) were arrested a few days after Xmas and put into the ghetto. The Legation and all Swedish houses robbed by the nyilas. The real Swedes and some of the Jews were taken back to their houses in three days time and under G. custody.

Meantime stealing of private property by G. soldiers is going on. At Derék utca (where Mr. Fledderus, the Dutch consul is living too) three houses were robbed by G. soldiers and their drunk "girlfriends." When the inhabitants of the villas came upstairs from the cellar, to see, what is going on, these soldiers dressing their partners into the silk underwear, they found in the drawers. With some silver trays under their arms, they left. [. . .]

At Tamás u. 14. the inhabitants were evacuated last week by G. soldiers. Yesterday they could go back to their home but found all clothing and food stuff missing. People are not even astonished at these stories, the unusual thing is, when anything is left at the spot.

This is the eighteenth day of the siege. At the beginning we believed, we can hold out but two weeks food. I got food in the meantime from the Lángs, the Horchlers, from Pubi and Charlie, Klári B. and Elly are helpful too, Klári even with fuel. She promised to give me firewood, when I am out of mine, which will be in about five or six days. With my present reserves (yesterday two canned lecso's from the Kürty shop) I still hope to hold out a fortnight. The worst thing is the unhappy and despairing face of people coming here. It is a shock every time I have to open the door.

At Döbrentei utca, according to Pali, well dressed people, ladies in beautiful furcoats are gathering around horse cadavers and cutting them up for use. At other places soldiers have the right to cut and sell. [. . .]

Here, on the corner of Margarite street a grave was dug the day before yesterday.

People have terrible dreams, Elly, Amélia, even our boy, Frédi. He has dreams about his father in the ghetto [. . .] It is phantastic to live without reliable news for such a long period.

STILL JAN. 11, THURSDAY.

We have a little hope, since the morning, when Mr Mikolay, who had intention to go over to the Pest side, come back with news of a police man. This stated the G.s have withdrawn from Pest to the bridges and are retreating out of town towards Budafok. They hope to find a gap there, to ship out the relief army. This would be welcomed by us, the damage done by them is much as it is. I got a newspaper today, how strange to see one after twenty days.

An intense airactivity over us since the morning. The retreating troups are heading across the Danube. The weather is mild, thawing if everything would not be covered with snow, one could say it is spring (+5C).

JAN. 12, FRIDAY.

I took a barbiturate the night, just a light dose, so I did not lay for hours awake. The night was quiet, too quiet for my taste, but this morning violent artillery, may be infantry action began South and South west from us. It seems the Svábhegy hillside[54] and the Sashegy-Gellérthegy junctions (where Hegyalja ut and Wolf Károly ut meet) are in the foreground, the latter would be important to the retreating G. army. The air is fresh Atlantic breeze is felt and almost no people on the streets. I ventured out to see the pharmacist but the shop was closed, neither did I found the grocer on their place.

Our friends in the house (Klári's Tibor and Laci) feel more hopeful, Elly has seen the Gorrieris (the nyilas leader of Weiss Manfred works) yesterday go out of the house with heavy knapsacks. Who is leaving the house with heavy knapsacks these days? Evidently somebody who is looking for another place to live in. These small signs have meaning these days they feel the end near and try to disappear in houses where they are not known.

Somehow—may be, it is the weather outside—we feel the change in our bones. We plan since yesterday to go far out, to see the city and see, what happened to friends. Poor Lacy, she feels the anguish, what is she going to find: brothers home, all, that used to belong her. Klári's friends have the certainty, their father and mother and sister were lost.[55] [. . .]

JAN. 13, SATUR.

Nineteenth day of the siege. The morning we heard a violent tank battle, not far off, at about 9 a.m. air activity joins the noises. According to the news of Mrs. Németh, who was here last night (Elly & mother here, Lacy and Frédi hidden in the bathroom), Pest will be given up entirely in two or three days and fighting will go on on our side, Buda. The army officers are not in the least in clear about the situation and have no word about the so called relief army.

54. The Svábhegy hillside, on the Buda side of the Danube, was still within the German-held lines on January 18 (see map 4).

55. Mádi's subsequent annotation: "1969. The sister came back, I met her."

Mrs. Németh came to pay me for my visit to her husband. Compared with the siege values, the compensation was not so bad: about 2 kgs of flour, ½ kg of lard and four eggs. With water, I mean drinking water, we are not at all well off. I have planned to go and haul some today but as it is a sunny day, it seems impossible to go out with air bombardment all around.

I hear from Maria Pató, that your friend Pokker[56] left for Germany, together with other Nazis from the Maort. It is strange that Mr. Ruedeman[57] gathered around him so many nazis, as Miss Osán, Mr Hauer, Apzinger, Pokker, etc., all in leading positions. Hauer's son served during all the war as a German (SS) soldier.[58] I hope, they all will stay in Germany. What a pleasure trip!

Mrs Borbás was just here (as patient), she has the news, Russian troups have occupied the Eastern station and are on Rákóczi ut already. So the Pravda family is in safety if they could survive the preliminaries.

SAME NIGHT.

The afternoon Klári B, Elly, Mr. Lang and myself went up Levendula utca[59] to the Borbás, to get water. Bullets whistled around air attacks, going on not far away, but I got five liters of drinking water. There are rumours in town, that the encircled army has provisions but until the 20 of January. Horses are starving. If only the ammunition would be out! Many G. and nyilas soldiers do pillage shops and houses.

JAN. 14, SUNDAY.

At 8 a.m. the Hermanses were down in our flat, the day is sunny and all sorts of activities (air, artillery, tanks) going on. They can't stand detonations in their second floor flat. At about 10 a.m. relative silence set in, so they left for their flat and soon after knocking was heard on the door, a nurse came from the next house, with a three years old little French girl, in high fever. The parents of the little girl were of French legation, their balcony next to the Hermanses,

---

56. Ernő Pokker (1914–48), chief engineer of MAORT. He committed suicide before he could be arrested by the Communist police in 1948. Simon Papp, *Életem* (Budapest: Zalaegerszeg, 2000), 204, accessed April 21, 2021, https://library.hungaricana.hu/hu/view/SZAK_OLAJ_Sk_2000_Papp.

57. Pál Ruedemann was the president of MAORT. See his role in the "MAORT sabotage" trial of 1948, described in "Hungary's Seizure of Oil Hit by US," *NYT*, December 3, 1948.

58. Mádi's subsequent annotation: "1969. Hauer died in Venezuela. He could not come to the U.S."

59. A cross street of Németvölgyi ut, about a two-block walk for Mádi from her 19 Margáreta utca flat.

they used to exchange a few words. We believed, they were off somewhere in safety, but the nurse told me they were arrested a month ago by the Gestapo their two small children were left here. We have no idea of the tragedies in our closest vicinity.

The afternoon. Water was to have on the ground floor faucets. A terrible fuss over it, I was down at least six or seven times and filled all bottle, even refilled partly the tub. [. . .] It is a bit sadistic as the Russians let us sit starving, without water, fuel, light and gas. I can see their point of view perfectly but still it is cruel.[60]

JAN. 15, MONDAY.

The twenty second day of the siege—and no change. At least, not here, where we could see. Yesterday we heard vague rumours about the Russians having occupied Pest until the Boulevards (Nagykörút [. . .]).[61]

I sleep with barbiturates and am afraid of everyday, as one is like exactly to the other. The worst noise is better, danger is easier to bear, as the monotony of stagnation. Amália (Mrs Brunovszky), Elly's mother who is a 76 year old real lady said yesterday "Ich war empört über die Ruhe."[62]

So we are all. My little French patient was here this morning, a bit better but still in danger.

We had a good lunch today. The second half of our last can of tomatoes, as soup. Beans. Cake (mákoskalács), Mrs Láng made me out of my last flour. In the evening beans again, but with the last of our bottled pork. In spite of comparatively sufficient food and almost no possibility of exercise, I am losing weight. I do not know, what I weigh, but my clothes are hanging loose on me. Elly's mother is declining and Klári Bálint with her pernicious anemia is by day worse off.

JAN. 16, TUESDAY.

The early morning, just the same as last afternoon began with seemingly violent tank, artillery and air action but soon a slowing off set in. So the day is sunny and clear, air bombardment is going on, without any visible damage in our parts. For me war seems to be the most senseless pass time. Here at least nothing happens on the surface, during these twenty three days I have not seen more then

60. Mádi's subsequent annotation: "1969. A la Warsaw and General Bor." General Bor was the nom de guerre of the Polish Home Army commander in the Battle of Warsaw (1944).

61. The front line had reached the Nagykörut (Grand Boulevard) by January 15 (see map 4).

62. Mádi's subsequent annotation: "1969. I was shocked by the Silence."

three or four G. soldiers, one of them a cook, about a dozen of H. soldiers, nothing else. This would be announced as fierce resistance and street fighting and you, dearest will eat your heart out of worry and anxiety what happens with me.

JAN. 17, WED.

The day almost out (at least daylight which counts) the morning at 7 a.m. a big explosion took all windows of our house on the North west and Northern side. The heavy panes of the housedoor are out as well. The wall is spotted with holes, caused by splinters. We had to open the balcony door and remained in bed until noon, between a visit from Elly and Amélie, their bathroom window, the outer one is out too. At noon I dressed, very little washing as the water out of the tub is almost gone. People did not find any water, not even at the water works.

I went to see the Làngs, she is ill in bed, I had to get my bag and supplies and she seems better off. Last night it was a visit with the Székelys, he is unwell. Coming upstairs—all the way shells exploding outside—we began to cook our lunch, *krumplis gombóc* with plums—Klári Bálint came with the news, the Böszörményi ut[63] below us, is crowded with G. and H. soldiers, horse, vehicles, etc. So they are target of this continual air bombardment. The explosions are heavy but no real damage can be seen in our street. The day light has faded out, so goodbye!

SAME NIGHT.

By candlelight I have to to tell you, what two of our men from the house did tell. The Parliament's Tower was burning yesterday, the Danube embankment, the hotels Dunapalota, Hungaria Carlton, Bristol all in ruins, the Váci utca does not exist anymore, etc, etc. Even if the news are exaggerated, the damage ought to be appalling. [. . .]

[Az Ostrom fucsaságai: néhány primítiv asszony, akiknek van elég ennivalójuk, azon panaszkodik egész nyiltan, hogy a sok menekült családtag miatt a kis lakásokban nem tudnak bizalmasan együtt lenni. . . . Mikolay páncélsisakban jár az clo-ra, sb a fölszinten lakik. Pató Mária kijelentette, hogy mivel a W.C-T nem tudja kiöblíteni, ő ezután nagydolgoni dobozba fog. Hogy ezt azután hová teszi, a technikai kivitelre még nem gondolt][64]

63. Street running parallel to Nemétvölgyi út and perpendicular to Margaréta utca one block east.

64. People of the siege: some primitive women who have sufficient food to eat complain openly about their family members crowding into their little flats. . . . Mr. Mikolay, who wears the helmet, waits in the toilet upstairs. Mária Pató says that the WC is not usable, she plans to shit in a box. She has not thought about how to dispose of it.

JAN. 18, THURSDAY.

The morning by explosions followed one another we are told by Mr Bencze, who was down allegedly in town, that over last bridges, Elizabeth and the chain bridge were blown up by the G.s the others gone already yesterday.[65] Pest is given up and the soldiers around us (Böszörményi ut, Németvölgyi ut, etc) retreated from Pest. A hopeless situation.

It happened also this morning, that something stuck our house, broke the iron railings before the garden, made a hole in Németh's livingroom wall, also on the balcony next mine, then settled into the small front yard of the house, before Lángs' door, unexploded. It is a 15 cm Russian grenade and we eye it suspiciously. Is it going to explode or is it not?

With the Hermanses we organize a mákos kalács in common. Mrs Láng (in bed) after a tonic administered to her, told me the secret of ingredients. At Hermanses we weighed in flour, shortening, sugar, egg, etc. Lacy worked the dough, Amálie will fill it and myself take it down for baking to the Lángs, when she will get her evening injection.

JAN. 19, FRIDAY.

The night I had a regular camp in my room, five persons slept in the tiny place. Elly and mother came to us, to have a night's rest, as in their flat everything is shaking when the shelling goes on or air bombardment follows. Frédi got two big armchairs to sleep in and we four slept on the couch diagonally like the photos of the Canadian quadruplets.[66] The other inhabitants of the house—except Klári B—slept in the cellar again, after a few days leisure. [. . .]

Having done my rounds by my patients, Amélie came to tell, there is water at the basement so I began being camel and run up and down the two floors to get up enough drinking water and to fill the tub. Between two ways a patient with a five year old little girl stood at my door, I had to hide Lacy and Frédi (their fourteenth week of stay) had to diagnose a case of chickenpox and sent the malicious message to the next house commander, to isolate them. They all live in the cellars about fifty persons. She too did not contribute to our household, money I did not take as it is no use, food she does not have, being, as she told me a refugee. So this is my luck. The only exceptions are the Lángs, who even today sent me a big bottle of lard and some pork.

65. Bridges were dynamited on January 18. See Ungváry, *Siege*, 148.

66. A reference to the Dionne quintuplets, who were born in 1934. See Pierre Berton, *The Dionne Years: A Thirties Melodrama* (New York: Norton, 1978).

JAN. 20, SATURDAY.

The morning was spent in carrying firewood up to Klári Bálint and into my own place. I told you already, my fuel was out, astonishingly soon, but so are all people in the house, I mean, they are not yet out but their fuel is dwindling away. The janitor family is wonderfully well off with fuel. I lent out my empty cellar to the Bencze family, for a basket of firewood and now Klári lends me out of her own, which means a lot, as she herself is not so well off. The noon I had to see Mrs Láng, then work at home, lunch a vegetable soup with bread dumplings. We have satisfied our hunger. Shooting goes on all the time. Mr Láng has news, the Gellért hill would be in Russian hands and they are already on Szebeny Antal tér.[67]

The afternoon I had a wonderful wash all over as the water began to run even here in my bathroom. For several days, I could wash myself partly. See coming epidemics!

JAN. 21, SUNDAY.

The morning Gizi and Ancy came to see us, a risky venture, I have to say for them. They brought us potatoes, a can of beans and one of tomatoes, beside a little herba maté, the Paraguyan tea (green), which I knew only out of pharmacology. They knew about the giving up of Pest before three days but do not know anything about Gellérthegy's occupation. After they left, I did my rounds at home a young girl came to pay me for the French girl, about 15 dks of very good coffee, which means a fee of about 150–200 Ps. So you see, one patient pays for the others, as many seem to believe, their doctor is living out of the air.

JAN. 22, MONDAY.

Yesterday, at about 3 p.m. (shooting went on rather sharply) I was called to a patient into number 9. I had to go, was lucky too both ways not to get a bullet. The night there was an ominous silence, but the morning began with five heavy artillery hits in our street, these were heavier as any before the house across was hit on three spots all corners, room, walls in ruins and one of the third floor flats in our house open to the elements too. I had to see Mrs Láng from the street entrance, demolition is around the house, they got two splinters in their room, the high basement flats have no windows, my own balcony door lost three of its panes again. To work on them, to nail them in with oilpaper was constant danger as planes are flying deep and machinegunning the place. We, our friends and myself agree upon, that we do not mind the whole business, if

67. Szarvas tér in present-day Budapest.

there will be a progress, a development of the situation. But if it remains unchanged, I shall be furious. The flat is cold, of course, we have to live and sleep in our furs and even so we are shivering.

JAN. 23, TUESDAY.

We live in darkness. The night comparatively quiet the morning again the usual artillery fire, this time not us as target. For three consecutive days we had water in the daylight hours, since yesterday again no drop, but we have reserves. Of course we are neglected, our clothes overworn. I could have never imagined, that organized life could cease for a whole month, may be, even considerably longer. Since the 23. Dec. no shops were open, but for the spell when a plundered grocery opened for two or three hours. Again I have no phantasy how organized life will begin after the siege. No bridges in a town of about two million inhabitants, most of them living on one side of the Danube and having to work on other side. [. . .]

Lacy dreamt the night, she was listening to the radio when a commentator spoke about the sieges of the different capitals. Belgrade was taken in nine days—the voice announced—Warsaw's siege lasted for ten weeks, Budapest's for thirty. . . . —here she listened sharp, to hear the exact number but she woke. [. . .]

In such times as this people's real character can be judged. The Lángs (Mr. Láng a shoemaker before accepted but luxury work), now taking all sorts of repair in return for food, share everything with the "family" that is Klári Balint and myself. Klári is all help, the Hermanses too. Poor Maria Pató would be helpful too, but is so mixed up it is better not to start with her. Before we (our family) used to be on friendly terms with the Székelys, the husband a Jew and on labour service. Now he is at home secretly but they behave so abnormally selfish, we are all disgusted by them. Some weeks ago, when milk was no more in the shops, not even on baby-ration cards, Mrs Brumovski, Elly's 78 year old mother supplied her daily with an excellent milk, she got secretly for her own use with the help of her own son in law. Now when the Hermanses are almost starving and I fully explained this to the Székelys, Mrs Székely did not contribute even with a little flour to their living, though we know she has ample supplies. This is disgusting. The other inhabitants of the house have plenty of food, but we were never on friendly terms with them, I should not dream to expect any help from them. [. . .]

This affair of supplies needs explanation. It was not a question of carelessness, that we do not have supplies. Canned food was not available for about two years. Even vegetables were rather scarce since the middle of October, when the Russians began to siege the Pest outskirts. All other things were rationed and even rations were not distributed regularly since October. So we, just ordinary, non nyilas and non nazi people, could only scarcely get our daily living.

JAN. 24, WEDNESDAY.

A wonder if I still remember the date as I have no calendar. The weather is cold, 10°c below, the night we could not sleep for hours because of the cold, though over the blankets I had my fur.

The morning Elly came with the usual pot of tea (it is with Gizi's Paraguayan tea) I was washed and dressed, then went off to see Gizi et Co. They got hit on their staircase last Sunday, not much damage done. A corpse is a few meters distance from their garden gate, shot on the nape (tarkó lövés),[68] undressed, no sign of identity. It was murder of course, deliberate murder, good old G. methods, it has been laying there for a week unburied. Last night when the shooting was sharp a G soldier came into the house, he was a seventeen year old only son of a Cologne factory owner, is soldiering since one and a half year, was drafted at the age of 15½.

JAN. 25, THURSDAY.

Counting the siege days from Xmas Eve, this is the thirty third day. Neither our friends, nor ourselves did believe, we could hold out as long as that. Patients coming every day, yesterday Mrs. Gorrieri the first, born Korbuly, may be an aunt of Emmy Korbuly.

Last night strong artillery fire, so this morning. The day bright but very cold, inside the flat +6°c, that is not much, though heating is going on and the missing windows mended with oilpaper. All the day strong air activity, just now leaflets dropped, G. language and addressed to G. officers and soldiers. The capture of Warsaw, Krakow, Lodz and Czestohowa announced. This is almost the liberation of Poland, devastated, of course, while Chechoslowakia remains untouched, the G.s. will have to evacuate it at great speed. This is luck and influence of Benes.[69]

We are still not hungry or at least not often. For a change today we had dry peas (it is either beans or peas with all of us these days). Our bread will be gone tomorrow morning and either do we use our last flour for bread or we use it for cooking for both ends it is not enough.

68. Neck shot.

69. "Benes" is Edvard Beneš (1884–1948), president of Czechoslovakia before the Munich Agreement and president of the Czech government in exile (1939–45).

JAN. 26, FRIDAY.

Thirty fourth day. The night I slept soundly. Not much noise, the dawn probably G. transport planes over us as there was no shooting upon them from these quarters. The wildest rumors in nazi families. The small Russian force is encircled and they wish to escape through Buda. This morning men were gathered from the opposite municipality houses, 29 of them about the ages of 18–50 it seemed. As there is no more question of taking them anywhere out, it is only to let them die inside the siege ring. Yesterday, we heard the Russian megaphones, not so far off, but understand we could not. Intermittently speech and music could be heard.

Somehow though without hope, I begin to prepare for the after siege period. We have no bread (Elly gave us this morning three slices of bread with bacon, what they have scarcely for them left) but I expect in the near future we shall get bread again on rations. I can see the difficulties in finding anybody or anything in a demolished town. I am told, in houses at the Széll Kálmán square the G.s. put heavy artillery on the second and third floor, of course the houses were demolished by airattacks. [. . .]

I mentioned before the disregard towards the population is unspeakable. During these 34 days we got bread with the help of authorities but thrice 80 gms per head at all. With me it had to suffice for us three as Lacy and Frédi are here illegally.

The so called defense of Buda continues, that is the ruin of all we had. I am told the Krisztinaváros area is unrecognizable, so the Margit körút– Statisztika parts too. The Todt organization had its headquarters there.

JAN. 28, SUNDAY.

The military situation unchanged, though last night Russians were reported at Tóth Lőrinc utca,[70] close to us. I was called to a patient after curfew (5 p.m.), a few houses distance, bullets whistling around. The case nothing but hysteria. I do not mind risking my life in serious need but I can be furious when I have to risk it for nothing. Experience: people begin to go out of their food reserves. Pay they can not, money I can not have, I tell them flour, potatoes, fuel, not to mention bacon or canned food, they have not or may be just lying to my face. Home news: Frédi in bed with belly ache. At Lángs: the boy with a serious infection on his right toe. A misery to be without hospital facilities.

I ate horse meat. I can not say I care for it but well prepared, it is not repugnant.

70. Just west of Déli Pályaudvar (Southern Railway Station) (see map 2).

In spite of the sunshine, the day is desperation for us. We hoped so much last night, no sound was heard, but Russian air activity, so we supposed, all resistance ceased in these quarters. The night and at dawn all began, all over again, AAC, machineguns, rifles, etc. No change in the situation. It is the thirty-sixth day beginning with Xmas eve, the sixth week begins. Yesterday's wind tore down the papers from the balcony door, so we are living almost in open air. It is cold. Some firewood come from two patients at least the stove will be hot and alternately we shall be able to lean against it. We all are losing weight, wrinkles, some dirt accentuates it even more, as it is more then ten days, we did not get any water. Last night no megaphon speeches. Today two of our men from the house (one of them Mr. Láng) had to report to Mészáros utca[71] only to receive the latest propaganda stuff, called recent news, about relief armies, for the benefits of the house inhabitants. To go there meant serious danger. It is just our bad luck that since Xmas—with exception of one or two days—it is so cold. More fuel is needed and in spite of heating my feet are always like ice. [. . .]

JAN. 29, MONDAY.

The thirty seventh day. All night machine gun fire under our window. No progress though. This morning artillery fire directed on the vicinity, we get big shakes every minute. The weather very cold, inside the room it is about 5–6°C. Elly won't be able to bring our morning tea, because of the danger in the staircase. It is all open to the Northside and many bullets have been found in it already.

I do not feel any more interest in this siege business. To help: it is beyond my power. It is but theoretic interest: how long it is going to last? But for myself, I do not mind a bit, what is going to happen. I am at the bottom of all miseries, anything would be welcomed as a change, even destruction.

The noon. I have been out of the house, on my rounds. The cold and the wind is bitter, like in Siberia. Bullets flying in several directions. Took down my bucket for snow (for cleaning) Mr. Láng, out of gratitude not only filled it for me under danger, but took it up to my door. What a contrast to the other men in the house, and he a shoemaker, the other so called intelligentsia!

On such days as this, the coffee from the French girl helps to survive. Last night we had but dry bread (cut up into slices months before) soaked into water. The taste is just the same, this sort of conservation proved excellent. For the next siege we shall be prepared entirely, we have all the experience needed.

71. Mészáros utca is adjacent to the Southern Railway Station, about a one-mile walk that Mr. Láng was compelled to make by Arrow Cross gunmen.

It is almost silly, but I could go on and on telling you the smallest details of our life, just to be with you for a while. This is my excuse for scribbling nonsense—I feel, I am with you. Do you notice how my English is deteriorating? I did not listen to radio news for weeks. Some words escape me, I miss some ways of expressions, I have to look for the exact word and do not find it. [. . .]

JAN. 30, TUESDAY.

The thirty eighth day. Still alive, though last night and this morning a vehement heavy artillery fire was concentrated upon us. The top of the house the upper part of the staircase and the Lajtai flat are destroyed. We remained in bed during all the time, temperature +5° in the room. This morning the sunshine is lovely, in consequence we laugh with Lacy all our miseries. The bathroom smells terribly, in lack of flushing of the lavatory (we wash it with melted snow, but in other flats they seem little to care for it) so we call it the gas chamber, dangerous to enter. [. . .]

We use for kindling the wood from the top beams Mr Láng brought in this morning. During the time, I am writing, we are attacked incessantly by Russian light planes. One gets used to all these.

JAN. 31, WEDNESDAY.

The morning about 9 a.m. several hits on our house, heavy artillery fire. A big hole on the top of the staircase, the Gorrieri and Bencze flats got hit, the latter on the spot, where I was consulted by them a day before. We were in bed still with balcony door ajar, when I was urgently called into the next house (this is not forbidden!). A man was hit by a splinter in his groin. Of course, I was told, the splinter got into the abdomen but no sign indicates this. People as a rule, like to overstate facts. Shelling was heavy, when I had to go over, even my dear fellow inhabitants, creeping in the basement were anxious for my safety and put a raincoat over my fur, so I should not be visible in the snowy street. On my return I dropped in to the Lángs, the boy there is a bit better, improving, no fever.

This is the thirty ninth day of the siege. Nothing indicates the end. This is eternity in hell. Yesterday we were told, we can't even expect to get water, the snow is dirty when melted. Temperature, inside my room with door shut and stove alright +5°c, this goes up by the evening to 10° almost.

FEBR. 1, THURSDAY.

The night at 1 a.m. knocking on my door, it was the janitor's wife, to call me to Mrs. Migrány in labour.

I won't retail all that happened, just the fact that heavy artillery fire began at 9 a.m. torn off the window of the labour-room, lent by Mikolay. Our house was shot at, several hits and splinters, as I have seen later one on my own balcony door (a splinter), which went over Bö's Persian rug and made a hole in the hall glass door, touching the mean time the wall. During the actual birth period the shelling was intensified, so as I finished the mother, the bathing of the baby was not done properly. I had no midwife to help, just the janitor's wife and I did not want to risk my life for a baby-bath even if I risked it for the birth. It happened at 12:15 p.m., among the respect of all inhabitants of the house, pity, I can not feed my family (Lacy and Frédi) out of their admiration.

Meantime two G.s soldiers forced their entrance into our house, looking for an observation post for their artillery. They decided the place was too exposed for this purpose and went away, as we were heavy shot at the whole time and the house half finished. This is the way, they destroy all civilian habitations and this is the reason our position seems rather hopeless. Exposed to heavy attacks all the time since, weeks and no progress in the situation. So inhuman.

My salary for the birth was until now 75 of Memphis cigarettes, two cups of tea, one cup of coffee (all surrogate) a slice of bread add two scrambled eggs, one plate of horse gyulyás[72] stew and a pot of potatoes with a goose ham, all this during the labour period or immediately after.

FEBR. 2, FRIDAY.

Dearest, the whole day long I did not have light enough to write. It is almost 9 p.m. and I burn our last candlestick (the light will not burn tonight). The morning again a windowpane lost and all the surrogate panes (out of paper) torn out several time by suction bombs. Some more splinters in the flat. My patient with the baby ok. Shelling was very heavy the morning and the afternoon, I hardly could go down the two flight of stairs to see them. As the balcony door is open to the air and splinters we put the wardrobe before it there is not much light. The cold is not so bad today, let us hope, it will subside. The evening we all three went to see the Hermanses, a big gathering with Klári and her two friends, we were nine persons alltogether.

FEBR. 3, SATURDAY.

Forty second day. Not very much to eat. A piece of dried bread the morning. At 7 a.m. G. artillery provoked a terrible shelling from the other side, again a pane lost from the balcony door. The morning temperature +7° in our room, pretty good our destruction seems almost inevitable. The good old G. method to nest in residential areas with their remaining forces guarantees it. On the next opposite municipality house sits the G. artillery observer, the heavy cannons

72. Goulash.

are so close somewhere, their sound is almost as deafening as the Russian hits. This is the situation since Xmas, we can see no change and we do not notice that any of the G. batteries would be silenced by the Russian guns.

Don't believe for a moment, I am afraid because I am not. I only loathe the whole affair, it is so pointless. We shall be destructed by explosions or starvation long ago, when the G.s will be still flourishing, well fed, plenty of ammunition, they only have to change their observation post for another, when one house is shot to pieces after the other. To go anywhere else is impossible, in other places they don't accept newcomers as the shelters are so crowded. Besides yesterday the entrance stairs to our house was demolished, today, almost the same spot, the central heating room was hit. Poor Marie Pató, who is living now with the Hermanses was here with Elly's tea, really in danger.

The evening. My fee for the birth came in the morning: 5 kgs of flour (this means three breads, shared with Klári), about 20 dks of fat, five cans of meat and fish and about half a pound of very queer coffee, smoky, brown in color but raw, it seems to have been in a warehouse. It has a smoky, funny, not very agreeable smell, taste a bit better. These Migrany people have 5 kgs of it, so I intend to get more of it as caffeine is caffeine, even with an oily flavor.

Artillery fire was tremendous today, but a new feature appeared motor cars were heard to rush down the road and machinegunning so strong and loud as never before.

8:30 p.m. Klári just here with the news, ten armed G. soldiers are in our house; two in the staircase, three up on the third floor and five in the flat opposite mine. They wanted pots, are in darkness but cooking their meal. This may be our end. They ordered all people into the cellar. I won't go, if possible (Frédi in bed with chicken pox) Klári won't go and I suppose, neither the Hermanses.

CHAPTER 7

Soviet Occupation, February 1945

Chapter 7 includes the entries Mádi wrote during and after the arrival of the Red Army to her Margaréta utca neighborhood. This was an event she had long awaited with a mix of hope and fear. The doctor had written in her diary many times of her dread of Communism, based on Hungary's 1919 experience. Hungarian and German news reporting throughout the summer and fall of 1944 warned of the Red Army as a murderous and pillaging invading force, but Mádi thought such reports were exaggerated. She scoffed at news that the cardinal primate of the Roman Catholic Church had ordered all priests to remain at their churches and suffer "martyrdom" at the hands of the godless "Asiatic" invaders. She saw no reason why the Red Army should murder priests and nuns. Mádi wrote about stories and rumors she heard of Soviet soldiers, some with favorable expectations of the coming encounter, some chilling. She recorded one story about a Hungarian encounter with a Soviet officer. The Russian seemed highly cultured in her eyes because he spoke several languages and wished to discuss literature with the Hungarian civilians he met. On the other hand, she repeated a story of Soviet troops who were Jewish but showed no concern for Hungarian Jewish survivors of the Holocaust, instead regarding all Hungarians, including Jews, as enemies of the USSR. By early February 1945, she had witnessed so much theft and violence from occupying German troops that she welcomed the arrival of the Red Army, if only to stop the looting of stores and private flats in her neighborhood.

February 3 might have been the most dangerous day of the siege as a German mortar unit sought to place a team atop the 19 Margaréta utca building, a move that would have soon brought Soviet counterbattery fire and the destruction of the building and its inhabitants. Still, there were ten German soldiers in the building, and they set up a barricade of furniture inside the front door to the building, as well as firing positions in some of the flats. They ordered all the residents to the basement shelter. The pro-German and anti-Nazi tenants were huddled together. Dr Mádi brought Lacy and Frédi with her. There was no chance of hiding them in the flat, and to her surprise, one of the pro-Nazi families was actually kind to Frédi, making sure he had a shelter bed. Fortunately for the residents, the Germans abandoned the block between the evening of February 3 and the morning of February 4 and slowly retreated southeast toward their Gellért Hill redoubt. The advance forces of the Red Army arrived and brought with them water and food to share with the residents of 19 Margaréta utca.

Soviet military intelligence ("GPU" in the diaries) had preliminary information about the residents of Mádi's building. The Soviets killed the janitor, Mr. Jancik, who was an Arrow Cross sympathizer, even as one of the junior officers in the Red Army greeted Mádi in Russian as "*doctor, dobre*" (doctor, good). That officer affixed a red cross to her overcoat, which allowed her to move around the neighborhood without being disturbed by other Soviet soldiers. "My red cross sign on my furcoat causes great respect," Mádi wrote on February 6, "and I feel perfectly safe." For a day, she was assigned to work at a Red Army battlefield first aid station.

Even as the red cross lapel pin provided some protection to the doctor, other residents of her building became victims. Mrs. Gorrieri, one of the pro–Arrow Cross women in the 19 Margaréta utca building, was gang-raped the first night of the Soviet occupation. Soviet military intelligence arrested that woman's husband and son and detained them for being Arrow Cross men. Mádi expressed little sympathy, at first, for Mrs. Gorrieri, writing coldly that the wife of the building's Fascist leader was raped "willingly and proud." The doctor also, at first, minimized the sexual violence of the Red Army soldiers. Although she had heard that "6–7 women" in the 19 Margaréta utca building had been raped, she thought that the actions of the soldiers "seem to be understandable, even if deplorable." Mádi soon began treating Mrs. Gorrieri as a patient, and the doctor's attitude softened a bit after seeing the woman's suffering and learning that the two shared a hitherto unknown family connection.

The frontline soldiers of the Red Army who took the building on February 4 were replaced several days later by other, rear-echelon troops. Looting was widely practiced by Soviet soldiers in their conquest of Budapest. One soldier looked at a framed photo of Hilda and then pocketed it. Another took some jewelry that Bö had left with Mádi. Several of Mádi's friends in her old Gellért Hill neighborhood were raped on February 8. The women came to the doctor's flat for medical attention and for shelter. Her one-bedroom apartment then held half a dozen women residents and Frédi. On February 9 a new Red Army detachment came to 19 Margaréta utca, and in the evening darkness, drunken Soviet soldiers pounded on Mádi's locked door. The doctor opened the door and met them in the hallway. A pair of soldiers seized her watch and jewelry at gunpoint. They demanded access to the traumatized women in the flat, but she screamed at them in Hungarian, "nem szabad" (not available), and used her fists to drive them away. She wrote that this was "one of the most terrible experiences in my life." She could only wish that the next neighborhood "would be taken by them and this will help us as much, they will plunder there and let us hope, here no more."

The doctor never did call the Red Army "liberators" or their arrival a "liberation" except when writing of the liberation of Budapest Jewry from the Nazis and Arrow Cross. Lacy and Frédi were liberated by the Soviets, and Mádi knew it. "Gentiles" like herself experienced the arrival of the Red Army more as an invasion of looting and sexual violence. Scholars estimate that as many as fifty thousand Budapest women were raped by the soldiers of the Red Army. The Soviets appointed civil authorities to replace the members of the Arrow Cross who fled or died in the siege, and the new officials complained to Soviet commanders about the mass rapes, but to no avail. Even the Hungarian Communist leadership asked the Soviets to halt the war crimes committed against Hungarian civilians, but again, no response came from the Red Army's leaders. In February 1945 the Soviets began their economic pillaging of what was left of Hungarian agricultural and industrial production. That included the kidnapping of Hungarian civilians, who were misclassified as enemy prisoners of war and deported to work in Soviet war reconstruction. Scholars estimate that one hundred thousand Hungarian civilians were kidnapped in the winter of 1944–45 as the Soviets fought to capture the city, with another half-million soldiers and civilians, especially Hungarians who were ethnic Germans, sent to forced labor later that year. Many died under appalling conditions, and those who survived did not return for years.

The entries in chapter 7 close with Mádi's thoughts about the previous years of Hungary at war. She felt resigned to the hardships of occupation, even as she welcomed the end of the siege. "No use, I hated this nazi war from the beginning," she wrote on February 18. "I have to take all the consequences of a lost war and destroyed civilization." She thought about ending the diary now that the war, at least so far as Hungary was concerned, was at an end. However, her sense of duty in serving as a witness for Hilda continued. "Still, as long we can not communicate by mail, I am going to tell you the small events of my everyday life." She continued to write diary entries after February about Budapest under Soviet occupation until postal service was restored between Hungary and the United States in the fall of 1945.

For Further Reading

The diary entries in chapter 7 include harrowing accounts of rape by Soviet forces occupying Budapest. Mádi wrote only a few entries on this topic. For many years after the war, the history of mass rape by Red Army troops was not the subject of scholarly attention, but in recent years there have been several published accounts, starting with Andrea Pető, "Memory and the Narrative of Rape in Budapest and Vienna," in *Life after Death: Approaches to a Cultural and Social History of Europe during the 1940s and 1950s*, edited by Dirk Schumann and Richard Bessel (Cambridge: Cambridge University Press, 2003), and subsequent reflections by Andrea Pető and Ayşe Gül Altınay in *Gendered Wars, Gendered Memories: Feminist Conversations on War, Genocide, and Political Violence* (London: Routledge, 2016). Deborah Cornelius, *Hungary in World War II: Caught in the Cauldron* (New York: Fordham University Press, 2011), has a chapter on the subject. Mádi also wrote of the Hungarians kidnapped off the street and sent to the USSR for war rehabilitation work. This subject, too, has become of interest to historians; see Tamás Stark, who has studied the records of the *malenki robot* (little bit of work) victims in "'Malenki Robot': Hungarian Forced Labourers in the Soviet Union (1945–1955)," *Minorities Research* 7 (2005): 155–67. The archivists at the Hungarian National Archives have created a searchable web database of more than six hundred thousand records of individuals sent to forced labor in the Soviet Union; see "Szovjet táborok magyar foglyai" (Hungarian prisoners in Soviet camps), Magyar Nemzeti Levéltár, Adatbáziok, accessed April 21, 2021, https://adatbazisokonline.mnl.gov.hu/adatbazis/szovjet-taborok-magyar-foglyai. Finally, Mádi lived in fear that the building janitor at 19 Margáreta utca would learn that she was hiding Lacy and Alfred, but when the Red Army arrived, the janitor was promptly killed. The doctor regarded him as pro-Nazi, but it is not clear from the diaries if he was such an active collaborator that he sent people to their deaths. István Pál Adám has written of the janitors and concierges of Budapest and their behavior during the German occupation, the Holocaust, and the Soviet occupation in *Budapest Building Managers and the Holocaust in Hungary* (Cham, Switzerland: Springer, 2016).

~

FEBR. 5, MONDAY.

At 9:30 a.m. the Russians in our house.[1] I have to tell you the whole story. Yesterday at 5 a.m. Lacy woke me (we slept with our clothes on because of the news, G.s in the house), she heard knocking on my door. It was the janitor, to tell my young patient with the baby has to be carried down to the shelter and everybody is ordered down by the G.s [. . .] so we went down into the cellar, with Lacy and Frédi, the first time since they are living with me. So did Klári

1. Ungváry, *Siege*, 162–63, presents a map showing Mádi's street liberated by the Red Army on February 4.

with their friends and the Hermanses. Going down the staircase in the dawn, misty, faint contours of houses and trees, behind the staircase windows the silhouettes of G. soldiers, it was ghastly.

In the cellar a terrible crowd, sleeping there, since weeks. They were rather friendly and helpful, took the child into a bed, against all my protestations. So the Bencze boys will develop chicken pox within twelve days. The day was terrible with all its horrors of darkness, hunger, thirst, and the G.s noise with machineguns above us. The house shook with all the artillery and aircraft hits until 6 p.m. then relative silence reigned until about 4 a.m. We had no proper room in the cellar, we were cold, painfully tired and in spite of it sleepless.

The morning I despaired and I had to despair this morning too, when at 4 a.m. I could distinctly hear German voices in the emptied shoemaker's shop. Unchanged situations—thought I and was ready to die any moment. At 6 a.m. Klári Bálint came to me, whether we should venture up into our flats [. . .]. We found our flats habitable, not much damage since we left it, so ate hastily some mouthful of canned food and returned to get our friends, before the big shootings would start. [. . .] The door of the house was barricaded by furniture from the basement flats, these were used to machinegun barricades too in the rooms. Other furniture, radios, lamps, etc. were thrown out of the windows, just to destroy them. My flat and Klári's and the Hermanses were not entered by them.

From about 6:30 a.m. until 9 a.m. a terrible artillery fire broke out, we just lay in bed and awaited death. We had no hope at all and then a knocking on my door, three soldiers, accompanied by Mr. Bencze and janitor's János came in, whom I believed to be G.s (in the twilight, as we cannot open the blinds) just looked round and said *doctor, dobre*[2] and went out. They were clean, clean-shaven and well fed, clothed, looking much better then we, dirty and starved.

Well, I have to finish, only tell, two other R. soldiers came in later, did not take watches or jewels from us, as it is said, they took down the shelter. I gave to one of them a bottle of Eau de Cologne, he accepted with difficulty but took your photos in his hand and admired very much, for a long time. So we hope to be free and safe, I hope to be able to cable you soon. The darkest moment of my life was the dawn of the 4 Febr., when going down the stairs I have seen the absolutely unhuman G. faces, without any thought, whether it was right or not, they were doing, whether there was any purpose or reason in the unbelievable destruction they were causing, their only thought: orders. One of them told to Mrs Gorrieri "our orders are: to hold out until the last man and the last house." Well, the houses are finished. With utmost difficulty

2. Doctor, good (Russian).

I could go out of the house this afternoon, its top and walls have suffered so much, ruins lay around knee deep everywhere. The opposite house looks like that[3] or even worse, I draw it as I can just remember as I have seen it for a few minutes.

The best moment again was, when I realized the soldiers in my flat were no G.s but Russians and I really could have a good impression about them, in any case they were no barbarians, well meaning, human creatures. Our friend the driver from Moscow, who was three times here, when offered a watch, refused and when offered a lighter refused too, promising to bring a bottle of gasoline for it use. Gs, on the other hand stole and took by force every conceivable object, yesterday one of them offered to Mrs. Németh silk stockings for a piece of bread. She felt sure they were her own silk stockings stolen from the drawer.

The Russians ought to be greeted very heartily on most places as the Hungarian words, they learned until now are: köszönöm szépen (many thanks) and viszontlátásra (au revoir). On other places they let people drink from the water before them, in me they had so much confidence, they took it directly, one of them, very exhausted, even took a pill from me without contradiction. It was Aktedron[4] poor boy, he wont sleep much the night as it makes you quite alert.

FEBR. 6, TUESDAY.

I venture to the other side of the street to the pharmacist, as my reserves are nearly exhausted. The night I was called down to the shelter twice, the janitor was dying of a wound in his abdomen. At midnight the men from the over house came home very tired, they had to work from morning on, carrying corpses, ammunition with and even heavy guns. Mr. Bencze did not return with them, he got a G. bullet and died there are no ceremonies these days, he was not even carried home. The janitor will be buried in the backyard, some deeds of the Russians soldiers are told, rape (though from 160[5] inhabitants of the house it is stated 6–7 women, in our house Mrs Gorrieri willingly and proud), some taking of watches and jewels, but to be just, what are the facts in comparison with the G.s in Russia or Poland and their deeds here, in a so called allied country, when they destroyed the house and belongings of hundred thousand on the other hand, these Russian soldiers are in war since three and half years, they have seen cruelties committed by G.s and very probably Hungarians, the taking of some valuable and these women affaires (mostly willing), never two or more men with women, seem to be understandable, even if

3. Mádi inserted an ink drawing in vol. 14, p. 35, of the diaries.

4. Amphetamine phosphate.

5. Mádi likely meant to write 60 inhabitants.

deplorable. Some of them are really nice, my red cross sign on my furcoat causes great respect and I feel perfectly safe, they will never take a needle from me. [. . .]

The two Gorrieris, father and son have been taken from work yesterday morning and disappeared since—both great nyilas leaders from the worst sort. It seems, these Russian soldiers coming into our house regularly, seem to be rather well informed about us. They do not let people to return upstairs whom they found down in the shelter but don't disturb us living upstairs. This morning, not even 24 hours after entering the house, they gave us one sack of flour, a box of lard and unknown quantity of sugar to make common use of it. The funny thing is, they come to us at 9:30 a.m. Monday and in number 17 and 15 they have been already Sunday night. If we had known it! It was the night of horrors for us. [. . .]

FEBR. 8, THURSDAY.

I can go everywhere freely, nobody disturbs me. Yesterday the morning I have dropped in the Horchlers. They are all well, Ancy was approached by a R soldier but another soldier run for their captain who turned out to be a twenty years old pretty girl and who reprimanded the soldier and turned him out of the house.

The afternoon I went up to Farkasrét, above the graveyard, to have news about Lily (Elly's sister) and family. [. . .]

Coming back I thought, I have lost my way, the cemetery chapel part was unrecognizable. Further down I was held up by a Russian tank, the soldier called their officer and he asked me to see three civilian wounded on the Sashegy (Fohász lépcső 19). They had found an M.D. colleague already but he did not dare to go up as the street was shot at. I told him I am willing to only don't have anything so their first aid station with a nice girl-colleague in it, lent me a syringe and antitetanus serum. I could go but down no more, the R guard aimed his rifle at me and chased me back to the house, the block was a battlefield under artillery and infantry fire. The G.s seemed to come back on the Sashegy, so I could so nothing else, but stay there for the night. Twelve people in the basement room, I got some food, cigarettes, as my fee a brand new hundred P banknote, issued by the red army. At present I do not see, how I can use it as there is nothing to buy. Prof. Kállay[6] from the Debrecen University gave his bed up for me, I was warm but very anxious for my people at home, who probably believed I was killed somewhere. The morning a R boy (about 15 years) came into my room and ordered Mrs Raskó to go to their captain. I told him she is

6. Kálmán Kállay (1890–1959), Reformed Church theologian (*MEK*).

ill (*bolnaj*)[7] and went myself, so getting down to Németvölgyi ut and home, to Lacy's great relief.

In this house this morning the G.P.U.[8] went round, looking for Lajtai and Ubrizsi the chief nyilas in this house but they have been out of the country long ago. To me they also came, a Jewish boy (Hungarian) and a Russian soldier, who gave me three cigarettes, the first asked some analgetic,[9] luckily I could give him.

After all, I have seen my impression are, the town is destroyed for about 60–70 percent, pillaged all, but most destruction and a part of the pillage was done by the G.s and only continued by the Russians, who, after all came as enemies and had plenty reason to hate us.

The G.P.U. soldier and his civilian companion returned to our house the afternoon, to the Székelys. Mr Székely makes great efforts to have something to do with them, or at least to appear so.

FEBR. 9, FRIDAY.

Some routine work the morning. Gizi and Ancy came to see me, to have my help, how to unload their house from the burden of soldiers' night visits.[10] These are terrible events and as I talked it over with a civilian R official, they will be prevented as soon the frontline moves farther. Until then there is nothing to do. I told Gizi, they should come here, as my flat was respected by all. There is no denial war is terrible. To complete the picture a drug addict came to me the afternoon a case of cancer of the uterus but did not accept anything else, just morphine, what I had not. Two R. soldiers helped me to get rid of her, as she insisted on staying here, promised gold, jewels, all.

FEBR. 10, SATURDAY.

Yesterday the dramatic events went on. Gizi, Lujzi and Anci fled to me for the night, to be safe. Unfortunately, the latter two had their experience already one night, at Muskátli utca. Until then I was never molested by R soldiers, but hardly had they been placed here, two soldiers came and though were not disagreeable, they said, they want to sleep in the flat and were difficult, to send away. At 9 p.m. when we were all in bed, other two soldiers came and I had to fight them alone in the hall, they took two wristwatches from my arm and put out the light whenever I lighted a match. In the darkness and barefoot, as I

7. Ill (Russian).

8. The Soviet military intelligence agency.

9. Analgesic, pain-relief medication.

10. A reference to rapes.

had to run out, I would not be energetic enough at the beginning and so I lost my own watch and Lacy's brother's. In vain I told them, I am a doctor and mentioned the Russian first aid station across. When they turned to go into the room (I was all anxiety for my five people inside), I told them boldly: nem szabad[11] and so they turned and went out. They were not rude or cruel, like the G.s but I had one of the most terrible experience in my life. I am a little afraid of them in the future. Allegedly our Gellért hill would be taken by them and this will help us as much, they will plunder there and let us hope, here no more. [. . .]

Don't believe, I am shaken or broken, because I am not. Lacy is in bed with an angina, I shall have to do the cooking today, Frédi cut his hand, just to cause trouble as usually. What a life.

This noon one of Klári Bálint's friends got a bucket full of bean soup from the Russians, when he helped him carry water. He gave us a potful of it, we ate this for lunch.

FEBR. 11, SUNDAY.

Routine work. The afternoon, Mr Vertán, Gizi's friend came to get me, he has a Russian captain in his kitchen (they did not turn him out of his room, imagine a German in his place!) who has high fever and asked for a Hungarian doctor. They have apparently but surgeons with them. I did what I could for him, for a fee I rather would have accepted bread or cigarettes but he had money, so I had my fourty pengös. If only I could buy something for it! No shops yet open, but order seems slowly to return. The frontline is moving on further. Officers seek rooms in private lodging, that means safety for the looting and rapes. Our house got a good looking R. officer too, in the Németh's flat in my absence he was in my flat too, Lacy sick in bed, he excused himself and went out. We shall sleep quietly this night. Poor Mamuci's they begin to have the worst part only now.

At 7 p.m. I had a glance on the street: no more black-out. There is no current, of course but in the rooms inhabitants candle light shows upon the street. What a humbug about German air superiority!

We are told by some soldiers, Vienna and Pozsony were given up by the G.s. If true, there must be dissident generals, the Hitler-Himmler pack would never dream of giving them up.

FEBR. 12, MONDAY.

The loveliest possible spring day, sunshine, changing clouds, warm breeze and terrible filth on the streets. Melting snow flowing on the pavement ankle deep.

11. Go away (not available)!

We got water at the water plant from faucets, allegedly it would be clean. High time, there would be more of it, at present it means an hour's walk with a 5 liters bottle. We have many dysentery-like case. [. . .]

Still no water supply, no gas, no current and no rations. The Russian soldiers give freely cigarettes to the men here, I got one Penzetyős and two Honoid from two civilians waiting on the same place. Would you ever believe, I shall beg on the street for cigarettes? Though, to be exact, I did not beg, they offered it.

FEBR. 13, THURSDAY.

At 6:30 a.m. knocking on my door I was called in an OB case in the next school building. [. . .] Two families are living in the schoolroom, but none of the women dared to touch the poor creature, so I had to begin with child and mother at the first instant. As fee I got about 5 kgs of flour and mák (poppy-seed), 100 gms of tobacco, the covering paper of the latter soaked in at some spots with blood, I am afraid, but I am going to smoke it. The fee was abundant, money so called "better" people promised but do not keep their word. The flour we divided between the Hermanses, Klári Bálint and ourselves, including Mrs Láng and the boy there, it means one more bread for each of us. With food we are at our wit's end, today we plan to go a R. military kitchen and beg some foods, people say, they give freely and we need it. When I came out of the school building, R. soldiers moved out of it already, further down hills. People say, the fortress has fallen Sunday, so the siege would be finished in 50 days. Let's hope, work and reconstruction will follow now. [. . .]

The afternoon a gentleman (councillor in the war office here), as patient: he has lice. Nine days after these quarters have fallen, they are still living in the shelter. At 3 p.m. we went to see the Horchlers with Lacy. They were in their airless, lightless shelter too, all sleeping. Their flat is not destroyed just turned upside down, it needs but one or two days hard work, to put it into order and they can not begin. People seem to be paralyzed by events.

The German resistance around Pasarét is said to be still existing and we heard a lot of shooting, guns, aircraft from there. As the fall of Budapest was not yet announced (may be in the radio and at Moscow, but not here on megaphone) it seems to be considerable in force today all Russian troupes move on from here. [. . .][12]

12. See "Budapest, in Ruins, Starts Life Anew: Famous Buildings Wrecked, Whole Districts Leveled—People Leave Cellars—Life Revived amid Ruins—Germans Boast of Defense," *NYT*, February 15, 1945.

FEBR. 14, WEDNESDAY.

Nothing happened the night. Air bombardment can still be heard from a distance. These parts are almost empty from soldiers and life seems to begin. People go in hundreds for water, where only two faucets are available, so they have to stay in line for hours. I had eight patients today—the day is not yet over, 3 p.m. only—it seems, I shall not have much time for doing household chores. We clean the flat ferociously, so many people are coming in and carry dirt on their shoes. Filth on the streets is unbelievable, the luck is, thaw has set in and much of the dirt is washed away. Lacy is out with the child, to get water, so for a short time I am alone. Klári's nerves are breaking down, she has five people in her tiny flat, among them two sick.

It is said, typhus (exanthematicus) is raging on the Pest side and isolation of the two parts ordered. We seem to be on the verge of it. [. . .]

If typhus and dysentery sets in, I shall be powerless, no pharmacies, no medicine, but not even food, to beef up our resistance. If only I could know for sure, that you are all right. [. . .]

Again a district nurse called for help and directions. I organize the few ones, who are able to help. You see, in times before I believed, other colleagues can do medical work so much better, but now, when other M.D.s seem to have entirely disappeared, I feel, I have to do it and I am willing to take the responsibility. [. . .]

Damaged buildings collapse from hour to hour in our vicinity. Sooner or later our own house, or part of it will follow, the roof is in shambles. I hope though, my first floor flat will hold, even if the staircase disappears. I could use a ladder from the balcony. There is no choice, one has to stay.

FEBR. 15, THURSDAY.

The morning, at about 9 a.m. Pali jr. arrived with two pots of water. The quarters they are living at, have fallen on the 11th. They are all alive, safe, though nervously broken, especially Apu, who is not able to do manual work. Their flat, with exception of our room, is destroyed. The destruction on these parts—Mihály utca, Kisgellért hegy—is unbelievable, I am not able to describe it. I went to see them this noon, after my routine rounds done and I came home depressed with much difficulty. On many streets still booby traps, trenches across, kneedeep mud and filth, filth, filth. Shooting and air bombardment can still be heard somewhere above Hűvősvölgy, where allegedly 15,000 G. soldiers have broken out from the fortress. Mrs. Bencze has seen yesterday on the Krisztina Körút several hundred G. prisoners driven by R. soldiers, running. Many of its bystanders shook their fist at them, only in my opinion, too late.

I have done much work today, made only 50 P and still nothing to buy for it. Lacy, just home from a walk, tells me, fires all over the Fortress can be seen. Apu was told, it is a heap of ruins.

FEBR. 16, FRIDAY.

Stray G. soldiers are somewhere in these quarters, shooting is heard here and there and last night—after some days pause—again Russian soldiers searched the house. I had three of them in the flat, they were looking for arms but searched every drawer, wardrobe, trunk and took our electric flashlight and poor Bö's bracelet. I felt rather sick after the event, it is the hopelessness, to have peace and order and security. They took in much mud on their boots and took almost all our money, Kartal's too, took two packs of tobaccos out of these. The G.s would have taken all. I had to fight it out alone this time again, Lacy and Frédi hiding in the bed under covers. They were clever to do it, they could not help me in any way but still, I felt very much alone. These soldiers were not at all rude, only determined, to have something. [. . .]

FEBR. 17, SATURDAY.

With the fact, the Germans are driven out of Budapest I could stop writing. The official announcement of the occupation happened Wednesday, on the 53rd day of the siege. Still, as long we can not communicate by mail, I am going to tell you the small events of my everyday life.

Yesterday, about at 2 p.m. László Lakos, Frédi's father arrived. He started at 5 a.m., had to walk down to Csepel, cross on a ferry boat to Budafok and so to us. Exhausted by the exertion, he still was happy to find his sister and son safe. Things have not much developed on the other side of the Danube but water supply they have already. The city is deserted, a few people here and there, there is no house to live in. Lacy's Magyar utca[13] flat is destroyed too, with exception of one room. Károly sleeps there in the shelter. They both escaped dangers and famine, many of their friends too, but of course there are quite some missing. Frédi's father brought us white bread, some canned food, a jar of apricot jelly and a piece of bacon. They—he and Frédi—are off this morning, early, they have to do a good day's walk and the child is untrained. They plan to go to Kecskemét soon, allegedly normal circumstances reign there.

Lacy has staid on with me, in spite of my disapproval. I know, she wants to be with her own people and she believes only, it is her duty to stay and take care of me. Sure, I had a lot more work, were she off, but on the other hand I could appreciate the luxury of living alone. With stray, looting soldiers we have to

13. On the Pest side near the Inner Boulevard, near the National Museum.

take care in the future too, it happens on the Pest side too, the frontline is still too close. Housedoors are closed now for the night and for the daytime too at No 9 in our street regular soldiers were looking yesterday morning for the looting ones.

Miklós Vertán, one of the Horchler's friend, who lives in the opposite house and has my Russian captain patient in his flat, was here the afternoon. I asked him for a Russian paper from the captain, which I could put on my door for safety's sake. He came to tell me, the captain was not home the last night. I lent him the Szabadság paper,[14] Lacy's brother brought us yesterday. It is read with utmost interest already on the fifth place, we have not seen any paper since Xmas.

Elly was to see the Dutch consul today, he was bombed out and robbed too, as I understand and have no idea, what about other Dutch subjects. It does not seem to be of much help in these turbulent days.

We hear, allegedly Bucarest would be under American military occupation. It is possibly because of the Ploesti oilfields and so soon American Standard men will be working there. I hope, you are not thinking about coming back in these times. I do not want you to come, even if I could join you there what is not very probable.

FEBR. 18, SUNDAY.

No use, I hated this nazi war from the beginning, I have to take all the consequences of a lost war and destroyed civilization. This morning we got up at 5 a.m. to get water in time, but although it was still dark, when we got there, a long line was waiting impatiently already. My luck was, some people recognized me with my red cross on the fur and gave me room at the head of the line. [. . .]

I have no urgent case for today, so I should like to spend the day somehow like Sunday, may be to go for a walk or read a bit. Until now, beginning from Xmas eve on, I could never have this Sunday feeling, all days were uniformly ghastly.

14. A newly established Budapest newspaper published under Soviet occupation.

CHAPTER 8

After the Battle of Budapest, March–November 1945

This abridged volume of Mádi's diaries includes only a few more entries written after February 1945. Frédi's father survived his labor battalion frontline service and came to the apartment to be reunited with his son and his sister. The Soviets slowly restored water, telephone, and electricity services to Budapest residents. However, food remained in short supply for months. Mádi did not return to work at Oti but instead built up a primary care practice in her neighborhood.

On the anniversary eve of the German occupation of March 19, 1944, she wrote in her diary, "The German infested year finished. Tomorrow will be a year. they invaded the whole country, it was a most sinister year, but I truly hope, we are over the worst." By the summer, she began to receive regular packages from Hilda in the United States. Her daughter sent food, cigarettes, and even a pair of new shoes from Bergdorf Goodman department store in New York. Hilda slipped some US currency into one parcel. Mádi welcomed dollars, which had value in Budapest, unlike the rapidly depreciating Hungarian pengö.

Mádi turned her thoughts to immigrating to the United States to join Hilda, George, and Barbara. US military officials arrived in Budapest to join the Allied Control Commission, even as Soviet officials held the power in the country their army occupied. Mádi began preparing her application to emigrate from Hungary to the United States. She had to reassemble personal documents, including a birth certificate, marriage certificate, divorce (annulment) certificate, and papers she had given away to protect others during the German occupation. She next had to acquire a passport from the new Hungarian civil administration and then transit visas to cross into occupied Austria, neutral Switzerland, and France for her departure to the United States to rejoin her family. That family—Hilda, George, and Barbara—had in the meantime been assigned by George's employer to petroleum prospecting in Peru. When Mádi finally got her entry visa, she went directly from New York City to Indiana, where George Walton's mother, Flossie, nursed the malnourished and underweight doctor back to health. Her health restored, Mádi sought to gain a medical license to practice her profession and secured employment in Massachusetts at the Westborough State Hospital for the Insane, initiating her second career, working in mental health from 1947 through 1966 in the United States.

Mádi kept her diary until November 5, 1945, a few weeks before the resumption of regular mail service between Hungary and the United States. The practical physician wrote in her last entry, "This is the end with scribbling. Last night I addressed my first direct letter to you, from now on there is no more sense in writing this diary."

For Further Reading

Mádi continued to live at 19 Margáreta utca until her departure from Hungary in 1946. Her diary entries in the summer and fall of 1945 do not mention the beginning of the trials of Hungarian war criminals by the Budapest People's Tribunals. The trials called for a different type of witnessing by Hungarians, that is, different from the witnessing that Mádi performed as a diarist for Hilda. Andrea Pető and Ildikó Barna, *Political Justice in Budapest after World War II* (Budapest: Central European University Press, 2015), offer a statistical analysis of the case files from the trials. Mádi spent a great deal of time trying to get an emigration visa to leave Hungary and an immigration visa to enter the United States. In this effort she was one of millions of persons across Europe in 1945 and 1946 seeking a new home, a history told in David Nasaw's *The Last Million: Europe's Displaced Persons from World War to Cold War* (New York: Penguin, 2020). The United States, which admitted Mádi to entry in 1946, also eventually accepted thousands of other Hungarians who fled the country. Steven Béla Várdy and Ágnes Huszár Várdy tell the story of the "1945ers" who arrived in the United States from displaced persons camps in occupied Germany and the "1947ers" who came to the United States after leaving Hungary to escape the Communist takeover. See their *Hungarian Americans in the Current of History* (Boulder, CO: East European Monographs, 2010). Finally, in the last few years of her life, Mádi returned to reading and editing her diaries and thinking about what she had witnessed twenty-five years after what she called the "German infested year" of March 1944–February 1945. Readers may wish to consult the leading scholar of the Holocaust in Hungary for his reflections on that history near the end of his life: Randolph L. Braham, "Hungary: The Assault on the Historical Memory of the Holocaust," in *The Holocaust in Hungary: Seventy Years Later*, edited by Randolph L. Braham and András Kovács (Budapest: Central European University Press, 2016).

~

MARCH 5, MONDAY.

It is a month, we have been liberated from the Germans. According to a recent command, black out still has to go on here in town, but as there is no current our flashlights have been taken from us, candles and lights are scarce, no policeman or patrol on the streets and last but not least, no neighbours, as the opposite house is ruined, there is nobody to check whether the windows are dark or not. [. . .]

MARCH 12, MONDAY.

After two weeks, I could lay my hand on a fresh newspaper. The occupation of Cologne, the crossing of the Rhine are good news, the fight for Breslau, the siege of Danzig and Stettin too, rather promising as to the end of war. The Corvin picture house plays an American picture, 3 Ritz brothers,[1] but, oh, British troups still before Bologna, just the same, as before Xmas! [. . .]

MARCH 15, THURSDAY.

This is a long promised day, civil administration would take the place of military command—well, I do not think, it can be done, the frontline is still too near. But our daily life is quiet, no more visit from stray, R. soldiers. Several of them had been arrested and punished for molesting the civilian population. Daily more and more of VD and pregnancy are turning up difficult to deal with.

MARCH 18, SUNDAY.

Blue skies and sunshine and the German infested year finished. Tomorrow will be a year. they invaded the whole country, it was a most sinister year, but I truly hope, we are over the worst.

MARCH 31, GOOD SATURDAY.

I had Bö here this morning, we both felt happy about it, after all, we survived together. She has lost almost everything, starved and else had no easy time, but is living and healthy. He [*sic*] took the loss of the bracelet splendidly.

APRIL 7, SATURDAY.

The red army is before Vienna, Pozsony[2] has fallen in one day, what luck they had! It seems our poor Balaton region had to be destroyed in order of saving Vienna's skin. They will not have the almost two month's siege, Budapest had and Székesfehérvár changing hands seven times, Esztergom four times.

APRIL 13, FRIDAY.

Today's paper the death of President Rosewelt. To my surprise I read, there will be no elections, the vice-president stepping into his place. I believe war and

1. *The Three Musketeers*, starring Don Ameche and the Ritz Brothers (Twentieth Century-Fox, 1939).

2. Bratislava, the capital of Slovakia.

peace can be conducted on many lines, but, as it was conducted under him until now, it would be better to go the same time, as plans have been made before on the several conferences. This morning I went to see Editke at the former American legation building. A line was standing on the street, an English marine and two Hungarian policemen before the door. It was funny, to hear English speech openly. Inside I heard, one can send a short message to folks over in your country, so I scribbled hastily a few words, made it for a lady too, who's son is out at Oregon and gave it to Editke. She states, office hours will be only from the 1 of July on, visa first only for American citizens, other subjects only after one year or so, this would not be so bad, as I counted with two years at least.[3]

One good story about a recent performance at Uránia picture house, where the Yalta conference, Churchill's meeting with Stalin was photographed. Stalin, advancing towards Churchill, to shake hands (his hand in the air) then somebody on the audience said: Óra van? Óra nincs? (Have you a watch? Don't you have a watch?)[4] The Russians words, they took almost all watches from the inhabitants of Bpest, may be, with Hungary. Scandal followed, the picture house had to be evacuated. I really do not mind our watches, but the remark was witty.

MAY 7, MONDAY.

The evening news arrived, the armistice between the allies and Germany has been signed. This after American, British declaration (days ago) that on their parts the armistice is practically accomplished. I suppose, there was a bit of play in the meantime, an interlude—why hurry, when the nazis could wait almost six years, it was not urgent until now. Anyway, I hope, things will improve now.

MAY 8, TUESDAY.

Last night all inhabitants of these quarters were ordered out by the communist party, to demonstrate before the Russian command house. Three Hungarian speeches were made there, not a single word about the allies role in winning the war. The Russian army celebrates today. They got alcoholic drinks, are driving up and down the roads on horse carts, singing. [. . .]

---

3. Editke's prediction was accurate. Mádi received an exit visa to emigrate from Hungary in May 1946, an immigration visa from the United States for family reunification in July 1946, a transit visa from the Austrians and Swiss to transit their countries en route to Paris in July 1946, permission to enter France for purposes of continued travel in October 1946, and passage on a Pan American Airways flight, Paris–New York, in December 1946.

4. Ungváry, *Siege*, 360, has a variant of this story featuring Stalin and Roosevelt.

MAY 17, THURSDAY.

We are told, Carpathian Russia declared they wish to join the Soviet Union.[5] We shall have Russian borders inside the Carpathians. Tito's troups at Klagenfurt and Trieste are just the same surprises.[6] About Poland we are told by our papers, there is no more problem: the Polish people declared her wish already. With regards public mentality—I have told you scores of times, how alone I felt, when taking care of Lacy—there is no one now, who did not save at least a dozen Jews. On the other hand, there is no one, who was not entirely robbed and looted.

MAY 25.

Friday Famine is threatening again, this time because of prices. One lettuce 12-16-20 P bread and bacon just for *one* breakfast 50 P, it is not possibly to earn enough. I do not see, how people can do, who have no help from countryside. With the present vaccinations there are days, I earn several hundreds, but it goes out immediately and besides, I am hungry.

JUNE 2, SATURDAY.

I am terribly excited, Maria Pató just left, she came with the news (Mr Ruedeman to major Hagy) that you are well, bought a house (where?) and are bound for Venezuela.[7] These news are from the 22nd and 24th of May.

AUGUST 17, FRIDAY.

Dearest, I am just home with your parcel, wonderful, marvels you were able to put into it. Am just getting acquainted with this sort of coffee, milk powder works splendidly, the bouillon cube is high above all I have ever tasted. With stockings I shall be safe for the winter. How fine is your sugar, not to mention your blue ribbon on it! And those lots of cigarettes! Darling, you know, you are spoiling me. So many thanks.

SEPT. 6, THURSDAY.

People, especially our class of people are incorrigible. They have a nostalgia towards their Germans, hate the Russians, as if they would be the only cause

---

5. "Czech Province Would Join Russia: Ruthenia Forms Autonomous Regime," *NYT*, May 16, 1945. Subcarpathian Ruthenia had been part of Czechoslovakia until March 1939, when Hungary seized the territory by force. Prior to 1919, the area had been part of the kingdom of Hungary.

6. "Trieste Peaceful Despite Dispute," *NYT*, May 13, 1945.

7. George Walton accepted an appointment to Standard Oil of Peru in 1945, and the Walton family lived there until 1950.

of present misfortune and have vague, nebulous plans and hopes, all against Russians and the present system. Antisemitism is raging, you can hear everywhere, that more Jews returned, than have left the country. In our circles you can not hear a single word of sympathy for all their sufferings, though papers write about it every day. [. . .]

SEPT. 25, TUESDAY.

I went early to town this morning, had to arrange for the eyeglasses of your aunt Margit, etc. then ran to the American Military Mission, where I got my parcel (No 2) *and letter* (I did not know of the letter before). How clever, you put the two five dollar bills into the letter [. . .]. The value of the 10$ is 44,000 P today, but it is not sure, whether it will be enough for one month. Apples are above 200 Ps today, grapes 200, poultry (without its fat) 900–1000 P per kg and so on. Your letter is sweet and clever. I am very happy with it, with recent photos and with the marvels of the package. And so many medicines! My patients got already from the quinine and tincture of Iodine. And nine packages of Camels! In Berlin, I am told, three American cigarettes are sold for a dollar.

OCT. 1, MONDAY.

Maria Pató just here to announce a new parcel from you. You are spoiling me, you know, Darling. I am afraid, you will get tired of me in no time, if you have so much trouble with me. Thanks! I am feeling so safe from want. The $ = 7800 P.

OCT. 3, WEDNESDAY.

Yes, your packages are just the same, like Tante's, all good concentrated in a box. This third one contained milkpowder, coffee, sugarcubes, a rawsilk shirtblouse, a pair of woollen socks, two pairs of stockings, a brassière, chocolates! (the first I had since about a year), to put it in figures, together with plenty of cigarettes, about 50,000 Ps value here. You are spoiling me and it is nice, to be spoilt by you.

OCT. 11, THURSDAY.

The fourth package from you! Powdered sugar, chocolates (almond-milk too) and gelatins in it. Gave a bit just to taste to the violinist Philippine Zipernovszky,[8] she was so happy. I am rich with these treasures, Dearest you have

8. Mária Zipernovszky (1900–1974) was a violinist who formed a string quartet with her sister, Fülöpke (*MEK*), who may be the Philippine Mádi references here.

no idea, what it all means here. I see, this is the first Xmas parcel, you could post on the 15th Sept., the one you mentioned in your Sept 8. letter, is not here yet. This parcel's value is above 20,000 Ps here, the third one's, with the silk blouse about 50,000 Ps [. . .]

OCT. 30, TUESDAY.

A crowded day yesterday. The morning I went over to the Mission to get my package. It was heavy. Coming home on the barge somebody carried a pair of good sports-shoes, which I viewed enviously, not knowing, I am carrying the same in the parcel. Really Hilda, this is too much, sending me your Bonwit[9] shoes, which I know, have been an extra luxury even in the States. Else, with your parcels, it is easier to state, what is *not* in them. You can put so much into every of them and so cleverly chosen! A thousand thanks, my Dear.

NOV. 1, THURSDAY.

This morning I got the eighth package from you. Thank you! Your solidarity with me is marvelous. Medicines, vitamine E (!), crackers, lipstick, powder, shoelaces, cocoa. The cocoa tin was smashed, opened and everything got impregnated with cocoa, but it could be not only cleaned, even cocoa too could be saved in 70–80 percent. Gizi and Pali were here and we enjoyed it tonight.

NOV. 5, MONDAY.

This is the end with scribbling. Last night I addressed my first direct letter to you, from now on there is no more sense in writing this diary. Still no mail service between our countries but the goodwill and understanding of your countrymen bridges over all difficulties. I feel a deep gratitude towards the country, where such men are brought up.

9. The Bonwit Teller department store, Fifth Avenue, New York.

www.ingramcontent.com/pod-product-compliance
Lightning Source LLC
Chambersburg PA
CBHW060809310726
48980CB00002B/284

* 9 7 8 0 2 9 9 3 4 3 1 0 1 *